Twentieth-Century
Russian Plays

IN THE NORTON LIBRARY

Nineteenth-Century Russian Plays   (N683)
edited and translated by F. D. Reeve

Twentieth-Century Russian Plays   (N697)
edited and translated by F. D. Reeve

Twentieth-Century Russian Plays

AN ANTHOLOGY

Edited, Translated, and Introduced by

F. D. REEVE

The Norton Library
W·W·NORTON & COMPANY·INC·
NEW YORK

For

Elena Borisovna

and

Maksim Osipovich

COPYRIGHT © 1963 BY F. D. REEVE

First published in the Norton Library 1973
by arrangement with Random House, Inc.

ALL RIGHTS RESERVED
Published simultaneously in Canada
by George J. McLeod Limited, Toronto

Books That Live
The Norton imprint on a book means that in the publisher's estimation it is a book not for a single season but for the years.
W. W. Norton & Company, Inc.

Originally published under the title *An Anthology of Russian Plays, Volume II*

Library of Congress Cataloging in Publication Data
Reeve, Franklin D. 1928–   comp.
  Twentieth-century Russian plays: an anthology.
  (The Norton library)
  A reprint, v. 2 of the compiler's An anthology of Russian plays, published by Vintage Books, 1963, which was issued as vol. V-732 of Vintage Russian library.
  CONTENTS: Introduction.—The seagull, by Anton Chekhov.—The lower depth, by Maskim Gorky. [etc.]
  1. Russian drama—20th century—Translations into English. 2. English drama—Translations from Russian. I. Title.
[PG3245.R4   1973b]   891.7'2'408   73-9779

PRINTED IN THE UNITED STATES OF AMERICA

1 2 3 4 5 6 7 8 9 0

Contents

Introduction 3

The Seagull / **Anton Chekhov** 23

The Lower Depths / **Maksim Gorky** 83

The Puppet Show / **Aleksandr Blok** 163

He Who Gets Slapped / **Leonid Andreyev** 177

The Days of the Turbins / **Mikhail Bulgakov** 255

The Bedbug / **Vladimir Mayakovsky** 335

The Shadow / **Evgeny Shvarts** 381

Twentieth-Century
Russian Plays

INTRODUCTION

No one has ever decided definitively which came first, the chicken or the egg. But in the theater the question answers itself. Without a live, grand, experimental theater, which a society, as audience, finds expressive of the meaning of its manners and ambitions, there are no fine plays—or very few.

The dramatic accomplishments in Western Europe, Britain, and America in the last ten years follow from the revival of the little theater; indeed, the failure of some little theaters to stay little—their tendency to become middle-class successes —threatens the entire theatrical renascence.

In Russia, almost a hundred years ago, Ostrovsky argued for the establishment of a national theater to satisfy the demands and cultural needs of the middle class, about which he himself had written much and well. The economic rise of the middle class and its desire for *entertainment* shaped the theater's repertoire. The approved and popular playwrights— such as Dyachenko, V. Krylov, Shpazhinsky, and Nevezhin —were untalented imitators of foreign playwrights such as Sardou, Scribe, Dumas *fils*, and, later, Pinero.

The new, plain style of acting introduced by Shchepkin had degenerated into extravagant showmanship *à la* Henry Irving. Saltykov-Shchedrin, one of the great satirists of the nineteenth century, said that Samoilov, a leading actor, was "an actor of all countries and times, but chiefly of all costumes." He said Samoilov would be just fine—in ballet.

Besides plays whose sole purpose was entertainment, there were, before the turn of the century, satirical plays (Saltykov-Shchedrin's *The Death of Pazukhin*), fantasies with patent social criticism (Sukhovo-Kobylin's trilogy *Krechinsky's Wedding*, *The Affair*, and *The Death of Tarelkin*), historical dramas (A. K. Tolstoy's *The Death of Ivan the Terrible*), social comedies of manner with sensitive psychological portraits (Turgenev's *A Month in the Country*), and outright, realistic attacks on social abuses (Pisemsky's *A Bitter Fate*). And there was, of course, some fine acting.

There were people both inside and outside the theatrical world who hoped and worked for a theatrical revival. But it was a long, slow process, this effort to return meaning to the theater, and its success came only after several years of critical commentary and powerful persuasion—and after a change in the social attitudes of the audience. It came, roughly speaking, around 1900, when, for a brief period, all of Russian intellectual life, penetrated with a special liberalism, was as bright and promising and *exciting* as the intellectual worlds of Paris and of Berlin forty years ago.

The theater with which this revival is popularly associated is the Moscow Art; the playwright, Chekhov. But the revival did not begin until almost 1900. Back in 1884, over the signature "My brother's brother," Chekhov published a satiric skit against the New Dramatic Theater opened in Moscow in 1883 by M. V. Lentovsky, an actor and producer specializing in operettas. The skit ridicules the theatrical tone of the times and shows what any theatrical reform had to oppose and overcome. The title of the skit is itself a parody on a play, adapted from the German, by K. Tarnovsky called *The Pure and the Leprous*.

THE IMPURE TRAGEDIANS AND THE LEPROUS PLAYWRIGHTS

A DREADFULLY-TERRIBLY-SHOCKINGLY-DESPERATE TRRRAGEDY

LOTS OF ACTS   EVEN MORE SCENES

DRAMATIS PERSONAE

MIKH. VAL. LENTOVSKY, a man and entrepreneur

TARNOVSKY, a heart-rending man; *tutoyer*s devils, whales, and crocodiles; pulse 225, temperature 109.4°

PUBLIC, a lady pleasing in every sense; eats everything she's served

KARL XII, King of Sweden; has the manners of a fireman

BARONESS, a brunette not without talent; doesn't refuse trifling roles

GENERAL ERENSWERD, a terribly huge man with the voice of a mastodon

DELAGARDI, an ordinary man; plays his role with the easy familiarity . . . of a prompter
STELLA, the entrepreneur's sister[1]
BURL, a man brought in on Svobodin's[1] shoulders
HANSEN[1]
OTHERS

Epilogue*

The crater of a volcano. At a desk, covered with blood, sits TARNOVSKY; *on his shoulders, instead of a head, there is a skull; sulphur is burning in his mouth; little green devils suspiciously smiling are jumping out of his nostrils. He dips his pen not into an inkwell but into the lava which witches are stirring. It's terrible. Shivers that creep up your spine are flying through the air. Upstage, quivering quakes are hanging on red-hot hooks. Thunder and lightning. Aleksei Suvorin's (the provincial secretary) calendar is lying right here with the impartiality of a bailiff foretelling the collision of the Earth with the Sun, the annihilation of the universe, and the increase in prices in pharmaceuticals. Chaos, terror, fear . . . The reader's fancy can supply the rest.*

TARNOVSKY (*gnawing his pen*). How'm I going to write something like that, goddddamn it? Can't think of a thing! There's already been *A Trip to the Moon* . . . and a *Hobo*, too . . . (*Drinks boiling oil.*) Got to think up something else . . . something so that the middle-class merchant women in Zamoskvorets dream of devils three days in a row . . . (*Rubs his frontal bone.*) Hm . . . Bestir yourselves, great brains! (*He thinks; thunder and lightning; there is heard the volley of a thousand cannons, executed from a drawing by Mr. Shekhtel; a dragon, vampires, and snakes crawl out of the cracks; right into the crater falls a huge trunk, out of which comes* LENTOVSKY, *dressed in a huge poster.*)

LENTOVSKY. Hello, Tarnovsky.

TARNOVSKY }
WITCHES } (*together*). All hail, Excellency!
OTHERS }

LENTOVSKY. Well, so? Play ready, godddamn it? (*Waves a cudgel.*)

TARNOVSKY. Not at all, Mikhail Valentinych. I keep thinking,

---

* I was about to put down *Prologue*, but the editor says that the more improbable this all is the better. Whatever he wants! (Type-setter's note.)

---

[1] Lentovsky's sister had become an actress in his theater; P. M. Svobodin was one of his employees, also, and Hansen was his ballet-master.

now, sitting here, and can't think of a thing. You gave me too hard an assignment! You want my play to make the public's blood freeze, for there to be an earthquake in the hearts of the Zamoskvorets middle-class merchant women, so that the lights'll go out from my soliloquies . . . But admit it, now, this is impossible, even for such a great dramatist as Tarnovsky! (*Having praised himself, he is embarrassed.*)

LENTOVSKY. Nonsense, godddamn it! Some more powder, more Bengal lights, more high-flown soliloquies—that's all there is to it! In the interests of the costumes, use high society, godddamn it . . . Betrayal . . . Prison . . . The girl the prisoner loves is married off to the villain by force . . . We'll give Pisarev the role of the villain . . . Then there's a flight from prison . . . shooting . . . I won't spare the powder . . . Then there's a baby, whose noble birth is revealed only later on . . . And in the end there's shooting again, a fire again, and the triumph of virtue! In short, cook up something trite, the way Rocambole and the Counts of Monte Cristo do . . . (*Thunder, lightning, hoarfrost, dew. The volcano erupts.* LENTOVSKY *is thrown outside.*)

ACT ONE

PUBLIC, USHERS, HANSEN, *and* OTHERS.

USHERS (*taking off the public's coats*). A little something from Your Worship! (*Not having received a tip, they grab the* PUBLIC *by the tails of their coats.*) O, black ingratitude!!! (*Are ashamed for mankind.*)

ONE OF THE PUBLIC. So, Lentovsky's well again?

USHER. Already started fighting; means he's well!

HANSEN (*dressing in his dressing room*). I'll astound them! I'll show them! All the papers'll start talking!
(*The act continues, but the reader is impatient; he craves the second act, and so—curtain!*)

ACT TWO

The Palace of KARL XII. *Behind his back,* VALTS[2] *is swallowing swords and red-hot coals. Thunder and lightning.*
KARL XII *and his* COURTIERS.

KARL (*strides around stage and rolls his eyes*). Delagardi! You've betrayed your country! Hand your sword over to the captain and please march off to jail!

---

[2] K. F. Valts was a scene-painter and the head stage technician in the Imperial theaters in Moscow; he also worked for Lentovsky.

INTRODUCTION 7

DELAGARDI (*says a few heart-felt words and goes off*).

KARL. Tarnovsky! In your heart-rending play you made me go through ten years of my life! Please head off to prison! (*To the* BARONESS.) You love Delagardi and have had a child by him. In the interests of the plot I'm not supposed to know this, and have to marry you off to a man you don't love. Go marry General Erenswerd.

BARONESS (*marrying the* GENERAL). Ah!

GENERAL ERENSWERD. I'll roast 'em! (*Is made superintendent of the prison where* DELAGARDI *and* TARNOVSKY *are imprisoned.*)

KARL. Well, now I'm free right up till the fifth act. I'll go into the dressing room!

ACT THREE AND FOUR

STELLA (*plays, as usual, not badly*). Count, I love you!

YOUNG COUNT. And I love you, Stella, but I adjure you in the name of love, tell me why in hell Tarnovsky got me mixed up in this mess? What does he need me for? What have I got to do with his plot?

BURL. But Sprut did all that! It was on account of him I ended up in the army. He beat me, hounded me, bit me—and may I not be Burl if it wasn't he who wrote this play! He'll do anything just to keep after me!

STELLA (*having found out her origin*). I'm going to set father free! (*On the way to the prison runs into* HANSEN. HANSEN *does an* entrechat.)

BURL. On account of Sprut, I ended up in the army and am taking part in this play. It's probably this Sprut made Hansen dance, too, just to keep after me and get me! But just you wait! (*The supports give way. The stage collapses.* HANSEN *executes a leap which causes all the old maids in the audience to feel faint.*)

ACT FIVE AND SIX

STELLA (*meets Papa in the prison and thinks up a plan of escape with him*). I'll save you, Father! But how can we do it so that Tarnovsky doesn't come with us? Once he escapes from prison, he'll write a new play!

GENERAL ERENSWERD (*tortures the* BARONESS *and the* PRISONERS). Since I'm the villain, then I mustn't look like a man at all! (*Eats raw meat.*)

DELAGARDI *and* STELLA (*escape from prison*).

ALL. Hold them! Catch them!

DELAGARDI. No matter what it's like there, we'll escape nevertheless and stay in one piece! (*A shot.*) Who cares! (*Falls dead.*) And who gives a damn about that, either! The author does the killing; and he does the resurrecting, too! (KARL *comes out of the dressing room and orders Virtue to triumph over Vice. General exultation. The Moon smiles, and the Stars, too.*)

PUBLIC (*pointing* TARNOVSKY *out to* BURL). There he is, that Sprut! Catch him!

BURL (*strangles* TARNOVSKY. TARNOVSKY *falls dead but immediately jumps up. Thunder, lightning, hoarfrost, the murder of Coverley,*[3] *a great migration of nations, shipwreck, and the bringing together of all the parts.*)

LENTOVSKY. But I'm still not satisfied! (*Vanishes through the floor.*)

Chekhov wanted words to be restored to their meanings; he wanted actions in the theater to be significant again. In a letter to Gorky, he wrote:

> It's understandable when I write, "A man sat down on the grass"; this is understandable because it's clear and doesn't draw attention to itself. On the other hand, it's confusing and mentally oppressive when I write, "A tall, narrow-chested man of medium build with a red beard sat down on the green grass already trampled and turned brown by people walking on it—sat down silently, and shyly and timidly looked around."

In the second description, the action is lost; the words work against themselves. The words are made to take on more than they, as gesture, can carry. The words set up definitions; the words describe poses; but the deadness of the words kills the language of gesture (to take Richard Blackmur's brilliant phrase), that action of meaning beneath the surface of the words which Aristotle called the soul of tragic drama.

The drama, of course, came out of dance, and dance is all gesture. Gesture informs the movement and determines the proportions of the dance. It is a kind of ritual in which the delicacy of the assigned movements changes them into meaningful gesture. It fits what it wears, and it brings what it wears to life. Nijinsky said that the costumes of ballet determine what the gestures will be. Chekhov showed us that the habits of life fix the gestures of meaning.

Chekhov's plays have no plot, in the usual sense of that word. In *The Seagull*, for example, the narrative thread is

[3] *The Murder of Coverley*—a melodrama, translated from the French.

simple: a young man who wants to be a great writer fails and therefore shoots himself; the young girl he loves is perhaps ruined by dedicating her life to something for which she has only imperfect talent. As Chekhov jotted in his notebook, "Treplyov has no definite goals, and that has ruined him. His talent has ruined him. He says to Nina in the finale: You've found your way, you're saved, but I'm lost."

The play has no thesis, in the usual sense of that word. It is not an illustration of the class struggle, or of the virtues of art over life or life over art, and it is not a nostalgic apology for the old way of life. Like Chekhov's other plays, it is not addressed to the mind, or to the heart, but to the histrionic sensibility. It is an imitation of action in an Aristotelian sense: the "events" of the play are arranged to be a definition of a total action that has a beginning, a middle, and an end in time. The habits of ordinary life present on the stage an underlying life of change, of the suffering of change.

The absence of mechanical plotting makes the playing seem even more real and is possible because the mode of action through which the underlying life is expressed is immediately perceptible pathos. Everything is directly perceived. Nothing is to be guessed at or "revealed"; nothing is to be demonstrated morally. All that there is are the separate, significant moments in the lives of the characters when they somehow catch themselves and immediately, directly, perceive their condition and their destiny. These are not rational moments; they are not moments when a man deliberates or expostulates: they are moments when a man simply feels himself inexorably involved with a total condition. The action of the play is the epitome of these moments, the sum of these gestures of awareness and meaning, dramatically expressed as each man's attempt to be a seagull, and his compromise with his failures.

Each character attaches himself to this central action, which is also given as a dramatic symbol. He puts some value in it: you might say that Arkadina was a seagull, that Treplyov wants to believe in seagulls, that Nina may still be a seagull, that Trigorin uses seagulls, and so on. Each character's values become an analogy to the common value of all. The interplay of social forces gives a deeper and more extensive meaning to the change that *is* life than any one character can. The focus of the play is always on the general action, as it is expressed in the separate characters' continually changing perception of the action. Pauses, sounds in the background, and so forth, are devices to sharpen the audience's perception of the central action.

A brilliant episode, in which all this is focused, is the lotto game in the last act of *The Seagull*. There are a number of movements, each repeating itself and being broken by the others to establish a meaning. There are the words repeated without regard to their ordinary denotation, to their ordinary usage even—just "numbers" corresponding to numbers on the cards. There are the repetitions of consciousness—Arkadina's harping on her past success. There are the repetitions of habit—Arkadina's putting the brooch on the table. There are the repetitions of judgment, the clichés we use to avoid getting involved with another person—Trigorin's comment on Treplyov's literary ability. And there is the repetition of the music, that suggestive intrusion of mood which helps persuade us to our perception of inexorable change.

The dialogue is naturalistic, yet fractured; a peculiar pattern is imposed on the rhythm of ordinary speech, infected with alien repetitions that are, also, gestures of meaning. At first, the characters participate in the game with the conscious gestures of indulging in a fresh activity, but they quickly return to what their conditions were before the new pattern was adopted, and the pattern around the game, like the pattern of the music, stands itself as a gesture distinct from the ordinary gestures of ordinary life. Even the numbers in Arkadina's report of her ovation are different numbers than those in the game; they represent values in a different conventional gesture. In the end, the monotony of the numbers is caught up in the terrible words of Trigorin's judgment: "Not a single living character." The scene is transfixed as a moment startled into maximum life. When, a few moments later, Treplyov talks about the important thing in writing being not old or new forms but the spontaneity of emotion and its aptness, we see, with him, how the total gesture of which he dreams is as impossible for him, in his way, as for the other characters, in theirs—and, perhaps, as for us.

By narrowing the scope of "naturalism," by discarding the

INTRODUCTION

mechanical plot, and by exploiting his self-imposed restrictions, Chekhov perfected modern "realistic" techniques. He returned drama to its ancient, tragic root—the immediate, mimetic response—and opened up new possibilities for the theater.

The founding of the Moscow Art Theater helped realize these possibilities. No other modern theater has achieved so great a reputation throughout the world or had so great an effect—both good and bad—on theatrical style. In *My Life in Art*, Stanislavsky comments on the reasons for his famous all-night meeting with Nemirovich-Danchenko:

> He, like me, thought the theater's situation hopeless, for the brilliant traditions of the past had degenerated into a plain collection of easy, technical devices. I'm not talking of certain exceptional talents, of course; thanks to the new theatrical schools, the mass of actors was better educated, but there were no real talents, and the theater was in the hands of dilettantes and bureaucrats.
>
> In June 1897, I received a note from him inviting me to have a talk with him in a Moscow restaurant, the Slavyansky Bazaar. There he explained to me the purpose of our interview. This was the creation of a new theater by combining our two ensembles of actors.
>
> An international conference doesn't study important political questions with greater exactness than we debated the conditions of our projected work, problems of pure art, ethics, staging techniques, organizational and repertory questions, our mutual understandings.
>
> "Take actor A.," we would say to each other, "do you think he has ability?"
>
> "Of course."
>
> "Shall we take him on?"
>
> "No."
>
> "Why?"
>
> "He's getting ready to make a career and fashions his talent to suit public taste, his character to follow the whims of a director, and himself to be a model of current theater. One so infected can't be cured."
>
> "What about actress B.?"
>
> "A good actress, but not for us."
>
> "Why?"
>
> "She doesn't care about art; she cares only about herself in art. . . ."

Stanislavsky thought his approach one that would expose the "true" and the "real." His method was to dramatize or to visualize on stage the small and isolated gestures by which playwrights like Chekhov trapped understanding of man's condition, to associate meaning with intention by an economy of environment and by a parsimony of movement, to build up through conventional responses an individual, non-conventional importance. He never assumed that the surface movements were real apart from the central context, the "goal" toward which they moved. The reality of his theater is, in this sense, *un*real; only after it has been realized—imitated in dramatic action—do we apperceive it, do we apprehend it in immediate response.

Stanislavsky's method was, further, an effort to break through the narrow traditions of the stage-drawing-room and of the well-made, or "thesis," play. Art, not life, is coherent. On the stage, Stanislavsky said, what is superfluous is vulgar. The actor is not a reporter, he said, but a creator, one who feels compelled to demonstrate externally what is locked inside him, one who is animated by a complete moral and physical concentration. The "reality" or "truth" which is the goal of the play and of the players is imaginary. The coherence is an illusion, but the accomplishments of coherence are real.

"They are wrong," said Stanislavsky, "who, when playing Chekhov, try to act, to represent. In these plays, one must be, that is, one must live, exist, in accordance with the governing train of emotions in the profundity and subtlety in which it lies hidden." He tells of an experiment he once made with Olga Knipper. Out in the country, along the banks of the Dnepr River, they decided to play a scene from Turgenev's *A Month in the Country*: "We walked down a long alley of trees, as the play calls for, then we sat down on a bench, as the directions say, and we continued talking. . . . And then we suddenly stopped, unable to go on. My acting in live nature seemed to me a lie." The aim of drama becomes the creation of such patterns that the silences of the moments of greatest dramatic intensity are charged with meaning. In nature, there are no silences. One must live *in art*.

Of the small, important experimental theaters which sprang up before the Revolution of 1917, perhaps the most distinguished was Vera Kommissarzhevskaya's. She herself was an actress of much skill whom Chekhov admired. The first production of *The Seagull* in her theater was not successful, though subsequent performances were. Her theater became important, however, for its productions of Symbolist dramas. It was here that the brilliant director Meyerhold first attracted wide attention, and it was here that Blok's *The Puppet Show* was performed. Aroused by the work of Wagner, drawing on such Western European playwrights as Maeterlinck, supported by the talent of such designers as Golovin, this theater was for a time the center of the Symbolists' efforts to express the dramatic content of the unifying principle of mystery, by which, they believed, all life was informed.

In Blok's play, the conventions surrounding mystery are mocked in order to establish the purity of mystery at the center, the purity of real love. Like Yeats' little dance-plays, the play works away from the stylization of gesture—the formal gestures of repetition: the dance, the musical accompaniment, the poses of love, the pretenses of the Mystics with their cardboard shirts, the deliberately artificial diction, and even the ancient love-triangle—toward the gesture of despair, that final moment of perception of change which can be contained and communicated only in a symbol.

In a review of the state of Symbolist theater, Andrei Bely, an outstanding poet and leading Symbolist critic, said of Blok's play that the movements of the actors were successful only insofar as they approached the mechanical, hypnotized motions of marionettes. He was angered by Blok's ironic suggestion that the Fiancée, the putative incarnation of Eternal Femininity or the Divine Sophia, might be only cardboard. He thought this blasphemy.

> And the poet tried to resolve the basic contradiction between the necessity for mystery and its impossibility in the setup of present-day life, by introducing the technical tricks of marionette-like movement into the very realm of symbols, instead of just leaving aside any concern over the method of enacting symbolic drama. After all, the meaning of tragedy lies in purification and elucidation.

Blok had never become as involved in the principles connected with the religious aspects of Symbolism as Bely had, and by 1906 he had begun to regard irony not only as a literary device but also as an aspect of the general attitude of his time.

Nevertheless, Bely reproached him for betrayal of faith and doctrine (they also had a personal falling-out) and asserted that the Symbolist theater had to move toward the expression of mystery in mime if it were to have meaning at all.

Literary "movements" do not last long; often, they are merely labels attached to the work of some writers by non-literary historians. Always, if the writers be strong talents, their own development forces them to be working in some different direction by the time the label has been pinned onto them. They are out of the movement, or the movement is dead, by the time it is recognized. Bely's later adaptations of his Petersburg and Moscow novels for Meyerhold's theater—adaptations attuned to Meyerhold's later style (1920's)—show how far he himself moved from his earlier position. On the other hand, there clearly are similarities in the dramatic works of, say, Blok, Sologub, and Bryusov which persuade us to separate them generically from the work of, say, Gorky. Judging by what they said of Gorky, we may be sure they would be glad if we did.

The Lower Depths has been very successful ever since it was first produced. It is skillfully constructed, with that distinguished facility and earnestness which made young Gorky widely renowned. But it does not present anything new artistically. Chekhov was hoping to create a new kind of drama that would wholly express man's actual condition. Blok was hoping to use old devices of drama to express new principles of understanding of life's actual conditions. Gorky took the tricks and the condition together. He describes a society of outcasts who live in the present physically by begging and robbing, and spiritually by grandiloquently remembering the past. In the midst of them is Luka, a sort of Greek chorus, who keeps them from running all over each other, who reminds the audience of the value of human dignity, and draws some lesson from the present with which to shape the future.

In Chekhov's plays, the future, which is continually invoked, is an unattainable freedom; it is unrealizable. The great dramatic power of his plays is in the perception of a present, dramatic moment in its entirety: a moment akin to the moment just before Oedipus, off-stage, puts out his eyes; a moment when he has come to full consciousness, can press no farther, can only respond with that gesture of despair. In *The Lower Depths*, the despair lies within the conventions of the naturalistic theater; it is a series of examples of pathetic humiliation and failure. The consciousness lies within the conventions of romanticism; the individual, it is asserted, has the power to transcend his condition, if not actually to transform it. Though we can no longer believe in the "truth" behind this play with the same enthusiasm with which it was offered sixty years ago, we can still admire its dramatic effectiveness. The contrast between what is "actual" and what is "real," about which we always have misgivings, forebodings, or downright concern, is here, read to the life, before our very eyes.

Andreyev was at one time closely associated with Gorky in a common literary program. His work, however, fits neither among that of the "realists" nor among that of the "symbolists"—or, perhaps, fits among all. At times a sententious, expository writer, he was also the author of *The Life of Man*, an overtly symbolic drama, a moralistic allegory on the chief stages of human life and the worth thereof. A play such as *He Who Gets Slapped* is realistic *and* symbolic. The clowns in the play are those marionettes Bely was referring to brought to life, "the musical clowns." The tigers and the fey ingenuousness of Consuelo are real.

The play has an exotic, deliberately artificial setting: it occurs in France; failure is always imminent—the need to please the public; and the characters' profession is to pretend. On top of it all, the central, depersonalized role is assigned to a figure who has literally upset society: a gentleman who, for special reasons, has determined to become society's scapegoat and, by suffering the pretense of being a clown, become "really" the representative of the values by which human life may be said to be worthwhile.

We are continually shown the backside of the circus performers' pretense—for example, the way our response is manipulated to Zinida's off-stage playing with her tigers. We are also shown the anonymous mask assumed by HE in order to lead us, with Consuelo, to apperception of the "truth." Though HE dies for it with Consuelo, we are left to live with it, alone.

The lesson is clear: unless we assume a higher value in the name of which to assume our role in life, we cannot successfully pretend to serve at all. And the immediate force of the dramatic presentation is such that we cannot adequately respond other than by instantly looking to our faith and to our role. The seemingly "philosophic" symbol here becomes immediate, dramatic. The play seems to me, therefore, a far greater theatrical accomplishment, even in Symbolist terms, than, say, Blok's dance-play, precisely because the ultimate terms by which life is held to be meaningful are given actual, dramatic embodiment in the context of the stage. The symbols in the mind become the symbols on stage; HE'S pretense—what he would become—is actualized; as he dies, he *is*. He has recreated himself. We see clearly that this cannot be denied, even though the world marks him down a failure. HE has recreated the values by which we live. We understand this, even though these values often lead us, also, to our deaths. What HE has, that we lack, is the courage and conditions successfully to assume the pretense. But isn't it precisely the measure of the artist that he has the skill, the talent, to put on the masks of drama, to bring reality to life? In this play the slaps of irony become a transformational gesture.

Not long after this play was written and first performed, the world around it, so to speak, changed. Bulgakov's *The Days of the Turbins* is a play that remains remarkable and historically significant for its fidelity to political "gesture." Although adapted by the author from his own novel, the play has been more successful than the novel and has come to be considered the most excellent dramatization of the real-life conflict between Red and White Russians. Although actual political conflict lies behind the events which make up the play's action, the basic conflict in the play is not between alternatives of political action. It does not matter, really, which color is which. The play is about a profound change in people's lives, and presents—from absurdity to heroism—the gestures with which people really respond to change.

INTRODUCTION

In the end, of course, after the jokes and the irritation and the shooting and the betrayals, there is no response other than the final, ambivalent gesture of understanding. History, like chance, may force choice on us, but who can meaningfully say what is prologue and what is epilogue? The bravest of men may die for his faith in the dignity of life and the rightness of his cause, but what are we to say who are left to live on? The drama of valor is comprehensible only in the perfectly illusory world of the stage, where we can respond with a mimetic, untranslatable gesture. I suppose Hegelian terms for tragedy could be fitted aptly to this play: that the claims which each figure advances for his side and to which he pledges allegiance are only, bitterly and hopelessly, partial. We the audience perceive the total catastrophe and, in our gestures of response, presume the epiphany.

History, as we know it, has little to do with epiphanies. The history that followed the 1917 Revolution was never concerned with that. Indeed, the political conflict that at first seemed so expressive of real human change, of the fact of suffering and loss, soon seemed to have become as institutionalized and as inhuman as the political organization which the conflict was supposed to destroy.

Into this context comes Mayakovsky's *The Bedbug*. It is a sort of vaudeville, with plot, satirizing the abuses of institutionalization. It is reformist, not Symbolist.

The gestures of comedy are the gestures of convention. The effort of comedy is to restore the aberrations of the non-conventional figure or the abuses of convention to the rectitude which, it is assumed, the convention really represents. The comic figure is, essentially, a harmless exaggeration of what is usually, normally acceptable behavior. Even the bedbug in this play is only an insistent vitality *out of place*. On the other hand, there is much satire here, much inverted lyricism. For Mayakovsky was a wild, unreconstructed Romantic, and the fact that the good world in which he believed did not come into being, and the fact that he never found "the love" which he craved, made him bitterly disillusioned. The conventions within which the play works are the tricks and terms of farce. Its electricity is the anger of a disinherited lover, a rejected son, who thought he had successfully pledged himself and his talent to the change of the future, only to find that things do not "really" change. A man is always, really, alone.

In the theater, though, no one works alone. Those experiments or changes in technique which were of major significance were made by groups directed by strong, inventive individuals. The theater which Vakhtangov established exploited theatricality and theatrical conventions, at the same time purging them of effeteness. Perhaps the clearest notion of what he did comes from reading his directive prologue to his staging of Gozzi's *Princess Turandot*:

> Music. The curtain rises. From the stuff which they have around them, the actors improvise costumes. Lightly, to the music, they throw pieces of the material from one to another, which "plays" in their hands. They rise. They group themselves as if figures of a perfect composition.

Vakhtangov exploited the relation of audience to play. He made a conscious effort, through convention, to create in the audience emotions corresponding to the movements on stage. He argued that a play should be made as complete a world as possible, that the meaning of a play lies in the connections among the responses it engenders. In acting style, in delivery of text, in attitude toward the part, in design of costume, in tone of incidental music—in everything, he tried to give a theatrical, not a psychological, significance to the facts and forms before an audience. He wished to emphasize "playing in the theater," to express the power of action and of theatrical conventions, to achieve a theater of perfected technique. His efforts probably came as close as the theater can come to the condition of music.

Meyerhold's theater was deliberately stylized. The conventions were intended to evoke specific responses, but not necessarily ones corresponding to movements. In music, for example, a series of notes provokes a specific response. You cannot precisely describe what you feel without replaying the notes. The music *is* your feeling. In Meyerhold's theater, the convention was used to create a response that would obtain independently of the provocation. The skill of the actors was to be directed, through mimetic convention, to expression of ultimate meaning. Meyerhold's work is often aligned with that of the Constructivists but, it seems to me, not less adequately described, in brief compass, by understanding of his earlier and, to be sure, somewhat different work among the Symbolists. Bryussov, a Symbolist poet and playwright, said that movements in the theater should be indicative tools in the poet's world of reality:

> Imitation of nature is, in art, a means, not an end. Naturalistic theaters aspire to a production as true to life as possible. These theaters are an asylum for people of feeble imagination. Their innovations . . . are, in fact, secondary, and leave the stage traditions intact. . . . But even if the theater were more audacious, it could not realize all its intentions at once. To reproduce life faithfully on the stage is impossible. Above all, where there is art, there is convention. By its very essence, the stage is conventional. There are two kinds of conventions. The first comes from a certain incapacity when one is concerned with trying to create truthfully what one wants. But there is a convention of a totally different sort, a deliberate or conscientious convention. The stage must supply everything which helps the spectator reconstruct, by imagination, the ambience drawn by the subject of the play. There is no need to conceal it; rather, it must be obviously conventional. It must be, in other words, stylized.

The center and the power of representation in the theater is the systematization of the artificial relationships imposed on the audience—and perhaps the play—by the skill of the director.

Tairov's Kamerny Theater was Futuristic. The theory on which it operated presumed the actor as the focal agent in *making* drama. The actors were to work with, and across, each other to weave a wholly sufficient theatrical life. The method was disciplined and eclectic, so that the group could and did play not only tragedy or drama but also comedy, farce, and harlequinades. The techniques themselves were to create life on stage. "I want to find in a classic play," said Tairov, "everything which prevents it from dying, and to focus on this the whole resonance of the play."

A pupil of Meyerhold's, and much later a supporter of Stanislavsky, Okhlopkov for a time headed the Realist Theater. What his theater represented is perhaps best seen from what he himself said he wanted:

Stanislavsky's theater was not what I wanted: there, the spectator had to be behind a fourth wall by which the actors separated themselves from the public—something I didn't want at all. Meyerhold's theater was no more satisfactory, because the actor became vulgar, playing directly to the pit, like a clown. One day, during the Civil War, I found myself in a station. A troop train came in and halted. A moment later another train came in from the opposite direction and stopped on the other side of the platform. The soldiers got out to . . . walk around. A young, cheerful fellow got out near me. Another got out from the other train. They looked at each other, threw their arms around each other's neck, and embraced, unable to speak for their overpowering emotions. . . . In that moment I understood what my theater must be: a meeting place, where two intimate friends express the harmony of their emotions. . . . In my theater, the actor and the spectator must shake hands like brothers. . . . In my theater, when a mother cries, a dozen people in the audience must be ready to jump forward to wipe away her tears.

In 1936, Okhlopkov's theater merged with Tairov's. Later, there was another merger with the Theater of the Revolution, once headed by Meyerhold; finally, there came about the Mayakovsky Theater, which Okhlopkov now heads. Okhlopkov has become an advocate of the so-called Stanislavsky "method." Such theatrical realignments are not surprising. What is surprising, perhaps, is the tenacity of a theatrical point of view toward the world of the theater.

There does not now seem to be a finer example of this tenacity than that of Nikolai Akimov, director of the Leningrad Theater of Comedy, a fine painter and scene designer, and a brilliant director continuing the vivid reforms in the theater that were begun almost sixty years ago. By his staging, first in 1940, and then again in 1960–61, of Shvarts' *The Shadow*, Akimov has shown his awareness of how the conventions of the stage, properly exploited, bear meaningfully on the conventions of actual life. The chief convention of comedy is talk. In the seventeenth century the chief source of wit was the court; in the eighteenth century, the upper class. Now, it is the bureaucracy, that self-serving legion of dutiful cowards who manipulate the affairs of this world for good or ill. Shvarts wrote his play against them; Akimov used the conventions of the theater to expose the pretenses of actual life. Indeed, for this play, the more stylized the conventions on stage, the more immediate the audience's response. The play does not deny the need for *a* system; it only insists on a decent system. The Scholar in the play, having made his final reckoning, avoids the corrupt system by taking his new-found, sweet love home. But how will we ever do that? Having come to the play's end with an appropriate gesture, how will we ever put it to the life? How will we ever become what we have seen of ourselves, what we have made of ourselves in the theater—except by going to the theater again?

F. D. Reeve

The Seagull

A COMEDY
IN FOUR ACTS

Anton Pavlovich Chekhov

A NOTE ON THE PLAY

Chekhov's *Ivanov* caused a furor when first produced in Saratov and Moscow in 1887, and received mixed reviews in St. Petersburg in 1889, but his *The Wood-Demon*, presented in Ambramova's Theater in Moscow in 1890, was sharply attacked. Chekhov stopped writing plays for a while after this, never again let *The Wood-Demon* be performed, and omitted it from his play collections.

In the spring of 1895, however, he again thought of writing a play. The weather was warm, he wrote his friend and occasional collaborator on dramatic projects, A. S. Suvorin, the editor of *New Time*, and he had an idea of setting to work on a play in the fall "if I don't go abroad." Nemirovich-Danchenko, one of the founders of the Moscow Art Theater, and Sumbatov-Yuzhin had persuaded him to return to writing for the theater. Suvorin had also urged him, suggesting he follow his own example. The play was written in the late fall and early winter of 1895–96 and sent to the censor in the middle of March, 1896. After some changes required by censorship—chiefly to de-emphasize the illicit relationship between Arkadina and Trigorin—and some minor changes by Chekhov, the play was approved for presentation and entered the repertoire of the Aleksandrinsky Theater, October 17, 1896. With extensive further revisions, it was first published in *Russian Thought* in December of that year.

Chekhov was aware of the theatrical and dramatic innovations his play offered and doubted it would succeed. He felt that he himself was "not much of a dramatist" and wrote Suvorin that he was "more displeased than pleased" with his new play. He attended almost every rehearsal, often interrupting the actors to explain a sentence, a gesture, an image. "The main thing," the director of the theater, Karpov, remembers Chekhov telling the actors, "is not to be theatrical. . . . Everything has to be simple . . . Absolutely simple . . . They're all simple, ordinary people." Chekhov was so worried, Suvorin noted in his diary, that after the dress rehearsal he did not even want the play performed.

The première was a failure. The reviewers criticized the play severely, calling it "confused and obscure," "absolutely absurd," "a badly conceived, incompetently executed play with an extremely odd content, or, more accurately, with no content at all." Each act was said to reek of hopeless despair, artificiality, and ignorance of life and people. After the second performance, Vera Kommissarzhevskaya, who played the role of Nina and was later to found a modern theater of her own, wrote Chekhov that the evening had been "a complete and unanimous success, just as it ought to be!" The audience had understood the play, she said, just as she herself felt she had grown into her role.

After the eighth performance, the play was taken out of the theater's repertoire.

Two years later, having with difficulty persuaded Chekhov to grant permission for its presentation, Nemirovich-Danchenko presented the play, in repertory, in his and Stanislavsky's new Moscow Art Theater. The first performance took place December 17, 1898. Its success was "colossal," Nemirovich-Danchenko wired Chekhov, "right from the first act." The audience understood everything: all that was said, the plot, the tone, the ideas, and all the psychological gestures, he added. When he saw a special performance in May, 1899, Chekhov did not like Stanislavsky's acting of Trigorin: ". . . he kept walking around and talking like a paralytic; [Trigorin] has 'no mind of his own,' and the actor understood this in a way that made me sick to look at." But he said that the staging was striking, paling anything the Maly Theater had done, and that even the Meinningen players had a long way to go to catch up to the new Art Theater. On a medallion he presented to Nemirovich-Danchenko he had inscribed: "You gave my 'Seagull' life. Thank you." The sensitivity and skill of the Art Theater's company made clear to the audience the new kind of play Chekhov had introduced into the theater—made clear the psychological portraits against a real-life background, the lyric outpourings and the discussion of literature on stage, and the frequent pauses which retarded the action but helped set the tone of the play.

As the seagull is still the emblem of the Art Theater,

embroidered on the theater's great curtain and worn as a lapel button by all its members, so the play *The Seagull*, in literary terms and by its history on the stage, may be considered emblematic of the change in Russia from the "old" theater to the "new."

This translation was made from the 1902 text, as reprinted in Chekhov's *Polnoe sobranie sochinenii i pisem*, Vol. XI, Moscow, 1948.

DRAMATIS PERSONAE

Irina Nikolayevna Arkadina [by marriage, Treplyova] an actress
Konstantin Gavrilovich Treplyov, her son, a young man
Pyotr Nikolayevich Sorin, her brother
Nina Mikhailovna Zarechnaya, a young girl, daughter of a rich landowner
Ilya Afanasyevich Shamrayev, a retired Lieutenant, Sorin's estate-manager
Polina Andreyevna, his wife
Masha, his daughter
Boris Alekseyevich Trigorin, a novelist
Evgeny Sergeyevich Dorn, a doctor
Semyon Semyonovich Medvedenko, a teacher
Yakov, a workman
A cook
A maid

The action takes place on Sorin's country estate.
Two years elapse between the third and fourth acts.

ACT I

A section of the park on SORIN'S *estate. A wide alley leading away from the audience into the depth of the park toward a lake, blocked off by an open stage hastily put up for a home performance, so that the lake cannot be seen at all. Left and right of the stage, shrubbery. Several chairs, a little table.*

The sun has just gone down. YAKOV *and other workmen are on the stage behind the lowered curtain; coughing and tapping are heard.* MASHA *and* MEDVEDENKO *come from the left, returning from a walk.*

MEDVEDENKO. Why do you always go around in black?

MASHA. It's mourning for my life. I'm unhappy.

MEDVEDENKO. Why? (*Deep in thought.*) I don't understand . . . You're healthy; your father, though he's not rich, has a good income. It's a lot harder for me than for you. I make only twenty-three rubles a month, and, besides, my retirement pay is deducted from that, but still I'm not wearing mourning. (*They sit down.*)

MASHA. It's not a question of money. Even a poor man can be happy.

MEDVEDENKO. That's in theory, but in practice it works out like this: there's me, and my mother, and two sisters, and my little brother, but my earnings are only twenty-three rubles. You have to eat and drink, don't you? Need tea and sugar, don't you? Tobacco? It takes some doing.

MASHA (*glancing at the stage*). The performance is going to start soon.

MEDVEDENKO. Yes. Zarechnaya has a part in it, and the play's the work of Konstantin Gavrilovich. They're in love with each other, and today their hearts will flow together aspiring to give one and the same image in art. But my heart and yours haven't any common points of contact. I love you—get so depressed I can't stay home, walk six versts here every day and six back and meet only indifference on your part. It's understandable. I have no means, my family's large . . . How can there be any desire to marry a man who doesn't have anything to eat himself?

MASHA. That's nothing. (*Snuffs tobacco.*) Your love is touching, but I just can't reciprocate your feelings, that's all. (*Holds the snuffbox out to him.*) Help yourself.

MEDVEDENKO. Not for me. (*Pause.*)

MASHA. It's stifling—probably means a thunderstorm tonight. You're always being philosophical or talking about money. The way you see it, there's nothing worse than poverty, but it seems to me that it's a thousand times easier to go around in rags and beg than . . . But you wouldn't understand it . . .

(SORIN *and* TREPLYOV *come in from the right.*)

SORIN (*leaning on his cane*). In the country I somehow don't feel myself, and, naturally, I'm never going to get used to it here. Yesterday I went to bed at ten, and this morning I woke up at nine with the feeling that from so much sleep my brain had got stuck to my skull and all that sort of thing. (*Laughs.*) After dinner I inadvertently fell asleep again, and now I'm all done in—feel as if I were in a nightmare, when all's said and done . . .

TREPLYOV. True, you need to live in town. (*Having seen* MASHA *and* MEDVEDENKO.) Ladies and gentlemen, you'll be called when it begins, but you mustn't be here now. Please leave.

SORIN (*to* MASHA). Marya Ilyinichna, be so good as to ask your papa to see to it that the dog is untied, because otherwise it howls. My sister didn't sleep all night again.

MASHA. Talk to my father yourself. I won't. Spare me that, please. (*To* MEDVEDENKO.) Let's go!

MEDVEDENKO (*to* TREPLYOV). Now, have them come tell us before it begins. (*They both go out.*)

SORIN. That means the dog will howl all night again. It's the same old story: I've never lived in the country the way I wanted to. Used to be you'd get twenty-eight days off and you'd come here to rest up and everything, but once here you'd be pestered with such nonsense you'd want to get away the same day you came. (*Laughs.*) I always left here with pleasure . . . But, now I'm retired, with no place to go, when all's said and done. Want to or not, you've got to live . . .

YAKOV (*to* TREPLYOV). We're going to go bathe, Konstantin Gavrilych.

TREPLYOV. All right, only be back in your places in ten minutes. (*Looks at his watch.*) It'll start soon.

YAKOV. Yes, sir. (*Goes out.*)

TREPLYOV (*glancing over the stage*). There's a real theater for you. A curtain, then the first wing, then the second, and empty space beyond. No scenery at all. The eye reaches right out to the lake and the horizon. We'll raise the curtain exactly at half past eight, when the moon comes up.

SORIN. Splendid.

TREPLYOV. If Zarechnaya is late, why, of course, the whole effect will be lost. She ought to be here now. Her father and stepmother keep their eye on her all the time, and it's as hard for her to get out of the house as out of a prison. (*Fixes his uncle's tie.*) Your hair and your beard are all dishevelled. You ought to have it cut and trimmed, shouldn't you? . . .

SORIN (*combing his beard*). The tragedy of my life. Even when I was young I always looked as if I'd been off on a drinking bout and everything. Women never liked me. (*Sitting down.*) Why is my sister out of sorts?

TREPLYOV. Why? She's bored. (*Sitting down beside him.*) And jealous. She's against me and against the performance and against my play because it's not she who's playing, but Zarechnaya. She doesn't know my play, but she already hates it.

SORIN (*laughs*). What you make up! really! . . .

TREPLYOV. She's already annoyed that here, on this little stage, the success will be Zarechnaya's, and not hers. (*After looking at his watch.*) A psychological oddity—that's my mother. She's unquestionably talented, clever—capable of sobbing over a book, can rattle off all of Nekrasov to you from memory, goes and takes care of the sick like an angel —but just try and praise Duse when she's around. Oh-ho! You have to praise only her, have to write about her, raise a clamor, go into ecstasies over her remarkable playing in *La dame aux camélias* or in *The Smoke of Life*.[1] But because

[1] The first is Alexandre Dumas *fils*' play—in English, *Camille*—from his novel of the same name. The second is a play—in

here in the country there aren't any of these narcotics, she's bored and in a bad temper, and we're all her enemies, we're all to blame. And then, she's superstitious—afraid of three candles, the thirteenth of the month. She's stingy. In the bank in Odessa she has seventy thousand—I know this for sure. But just you ask her for a loan, she'll start crying.

SORIN. You've imagined that your mother won't like your play, and you're already getting all upset and everything. Relax, your mother worships you.

TREPLYOV (*plucking petals from a flower*). She loves me—she loves me not—she loves me—she loves me not—she loves me—she loves me not. (*Laughs.*) See? my mother doesn't love me. And how! She wants to live, to love, to wear light-colored blouses, but I'm already twenty-five, and I'm a continual reminder to her that she's not young any more. When I'm not around, she's only thirty-two; but when I am, she's forty-three, and for that she hates me. Also, she knows I don't approve of the theater. She loves the theater, believes she's serving mankind, sacred art; but as I see it, the contemporary theater is just a hidebound routine, just prejudice. When the curtain goes up and, there in the evening lighting in a three-walled room, those great talents, the priests of a sacred art, show people eating, drinking, loving, walking, wearing their coats; when they try to fish a moral out of banal scenes and phrases—a little moral, comprehensible and useful in the household; when in a thousand variations I'm offered always the same old thing, the same old thing, the same old thing—then I run and run, as Maupassant ran from the Eiffel Tower, weighing down his brain by its banality.

SORIN. Can't do without the theater.

TREPLYOV. It needs new forms. New forms are needed, but if there aren't any, it'd be better to have nothing. (*Looks at his watch.*) I love my mother, love her very much, but she leads

---

Russian, *Chad zhizni*—by B. M. Markevich (1822–84) from his novel *Bezdna* (*The Chasm*). Chekhov wrote a parody of the play, which he chose not to publish, and a very sharp review (1884), in which he called Markevich a "well-known Moscow dandy and drawing-room man" and said "the play is written with a broom, and stinks."

a mixed-up life, eternally making too much of a fuss over this novelist; her name is constantly splashed all over the papers—and this wears me out. Sometimes the simple egoism of an ordinary mortal speaks up in me. I regret that I have a famous actress for a mother, and I feel I would be much happier if she were just an ordinary woman. Uncle Pyotr, what can be more awful and more stupid than my position? Sometimes she's visited by nothing but celebrities, famous actors and writers, and among them all I'm the only one who amounts to nothing. They put up with me only because I'm her son. Who am I? What am I? I dropped out of the third year at the University, under circumstances for which, as they say, the editors are not responsible. I have no talents, absolutely no money, and in my passport I'm a Kievan bourgeois.[2] My father, of course, was a Kievan bourgeois, though he was also a famous actor. So whenever all these actors and writers in her drawing room have turned their gracious attention to me, I've felt their eyes were measuring up my insignificance; I guessed what they were thinking and suffered from humiliation . . .

SORIN. Tell me, by the way, please, what sort of man is this novelist? Can't make him out. He never talks.

TREPLYOV. An intelligent man, simple—a little, well, you know, melancholic. Very decent. He's got a way to go yet before he's forty, but he's already famous and had his fill . . . As far as what he's written is concerned, well . . . How shall I put it? It's nice, talented . . . but . . . after Tolstoy or Zola you won't want to read Trigorin.

SORIN. But now I, my boy, like literary men. Once upon a time I passionately wanted two things: I wanted to get married, and I wanted to become a man of letters, but I didn't manage one or the other. Yes. It's nice to be even a little man of letters, after all.

TREPLOYOV (*listens*). I hear footsteps . . . (*Embraces his uncle.*) I can't live without her . . . Even the sound of her footsteps is beautiful . . . I'm wildly happy! (*Hur-*

[2] In Russian, *meshchanin*, meaning a member of the lower middle-class.

riedly goes to meet Nina Zarechnaya, coming in.) Enchantress, dream of my life . . .

NINA (*anxiously*). I'm not late? . . . Of course, I'm not late . . .

TREPLYOV (*kissing her hands*). No, no, no . . .

NINA. I was upset all day, I was so terrified! I was afraid my father wouldn't let me go . . . But he and my stepmother have just gone out. A red sky, the moon's even beginning to rise, and I rode the horse hard, really hard. (*Laughs.*) But I'm glad. (*Squeezes* SORIN'S *hand hard.*)

SORIN (*laughs*). Those little eyes, I think, have had tears in them . . . He-heh! That's not good!

NINA. Oh, that's just . . . You see how I'm panting. I'll go in half an hour—have to hurry. You mustn't, you mustn't, for the Lord's sake, don't keep me! Father doesn't know I'm here.

TREPLYOV. As a matter of fact, it *is* time to start. Everybody has to be called.

SORIN. I'll go do that and everything. Right away. (*Goes to the right and sings.*) "*Two grenadiers to France did come . . .*"[3] (*Turns around.*) Once I began singing that, and one of the assistant prosecutors says to me: "Why, Your Excellency, you've got a powerful voice." Then he thought a moment and added: "But . . . a rotten one." (*Laughs and goes out.*)

NINA. Father and his wife won't let me come here. They say it's a Bohemia here . . . they're afraid I might take after the actresses . . . But, just like a seagull, I long to come here to the lake . . . My heart is filled with you. (*Glances around.*)

TREPLYOV. We're alone.

NINA. I think there's somebody there . . .

TREPLYOV. Nobody. (*They kiss.*)

NINA. What kind of tree is this?

TREPLYOV. An elm.

NINA. Why is it so dark?

TREPLYOV. It's already evening; everything gets dark. Don't go early, I beg you.

NINA. I have to.

[3] A *lied* by Heine—"Zwei Grenadieren"—set to music by Schumann.

TREPLYOV. But if I go over to your place, Nina? I'll stand in the garden all night and watch your window.

NINA. You mustn't, the watchman'll see you. Tresor isn't used to you yet, and he'll bark.

TREPLYOV. I love you.

NINA. Shhh . . .

TREPLYOV (*having heard footsteps*). Who's there? Is that you, Yakov?

YAKOV (*behind the stage*). That's right.

TREPLYOV. Take your places. It's time. The moon's coming up?

YAKOV. That's right.

TREPLYOV. You have the spirits? The sulphur? When the red eyes appear, it has to smell of sulphur. (*To* NINA.) Go on, everything's ready there. Are you nervous?

NINA. Yes, very. Your mama doesn't matter, I'm not scared of her, but you have Trigorin with you . . . I'm terrified and ashamed of playing in front of him . . . A famous writer . . . Is he young?

TREPLYOV. Yes.

NINA. He has written such wonderful stories!

TREPLYOV (*coldly*). I don't know, never read them.

NINA. It's hard to do your play. There are no live characters in it.

TREPLYOV. Live characters! Life has to be shown not as it is and not as it ought to be, but as it appears in dreams.

NINA. There's little action in your play, just a lot of talk. And in a play, I think, there absolutely has to be love . . . (*Both go off behind the stage.* POLINA ANDREYEVNA *and* DORN *come in.*)

POLINA ANDREYEVNA. It's getting raw. Go back and put on your galoshes.

DORN. I'm hot.

POLINA ANDREYEVNA. You don't take care of yourself. It's stubbornness. You're a doctor and know perfectly well that damp air is bad for you, but you just want me to suffer; you deliberately sat out on the terrace all last evening . . .

DORN (*croons*). "*Don't tell me that I threw away my youth.*" [4]

---

[4] From a poem by N. A. Nekrasov, "*Tyazholy krest dostalsya ey na dolyu*" ("It Was a Heavy Cross Fell to Her Lot") (1856).

POLINA ANDREYEVNA. You were so carried away by talking to Irina Nikolayevna . . . you didn't notice the cold. Admit it: you like her . . .

DORN. I'm fifty-five.

POLINA ANDREYEVNA. Fiddlesticks, for a man that's nothing. You're wonderfully preserved and women still find you attractive.

DORN. So, what do you want?

POLINA ANDREYEVNA. You're all of you ready to prostrate yourselves before an actress! All of you!

DORN (*crooning*). "*Again I stand before you . . .*"[5] If actors are liked in society and treated differently than, for example, merchants, why that's quite natural. That's idealism.

POLINA ANDREYEVNA. Women have always fallen in love with you and thrown themselves around your neck. Is that idealism, too?

DORN (*shrugging his shoulders*). Well, so? In women's relations with me, there's been a lot that's good. It's chiefly the splendid doctor in me they've loved. Ten—fifteen years ago, you remember, I was the only decent obstetrician in the whole province. And besides, I was always an honest man.

POLINA ANDREYEVNA (*takes him by the arm*). My darling!

DORN. Quiet. They're coming.

(ARKADINA *arm-in-arm with* SORIN, *followed by* TRIGORIN, SHAMRAYEV, MEDVEDENKO, *and* MASHA *come in.*)

SHAMRAYEV. In 1873 at the fair in Poltava she played wonderfully. It was a pure delight! Played marvellously! And I also wonder what's happened to the comedian Chadin, Pavel Semyonych? As Rasplyuyev[6] there was nobody like him—much better than Sadovsky,[7] I swear, my lady. Where's he now?

---

[5] "Again I stand before you [captivated] . . ." From a poem by V. I. Krasov, "*Stansy*" ("Stanzas") (1840).

[6] A character in Sukhovo-Kobylin's comedy *Krechinsky's Wedding* (1856).

[7] Prov Sadovsky [Ermilov, 1818–72], a great dramatic actor who created the leading roles in many of Ostrovsky's plays and contributed substantially to their success. He is associated with Ostrovsky in the theater as Shchepkin is with Gogol.

ARKADINA. You keep asking about some antediluvian or other. How should I know! (*Sits down.*)

SHAMRAYEV (*sighing*). Pashka Chadin! There aren't any like that any more. The stage has gone down, Irina Nikolayevna! There used to be mighty oaks, but now we see only stumps.

DORN. There aren't many brilliant talents now, that's true, but the average actor is on a much higher level.

SHAMRAYEV. I can't agree with you. However, it's a matter of taste. *De gustibus aut bene, aut nihil.*[8]

(TREPLYOV *comes out from behind the stage.*)

ARKADINA (*to her son*). My sweet son, when's the curtain?

TREPLYOV. In a minute. Please be patient.

ARKADINA (*recites* Hamlet).[9] "O Hamlet! speak no more: Thou turn'st mine eyes into my very soul, And there I see such black and grained spots As will not leave their tinct."

TREPLYOV (*from* Hamlet). "Nay, but to live In the rank sweat of an enseamed bed, Stew'd in corruption, honeying and making love Over the nasty sty,—"

(*A horn is played behind stage.*)

Ladies and gentlemen, the curtain! Your attention, please! (*A pause.*) I begin. (*Raps with a little stick and speaks loudly.*) O you venerable old shadows who weave back and forth in the night over this lake, entrance us and let us envision what will be in two hundred thousand years.

SORIN. In two hundred thousand years there'll be nothing.

TREPLYOV. So let them show us this nothing.

ARKADINA. Let them. We're asleep.

(*The curtain goes up: a view to the lake is opened; the moon is just above the horizon, its reflection on the water;* NINA ZARECHNAYA, *all in white, is sitting on a big rock.*)

NINA. Men and women, lions, eagles and partridges, great stags, geese, spiders, silent fishes dwelling in the deep,

---

[8] A confusion of *de gustibus non disputandum* and *de mortuis aut bene aut nihil.*

[9] *Hamlet*, III, iv, 88–94. A literal translation of the Russian translation would read: "My son! You have turned my eyes inside my soul, and I have seen it in such bloody, in such deadly sores that there is no salvation!" "Why did you yield to vice, why looked for love in the chasm of transgression?"

starfish and those the naked eye could never see—in short,
all living things, all living things, all living things, having
completed their mournful circle, have died out. For
thousands of centuries now the earth has not borne a single
living creature, and this poor moon vainly lights its lamp.
No longer do the cranes awake with a shriek in the meadow,
and the cockchafers are not heard in the linden thickets.
It's cold, cold, cold. Empty, empty, empty. Terrible,
terrible, terrible. (*A pause.*) The bodies of living creatures
have vanished into dust, and eternal matter has turned
them into stones, into water, into clouds, and the souls of
all of them have merged into one. The common soul of the
world—it is I . . . I . . . I am the soul of Alexander the
Great and of Caesar and of Shakespeare and of Napoleon
and of the lowest leech. I am the consciousness of humans
merged with the instincts of beasts, and I remember everything, everything, everything, and in myself I relive every
life anew. (*Swamp lights appear.*)

ARKADINA (*softly*). This is something decadent.[10]

TREPLYOV (*imploringly and reproachfully*). Mama!

NINA. I am all alone. Once every hundred years I open my
lips to speak, and my voice resounds dolefully through this
waste, and no one hears . . . Even you, pale lights, do not
hear me . . . Toward morning the festering swamp gives
you birth, and you wander until dawn, but without thought,
without will, without a flicker of life. Fearing lest life arise
in you, the father of eternal matter, the devil, every
moment effects a change of atoms in you, as in the stones
and the water, and you keep changing ceaselessly. In the
universe only the spirit remains constant and unchanged.
(*A pause.*) Like a prisoner hurled into a deep and empty
well, I do not know where I am and what awaits me. Only
one thing is not hidden from me—that I am fated to be
victorious in a fierce and stubborn struggle with the devil,

[10] Chekhov is satirizing the work—especially the plays and
dramatic dialogues—of the Russian Symbolists, their followers
and imitators. The Symbolist-Decadent movement had achieved
first notoriety with the 1894–95 publication of Briusov and
Miropolsky's translations and original poems in three little volumes, *Russkie simvolisty* (*Russian Symbolists*).

and that, afterward, matter and spirit will merge in beautiful harmony, and the reign of the world-will shall set in. But that will be only when, little by little, after a long, long series of millennia, the moon and bright Sirius and the earth will have turned to dust . . . But until that time, horror, horror . . . (*A pause. Against the background of the lake there appear two red dots.*) Here comes my mighty enemy, the devil. I see his terrible, crimson eyes . . .

ARKADINA. It smells of sulphur. Is it supposed to?

TREPLYOV. Yes.

ARKADINA (*laughs*). Of course, that's a stage effect.

TREPLYOV. Mama!

NINA. He is bored without a man . . .

POLINA ANDREYEVNA (*to* DORN). You took your hat off. Put it on or you'll catch cold.

ARKADINA. That was the doctor taking off his hat to the devil, the father of eternal matter.

TREPLYOV (*flaring up, loudly*). The play's over! Enough! Curtain!

ARKADINA. Why are you angry?

TREPLYOV. That's enough! Curtain! Let's have the curtain! (*Stamping his foot.*) Curtain! (*The curtain falls.*) My fault! I didn't keep in mind that only certain select people can write plays and act on stage. Me . . . I . . . (*About to say something more, but waves his hand in vexation and goes out left.*)

ARKADINA. What's the matter with him?

SORIN. Irina, you mustn't behave like that, dear, to young pride.

ARKADINA. What did I say to him?

SORIN. You hurt his feelings.

ARKADINA. But he himself said beforehand that it was a joke, and I treated his play as a joke.

SORIN. All the same . . .

ARKADINA. Now it turns out he wrote a great work! Oh, don't tell me! And so he arranged this performance and scented us with sulphur not as a joke but for a real demonstration . . . He wanted to give us a lecture on how you have to write and what you must put on. After all now, this is getting tiresome. These constant sorties against me and these

little pricks, if you please, would make anybody fed up!
A whimsical, touchy, little boy.

SORIN. He wanted to give you pleasure.

ARKADINA. Really? Then why didn't he choose some ordinary play, but made us listen to this decadent madness? As a joke, I'm willing to listen even to madness, but, you know, this had pretensions to new forms, to a new era in art. But as I see it there are no new forms here at all, just a foul disposition.

TRIGORIN. Everyone writes as he likes, and as he can.

ARKADINA. Let him write as he likes and can, only let him leave me alone.

DORN. Jupiter, you're angry . . .[11]

ARKADINA. I'm not Jupiter, but a woman. (*Lights a cigarette.*) I'm not angry; I'm only very sorry that a young man spends his time so dully. I didn't mean to hurt his feelings.

MEDVEDENKO. No one has grounds to separate spirit from matter, because it may be that spirit itself is the aggregate of material atoms. (*Animatedly, to* TRIGORIN.) Now, you know, what you ought to do is write a play about how we teachers live, and then put it on the stage. It's hard, awful hard for us to make out!

ARKADINA. That's very true, but we're not going to talk about plays or about atoms. The evening's so wonderful! You hear, everybody? there's singing! (*Listens.*) How nice!

POLINA ANDREYEVNA. It's on the other side. (*A pause.*)

ARKADINA (*to* TRIGORIN). Sit beside me. Ten—fifteen years ago, here, on the lake, you could hear music and singing continuously almost every night. There are six big country places here along the shore. I remember there was laughter, noise, shooting, and always love affairs, and love affairs . . . The *jeune premier* and idol of all six houses then was that one there. You'll like him (*nods in* DORN'S *direction*), Doctor Evgeny Sergeyich. Even now he's charming, but then he was irresistible. My conscience, though, is beginning to bother me. Why did I hurt my poor little boy's feelings? I'm worried. (*Loudly.*) Kostya! Son! Kostya!

MASHA. I'll go find him.

[11] The proverb (from the Latin) runs: "Jupiter, you're angry; that means, you're wrong."

ARKADINA. Please do, dear.

MASHA (*goes to the left*). Hoo-ooh! Konstantin Gavrilovich! . . . Hoo-ooh! (*Goes out.*)

NINA (*coming out from behind the stage*). Apparently there won't be any more, so I can come out. Hello! (*Exchanges kisses with* ARKADINA *and* POLINA ANDREYEVNA.)

SORIN. Bravo! Bravo!

ARKADINA. Bravo! Bravo! We enjoyed it. With such looks, with such a marvellous voice, you mustn't—it's sinful to—stay in the country. You certainly must have the talent. You hear? You absolutely must go on the stage!

NINA. Oh, that's my dream! (*Sighing.*) But it will never come about.

ARKADINA. Who knows? Here, let me present to you Trigorin, Boris Alekseyevich.

NINA. Oh, I'm so pleased . . . (*Embarrassed.*) I always read you . . .

ARKADINA (*seating* NINA *beside her*). Don't be embarrassed, dear. He's a celebrity, but he's a simple man at heart. You see, he's become embarrassed himself.

DORN. I suggest you can raise the curtain now, beause it's frightful here.

SHAMRAYEV (*loudly*). Yakov, pull the curtain up now, fellow! (*The curtain goes up.*)

NINA (*to* TRIGORIN). It is an odd play, isn't it?

TRIGORIN. I didn't understand anything. Though I watched with pleasure. You played so sincerely. And the setting was lovely. (*A pause.*) I suppose there are a lot of fish in this lake.

NINA. Yes.

TRIGORIN. I love to go fishing. There's nothing more enjoyable for me than sitting on the shore in the evening and watching your float.

NINA. But I would think that whoever has experienced the joy of creating—for him all other enjoyments don't exist.

ARKADINA (*laughing*). Don't talk like that. When people tell him nice things, he falls apart.

SHAMRAYEV. I remember at the Opera in Moscow once, the famous Silva hit low C. And just at that time, as if on purpose, one of our Synod choir basses was sitting in the upper balcony, and suddenly—you can imagine our extreme surprise—we all heard from the balcony: "Bravo, Silva!" —a whole octave lower . . . Like this (*in a low bass*): Bravo, Silva . . . The theater froze. (*A pause.*)

DORN. A silent angel flew past.

NINA. But it's time for me to go. Good-by.

ARKADINA. Where are you going? So early? We won't let you.

NINA. Papa's waiting for me.

ARKADINA. What a man, really! . . . (*They kiss.*) Well, what can you do? It's a shame, a shame to let you go.

NINA. If only you knew how hard it is for me to leave!

ARKADINA. Somebody'll go with you, sweet child.

NINA (*startled*). Oh, no, no!

SORIN (*begging her*). Stay!

NINA. I can't, Pyotr Nikolayevich.

SORIN. Stay for just an hour, and everything. Come now, really.

NINA (*having thought it over, through tears*). I can't! (*Shakes his hand and quickly goes out.*)

ARKADINA. An unhappy girl, actually. They say her mother, who's dead, willed her husband all her enormous fortune, down to the last kopek, and now the girl's left with nothing, since her father's already willed it all to his second wife. It's outrageous.

DORN. Yes, her little papa's really a first-class brute, to give him his due.

SORIN (*rubbing his cold hands*). Let us go in, too, good people, it's getting raw. My legs are aching.

ARKADINA. But just like wooden ones, yours hardly work anyway. Come, let's go, you ill-starred old man. (*Takes him by the arm.*)

SHAMRAYEV (*offering his arm to his wife*). Madame?

SORIN. I hear the dog howling again. (*To* SHAMRAYEV.) Be so kind, Ilya Afanasyevich, as to have them untie it.

SHAMRAYEV. Mustn't, Pyotr Nikolayevich; I'm afraid of thieves getting into the barn. I've got millet there. (*To* MEDVEDENKO, *walking alongside him.*) Yes, a whole octave lower: "Bravo, Silva!" And he wasn't a singer, mind you, but just a plain Synod choir member.

MEDVEDENKO. And what's the pay of a Synod choir member?

(*Everyone goes out, except* DORN.)

DORN (*alone*). I don't know, maybe I don't understand anything or have lost my head, but I liked the play. There's something there. When this girl was talking about loneliness, and then later, when the devil's red eyes appeared, my hands trembled from emotion. It's fresh, naïve . . . Look, here he comes, I think. I'd like to tell him some nice things.

TREPLYOV (*comes in*). Everybody's already gone.

DORN. I'm here.

TREPLYOV. Mashenka's looking for me all over the park. An unbearable creature.

DORN. Konstantin Gavrilovich, I liked your play very, very much. It's sort of an odd one, and I didn't hear the end, but still it makes a deep impression. You're a talented man; you have to go on.

(TREPLYOV *presses his hand tightly and impetuously embraces him.*)

Phew, what a bundle of nerves. Tears in his eyes . . . What was I going to say? You took your theme from the realm of abstract ideas. That was right, because a work of art necessarily must express some grand idea. Only what's profound is beautiful. How pale you are!

TREPLYOV. And so you say—I should go on?

DORN. Yes . . . But portray only what's important and eternal. You know, I've lived my life with variety and with taste; I'm content; but if I ever happened to experience that exuberance of spirit which artists get when they're creating, why, I think I'd scorn my material shell and everything that goes along with it, and let myself be carried away from the earth far up on high.

TREPLYOV. Excuse me, where's Zarechnaya?

DORN. And then, too, in a work of art there has to be a clear, distinct idea. You have to know what you're writing for, otherwise, if you go along this picturesque road without any distinct aim, you'll get lost and your talent will ruin you.

TREPLYOV (*impatiently*). Where's Zarechnaya?

DORN. She went home.

TREPLYOV (*in despair*). What'll I do? I want to see her . . . I have to see her . . . I'll go . . .

(MASHA *comes in.*)

DORN (*to* TREPLYOV). Relax, old man.

TREPLYOV. But I'm still going. I have to.

MASHA. Go into the house, Konstantin Gavrilovich. Your mama's waiting for you. She's upset.

TREPLYOV. Tell her I've left. And I beg you all, leave me alone! Leave me alone! Don't follow me around!

DORN. Now, now, now, boy . . . you mustn't . . . That's no good.

TREPLYOV (*through tears*). Farewell, Doctor. Thank you . . . (*Goes out.*)

DORN (*sighing*). Youth, youth!

MASHA. When there's nothing else to say, then people say "Youth, youth! . . ." (*Snuffs tobacco.*)

DORN (*takes the snuffbox from her and flings it into the bushes*). That's vile! (*A pause.*) Inside, I think, they're playing. Better go in.

MASHA. Wait a minute.

DORN. Why?

MASHA. I want to tell you something else. I'd like to talk to you a bit . . . (*Agitated.*) I don't like my father . . . but I'm fond of you. For some reason I just feel inside that you're close to me . . . Help me. Help me, or I'll do something foolish, I'll make my life a joke, I'll ruin it . . . I can't go on any more . . .

DORN. What is it? Help how?

MASHA. I'm suffering. Nobody, nobody knows my sufferings! (*Puts her head on his chest, softly.*) I love Konstantin.

DORN. How everybody's all nerves! Everybody's all nerves! And so much love . . . Oh, the bewitching lake! (*Tenderly.*) But what can I do, my child? What? What?

(*Curtain*)

ACT II

A croquet court. In the background on the right, a house with a large terrace; on the left one can see the lake in which the sun's reflection shines. Parterres. It is midday and hot. On one side of the court, in the shade of an old linden, ARKADINA, DORN, *and* MASHA *are sitting on a bench. A book lies open on* DORN'S *knees.*

ARKADINA (*to* MASHA). Let's get up and see. (*Both stand.*) We'll stand side by side. You're twenty-two, and I'm almost twice that. Evgeny Sergeyich, which of us is younger-looking?

DORN. You, of course.

ARKADINA. You see! And why? Because I'm working, I'm feeling, I'm constantly busy, but you're always sitting still in one place, you don't live . . . I have one rule: never look into the future. I never think either about old age or about death. You can't avoid what lies ahead.

MASHA. But I have the feeling that I was born long, long ago; I'm just dragging my life along behind me, like an endless train on my dress . . . And often I've no desire at all to go on living. (*Sits down.*) Of course, this all doesn't amount to anything. I have to pull myself out of this, shake all this off.

DORN (*softly crooning*). "*Now you tell her, flowers of mine* . . ."[12]

ARKADINA. On the other hand, I'm as proper as an Englishman. I keep a tight check on myself, as they say, my dear, and I'm always dressed and my hair done *comme il faut.* That I might let myself go out of the house, even just into the garden, in a blouse or without fixing my hair? Never. And therefore I'm well preserved, because I was never a sloppy person—didn't just let myself go, like some . . . (*Her hands on her hips, she walks back and forth along the court.*) Here, look . . . This is how you go on tiptoes. I could play even a fifteen-year-old girl.

[12] From Valentine's song from Gounod's *Faust*. In Russian, the line given here became a stock response to someone's assertion of obvious nonsense or impossible wishes.

THE SEAGULL 45

DORN. Well now, nevertheless, I'll continue. (*Picks up the book.*) We stopped at the corn dealer and the rats . . .

ARKADINA. And the rats. Do read. (*Sits down.*) On the other hand, let me have it and I'll read. It's my turn. (*Takes the book and searches in it for the passage.*) And the rats . . . Here it is . . . (*Reads.*) "And it goes without saying that for people of fashion to indulge novelists and attract them is just as dangerous as for a corn dealer to bring up rats in his barns. But, meanwhile, they love them. Thus, when a woman has picked a writer whom she wants to captivate, she lays siege to him by means of compliments, courtesies and pleasing ways . . ." Well, that's what the French do, maybe, but we have nothing like that, no programs at all. With us, a woman is usually head over heels in love with a writer before she tries to captivate him, you must admit. Without searching far for examples, just take me and Trigorin . . .

(SORIN *comes in, leaning on his cane,* NINA *with him;* MEDVEDENKO *wheels an empty chair along behind them.*)

SORIN (*in a tone of voice used for speaking affectionately to children*). Really? We have some joyful news? We're gay today, after all? (*To his sister.*) We have some joyful news! Our father and stepmother have gone off to Tver, and now we're free for three whole days.

NINA (*sits down beside* ARKADINA *and embraces her*). I'm so happy! Now I'm all yours.

SORIN (*sits down in his chair*). She's lovely today.

ARKADINA. Smartly dressed, interesting . . . For that you're a very good girl. (*Kisses* NINA.) But we mustn't praise her very much, or we'll spoil it all. Where's Boris Alekseyevich?

NINA. He's in the bathing hut, fishing.

ARKADINA. Why he isn't fed up with that! . . . (*About to continue reading.*)

NINA. What's that you have?

ARKADINA. Maupassant. *On the Water*, my dear.[13] (*Reads several lines to herself.*) Well, further on it's uninteresting and untrue. (*Shuts the book.*) I'm worried. Tell me, what's bothering my son? Why is he so dull and severe? He spends whole days on the lake, and I hardly ever see him at all.

[13] *Sur l'eau*, an account of a sea voyage, published in 1888.

MASHA. There's something on his mind. (*To* NINA, *timidly.*) Please, recite something from his play!

NINA (*with a shrug of her shoulders*). You want me to? It's so uninteresting!

MASHA (*restraining her enthusiasm*). When he recites something himself, his eyes flash and his face becomes pale. He has a beautiful, sad voice—and gestures, like a poet.

(SORIN'S *snoring is heard.*)

DORN. Good night!

ARKADINA. Petrusha!

SORIN. Huh?

ARKADINA. You asleep?

SORIN. Not a bit.

(*A pause.*)

ARKADINA. You're not taking a cure, and that's bad.

SORIN. I'd be glad to, but the doctor here won't have it.

DORN. Take a cure at the age of sixty!

SORIN. But even at sixty you want to live.

DORN (*showing vexation*). Eh! Well, take tincture of valerian drops.

ARKADINA. It seems to me it would be good for him to go to a spa somewhere.

DORN. Why not? He can go. He can also not go.

ARKADINA. Now understand that.

DORN. There's nothing to understand. It's all clear.

(*A pause.*)

MEDVEDENKO. Pyotr Nikolayevich ought to give up smoking.

SORIN. Nonsense.

DORN. No, not nonsense. Liquor and tobacco make you lose your individuality. After a cigar or a little glass of vodka you're not Pyotr Nikolayevich any more, but Pyotr Nikolayevich plus somebody else, too; your self all spreads out and you treat yourself like a third person—a he.

SORIN (*laughs*). It's all right for you to argue like that. You had your fling in your time, but me? I served in the Justice Department for twenty-eight years, but I haven't yet lived, never experienced anything, when all's said and done, and, naturally, I'd very much like to live. You're satiated and indifferent, and therefore you have an inclination for philosophy; I want to live and so I drink sherry at dinner and smoke cigars and all that sort of thing. There you are.

DORN. You have to deal with life seriously, and to take a cure at the age of sixty, to regret that you didn't have much of a gay time when you were young, that's being, I'm sorry to say, frivolous.

MASHA (*gets up*). It's time for lunch, probably. (*Walks with a lazy, languid gait.*) My foot's asleep . . . (*Goes out.*)

DORN. She'll go and down two glasses before lunch.

SORIN. The poor girl has no happiness in her personal life.

DORN. Nonsense, Your Excellency.

SORIN. You keep arguing like a man who's full.

ARKADINA Ah, what can be more boring than this lovely country boredom! It's hot, quiet, nobody's doing anything, everybody's philosophizing . . . It's good to be with you, friends, pleasant to listen to you, but . . . sitting in your hotel room by yourself and memorizing a role is much, much better!

NINA (*enthusiastically*). It's good! I know what you mean.

SORIN. Of course it's better in town. You sit in your own office, the footman doesn't let anybody in unannounced, the telephone . . . outside on the street there are cab-drivers and everything . . .

DORN (*croons*). "*Now you tell her, flowers of mine . . .*"

(SHAMRAYEV *comes in, followed by* POLINA ANDREYEVNA.)

SHAMRAYEV. Here you all are. Good day! (*Kisses* ARKADINA'S *hand, then* NINA'S.) Absolutely delighted to see you in good health. (*To* ARKADINA.) My wife says that you're planning to go over to town with her today. Is that true?

ARKADINA. Yes, we are.

SHAMRAYEV. Hm . . . That's splendid, but what are you going to go in, my good lady? We're carting in the rye today, all the men are busy. And with which horses, if I may ask you?

ARKADINA. With which horses? How should I know with which!

SORIN. But we have carriage horses.

SHAMRAYEV (*agitated*). Carriage horses? And where'll I get the collars? Where will I get the collars? This is amazing! This is beyond understanding! My good lady! I'm sorry; I stand in awe before your talent, I'm ready to give up ten years of my life for you, but I can't give you horses!

ARKADINA. But if I have to go? This is something odd!

SHAMRAYEV. My dear lady! You don't know what it means to run a place!

ARKADINA (*flaring up*). This is an old story! In that case, I'm going to Moscow today. Have horses hired for me in the village, or else I'll walk to the station!

SHAMRAYEV (*flaring up*). In that case I quit! Find yourself another manager! (*Goes out.*)

ARKADINA. It's like this every summer; every summer I'm insulted here! I won't set foot on this place again! (*Goes out left, in the direction of the bathing hut; a minute later she can be seen passing through into the house;* TRIGORIN *follows her with fishing rods and a bucket.*)

SORIN (*flaring up*). This is real impudence! This is God knows what the hell! I'm fed up with it, when all's said and done. Have them bring all the horses here right away!

NINA (*to* POLINA ANDREYEVNA). To refuse Irina Nikolayevna, the famous actress! Isn't her every wish, even whim, more important than your running the place? It's simply unbelievable!

POLINA ANDREYEVNA (*in despair*). What can I do? Look at it from my position: what can I do?

SORIN (*to* NINA). Let's go see my sister . . . We'll all beg her not to leave. Isn't that right? (*Looks in the direction in which* SHAMRAYEV *went out.*) Insufferable man! The despot!

NINA (*keeping him from getting up*). Sit down, sit down . . . We'll push you . . . (*She and* MEDVEDENKO *wheel the chair.*) Oh, how dreadful this is! . . .

SORIN. Yes, yes, it's dreadful . . . But he won't leave, I'll have a talk with him right away. (*They go out; only* DORN *and* POLINA ANDREYEVNA *remain.*)

DORN. People are tiresome. Actually, your husband should have been simply kicked out of here. But of course it's all going to end up with this old woman Pyotr Nikolayevich and his sister telling him they're sorry. You'll see!

POLINA ANDREYEVNA. He sent even the carriage horses out to the fields. And every day there are the same kind of misunderstandings. If only you knew how this upsets me! I get sick: you see, I'm trembling . . . I can't stand his coarseness. (*Imploringly.*) Evgeny, dear, my darling, take me to your place . . . Our time is running out; we're not young any more, and at the end of our lives at least we shouldn't have to hide, to lie . . . (*A pause.*)

DORN. I'm fifty-five, already too late to change my life.

POLINA ANDREYEVNA. I know you're refusing me because there are other women besides me who are near your heart. You can't have them all with you. I understand. Forgive me—you're sick and tired of me.

(NINA *appears near the house; she is picking flowers.*)

DORN. No, that's all right.

POLINA ANDREYEVNA. I'm suffering from jealousy. Of course, you're a doctor, you can't avoid women. I understand . . .

DORN (*to* NINA, *who comes up to them*). How are things there?

NINA. Irina Nikolayevna is crying, and Pyotr Nikolayevich has an attack of asthma.

DORN (*gets up*). Better go give them both some valerian drops . . .

NINA (*gives him some flowers*). Please!

DORN. *Merci bien!* (*Goes toward the house.*)

POLINA ANDREYEVNA (*going with him*). What lovely flowers! (*Near the house, in a low voice.*) Give me those flowers! Give me those flowers! (*Having received the flowers, she tears them up and throws them away. They both go into the house.*)

NINA (*alone*). How strange to see a famous actress crying, and for such a silly reason! And isn't it strange that a celebrated writer, a public favorite written about in all the papers, his picture sold all over, his work translated into foreign languages, that he goes fishing all day and is delighted when he catches two chub? I thought famous people were haughty, unapproachable, that they scorned the crowd and got even with it by their fame and the luster of their name for the crowd's putting noble birth and wealth above everything else. But here they are crying, fishing, playing cards, laughing and being angry, just like everybody . . .

TREPLYOV (*comes in without a hat, carrying a gun and a shot seagull*). You alone here?

NINA. Alone.

(TREPLYOV *places the seagull at her feet.*)

NINA. What does this mean?

TREPLYOV. I was nasty enough to kill this seagull today. I lay it at your feet.

NINA. What's happening to you? (*Picks up the seagull and looks at it.*)

TREPLYOV (*after a pause*). I'll soon kill myself just like that.

NINA. I don't recognize you.

TREPLYOV. Yes, ever since I stopped being able to recognize you. You've changed toward me; your look is cold; my presence makes you uncomfortable.

NINA. Lately you've become short-tempered, express yourself incomprehensibly all the time, in some kind of symbols. And now this seagull, too, apparently, is a symbol, but, I'm sorry, I don't understand . . . (*Puts the seagull on the bench.*) I'm too simple to know what you mean.

TREPLYOV. It all started that evening when my play failed so stupidly. Women don't forgive failure. I've burned everything, everything right down to the last scrap! If only you knew how unhappy I am! Your coldness is terrible, incredible; as if I woke up and saw that this lake here had suddenly dried up, or drained into the ground. You just said you're too simple to understand what I mean. Oh, what is there to understand! You didn't like the play, you scorn my inspiration, already think of me as mediocre, insignificant, like so many . . . (*Stamping his foot.*) How well I understand that, how I do! It's just as if there were a nail in my brain; damn it and my pride, too, which sucks my blood, sucks it like a serpent . . . (*Catching sight of* TRIGORIN, *who comes along reading a book.*) Here comes a real talent, strides along like Hamlet, and with a book, too. (*Mimicks him.*) "Words, words, words . . ." This sun hasn't yet reached you, and you're already smiling; your look has thawed out in his rays. I won't get in your way. (*Goes out quickly.*)

TRIGORIN (*noting something down in the little book*). Snuffs tobacco and drinks vodka . . . Always in black. Loved by the teacher . . .

NINA. Hello, Boris Alekseyevich!

TRIGORIN. Hello. Circumstances unexpectedly arose, because

of which we're leaving, I think, today. There's hardly a chance that you and I will ever meet again. And that's too bad. I don't often have the chance of running across young girls, young and interesting; I've long forgotten, and can't now picture to myself clearly, how they feel at the age of eighteen or nineteen, and so in my stories and tales the young girls are usually artificial. I'd very much like to be in your place, even for just an hour, to know how you think and, generally, what makes you what you are.

NINA. And I'd like to be in your place.

TRIGORIN. Why?

NINA. To know how a famous, talented writer feels. What is it like to be famous? How do you respond to the fact that you are?

TRIGORIN. How? I suppose, nohow. I never thought about that. (*Having reflected a moment.*) It's one of two things: either you're exaggerating my fame, or else generally it's not felt any way.

NINA. But if you read about yourself in the papers?

TRIGORIN. When you're praised, it's pleasant; when you're attacked, for two days afterwards you feel out of sorts.

NINA. What a wonderful world! How I envy you! If only you knew! . . . People's lots are different. Some barely drag out their dull, insignificant existence, each just like the rest, all of them unhappy; others, such as you, for example—you're one in a million—have had an interesting, bright life fall to their lot, a life full of meaning . . . You're fortunate . . .

TRIGORIN. Me? (*Shrugging his shoulders.*) Hm . . . Now here you've been talking about fame, about happiness, about some bright, interesting life, but for me all these fine words are, sorry, just so much marmalade, which I never eat. You're very young and very kind.

NINA. Your life is beautiful!

TRIGORIN. What's especially good about it? (*Looks at his watch.*) I have to go now and write. Excuse me, I haven't the time . . . (*Laughs.*) You've stepped, as they say, on my favorite corn, and here I'm beginning to get nervous and a little angry. Nevertheless, let's talk. We'll talk about my beautiful, bright life . . . Well, where shall we begin? (*Having thought a bit.*) There are such things as images a man can't get out of his head, times when he thinks day and night about, say, the moon; and I, too, have my own sort of moon. Day and night one and the same importunate thought possesses me: I have to write, I have to write, I have to . . . I've barely finished one story when, for some reason, I have to write another, and then a third, and after the third a fourth . . . I'm continually writing, as if always changing horses to gallop onward, and I can't do it any other way. What's beautiful and bright about that, I ask you? Oh, what a mad life! Here I am with you now, I'm becoming emotional, and yet all the time I keep remembering every instant that there's an unfinished story waiting for me. I see that cloud there, like a grand piano. And I think: got to mention it in a story somewhere, that a cloud sailed by shaped like a grand piano. There's the odor of heliotrope. Right off, I put it away for later: a cloying smell, a widow's color, to be used in describing a summer evening. I catch myself, and you, at every phrase, every word, and first thing, I hurry to shut up all these phrases and words in my literary storeroom: who knows, maybe it'll come in handy! When I finish work, I rush to the theater or off fishing; maybe there I can get away from it all, forget myself, but—no, already there's an iron-heavy kernel of something spinning around in my head—a new idea, and I'm already being pulled to my desk, and I have to hurry up again and write and write. And that goes on and on, always, and I have no peace from myself, and I feel I'm consuming my own life, that for the honey I give somebody far, far away, I'm cleaning out the pollen from my best flowers, picking the flowers themselves and trampling on their roots. Am I not mad? Do my closest friends and acquaintances behave toward me as toward a normal man? "What're you working on? What're you going to give us next?" The same old thing, the same old thing, and I think that this attention by acquaintances, this praise and admiration—it's all a fraud; I'm being deceived, like a sick man, and sometimes I'm afraid that they're just about to steal up on me from behind, grab me, and carry me off, like Poprishchin,[14] to the madhouse. And in those years when I was beginning, in those young, those best years of all, my being a writer was just sheer torture. A young writer, especially when things go badly for him, thinks himself clumsy, awkward, superfluous; his nerves are all tense and frayed; he irrepressibly hovers around people involved in literature and art, unrecognized, unnoticed by anyone, afraid to look anyone in the eye straight and boldly, like a passionate gambler who has no money. I didn't see the man who would read my work, but he somehow seemed in my imagination hostile, distrustful. I was afraid of the public, it was terrifying for me, and when a new play of mine would happen to be performed, every time I'd think that the brunettes were sharply against it and the blondes, coldly indifferent. Oh, it was so dreadful! What a torture it was!

NINA. That may be, but don't inspiration and the creative process itself afford you lofty, happy moments?

TRIGORIN. Yes. When I'm writing, it's pleasant enough. And it's pleasant to read the proofs, but . . . once the thing's published, I can't stand it and already see that it's not what I had in mind, that it's a mistake, that it shouldn't have been written at all, and I'm annoyed at myself; I have a sort of rotten feeling . . . (*Laughing.*) But the general public reads it: "Why, sure, it's nice, talented . . . Nice, but a long shot from Tolstoy"—or: "A lovely piece, but Turgenev's *Fathers and Children* is better." And so, right to my grave it'll always be just nice and talented, nice and talented—no more, no less, and when I'm dead, the people who knew me, going by my grave, will say, "Here lies Trigorin. He was a good writer, but not so good as Turgenev."

NINA. Excuse me, I just can't accept that. You've simply been spoiled by success.

TRIGORIN. What success? I've never thought well of myself. I don't like myself as a writer. What's worst of all is that I'm in some sort of a daze and often don't understand what I write . . . I love this water here, say, the trees, the sky;

[14] Poprishchin, Aksenty Ivanovich—the central figure, the narrator, in Gogol's "Notes of a Madman."

I have a feeling for nature; it fills me with passion, with an overwhelming desire to write. But of course I'm not just a landscape painter, I'm also a citizen; I love my country, its people; I feel that, if I'm a writer, I have a duty to speak about the people, about their sufferings, about their future, to discuss science, the rights of man, and so on and so on, and I do discuss everything: I keep hurrying, I'm driven on from all sides, people get angry at me, I rush from side to side like a fox brought to bay by the hounds; I see that life and science keep going farther and farther ahead, but that I fall farther and farther behind like a peasant who has missed his train, and, when you come right down to it, I feel I know how to describe only a landscape, and that in everything else I'm fake, fake right to the very marrow.

NINA. You've overworked yourself, and you don't have the time or the desire to realize your own importance. So what if you're dissatisfied with yourself! For others you're great and magnificent! If I were a writer like you, I'd give up my whole life to the public, but I'd be aware that its happiness lies only in its coming up to my level, and it would drive me in a chariot.

TRIGORIN. Come now, in a chariot! What am I, Agamemnon? (*They both smile.*)

NINA. For the happiness of being a writer or an actress I'd put up with my family's disapproval, with want, disillusionment; I'd live in a little top-floor room and eat only rye bread; I'd suffer from dissatisfaction with myself, from knowing my imperfections; but still, I'd demand fame . . . real, tumultuous fame . . . (*Covers her face with her hands.*) My head's going around . . . Ooogh! . . .

ARKADINA'S VOICE (*from the house*). Boris Alekseyevich!

TRIGORIN. They're calling me . . . Probably packing up. But I don't much want to leave. (*Looks around at the lake.*) Just look what bliss! . . . It's all right!

NINA. Do you see the house and garden on the other side?

TRIGORIN. Yes.

NINA. That's my mother's estate; she's dead now. I was born there. I've spent my whole life near this lake and I know every little island on it.

TRIGORIN. It's very nice here! (*Having noticed the seagull.*) But what's that?

NINA. A seagull. Konstantin Gavrilych killed it.

TRIGORIN. A beautiful bird. Really don't feel like going. Now, why don't you go talk Irina Nikolayevna into staying. (*Makes a note in his little book.*)

NINA. What are you writing there?

TRIGORIN. Nothing, just making a note . . . I had an idea . . . (*Putting the little book away.*) An idea for a little story: a young girl, something like you, has been living by a lake ever since childhood, loves the lake, like a gull, and is happy and free, like a gull. But by chance along comes a man, notices her and, just to pass the time, destroys her, like this seagull here.

(*A pause.* ARKADINA *appears in the window.*)

ARKADINA. Boris Alekseyevich, where are you?

TRIGORIN. Coming! (*Goes and looks back at* NINA. *By the window, to* ARKADINA.) What?

ARKADINA. We're staying.

(TRIGORIN *goes into the house.*)

NINA (*goes up to the footlights; after some reflection*). It's a dream!

(*Curtain*)

ACT III

The dining-room in SORIN'S *house. Doors on the right and left. A sideboard. A medicine cabinet. A table is in the middle of the room. A suitcase and boxes show preparations for departure.* TRIGORIN *is eating lunch;* MASHA *stands by the table.*

MASHA. I'm telling all this to you as a writer. You can make use of it. I'll tell you honestly: if he'd hurt himself seriously, I wouldn't have gone on living, not for one minute. But all the same I've got courage. So I up and decided: I'll rip this love right out of my heart, rip it out by the roots.

TRIGORIN. How will you?

MASHA. I'm going to get married. To Medvedenko.

TRIGORIN. That's the teacher?

MASHA. Yes.

TRIGORIN. I don't understand the need for it.

MASHA. To love hopelessly, to be waiting for something all the time, years on end . . . But once I'm married, there won't be any more question of love; new worries will drown out all the old things. And besides, you know, it's a change. Should we go over it again?

TRIGORIN. But won't it be too long?

MASHA. Why, sure! (*Fills their glasses.*) Don't you look at me like that. Women drink more than you think. The minority drinks openly, like me, and the majority secretly. That's the truth. And always vodka or cognac. (*Clinks glasses.*) To you! You're an unpretentious man, it's too bad to be saying good-bye to you. (*They drink.*)

TRIGORIN. I don't feel like leaving, myself.

MASHA. Then ask her to stay.

TRIGORIN. No, she won't now. Her son's behaving extremely thoughtlessly. First he tried to shoot himself, and now they say he's getting ready to challenge me to a duel. And for what? He's sulky, snorts, propagates new forms . . . But isn't there room for everyone now, for both the old and the new? Why push each other around?

MASHA. Yes, but jealousy! However, it's not my business.

(*A pause.* YAKOV *goes through from left to right with a suitcase;* NINA *comes in and stops by the window.*)

MASHA. My teacher isn't so terribly smart, but he's a good man and a poor one, and he really loves me. I feel sorry for him. And for his old mother. Well, sir, let me wish you the best of everything. Think kindly of me. (*Shakes his hand warmly.*) I'm very grateful to you for your good favor. Send me your books, and be sure to autograph them. Only don't write "My dear," but just put: "To Marya, who doesn't remember her family and is here in this world for no known reason." Good-bye! (*Goes out.*)

NINA (*holding her closed hand out toward* TRIGORIN). Odd or even?

TRIGORIN. Even.

NINA (*sighing*). Wrong. There's just one pea in my hand. I was trying to tell my fortune: should I become an actress or not? If only someone would advise me.

TRIGORIN. No one can about that. (*A pause.*)

NINA. We're parting and . . . probably won't ever see each other again. Please take this little medallion from me as a keepsake. I had your initials put on it . . . and on this side the title of your book, *Days and Nights*.

TRIGORIN. How lovely! (*Kisses the medallion.*) A charming present!

NINA. Remember me sometimes.

TRIGORIN. I will. I'll remember you as you were that clear day—remember?—a week ago when you had on the bright dress . . . we talked . . . and the white gull was lying there then on the bench.

NINA (*reflectively*). Yes, the gull . . . (*A pause.*) We can't talk any more, they're coming . . . Before you go, give me two minutes, I beg you . . . (*Goes out left. Simultaneously there come in from the right:* ARKADINA, SORIN *in a tail coat with a decoration, and then* YAKOV, *who is worried about the packing.*)

ARKADINA. Come on, old man, stay home. Why should you, with your rheumatism, go traveling around visiting? (*To* TRIGORIN.) Who's that just went out? Nina?

TRIGORIN. Yes.

ARKADINA. *Pardon*, we interrupted you . . . (*Sits down.*) I think I've packed everything. I'm exhausted.

TRIGORIN (*reads on the medallion*). "*Days and Nights*, page 121, lines 11 and 12."

YAKOV (*clearing the table*). Do you also want the rods packed?

TRIGORIN. Yes, I'll still need them. But give the books away to somebody.

YAKOV. Yes, sir.

TRIGORIN (*to himself*). Page 121, lines 11 and 12. What's in those lines? (*To* ARKADINA.) Do you have my books in the house?

ARKADINA. In my brother's study, in the corner bookcase.

TRIGORIN. Page 121 . . . (*Goes out.*)

ARKADINA. Really, Petrusha, you ought to stay . . .

SORIN. You're going; it'll be very hard for me without you.

ARKADINA. But what is there in town?

SORIN. Nothing special, but still. (*Laughs.*) There'll be the laying of the cornerstone of the district council building and everything like that . . . Even just for a little while I'd like to pull myself together and get out of this chirpy life, for I've gotten very stale, just like an old cigar holder. I've ordered the horses up for one o'clock; we'll leave together.

ARKADINA (*after a pause*). Come, now, stay here, don't feel lonely, don't catch cold. Take care of my son. Look after him. Set him right. (*A pause.*) Here, I'll be gone, and I won't know why Konstantin shot himself. I think the main reason was jealousy, and the sooner I take Trigorin away from here, the better.

SORIN. How'll I put it? There were other reasons, too. It's understandable; a young man, intelligent, living in the country, way out, with no money, no position, no future. Nothing to keep him busy. Ashamed and afraid of his idleness. I'm extremely fond of him, and he's attached to me, but still, when all's said and done, he feels he's extra in the house, that he's a hanger-on here, a sponger. It's understandable: pride . . .

ARKADINA. He's nothing but trouble to me! (*In deep thought.*) What about his going into the service, perhaps . . .

SORIN (*whistles, then hesitatingly*). I think the best thing would be if you . . . gave him a little money. First of all, he's got to dress humanly, and all that sort of thing. Just look at him: he's been wearing the one and the same jacket around three years now, goes without a coat . . . (*Laughs.*) And it wouldn't hurt the boy to go off and have a good time . . . Go abroad, maybe . . . After all, that doesn't cost a lot.

ARKADINA. Still . . . well, perhaps, I can still manage a suit, but as for going abroad . . . No, right now, I can't even manage a suit. (*Decisively.*) I have no money!

(SORIN *laughs.*)

ARKADINA. I don't!

SORIN (*whistles*). Ri-ight. I'm sorry, my dear, don't be angry. I believe you . . . You're a generous, noble woman.

ARKADINA (*through tears*). I have no money!

SORIN. If I had any, naturally I'd give him some myself, but I haven't a thing, not even five kopeks. (*Laughs.*) The manager takes away my whole pension and spends it on farming, cattle raising, beekeeping, and my money goes for nothing. The bees die, the cows die, and they never bring me the horses . . .

ARKADINA. Certainly, I have money, but, after all, I'm an actress: just the clothes alone ruin me completely.

SORIN. You're kind, my dear . . . I respect you . . . Certainly . . . But now again something's not right . . . (*Staggers.*) My head's going around. (*Grabs hold of the table.*) I feel faint and all that sort of thing.

ARKADINA (*frightened*). Petrusha! (*Trying to hold him up.*) Petrusha, dear . . . (*Shouts.*) Help me! Help! . . .

(TREPLYOV, *with a bandage on his head, and* MEDVEDENKO *come in.*)

ARKADINA. He's fainting!

SORIN. It's nothing, nothing . . . (*Smiles and drinks some water.*) It's gone . . . that's all . . .

TREPLYOV (*to his mother*). Don't be scared, Mama, it's not dangerous. That often happens to Uncle Pyotr now. (*To his uncle.*) You ought to lie down a bit, Uncle Pyotr.

SORIN. Just a minute, yes . . . But still I'm going to town . . . I'll lie down a minute and go . . . naturally . . . (*Goes out, leaning on his cane.*)

MEDVEDENKO (*escorts him by the arm*). Here's a riddle: what goes on four legs in the morning, on two at noon, and on three in the evening . . .

SORIN (*laughs*). Precisely. And on its back at night. Thank you, I can manage myself . . .

MEDVEDENKO. Well, now, what formality! . . . (*He and* SORIN *go out.*)

ARKADINA. What a scare he gave me!

TREPLYOV. It's unhealthy for him to live in the country. He feels miserable. But now, Mama, if you suddenly felt very generous and gave him a loan of one thousand five hundred or two thousand, why he could live in town a whole year.

ARKADINA. I haven't any money. I'm an actress, not a banker. (*Pause.*)

TREPLYOV. Mama, change my bandage. You do it well.

ARKADINA (*gets iodoform and a box of bandages out of the medicine cabinet*). The doctor's late.

TREPLYOV. Promised to be here at ten, but it's already noon.

ARKADINA. Sit down. (*Takes the bandage off his head.*) You look as if you had a turban on. Yesterday a visitor in the kitchen asked what your nationality was. Oh, it's almost completely closed. Just a tiny bit left. (*Kisses his head.*) But when I'm not here you're not going to do this click-click again?

TREPLYOV. No, Mama. That was a moment of mad despair, when I couldn't control myself. That won't happen again. (*Kisses her hand.*) You have hands of gold. I remember, very long ago, when you were still working in the government theater—I was little then—there was a fight outside in our courtyard. The laundress who lived in was badly beaten up. Remember? She was picked up unconscious . . . You took care of her the whole time, brought her medicines, washed her children in the tub. Don't you really remember?

ARKADINA. No. (*Puts on a new bandage.*)

TREPLYOV. There were two ballerinas living in the same house as us then . . . They used to come drink coffee with you . . .

ARKADINA. That I remember.

TREPLYOV. They were very sort of pious. (*A pause.*) Recently, these last few days now, I love you just as tenderly and wholeheartedly as when I was a child. Except for you, I have nobody left now. Only why, why do you give in to that man's influence?

ARKADINA. You don't understand him, Konstantin. He's the most noble person . . .

TREPLYOV. However, when he was told that I was planning to challenge him to a duel, all that nobleness didn't prevent him from being a coward. He's going. Disgraceful running away!

ARKADINA. What nonsense! I myself am asking him to leave here.

TREPLYOV. The most noble person! Here you and I are practically arguing over him, and he's somewhere in the drawing room or the garden making fun of us . . . trying to make Nina mature, trying to convince her once and for all that he's a genius.

ARKADINA. You simply delight in saying nasty things to me. I respect that man and I ask you not to speak ill of him in my presence.

TREPLYOV. And I don't respect him. You want me, too, to think he's a genius, but—I'm sorry, I don't know how to lie—his writing makes me sick.

ARKADINA. That's just envy. People with no talent but with lots of pretensions have nothing else to do but attack real talent. It's their only consolation!

TREPLYOV (*ironically*). Real talent! (*Angrily.*) I'm more talented than you all, for that matter! (*Yanks the bandage off his head.*) You, you conservatives, have grabbed first place in art and consider nothing valid and real but what you do yourselves, and everything else you stifle and stamp on! I don't acknowledge you! Not you, nor him!

ARKADINA. You decadent! . . .

TREPLYOV. Go on off to your darling theater and play your roles there in those pitiful, dull plays!

ARKADINA. I've never played in such plays. Leave me alone! You're not able to write even a pitiful vaudeville show! You Kievan bourgeois! You sponger!

TREPLYOV. You tightwad!

ARKADINA. You ragamuffin!

(TREPLYOV *sits down and cries softly.*)

ARKADINA. You nobody! (*Having walked back and forth, in agitation.*) Don't cry. Don't, don't cry . . . (*Cries.*) Don't . . . (*Kisses his forehead, his cheeks, his head.*) My precious child, forgive me . . . Forgive your guilty mother. Forgive wretched me.

TREPLYOV (*embraces her*). If only you knew! I've lost everything. She doesn't love me, I can't write any more . . . all I hoped for is gone . . .

ARKADINA. Don't give up hope . . . Everything will be all right. He'll be going very soon; she'll love you again. (*Wipes away his tears.*) Stop now. We're friends again.

TREPLYOV (*kisses her hands*). Yes, Mama.

ARKADINA (*tenderly*). Be friends with him, too. You don't have to duel . . . You don't have to, do you?

TREPLYOV. All right . . . Only, Mama, don't make me see him. It's very hard for me . . . more than I can stand . . . (TRIGORIN *comes in.*) There he is . . . I'm going . . . (*Quickly puts the medicines back in the cabinet.*) And the doctor'll do the bandage . . .

TRIGORIN (*looking in a book*). Page 121 . . . lines 11 and 12 . . . Here they are . . . (*Reads.*) "If you ever have need of my life, come and take it."

(TREPLYOV *picks the bandage up from the floor and goes out.*)

ARKADINA (*after looking at her watch*). The horses will be here soon.

TRIGORIN (*to himself*). "If you ever have need of my life, come and take it."

ARKADINA. All your things, I hope, are already packed?

TRIGORIN (*impatiently*). Yes, yes . . . (*In deep thought.*) Why do I hear a note of sorrow in this appeal of a pure soul, and why is my heart so painfully wrung? . . . "If you ever have need of my life, come and take it." (*To* ARKADINA.) Let's stay one day more!

(ARKADINA *shakes her head negatively.*)

Let's!

ARKADINA. Darling, I know what's keeping you here. But control yourself. You're a little high; sober up.

TRIGORIN. You be sober, too, be sensible, reasonable, I beg you; look at this all as a true friend . . . (*Presses her hand.*)

You're capable of sacrifice . . . Be my friend, let me go . . .

ARKADINA (*in extreme agitation*). You're so enchanted?

TRIGORIN. I'm being lured to her! Perhaps it's exactly what I need.

ARKADINA. The love of a little provincial girl? Oh, how little you know yourself!

TRIGORIN. Sometimes people sleep as they go; so now, as I talk to you, I seem to be sleeping and seeing her in my sleep . . . Sweet, delightful dreams have overcome me . . . Let me go . . .

ARKADINA (*shuddering*). No, no—I'm like any other woman, and I won't be talked to like that . . . Don't torture me, Boris . . . I'm terrified . . .

TRIGORIN. If you want, you can be remarkable. Young love, charming, poetic, a transport to the world of dreams—only it alone on earth can bring happiness! I've never yet known such love . . . When I was young, I had no time, I was haunting the editorial offices, struggling against want . . . Now, here, this love has come, has, in the end, allured me . . . What's the sense of running away from it?

ARKADINA (*in anger*). You're out of your mind!

TRIGORIN. Well, so?

ARKADINA. You've all made a pact today to torture me! (*Cries.*)

TRIGORIN (*grabs his head*). She doesn't understand! Doesn't want to!

ARKADINA. Am I really already so old and ugly that you can shamelessly talk to me about other women? (*Embraces him and kisses him.*) Oh, you're mad! My beautiful, marvellous . . . You, the last page of my life! (*Kneels down.*) My joy, my pride, my bliss . . . (*Embraces his knees.*) If you leave me, even for an hour, I won't be able to go on living, I'll lose my mind—my wonderful, my splendid sovereign . . .

TRIGORIN. Someone may come in. (*Helps her up.*)

ARKADINA. Let them; I'm not ashamed of my love for you. (*Kisses his hands.*) My treasure, my poor desperate dear, you want to behave like a madman, but I don't want you to, I won't let you . . . (*Laughs.*) You're mine . . . you're mine . . . And this forehead is mine, and these eyes are mine, and this lovely silk hair is mine, too . . . You're all mine. You're so talented, intelligent, the best of all modern writers; you're Russia's only hope . . . You have so much sincerity, simplicity, freshness, so much healthy humor . . . With just one stroke you can characterize a person or a landscape; your people seem alive. Oh, no one can read you without delight! You think this is just so much false praise? That I'm trying to flatter you? Come, look me in the eye . . . look at me . . . Do I look like a liar? There, you see! Only I know your real value; only I tell you the truth, my darling, my wonderful . . . You'll go? Yes? You won't leave me? . . .

TRIGORIN. I don't have a mind of my own . . . I never did . . . Nerveless, flabby, always submissive—can a woman really like that? Take me, carry me away, only don't let me out of your sight even one step . . .

ARKADINA (*to herself*). Now he's mine. (*Casually, as if nothing had happened.*) However, if you want to, you can stay. I'll go ahead alone, and you can come later, in a week. As a matter of fact, what's there for you to rush off to?

TRIGORIN. No, better go together.

ARKADINA. As you want. So, let's go together . . .

(*Pause.* TRIGORIN *makes a note in his book.*)

ARKADINA. What're you doing?

TRIGORIN. I heard a good expression this morning: "the maiden pines . . ." It'll come in handy. (*Stretches.*) So we're going? And again the trains, the stations, the buffets, the chops, the conversations . . .

SHAMRAYEV (*enters*). I regret I have the honor to announce that the horses are ready. It's time, my dear lady, to go to the station; the train arrives at 2:05. And, Irina Nikolayevna, do me a favor: don't forget to inquire about where the actor Suzdaltsev is now? Alive? Well? We used to drink together once upon a time . . . You couldn't beat the way he played in *The Mail Robbery* . . .[15] I remember the tragedian Izmailov was working with him then in Elisavetgrad— also a remarkable person . . . Don't hurry, my dear lady,

[15] A nineteenth-century French melodrama by Moreau, Sidorain, and Delacour which Chekhov as a boy had been fond of.

you have five more minutes. Once in one melodrama they were playing conspirators, and when they were caught red-handed, they were supposed to say: "We're trapped," but Izmailov says, "We're prapped . . ." (*Guffaws.*) Prapped! . . .

(*While he is speaking,* YAKOV *fusses around the suitcases, the* MAID *brings* ARKADINA *her hat, mantle, parasol, gloves; all help* ARKADINA *dress. The* COOK *peeks in through the left door, a little later comes in hesitantly.* POLINA ANDREYEVNA *comes in, then* SORIN *and* MEDVEDENKO.)

POLINA ANDREYEVNA (*with a little basket*). Here are some plums for you to eat on the way . . . They're very sweet. Maybe you'll want a treat . . .

ARKADINA. You're very kind, Polina Andreyevna.

POLINA ANDREYEVNA. Good-bye, my dear! If anything wasn't right, forgive us. (*Cries.*)

ARKADINA (*embraces her*). Everything was fine, everything was fine. Only now don't cry.

POLINA ANDREYEVNA. Our time's running out!

ARKADINA. And what can we do!

SORIN (*wearing a coat with a cape, a hat, and using a cane, comes in through the left door; going across the room*). Sister, it's time, so's not to be late, when all's said and done. I'm going to get in. (*Goes out.*)

MEDVEDENKO. And I'm going to walk to the station . . . to see you off. I'll be quick . . . (*Goes out.*)

ARKADINA. Good-bye, my dears . . . If we're all alive and well, we'll see each other in the summer again . . . (*The* MAID, YAKOV, *and the* COOK *kiss her hand.*) Don't forget me. (*Gives the* COOK *a ruble.*) Here's a ruble for the three of you.

COOK. Most humbly thank you, ma'am. Have a good trip! You've been good to us!

YAKOV. God grant you good luck!

SHAMRAYEV. Just a note would make us happy! Good-bye, Boris Alekseyevich!

ARKADINA. Where's Konstantin? Tell him I'm going. Must say good-bye. Well, think kindly of me. (*To* YAKOV.) I gave the cook a ruble. It's for the three of you.

(*All go out right. The stage is empty. Behind stage there is the noise of people seeing others off. The* MAID *comes back in to fetch the basket of plums from the table and goes out again.*)

TRIGORIN (*coming back in*). I forgot my cane. I think it's there on the terrace. (*Goes toward it and at the left-hand door meets* NINA, *coming in.*) It's you? We're leaving.

NINA. I had a feeling we'd meet again. (*In agitation.*) Boris Alekseyevich, I've irrevocably decided, the die is cast, I'm going to go on the stage. Tomorrow I'll be gone; I'm leaving my father, leaving everything behind, beginning a new life . . . I'm going away, just like you . . . to Moscow. We'll meet there.

TRIGORIN (*having glanced around*). Stay at the Slaviansky Bazaar . . .[16] Let me know at once . . . Molchanovka, Grokholsky's house . . .[17] I must hurry . . . (*A pause.*)

NINA. Just a minute more . . .

TRIGORIN (*in a low voice*). You're so beautiful . . . Oh, what happiness to think that we'll see each other soon! (*She leans against his chest.*) I'll see again these marvellous eyes, this indescribably beautiful, soft smile . . . these gentle features, this expression of angelic purity . . . My sweet . . . (*A long kiss.*)

(*Curtain*)

[16] A Moscow hotel of great elegance and chic.
[17] The house owner's name was used instead of the street number.

ACT IV

One of the drawing rooms in SORIN'S *house, turned into a study by* KONSTANTIN TREPLYOV. *On the right and left, doors leading to the inner rooms. Directly ahead, a glass door onto the terrace. In addition to the usual drawing-room furniture, there is a desk in the right-hand corner, a Turkish divan by the door on the left. A bookcase, and books on the windows and on chairs. It is evening. A single bulb under a lampshade is lit. It is semidark. The trees are rustling and the wind is howling in the chimneys. The watchman knocks.* MEDVEDENKO *and* MASHA *come in.*

MASHA (*calls*). Konstantin Gavrilych! Konstantin Gavrilych! (*Looks around.*) Nobody's here. The old man keeps asking every minute: Where's Kostya, Where's Kostya? . . . Can't live without him . . .

MEDVEDENKO. He's afraid of being alone. (*Listening.*) What awful weather! It's the second day now.

MASHA (*turning up the wick in the lamp*). There are waves on the lake. Huge ones.

MEDVEDENKO. It's dark in the garden. Must tell them to take down that theater. Stands there all bare, ugly, like a skeleton, and the curtain flaps in the wind. When I was going by last night, it seemed to me there was somebody crying in it.

MASHA. So, you see . . . (*Pause.*)

MEDVEDENKO. Masha, let's go home!

MASHA (*shakes her head negatively*). I'm going to spend the night here.

MEDVEDENKO (*imploringly*). Masha, let's go! The baby! I bet it's hungry.

MASHA. Never mind! Matryona will feed him. (*Pause.*)

MEDVEDENKO. I feel sorry for him. This is the third night without his mother.

MASHA. You've gotten tiresome. Before, you at least used to do a little philosophizing, but now it's all baby, home, baby, home—that's all a person can get out of you.

MEDVEDENKO. Let's go, Masha!

MASHA. Go by yourself.

MEDVEDENKO. Your father won't give me a horse.

MASHA. He will. You just ask, he will.

MEDVEDENKO. All right, I might. Means you'll be coming tomorrow?

MASHA (*takes a snuff*). Oh, all right. You've badgered me . . .

(TREPLYOV *and* POLINA ANDREYEVNA *come in.* TREPLYOV *has brought pillows and a blanket, and* POLINA ANDREYEVNA, *sheets and pillowcases; they put it all on the Turkish divan, and then* TREPLYOV *goes to his desk and sits down.*)

MASHA. What's this for, Mama?

POLINA ANDREYEVNA. Pyotr Nikolayevich asked for his bed to be made up in Kostya's room.

MASHA. Let me, I'll . . . (*Makes the bed.*)

POLINA ANDREYEVNA (*sighing*). Old men are as bad as children . . . (*Goes over to the desk and, leaning on it with her elbows, looks at a manuscript. A pause.*)

MEDVEDENKO. Well, I'll be going now. Good-bye, Masha. (*Kisses his wife's hand.*) Good-bye, Mother. (*Moves to kiss his mother-in-law's hand.*)

POLINA ANDREYEVNA (*vexedly*). Come, now! Take care of yourself.

MEDVEDENKO. Good-bye, Konstantin Gavrilych.

(TREPLYOV *puts his hand out without speaking;* MEDVEDENKO *goes out.*)

POLINA ANDREYEVNA (*looking at the manuscript*). Nobody ever dreamed that you'd make a real writer, Kostya. And now, thank God, you're even getting money sent back from the magazines. (*Passes her hand over his hair.*) And you've grown handsome . . . Kostya dear, good Kostya, be gentler with my Mashenka! . . .

MASHA (*making the bed*). Leave him alone, Mama.

POLINA ANDREYEVNA (*to* TREPLYOV). She's awfully nice. (*Pause.*) A woman, Kostya, doesn't need anything but to be looked at with affection. I know that from my own experience.

(TREPLYOV *gets up from behind the desk and goes out without speaking.*)

MASHA. And now you've made him mad. That's all he needed, was to be pestered.

POLINA ANDREYEVNA. I feel sorry for you, Mashenka.

MASHA. What do I care!

POLINA ANDREYEVNA. My heart's sore for you. Sure, I see it all, understand it.

MASHA. It's all nonsense. A hopeless love—that's something that's only in novels. It's nothing. Only you mustn't let yourself get out of hand, you must keep on waiting for something, for the wind to come in from the sea . . . Once love has started up in your heart, you have to get rid of it. Here, my husband's been promised a transfer to another district. Once we move there, I'll forget it all . . . tear it out of my heart by the roots.

(*A melancholy waltz is played two rooms away.*)

POLINA ANDREYEVNA. Kostya's playing. Means he's feeling lonely.

MASHA (*silently makes two or three waltz turns*). The most important thing, Mama, is not to look at what's in front of you. Just once my Semyon gets his transfer, then, believe me—there I'll have forgotten all about it in a month. There's nothing to it.

(*The left door opens.* DORN *and* MEDVEDENKO *wheel in* SORIN *in a wheelchair.*)

MEDVEDENKO. I've got six in the house now. And flour's seventy kopeks a pood.

DORN. It takes some doing.

MEDVEDENKO. It's easy for you to laugh. You're rolling in money.

DORN. Money? In thirty years of practice, my friend, of nerve-racking practice, when I couldn't call my time my own day or night, I managed to save up only two thousand, and I ran through that not long ago abroad. I have nothing.

MASHA (*to her husband*). You didn't go?

MEDVEDENKO (*guiltily*). How? When they won't let you have a horse?

MASHA (*in bitter annoyance, in a low voice*). I don't want to have to look at you!

(*The wheelchair stops on the left side of the room;* POLINA ANDREYEVNA, MASHA, *and* DORN *sit down beside it;* MEDVEDENKO, *saddened, goes off to one side.*)

DORN. But how many changes you've made! Made a study out of a drawing room.

MASHA. It's more pleasant for Konstantin Gavrilych to work

here. When he feels like it, he can go out in the garden and think there.

(*The watchman knocks.*)

SORIN. Where's my sister?

DORN. She went to the station to meet Trigorin. She'll be right back.

SORIN. If you thought it necessary to call my sister here, that means I'm dangerously ill. (*After a pause.*) That's a fine how-do-you-do for you: I'm dangerously ill, but in the meantime I'm not given any medicine.

DORN. What do you want? Valerian drops? Bicarbonate of soda? Quinine?

SORIN. Now, here the philosophy starts. Oh, what a punishment! (*Nodding toward the divan.*) Is that made up for me?

POLINA ANDREYEVNA. For you, Pyotr Nikolayevich.

SORIN. Thank you.

DORN (*croons*). "*The moon sails over the midnight skies* . . ." [18]

SORIN. Here, I want to give Kostya a subject for a story. It has to be called "The Man Who Wanted To." "*L'homme qui a voulu.*" One time, when I was young, I wanted to become a literary man—and I didn't; I wanted to speak elegantly—and I've always spoken rottenly (*mocks himself*): "and everything, and all that sort of thing, you know, now, not quite . . ." and I used to try and try to sum things up and just break out in a sweat; I wanted to get married—and I didn't; I always wanted to live in town—and here I'm ending my life in the country and all that sort of thing.

DORN. You wanted to become a full-fledged Councillor of State—and you did.

SORIN (*laughs*). I didn't try for that. That happened all by itself.

DORN. To express dissatisfaction with life at the age of sixty-two, admit it, is not magnanimous.

SORIN. What a stubborn man. Don't misunderstand me: I want to live!

DORN. That's frivolous thinking. By the laws of nature, every life must have an end.

SORIN. You're arguing like a man who is full. You're completely satisfied and therefore indifferent to life, nothing

[18] A nineteenth-century romance.

makes any difference to you. But you, too, will be terrified of dying.

DORN. The fear of death is an animal fear. It must be suppressed. The only people who consciously fear death are those who believe in eternal life, who are terrified of their sins. But, first of all, you're not a believer, and, secondly, what sins have you got? You served in the Justice Department twenty-five years—and that's it . . .

SORIN (*laughs*). Twenty-eight . . .

(TREPLYOV *comes in and sits down on the bench at* SORIN'S *feet.* MASHA *does not take her eyes off him the whole time.*)

DORN. We're keeping Konstantin Gavrilych from working.

TREPLYOV. No, that's all right. (*A pause.*)

MEDVEDENKO. May I ask you, Doctor, which city you liked most of all abroad?

DORN. Genoa.

TREPLYOV. Why Genoa?

DORN. There's a splendid crowd in the street there. When you come out of your hotel in the evening, the whole street is jammed with people. You move along then in the crowd without any aim, this way and that, in a broken line, live right along with it, become commingled with it psychically and begin to believe that a single world-soul is really possible, sort of like the one Nina Zarechnaya played in your play once. By the way, where is Zarechnaya now? Where and how is she?

TREPLYOV. I suppose she's well.

DORN. I heard something about her having led some kind of peculiar life. What happened?

TREPLYOV. It's a long story, Doctor.

DORN. Well, you make it short. (*Pause.*)

TREPLYOV. She ran away from home and took up with Trigorin. Did you know that?

DORN. I did.

TREPLYOV. She had a baby. The baby died. Trigorin stopped loving her and went back to his old ties, as was to be expected. As a matter of fact, he never left them, but, out of weakness of will, somehow managed to be both places at once. So far as I could understand from what I heard, Nina's personal life was a complete failure.

DORN. But the stage?

TREPLYOV. Even worse, it seems. She made her debut in a summer theater outside of Moscow, then went off to the provinces. At that time I didn't let her out of sight, and for a while wherever she went, I went, too. She kept taking on big parts but she played coarsely, tastelessly, howling and making crass gestures. There were moments when she'd give a scream with talent, or die with talent, but those were only moments.

DORN. Still, it means she has talent?

TREPLYOV. It was hard to know. Probably she does. I saw her, but she didn't want to see me, and her maid wouldn't let me in to her room. I understood how she felt and didn't insist on a meeting. (*Pause.*) What else is there to tell you? Then, after I'd come home, I kept getting letters from her. Intelligent, warm, interesting letters; she didn't complain, but I sensed that she was deeply unhappy; every line showed she was sick, her nerves all taut. And her fancy a little deranged. She would sign herself "The Seagull." In "*Rusalka*,"[19] the miller says he's a raven; so she in her letters kept repeating that she was a seagull. Now she's here.

DORN. What do you mean, here?

TREPLYOV. In town, at the inn. She's had a room there now the last five days or so. I was going to go see her, and Marya Ilyinishna did go, but she doesn't see anyone. Semyon Semyonovich says he's sure he saw her yesterday after dinner in the fields two versts from here.

MEDVEDENKO. Yes, I did. She was headed the other way, toward town. I greeted her, asked why she didn't come calling on us. She said she would.

TREPLYOV. She won't come. (*Pause.*) Her father and stepmother don't want to have anything to do with her. They've stationed watchmen everywhere, so as not to let her even get near the estate. (*With the doctor, moves over toward the desk.*) How easy, Doctor, to be a philosopher on paper and how hard in fact!

SORIN. She was a lovely girl.

[19] In English, "The Water-nymph"; a romantic narrative poem by Pushkin, later an opera by Dargomyzhsky.

DORN. What, sir?
SORIN. I said, she was a lovely girl. Councillor of State Sorin was even in love with her for a while.
DORN. You old Lovelace.
(SHAMRAYEV's *laugh is heard.*)
POLINA ANDREYEVNA. I guess they're back from the station.
TREPLYOV. Yes, I hear Mama.
(ARKADINA *and* TRIGORIN *come in, followed by* SHAMRAYEV.)
SHAMRAYEV (*entering*). We're all growing old, being worn away by the wind and the weather, but you, my dear lady, are still young . . . A bright blouse, vivacity . . . grace . . .
ARKADINA. Again you're out to ruin things for me, you tiresome man!
TRIGORIN (*to* SORIN). Hello, Pyotr Nikolayevich! What's this about you being sick all the time? That's not good! (*Having noticed* MASHA, *delightedly.*) Marya Ilyinishna!
MASHA. You recognized me? (*Shakes his hand.*)
TRIGORIN. Married?
MASHA. A long time.
TRIGORIN. Happy? (*Exchanges bows and greetings with* DORN *and with* MEDVEDENKO, *then goes hesitantly up to* TREPLYOV.) Irina Nikolayevna said you've forgotten the past and stopped being angry. (TREPLYOV *holds out his hand to him.*)
ARKADINA (*to her son*). Here, Boris Alekseyevich has brought the magazine with your new story.
TREPLYOV (*taking the magazine, to* TRIGORIN). Thank you. You're very kind. (*They sit down.*)
TRIGORIN. Your admirers send you their compliments . . . In Petersburg and in Moscow in general, they're interested in you, and I'm always being asked about you. I'm asked: what's he like, how old is he, dark or blond. For some reason everybody thinks that you're no longer young. And nobody knows your real name, since you publish under a pseudonym. You're mysterious, like The Man in the Iron Mask.
TREPLYOV. Are you staying long?
TRIGORIN. No. I think I'll be on my way to Moscow tomorrow. I have to. I'm in a hurry to finish a story, and I've promised to give something else to an anthology. In short—the same old thing.

(*While they are talking,* ARKADINA *and* POLINA ANDREYEVNA *put a card table in the middle of the room and open it;* SHAMRAYEV *lights some candles, puts chairs around. They take lotto cards[20] and disks out of a cupboard.*)

TRIGORIN. The weather has greeted me coldly. The wind is savage. Tomorrow morning, if it dies down, I'll go down to the lake and go fishing. At the same time I must have a look at the garden and that place—remember?—where they put your play on. I have a plot all set in my mind, just have to refresh my memory on the setting.

MASHA (*to her father*). Papa, let my husband have a horse! He has to get home.

SHAMRAYEV (*mimicking her*). A horse . . . get home . . . (*Harshly.*) You've seen for yourself: they just went down to the station. Can't send 'em running out again.

MASHA. But there are other horses after all . . . (*Seeing that her father is silent, waves her hand in disgust.*) To have anything to do with all of you is . . .

MEDVEDENKO. I'll walk, Masha. Really . . .

POLINA ANDREYEVNA (*sighing*). Walk, in such weather . . . (*Sits down at the card table.*) Come, ladies and gentlemen.

MEDVEDENKO. Because it's only six versts . . . Good-bye . . . (*Kisses his wife's hand.*) Good-bye, Mother. (*His mother-in-law reluctantly holds out her hand for him to kiss it.*) I wouldn't bother anybody, but the baby . . . (*Bows to all.*) Good-bye . . . (*Goes out with a guilty walk.*)

SHAMRAYEV. He'll probably make it. He's not a general.

POLINA ANDREYEVNA (*raps on the table*). Come, ladies and gentlemen. Let's not waste time, for supper will soon be ready.

(SHAMRAYEV, MASHA, *and* DORN *sit down at the table.*)

ARKADINA (*to* TRIGORIN). When the long fall evenings come, they play lotto here. Just look: old-fashioned lotto, which my mother used to play with us when we were children. Don't you want to play a round with us before supper? (*Sits down at the table with* TRIGORIN.) It's a dull game, but once you've gotten used to it, that doesn't matter. (*Gives everyone three cards.*)

TREPLYOV (*thumbing through the magazine*). Read his own

[20] The modern American word for the game is bingo.

story but didn't even cut the pages of mine. (*Puts the magazine on the desk, then heads for the left door; as he passes his mother, he kisses her head.*)

ARKADINA. And you, Kostya?

TREPLYOV. Excuse me, I don't feel like it . . . I'm going to take a little walk. (*Goes out.*)

ARKADINA. The ante is ten kopeks. Put it in for me, Doctor.

DORN. Agreed, madam.

MASHA. Everyone bet? I'm starting . . . Twenty-two!

ARKADINA. I have it.

MASHA. Three!

DORN. Right.

MASHA. You covered three? Eight! Eighty-one! Ten!

SHAMRAYEV. Take your time.

ARKADINA. How I was received in Kharkov! My gracious, my head's still in a whirl!

MASHA. Thirty-four!

(*Off stage, a melancholy waltz is played.*)

ARKADINA. The students gave me an ovation . . . Three baskets, two wreaths, and this . . . (*Takes off a brooch and tosses it on the table.*)

SHAMRAYEV. Yes, that's a thing . . .

MASHA. Fifty!

DORN. Exactly fifty?

ARKADINA. I was strikingly dressed . . . Really something, and I'm no fool when it comes to clothes.

POLINA ANDREYEVNA. Kostya's playing. He feels lonely, the poor boy.

SHAMRAYEV. He gets criticized severely in the papers.

MASHA. Seventy-seven!

ARKADINA. Why does he bother to pay attention!

TRIGORIN. He has no luck. He still somehow can't hit his own, real, right tone. There's something odd about his work, something vague, at times even rather like gibberish. Not a single live character.

MASHA. Eleven!

ARKADINA (*glancing at* SORIN). Petrusha, you bored? (*Pause.*) He's asleep.

DORN. The Councillor of State is asleep.

MASHA. Seven! Ninety!

TRIGORIN. If I lived on an estate like this, by a lake, would I take up writing? I'd overcome this passion in me and not do anything but go fishing.

MASHA. Twenty-eight!

TRIGORIN. To catch a ruff or a perch—that's such bliss!

DORN. But I have faith in Konstantin Gavrilych. There's something there! There's something there! He thinks in images, his stories are colorful, vivid, and I get very much involved in them. I'm only sorry he has no definite aims. He creates an impression, and that's all, but of course you can't go far with just an impression. Irina Nikolayevna, are you glad you have a son who's a writer?

ARKADINA. Just imagine, I haven't read his piece yet. There's never time.

MASHA. Twenty-six!

(TREPLYOV *comes in quietly and goes over to his desk.*)

SHAMRAYEV (*to* TRIGORIN). But, Boris Alekseyevich, we still have your thing here.

TRIGORIN. What thing?

SHAMRAYEV. One time Konstantin Gavrilych shot a seagull, and you asked me to have it stuffed.

TRIGORIN. I don't remember. (*Reflecting.*) Don't remember.

MASHA. Sixty-six! One!

TREPLYOV (*flings open the window, listens*). How dark! I don't understand why I feel such anxiety.

ARKADINA. Kostya, shut the window, it's drafty.

(TREPLYOV *shuts the window.*)

MASHA. Eighty-eight!

TRIGORIN. I have a row, ladies and gentlemen.

ARKADINA (*gaily*). Bravo! Bravo!

SHAMRAYEV. Bravo!

ARKADINA. This man always has all the luck in everything. (*Gets up.*) And now let's go have a bite of something. Our celebrity had no dinner today. After supper we'll continue. (*To her son.*) Kostya, leave your writing, let's go eat.

TREPLYOV. I don't want to, Mama, I'm full.

ARKADINA. As you like. (*Wakes* SORIN *up.*) Petrusha, supper time! (*Takes* SHAMRAYEV *by the arm.*) I'll tell you how I was received in Kharkov . . .

(POLINA ANDREYEVNA *puts out the candles on the table, then she and* DORN *wheel in the chair. All go out through the left door; on stage,* TREPLYOV *remains alone at his desk.*)

TREPLYOV (*gets ready to write; skims over what is already written*). I've talked so much about new forms, but now I feel that I am slowly slipping into a rut myself. (*Reads.*) "The poster on the fence announced . . . The pale face framed with dark hair . . ." Announced, framed . . . That shows no talent. (*Crosses it out.*) I'll start with the noise of the rain waking the hero up, and all the rest goes out. The description of the moonlit night is long and pretentious. Trigorin has worked out devices for himself, it's easy for him . . . He has the neck of a broken bottle shining on the dam and the shadow of the mill wheel looming black— there's the moonlit night all done. But I have a flickering light, and the soft shimmering of the stars, and the distant sounds of a piano fading away on the soft, fragrant air . . . It's unbearable. (*Pause.*) Indeed, I more and more come to the conclusion that it's not a question of old and new forms, but of what a man writes without thinking about any forms, writes because it comes freely straight from his heart. (*Someone knocks on the window closest to the desk.*) What's that? (*Peers out the window.*) Can't see a thing . . . (*Opens the glass door and looks into the garden.*) Somebody ran down the steps. (*Calls out.*) Who's there? (*Goes out and is heard quickly crossing the terrace; in half a minute he returns with* NINA ZARECHNAYA.) Nina! Nina!

(NINA *puts her head on his chest and sobs quietly.*)

TREPLYOV (*deeply moved*). Nina! Nina! It's you . . . you . . . I seemed to have a presentiment; all day my heart was in terrible anguish. (*Takes off her hat and talma.*[21]) Oh, my good one, my beloved, she's come! We won't cry, we won't.

NINA. There's somebody here.

TREPLYOV. Nobody.

NINA. Lock the doors, or they'll come in.

TREPLYOV. Nobody will come in.

NINA. I know, Irina Nikolayevna's here. Lock the doors . . .

TREPLYOV (*locks the right door with a key, goes over to the left*).

[21] A long cape or cloak, sometimes with a hood, worn by men and women in the nineteenth century; named after the French tragedian François Talma.

This has no lock. I'll put a chair up. (*Puts a chair against the door.*) Don't be afraid, nobody will come in.

NINA (*looks him in the face intently*). Let me look at you. (*Glancing around.*) It's warm, nice . . . Here there was a drawing room . . . Have I changed much?

TREPLYOV. Yes . . . You've gotten thin, and your eyes have become bigger. Nina, it's somehow strange to be seeing you. Why wouldn't you let me into your hotel room? Why haven't you come here until now? I know you've been here almost a week . . . Every day I've gone to your place several times, stood under your window like a beggar.

NINA. I was afraid you'd hate me. Every night I still dream that you're looking at me and don't recognize me. If only you knew! From the moment I arrived, I've been walking around here . . . by the lake. By your house a lot of times, but I didn't dare come in. Let's sit down. (*They sit down.*) We'll sit down and talk and talk. It's nice here, warm, comfortable . . . You hear—the wind? There's a line in Turgenev: "Lucky is the man who on such nights sits under his own roof, who has a warm nook."[22] I'm a seagull . . . No, that's not it. (*Rubs her forehead.*) What was I talking about? Oh, yes . . . Turgenev . . . "And may God help all homeless wanderers . . ." Never mind. (*Sobs.*)

TREPLYOV. Nina, you're again . . . Nina!

NINA. It's nothing; this makes it easier for me . . . I haven't cried for two years now. Late last night I went to have a look in the garden if our theater was still all together or not. It's still standing. I cried for the first time in two years, and I felt better, things were clearer inside. See, I'm not crying now. (*Takes him by the arm.*) And so you've become a writer . . . You're a writer; I'm—an actress . . . We've both fallen into a whole round of things to do, you and I . . . I was living joyfully, like a child—I'd wake up in the morning and sing; I loved you, dreamed of fame, but now? Early tomorrow morning I have to take a third-class train to Elets—with the peasants—and in Elets educated merchants will badger me with compliments. A dirty life!

TREPLYOV. Why to Elets?

[22] Both quotations are from the Epilogue in Turgenev's novel *Rudin*.

NINA. I've agreed to an engagement for the whole winter. It's time to go.

TREPLYOV. Nina, I cursed you, hated you, tore up your letters and pictures, but every minute I was aware that my whole being was tied to you forever. I just can't stop loving you, Nina. Ever since I lost you and began to be published, life has been unbearable for me—I'm suffering . . . My youth was suddenly cut off, and I feel as if I'd been in the world for ninety years already. I keep calling you, kissing the ground you've walked on; wherever I look, I always see your face, that warm smile which shone on me in the best years of my life . . .

NINA (*confusedly*). Why does he talk like that, why does he talk like that?

TREPLYOV. I'm all alone, not warmed by anybody's affection; I feel cold, as if in a dungeon, and no matter what I write, it's all dry, stale, gloomy. Stay here, Nina, I beg you, or let me go with you!

(NINA *quickly puts on her hat and talma.*)

Nina, why? Oh, please, Nina . . . (*Watches her put on her things. A pause.*)

NINA. My horses are standing at the gate. Don't go with me, I can make it myself . . . (*Through tears.*) Let me have some water . . .

TREPLYOV (*gives her a drink*). Where are you going now?

NINA. To town. (*Pause.*) Irina Nikolayevna's here?

TREPLYOV. Yes . . . Uncle Pyotr was bad on Thursday; we sent her a telegram to come.

NINA. Why do you say you've kissed the ground I've walked on? I ought to be killed. (*Braces herself on the desk.*) I'm so worn out! Just to rest . . . to rest! (*Raises her head.*) I'm a seagull . . . That's not it. I'm an actress. Yes, sure! (*Hearing the laughter of* ARKADINA *and* TRIGORIN, *she listens, then runs to the left door and peers through the keyhole.*) He's here, too . . . (*Going back to* TREPLYOV.) Yes, sure . . . Doesn't matter . . . Yes . . . He didn't believe in the theater, kept making fun of my dreams, and little by little I, too, stopped believing and lost courage . . . And then there were the problems of love, the jealousy, the constant fear for the baby . . . I became petty, worthless, played inanely . . . I didn't know what to do with my hands, didn't know how to stand on stage, had no control of my voice. You don't understand what it's like when you feel you're playing terribly. I'm a seagull. No, that's not it . . . Remember, you wounded a seagull? Along came a man, noticed her and, just to pass the time, destroyed . . . An idea for a little story . . . That's not it . . . (*Rubs her forehead.*) What was I talking about? . . . I was talking about the stage. I'm not like that now . . . I'm a real actress now; I play with delight, with enthusiasm, become intoxicated on stage and feel I'm beautiful. And now, while I've been living here, I've been walking and walking and thinking, thinking and feeling how with each passing day my spiritual strength grows more and more . . . Now I know, I understand, Kostya, that in what you and I do— it doesn't matter whether we act or write—the main thing isn't fame, isn't success, isn't what I used to dream about, but is being able to endure. Know how to bear your cross, and keep faith. I've kept faith, and it's not so painful for me, and when I think about my calling, then I'm not afraid of life.

TREPLYOV (*sadly*). You found your way; you know where you're going, but I'm still drifting in a chaos of dreams and images without knowing what for or who needs it. I have no faith and I don't know what my calling is.

NINA (*listening*). Shh . . . I'm going. Good-bye. When I become a great actress, come see me. You promise? But now . . . (*Presses his hand.*) It's already late. I can hardly stand up . . . I'm so weak, I'd like something to eat . . .

TREPLYOV. Stay, I'll bring you supper . .

NINA. No, no . . . Don't go with me, I can make it myself . . . My horses are close . . . That means she brought him with her? So what, it doesn't make any difference. When you see Trigorin, don't tell him anything . . . I love him. I love him even more than before . . . An idea for a little story . . . I love him, love him passionately, love him to despair. It was good before, Kostya! Remember? What a bright, warm, gay, pure life; what feelings—feelings like soft elegant flowers . . . Remember? . . . (*Recites.*) "Men and women, lions, eagles and partridges, great stags,

geese, spiders, silent fishes dwelling in the deep, starfish and those the naked eye could never see—in short, all living things, all living things, all living things, having completed their mournful circle, have died out. For thousands of centuries now the earth has not borne a single living creature, and this poor moon vainly lights its lamp. No longer do the cranes awake with a shriek in the meadow, and the cockchafers are not heard in the linden thickets . . ."
(*Embraces* TREPLYOV *impetuously and runs out through the glass door.*)

TREPLYOV (*after a pause*). It won't be good if someone runs into her in the garden and then tells Mama. That might distress Mama . . . (*During the next two minutes, he tears up all his manuscripts without saying a word and throws them under the desk, then unlocks the right door and goes out.*)

DORN (*trying to open the left door*). That's odd. The door seems locked . . . (*Comes in and puts the chair back in place.*) An obstacle race.

(ARKADINA *and* POLINA ANDREYEVNA *come in, followed by* YAKOV *with bottles, and* MASHA, *and then* SHAMRAYEV *and* TRIGORIN.)

ARKADINA. The red wine and the beer for Boris Alekseyevich put here, on the table. We'll play and drink. Let's sit down, ladies and gentlemen.

POLINA ANDREYEVNA (*to* YAKOV). Serve the tea, too, right away. (*Lights the candles, sits down at the card table.*)

SHAMRAYEV (*takes* TRIGORIN *up to the cupboard*). Here's that thing I was telling you about recently . . . (*Takes the stuffed seagull out of the cupboard.*) Your request.

TRIGORIN (*looking at the seagull*). I don't remember! (*After a moment's thought.*) Don't remember.

(*Off stage right, a shot; everyone shudders.*)

ARKADINA (*frightened*). What's that?

DORN. Nothing. I suppose something in my traveling kit popped. Don't worry about it. (*Goes out the right door, returns half a minute later.*) That's what it was. A vial of ether burst. (*Croons.*) "Again I stand before you captivated . . ."

ARKADINA (*sitting down at the table*). Phew, I was scared. It reminded me how . . . (*Covers her face with her hands.*) Everything went dark before my eyes . . .

DORN (*thumbing through the magazine, to* TRIGORIN). There was a certain article in here a couple of months ago . . . a letter from America, and I wanted to ask you, by the way . . . (*takes* TRIGORIN *by the waist and leads him down toward the footlights*) . . . since I'm much interested in this problem . . . (*A tone lower, in a half-whisper.*) Take Irina Nikolayevha away from here some place. The thing is that Konstantin Gavrilovich has killed himself . . .

(*Curtain*)

The Lower Depths

Maksim Gorky

[Aleksei Maksimovich Peshkov]

dedicated to
KONSTANTIN PETROVICH
PYATNITSKY

A NOTE ON THE PLAY

By the late 1890s, Gorky, born in the city that now bears his name (but then called Nizhny Novgorod), had published some romantic stories and anecdotes, which had drawn older writers' attention to him—most importantly, perhaps, Chekhov's. The establishment of the Moscow Art Theater and its initial success presented a special possibility: the new, "naturalistic" performance of—usually sententious—plays about what might be called the natural hollowness of then contemporary life.

The Lower Depths had its première, December 18, 1902, in the Moscow Art Theater and was greeted with extraordinary ovations. Gorky, thirty-four years old, became nationally famous, and the Theater, though identified with Chekhov's seagull, experienced its greatest success. The extent of the play's popularity may be surmised from the fact that in 1903 alone, the year it was published with the subtitle, "Scenes in Four Acts," it went through seventeen printings and over 100,000 copies were sold.

Gorky wrote the play in the summer of 1902, at Arzamas, where he had been deported from Nizhny Novgorod. His confinement to Arzamas temporarily delayed his working on the play with the Moscow Art Theater—members of which he had previously met on a visit to Chekhov—the theater with which he had agreed to collaborate. Nemirovich-Danchenko, producer and co-founder of the Theater with Stanislavsky, wrote what he remembered of the circumstances attendant on the play's production:

> I don't recall just what month Aleksei Maksimovich received permission to live in Petersburg and Moscow, but by the time of the November rehearsals of *The Lower Depths* he was already in Moscow. As one would have expected, *The Lower Depths* was absolutely forbidden by the censor. It was necessary to go to Petersburg to defend practically every sentence, reluctantly make concessions, and finally to win permission, but only for the Art Theater. From a series of conversations with the then head of the Central Press Office, Professor Zverev, I was left with the impression that *The Lower Depths* was authorized only

because the authorities were counting on the play's complete failure.

The censor's excisions and changes were extensive, of course. Lines like Luka's "Prison don't teach a man good" were cut, and, according to V. V. Luzhsky's memoirs, some of the cuts "were restored only this [1927] season by Gribunin, so accustomed had the actors become to the censored lines in the course of twenty-four seasons."

Performed in London, in Berlin, and in New York in 1903, the play has since become a favorite for theater workshops and amateur groups all over the world. It is still part of the the repertoire in Russia, of course. The present translation was made from the text in Volume V of Gorky's *Sobranie sochinenii*, Moscow-Leningrad, 1932.

DRAMATIS PERSONAE

Mikhail Ivanov Kostylyov ["Crutch"], keeper of a flophouse, 54
Vasilisa Karpovna, his wife, 26
Natasha, her sister, 20
Medvedev ["Bear"], their uncle, a policeman, 50
Vaska Pepel ["Ashes"], 28
Andrei Mitrich Kleshch ["Tick"], a locksmith, 40
Anna, his wife, 30
Nastya, a girl, 24
Kvashnya ["Dumpling"], a meat-dumpling hawker, about 40
Bubnov ["Diamonds" (cards)], a hatmaker, 45
Satin ["Sateen"] } approximately the same age, about 40
An Actor
A Baron, 33
Luka ["Luke," i.e., the Healer], a wanderer, 60
Alyosha, a shoemaker, 20
Krivoi Zob ["Crooked Double-chin"] } longshoremen
The Tartar
Several bums without names or lines

ACT ONE

A cellar resembling a cave. The ceiling is heavy with smoky stone vaulting and falling plaster. The light falls from the audience's side and down from above—from a square window on the right side. The right-hand corner is occupied by PEPEL's *room, fenced off with thin partitions; near the door into this room is* BUBNOV's *plank bed. In the left-hand corner is a big Russian stove; in the left stone wall there is a door into the kitchen where* KVASHNYA, *the* BARON, *and* NASTYA *live. Near the wall between the stove and the door is a wide bed covered with a dirty chintz canopy. There are plank beds all along the walls. In the foreground near the left wall there is a block of wood with clamps on it and a little anvil fastened to it, and another block, shorter than the first. On it, in front of the anvil, sits* KLESHCH, *fitting keys to old locks. At his feet are two huge bunches of various keys hung on a wire loop, a battered tin samovar, a hammer, and little files. In the middle of the flophouse there is a big table, two benches, a stool— all unpainted and dirty. At the table by the samovar,* KVASHNYA *is pouring tea. The* BARON *munches some black bread, and* NASTYA, *on the stool, is reading a tattered book, her elbows on the table.* ANNA *is coughing in the canopy-covered bed.* BUBNOV, *sitting on a plank bed, tries, on a blockhead squeezed between his knees, old, ripped-up pants, figuring out how to cut them. Beside him is a torn hatbox for visors, bits of oilcloth, rags.* SATIN *has just awakened, lies on his bed and—growls. Unseen on the stove, the* ACTOR *moves around and coughs.*
It is the beginning of spring. Morning.

BARON. Go on!
KVASHNYA. No-o, dearie, I'm telling you, you leave me alone now with that. I know all about that, let me tell you . . . and I wouldn't get married now for a hundred lobsters!
BUBNOV (*to* SATIN). What're you grunting about?
(SATIN *growls.*)
KVASHNYA. For me, now, I'm telling you, a woman free as the air, herself her own lady and mistress, to get her name written into somebody else's passport and give herself over

to a man's keeping—no! Even if he's an American prince, I wouldn't dream of marrying him.

KLESHCH. Nonsense!

KVASHNYA. Wha-at?

KLESHCH. Nonsense. You're going to marry Abramka . . .

BARON (*grabbing* NASTYA'S *book, reads the title*). "Fatal Love" . . . (*Laughs loudly.*)

NASTYA (*reaching out*). Give me . . . give it back! Now . . . don't play tricks!

BARON (*looks at her and waves the book in the air*).

KVASHNYA (*to* KLESHCH). You redheaded billy goat! Nonsense yourself! How dare you say something like that to me?

BARON (*hitting* NASTYA *on the head with the book*). You're an idiot, Nastka . . .

NASTYA (*taking the book away from him*). Give me . . .

KLESHCH. A big lady . . . But you're going to marry Abramka . . . That's all you're waiting for . . .

KVASHNYA. Sure thing! You bet! . . . What're you talking about! You, now, why you wore your wife out half to death . . .

KLESHCH. Shut up, you old thing! It's none of your business . . .

KVASHNYA. Ah-ha! Can't take the truth!

BARON. They're off! Nastka, where are you?

NASTYA (*without looking up*). Ah . . . Go away!

ANNA (*sticking her head out from under the canopy*). The day's begun! For God's sake . . . don't shout . . . don't swear at each other!

KLESHCH. She's started complaining!

ANNA. Each glorious day . . . at least let me die in peace!

BUBNOV. Noise doesn't get in the way of dying . . .

KVASHNYA (*going over to* ANNA). Ah, mother of mine, how did you ever live with such a wicked man?

ANNA. Stop . . . leave me alone . . .

KVASHNYA. Well, now! Ah, you . . . you're the soul of patience! . . . Isn't it a little lighter in your chest, now?

BARON. Kvashnya! Time to go to market . . .

KVASHNYA. Coming right away! (*To* ANNA.) I'll give you some hot meat dumplings . . . you want me to?

ANNA. Don't bother . . . Thanks. Why should I eat?

KVASHNYA. Now you eat some. Hot food'll make it easier. I'll put some in a cup and leave it here for you . . . Whenever you want to you can eat some! Let's go, sir . . . (*To* KLESHCH.) Uh, the old devil . . . (*Goes into the kitchen.*)

ANNA (*coughing*). O Lord . . .

BARON (*lightly pushing* NASTYA *on the back of her head*). Drop it . . . you idiot!

NASTYA (*mumbles*). Go away . . . I'm not bothering you. (*Whistling, the* BARON *goes out after* KVASHNYA.)

SATIN (*sitting up on the bed*). Who was it beat me yesterday?

BUBNOV. And what do you care? . . .

SATIN. Let's put it this way . . . What was I beaten for?

BUBNOV. Did you play cards?

SATIN. I did . . .

BUBNOV. And that's what you got beaten for . . .

SATIN. The bastards . . .

ACTOR (*sticking his head out from the stove*). Once you'll get beaten up dead completely . . .

SATIN. And you're a real thickhead.

ACTOR. Why?

SATIN. Because a man can't be beaten dead twice.

ACTOR (*after a pause*). I don't understand . . . Why "can't be?"

KLESHCH. And you come down off the stove now and clean up the place . . . What're you lying around for?

ACTOR. That's none of your business . . .

KLESHCH. Ah, here's Vasilisa coming now; she'll show you whose business it is . . .

ACTOR. The hell with Vasilisa! Today it's the Baron's turn to clean up . . . Baron!

BARON (*coming out of the kitchen*). I've no time to clean up . . . I'm going to the market with Kvashnya.

ACTOR. That's got nothing to do with me . . . Go to Siberia for all I care . . . but it's your turn to sweep the floor . . . I'm not going to do other people's work . . .

BARON. Ah, the hell with you! Nastenka'll do it . . . Hey, you, fatal love! Wake up! (*Takes the book away from* NASTYA.)

NASTYA (*getting up*). What do you want? Give it back! Naughty boy! And a gentleman besides . . .

BARON (*giving the book back*). Nastya! Sweep the floor for me . . . all right?

NASTYA (*going out into the kitchen*). A lot I need to do that . . . Sure thing!

KVASHNYA (*at the kitchen door, to the* BARON). And you go on! They'll straighten up without you! . . . Actor, you've been asked, now you do it . . . It won't kill you!

ACTOR. Well, now . . . it's always me . . . I don't understand . . .

BARON (*comes out of the kitchen carrying baskets on a yoke. In them is cheap pottery covered with rags*). It's heavy today for some reason . . .

SATIN. It was worth your while getting born a baron . . .

KVASHNYA (*to the* ACTOR). You be sure and sweep up now! (*Goes out into the entryway, having let the* BARON *go first.*)

ACTOR (*sliding down from the stove*). It's bad for me to breathe dust. (*With pride.*) My organism is poisoned by alcohol . . . (*Becomes lost in thought, sitting on the bed.*)

SATIN. Organism . . . organon . . .

ANNA. Andrei Mitrich . . .

KLESHCH. Now what?

ANNA. Kvashnya left me some dumplings there . . . Go ahead, eat them.

KLESHCH (*going over to her*). But you—you won't?

ANNA. I don't feel like it . . . What for? You're a working man . . . you . . . have to . . .

KLESHCH. You afraid? Don't be . . . it can still . . .

ANNA. Go on, eat! It's hard for me . . . seems that soon now . . .

KLESHCH (*moving away*). It's nothing . . . maybe—you'll get up . . . It happens! (*Goes out into the kitchen.*)

ACTOR (*loudly, as if suddenly waked up*). Yesterday, in the hospital, the doctor told me: "Your organism," he says, "is completely poisoned by alcohol."

SATIN (*smiling*). Organon . . .

ACTOR (*insistently*). Not organon but or-ga-ni-sm.

SATIN. Sicambrian.

ACTOR (*waves his hand at him*). Eh, nonsense! I'm talking—seriously . . . yes. If the organism is poisoned . . . means it's bad for me to sweep the floor . . . breathe the dust.

SATIN. Macrobiotics! . . . ha!

BUBNOV. What're you mumbling?

SATIN. Words . . . And then there's trans-scendental . . .

BUBNOV. What's that?

SATIN. Don't know . . . forgot . . .

BUBNOV. And what's the point of your talking?

SATIN. No reason . . . I'm fed up with all these words people have . . . all our words—fed up! I've heard every one of them . . . a thousand times, I bet.

ACTOR. In the play *Hamlet* it says: "Words, words, words!" A good play . . . I played the gravedigger in it . . .

KLESHCH (*coming out of the kitchen*). You going to start playing with that broom soon?

ACTOR. None of your business . . . (*Strikes his breast with his hand.*) Ophelia! O, remember me in thy orisons! . . .

(*Behind the stage, somewhere far away, there is a dull noise, shouting, a policeman's whistle.* KLESHCH *sits down at his work and scrapes away with a file.*)

SATIN. I like incomprehensible, rare words . . . When I was a boy . . . I worked in the telegraph office . . . read a lot of books.

BUBNOV. And were you a telegraph operator?

SATIN. I was . . . There are some very fine books . . . and a lot of interesting words . . . I was an educated man . . . you know?

BUBNOV. Heard about it . . . a hundred times! So you were . . . what's it prove? . . . Take me—I was a furrier . . . had my own place . . . My hands were so yellow—from the dye: dyeing furs I was . . . I always figured I'd never get it off till the day I died . . . That I'd die with my arms all yellow like that . . . And now, look at them . . . just dirty . . . sure!

SATIN. Well, and so?

BUBNOV. And that's it.

SATIN. What's your point?

BUBNOV. No point . . . just thinking . . . Comes out—no matter how you deck yourself out on the outside, it all wears off . . . it all wears off, yep!

SATIN. Ah . . . my bones ache!

ACTOR (*sits, his arms around his knees*). Education's nothing. The main thing's talent. I used to know an actor . . . spoke his roles syllable by syllable but could play heroes so . . . the theater'd shake and reel from the audience's delight . . .

SATIN. Bubnov, give me five kopeks!

BUBNOV. Only got two . . .

ACTOR. I tell you, talent, that's what a hero's got to have. And talent—that's faith in yourself, in your own strength . . .

SATIN. Give me five and I'll believe you've got talent, that you're a crocodile, a hero, a real bailiff . . . Kleshch, give me five!

KLESHCH. Go to hell! There's a lot of you here . . .

SATIN. What're you swearing for? Sure, you haven't got a thing, I know.

ANNA. Andrei Mitrich . . . I can't breathe . . . it's hard . . .

KLESHCH. What'll I do?

BUBNOV. Open the door into the entrance . . .

KLESHCH. All right! You're sitting on a bed, but I'm on the floor . . . Let me have your place and you go open . . . I've got a cold as it is . . .

BUBNOV (*quietly*). It's not me who has to open . . . your wife's the one who's asking . . .

KLESHCH (*sullenly*). Everybody's always asking for everything . . .

SATIN. My head's ringing . . . ah! Why're people always beating each other's brains out?

BUBNOV. They don't beat just the brains out, but all over the rest of the body, too. (*Gets up.*) Got to go buy some thread . . . And somehow we haven't seen our landlords for a long time today . . . as if they'd kicked the bucket. (*Goes out.*) (ANNA *coughs.* SATIN, *his hands up under his head, lies motionless.*)

ACTOR (*having sadly looked around, goes over to Anna*). Well? Not so good?

ANNA. It's stuffy.

ACTOR. You want me to—I'll take you out into the entryway? Well, get up. (*Helps the woman up, throws some kind of old rag over her shoulders and, supporting her, takes her out into the entryway.*) Now, now . . . steady! I'm a sick man myself . . . poisoned by alcohol . . .

KOSTYLYOV (*in the doorway*). Out for a walk? Ah, what a fine pair, the gent and his fair . . .

ACTOR. Now you—get out of the way . . . Don't you see, sick people are coming? . . .

KOSTYLYOV. Pass on, please do . . . (*Humming some hymn through his nose, he looks the flophouse over suspiciously and tilts his head to the left as if listening to something in* PEPEL's *room.* KLESHCH *fiercely rattles his keys and scrapes away with the file, sullenly following the landlord with his eyes.*) Scraping away?

KLESHCH. What?

KOSTYLYOV. Scraping away, I said? (*Pause.*) A-ah . . . now . . . What was it I wanted to ask, now? (*Quickly and quietly.*) My wife wasn't here?

KLESHCH. Didn't see her . . .

KOSTYLYOV (*cautiously moving over toward the door to* PEPEL's *room*). How much of my space you take up for just a couple of rubles a month! A bed . . . sitting there yourself . . . really! Five rubles' worth, honest to God! Got to add a half ruble to you . . .

KLESHCH. You'd throw a rope around my neck and knock me off . . . You'll soon kick off, and here you are all worried about half rubles . . .

KOSTYLYOV. Why knock you off? What's the use of that to anybody? Lord save you, live to your heart's content. And I'll add a little half ruble from you—buy some oil for the icon-lamp . . . and my offering'll burn there before the holy image . . . And my offering'll count up for me, and pay off my sins, and yours, too. You know you yourself never think about your sins . . . you see . . . Ah, Andryushka, you're a bad man! Your wife got all sick from your wickedness . . . nobody likes you, respects you . . . your work's screechy and scrapy, bothers everybody . . .

KLESHCH (*shouts*). What did you . . . come to persecute me? (SATIN *growls loudly.*)

KOSTYLYOV (*shuddering*). Hey now, you there . . .

ACTOR (*enters*). Put the old girl in the entryway . . . wrapped her up . . .

KOSTYLYOV. Now, what a good fellow you are! That's good . . . That'll all be counted up for you . . .

ACTOR. When?

KOSTYLYOV. In the next world, m'boy . . . There, it's all . . . everything we do is all reckoned up . . .

ACTOR. But you might reward me now for doing good here . . .

KOSTYLYOV. Now how could I do that?

ACTOR. Knock off half the debt . . .

KOSTYLYOV. Heh-heh! You're always joking, sonny, always playing something . . . How can you put the heart's kindness on a level with money? Kindness—it's the highest of all blessings. And what you owe me—well, that's what you owe me! Means you got to pay me back the debt . . . You got to show your kindness to me, an old man, free of charge . . .

ACTOR. You're a cheat, you old man . . . (*Goes out to the kitchen.*)

(KLESHCH *gets up and goes out into the entryway.*)

KOSTYLYOV (*to* SATIN). A scraper, isn't he? Ran away, heh-heh! Doesn't like me . . .

SATIN. Who, except the devil, does like you? . . .

KOSTYLYOV (*laughing a bit*). What a man for swearing! But I like you all . . . I understand you're my miserable, no-good, lost brethren . . . (*Suddenly, quickly.*) And . . . Vaska's home?

SATIN. Have a look . . .

KOSTYLYOV (*goes up to the door and knocks*). Vasya!

(*The* ACTOR *appears in the kitchen door. He is chewing something.*)

PEPEL. Who's that?

KOSTYLYOV. It's me . . . me, Vasya.

PEPEL. What do you want?

KOSTYLYOV (*stepping back*). Open up . . .

SATIN (*without looking at* KOSTYLYOV). He will, and she's—there . . .

(*The* ACTOR *snorts.*)

KOSTYLYOV (*anxiously, not loudly*). Ah? Who's there? That you . . . what?

SATIN. What? You talking to me?

KOSTYLYOV. What did you say?

SATIN. I was just talking . . . to myself . . .

KOSTYLYOV. You be careful! Don't carry your jokes too far . . . I mean it! (*Knocks hard on the door.*) Vasily . . .

PEPEL (*opening the door*). Well? What's bothering you?

KOSTYLYOV (*peering into the room*). I . . . you see . . .

PEPEL. You brought the money?

KOSTYLYOV. I got to talk to you . . .

PEPEL. The money—you brought it?

KOSTYLYOV. What money? Wait . . .

PEPEL. The money—seven rubles—for the watch. Well?

KOSTYLYOV. What watch, Vasya? . . . Ah, you . . .

PEPEL. Now you watch out! Yesterday in front of witnesses I sold you a watch for ten rubles . . . Three I got; hand over the seven! What're you batting your eyes for? Slops around here, bothers people . . . and doesn't know his own business . . .

KOSTYLYOV. Sh-sh! Don't get mad, Vasya . . . The watch—it's . . .

SATIN. Stolen . . .

KOSTYLYOV (*sternly*). I don't take stolen things . . . How can you . . .

PEPEL (*takes him by the shoulder*). You—what did you get me up for? What do you want?

KOSTYLYOV. Sure . . . I've—got nothing . . . I'm going . . . since you're like this . . .

PEPEL. Clear out! Bring me the money!

KOSTYLYOV (*goes out*). What vulgar people! Ai-yai . . .

ACTOR. It's a farce!

SATIN. It's good! This I like . . .

PEPEL. What was he doing here?

SATIN (*laughing*). You don't get it? Looking for his wife . . . and why don't you clobber him, Vasily?!

PEPEL. Am I going to ruin my life on account of such crap? . . .

SATIN. Do it clever. And then—you'll marry Vasilisa . . . you'll be our landlord . . .

PEPEL. That's a joy! Not just everything I have, but me, too —on account of my kindness—you'd drink up in the tavern . . . (*Sits on the bed.*) The old bastard . . . woke me up . . . And I was having a good dream: seemed I was out fishing and I hooked the biggest, greatest bream ever!

The kind of bream you only get in dreams . . . And here I'm playing him on my line and I'm afraid the line'll break! And I've got the landing-net ready . . . Now, I figure, all set . . .

SATIN. That was no bream; that was Vasilisa . . .

ACTOR. He caught Vasilisa long ago . . .

PEPEL (*angrily*). Go to hell, all of you . . . and her, too!

KLESHCH (*comes in from the entryway*). Freezing cold . . . cold as hell . . .

ACTOR. Why didn't you bring Anna in? She'll freeze to death . . .

KLESHCH. Natashka took her out into the kitchen . . .

ACTOR. The old man'll drive her out . . .

KLESHCH (*sitting down to work*). So . . . Natashka'll bring her in . . .

SATIN. Vasily! Give me five kopeks!

ACTOR (*to* SATIN). Oh you . . . five kopeks! Vasya! Give us twenty kopeks . . .

PEPEL. Better hurry up . . . before you ask for a ruble . . . There!

SATIN. Gibraltar! There's nobody in the world better than thieves!

KLESHCH (*sullenly*). It's easy for them to get money . . . They—don't work . . .

SATIN. A lot of people get money easily, but not many easily let go of it . . . Work? Fix it so's I like working and maybe I'll go to work . . . seriously! Maybe! When work's a pleasure life's good! When it's what you got to do, life's slavery! (*To the* ACTOR.) You, Sardanapalus! Let's go! . . .

ACTOR. Let's go, Nebuchadnezzar! I'll get myself drunk—like . . . forty thousand drunks . . . (*They go out.*)

PEPEL (*yawning*). So, how's your wife?

KLESHCH. Seems it'll be soon now . . . (*Pause.*)

PEPEL. I look at you—and see there's no point in your scraping away.

KLESHCH. But what can I do?

PEPEL. Nothing.

KLESHCH. And how'll I eat?

PEPEL. People make out . . .

KLESHCH. These? What sort of people are they? Bums, fake

bohemians . . . people! I'm a working man . . . makes me ashamed to look at them . . . I've been working since I was little . . . You think I'll never get out of here? I will . . . I'll skin myself, but I'll get out . . . You just wait . . . My wife'll die . . . I've been here half a year . . . but it might as well be six . . .

PEPEL. Nobody here's worse than you . . . you oughtn't talk like that . . .

KLESHCH. No worse! They've no honor, no conscience . . .

PEPEL (*indifferently*). And what'll you do with them—this honor, conscience? You're not going to put honor or conscience on your feet instead of boots . . . Honor and conscience is what the fellow needs who's got power and authority . . .

BUBNOV (*enters*). Oo-oo . . . I'm freezing!

PEPEL. Bubnov! You got any conscience?

BUBNOV. Wha-at? Conscience?

PEPEL. Yes.

BUBNOV. Conscience for what? I'm not rich . . .

PEPEL. That's what I'm saying, too: it's the rich fellow needs conscience, sure! But Kleshch is attacking us, says we have no conscience . . .

BUBNOV. What'd he want to do, borrow some?

PEPEL. He's got lots of his own . . .

BUBNOV. What's that mean, you're selling it? But nobody here's going to buy that. Now I'd buy some old cards . . . but on account . . .

PEPEL (*instructing*). You're a fool, Andryushka! You ought to listen to Satin about conscience . . . or the Baron . . .

KLESHCH. I've nothing to talk to them about . . .

PEPEL. They'll be wiser about it than you . . . even though they are drunks . . .

BUBNOV. And who's drunk and wise has got two good sides . . .

PEPEL. Satin says everybody wants the next fellow to have conscience, but nobody figures, see, that he needs to have it himself . . . And that's true enough . . .

(NATASHA *comes in. Behind her,* LUKA *with a stick in hand, a sack over his shoulder, a mess-tin and teapot at his waist.*)

LUKA. Good health to you all, honest folks!

PEPEL (*smoothing his mustache*). Ah-ah, Natasha!

BUBNOV (*to* LUKA). We were honest enough, but the spring before last . . .

NATASHA. Here's a new lodger . . .

LUKA. Makes no difference to me! I respect crooks, too; according to me there's not a single bad flea: all are black, all jump around . . . that's how it is. Where'll I keep my things here, dearie?

NATASHA (*pointing to the kitchen door*). Go in there, grampa . . .

LUKA. Thanks, girl! If there, all right—there! For an old fellow, wherever it's warm, there's his home.

PEPEL. What a funny old guy you've brought in, Natasha.

NATASHA. More interesting than all of you . . . Andrei! Your wife's with us in the kitchen . . . Come get her in a little while.

KLESHCH. All right . . . I will . . .

NATASHA. And I guess you better be a little more gentle with her now . . . it won't be long . . .

KLESHCH. I know.

NATASHA. You know . . . It's not enough to know; you—you must understand. Because dying's terrible . . .

PEPEL. Take me now, I'm not afraid . . .

NATASHA. What're you talking about! . . . Courage . . .

BUBNOV (*with a whistle*). And the threads're all rotten . . .

PEPEL. Really, I'm not! Right now even—ready to die! Go get a knife, strike in here to my heart . . . I'll die, and not even groan! Even die with joy, 'cause from a clean hand . . .

NATASHA (*going out*). Oh, go pull the wool over somebody else's eyes.

BUBNOV (*slowly*). And the threads're all rotten . . .

NATASHA (*in the door to the entryway*). Andrei, don't forget about your wife . . .

KLESHCH. All right . . .

PEPEL. A great little girl!

BUBNOV. The girl's all right . . .

PEPEL. Why is she like that with me? Rejects me . . . 'Course she'll get ruined here all the same . . .

BUBNOV. Get ruined by you . . .

PEPEL. Why by me? I feel sorry for her . . .

BUBNOV. Like a wolf for a lamb . . .

PEPEL. That's not true! I feel very . . . sorry for her . . . It's bad for her living here . . . I see that . . .

KLESHCH. You wait till Vasilisa sees you talking to her.

BUBNOV. Vasilisa? Right. She won't give up what's hers for nothing . . . a wild woman . . .

PEPEL (*lying down on the bed*). Go to hell, the both of you . . . prophets!

KLESHCH. You'll see! . . . just wait! . . .

LUKA (*in the kitchen, sings*). "Through the ni-ight . . . can't se-ee the wa-ay we're go-ing . . ."

KLESHCH (*going out into the entryway*). Listen to that . . . howling . . .

PEPEL. It's boring . . . Why do I keep getting bored? You're living along, making out all right—and suddenly it's like you froze: it's all boring . . .

BUBNOV. Boring? Hm-mm . . .

PEPEL. Honest to god!

LUKA (*sings*). "Eh, ca-an't se-ee the wa-ay . . ."

PEPEL. Hey, you, old man!

LUKA (*peering out of the door*). Who, me?

PEPEL. You. Don't sing.

LUKA (*comes out*). You don't like it?

PEPEL. I like it when it's good . . .

LUKA. You mean mine's no good?

PEPEL. Must be . . .

LUKA. Well now! And I thought I sang all right. That's the way it always is: a fellow thinks to himself, I'm doing all right! But, boop! people don't like it.

PEPEL (*laughing*). Right! That's true . . .

BUBNOV. You say it's boring, but you're laughing.

PEPEL. And what're you doing? You crow . . .

LUKA. Who's it boring for?

PEPEL. Me, that's who . . .

(*The* BARON *enters.*)

LUKA. Well now! And out there in the kitchen there's this girl sitting there, reading her book and crying! Really! Tears're pouring down . . . I says to her: "Dearie, what's that for?" But she says she feels really sorry! "Sorry for who?" I says. "Here," she says, "in the book." Is that what some folks spend their time doing? Must be on account of boredom, too . . .

BARON. She's an idiot . . .

PEPEL. Baron! You had some tea?

BARON. I did . . . Go on!

PEPEL. You want, I'll treat you to half a bottle?

BARON. Goes without saying . . . Go on!

PEPEL. Get on all fours and bark like a dog!

BARON. Idiot! What're you, a merchant? Or drunk?

PEPEL. Come on, bark! It'll be funny for me . . . You're a gentleman . . . There was a time when you didn't think fellows like me even human . . . and all that . . .

BARON. So, go on!

PEPEL. So! And now I'll make you bark like a dog, and you will . . . you will, won't you?

BARON. A lot I will! Blockhead! What kind of pleasure can you get from this when I myself know that I've become practically lower than you? You should have made me go around on all fours then, when I wasn't on your level . . .

BUBNOV. True!

LUKA. And me too: that's right! . . .

BUBNOV. What's gone is gone, and there's just a lot of little stuff left . . . No more ladies and gents here . . . everything's been sloughed off, there's just the naked man left . . .

LUKA. Means everybody's equal . . . And you, friend, were a baron?

BARON. What's this now? Who're you, you gorgon?

LUKA (*laughs*). I've seen a count and I've seen a prince . . . but this is the first time I've ever met a baron, and a ruined one at that . . .

PEPEL (*bursts out laughing*). Baron! And you were making me embarrassed . . .

BARON. Time to wise up, Vasily.

LUKA. Heh-heh! Just looking at you fellows, the way you're living—oi-yoi!

BUBNOV. Such a life that, once you're up in the morning, just for the howling, you'd . . .

BARON. We've lived better . . . that's sure! I . . . used to . . . wake up in the morning and, lying there in my bed, would drink coffee. Coffee! With cream! . . . That's the truth!

LUKA. And still you're human! No matter how you pretend, or how you stagger along, you're born a man and you'll die a man. And as I see it, people are getting smarter all the time, more interesting . . . and even if they're worse off, they want it to get better and better . . . stubborn things!

BARON. And who are you, old man? . . . Where'd you show up from?

LUKA. Who, me?

BARON. A wanderer?

LUKA. All of us on earth are wanderers. According to some, I've heard say, this earth of ours is a wanderer in the sky.

BARON (*sternly*). All right, but still—you have a passport?

LUKA (*not right away*). And who are you, a detective?

PEPEL (*delighted*). Good work, old man! Well, Barony, *you* got it, too, didn't you?

BUBNOV. Yes, the gentleman got it . . .

BARON (*embarrassed*). Come on, what do you mean? You know I was joking, old man! Friend, I haven't got any papers myself . . .

BUBNOV. You're lying!

BARON. That is . . . I have papers . . . but they're worthless . . .

LUKA. They're all, the papers I mean, are all like that. All of 'em are worthless.

PEPEL. Baron! Let's go to the tavern . . .

BARON. All set! So, good-bye, old man . . . you're pretty sly!

LUKA. There's all kinds, friend . . .

PEPEL (*by the door into the entryway*). Come on, let's go, what're you doing! (*Goes out. The* BARON *quickly follows.*)

LUKA. That fellow was a baron, actually?

BUBNOV. Who knows? A nobleman, that's for sure . . . Still is: you wouldn't think it, and then all of a sudden the gent in him shows through. Hasn't got unaccustomed yet, I guess.

LUKA. It's like—I mean, this nobility, now—is sort of like small pox . . . A man gets all well but the marks stay there . . .

BUBNOV. He's all right, just the same . . . Only he sometimes kicks up like that . . . like the way he did about your passport . . .

ALYOSHKA (*comes in, quite high, his accordion in his hands. Whistles*). Hey, residents!

BUBNOV. What're you shouting for?

ALYOSHKA. Sorry . . . beg y'r pardon! I'm a civil fellow . . .

BUBNOV. Tied one on again?

ALYOSHKA. Many times as y'want! Just now the Dep-'t'y Precinct Cap'n, Medyakin, kicked me out and says: "Don't le' me even smell you," he says, "on the street." Not a smell! I'm man of char'cter . . . But the lan'lor' snorts at me . . . But what's this—a lan'lor'? Phe-phew! Just a misun'erstan'ing . . . A drunk's what he is, the lan'lor' . . . An' I'm the kin' of fellow, who . . . not looking for anything! Don' wan' a thing, an' that's it! Here, y' can have me for twenty rubles, now! An' I—don' wan' a thing. (NASTYA *comes out of the kitchen.*) Gi' me a million—don' wan' it! An' for me now, a goo' fellow, to be ordered aroun' by my comrade—drunk that I am, don' wan' it! Don' wan' that!

(NASTYA, *standing in the doorway, shakes her head, looking at* ALYOSHKA.)

LUKA (*good-naturedly*). Ah, fellow, you're all mixed up . . .

BUBNOV. Human folly . . .

ALYOSHKA (*lies down on the floor*). Here, eat me up! An' I—don' wan' a thing! I'm a desp'rate man! Y' 'splain me why'm I worse? Why'm I worse'n others? See, Medyakin says, don' go out 'n the street, 'll bash your mug in! But I'm goin' . . . 'm goin' an' lie down right 'n the mi'le o' the street—g' on, run over me! I don' wan' a thing!

NASTYA. Poor boy! . . . Still so young, yet he's already trying to be such a big shot . . .

ALYOSHKA (*having seen* NASTYA, *rises to his knees*). Youn' lady! Mam'selle! Parlez français? . . . prix courant! I had a real spree . . .

NASTYA (*whispers loudly*). Vasilisa!

VASILISA (*quickly opening the door, to* ALYOSHKA). You here again?

ALYOSHKA. How d' y' do? . . . C'm in . . .

VASILISA. I told you, you puppy, to clear out of here for keeps . . . but you're back again?

ALYOSHKA. Vasilisa Karp'vna . . . wan' me . . . 'll play you nice fun'ral march?

VASILISA (*pushes his shoulder*). Get out!

ALYOSHKA (*moving toward the door*). Wait . . . no' like that! Th' fun'ral march . . . jus' learned it! 'S nice music . . . wai' now! No' like that!

VASILISA. I'll show you not like what . . . I'm going to set the whole street on you . . . you damned pagan . . . A boy like you going around barking about me . . .

ALYOSHKA (*running out*). A' right, 'm goin' . . .

VASILISA (*to* BUBNOV). And don't let him ever come back in! You hear me?

BUBNOV. I'm not your watchman . . .

VASILISA. It's none of my business who you are! You're living here on charity, don't forget! How much you owe me?

BUBNOV (*quietly*). Never figured out . . .

VASILISA. You watch out, I will!

ALYOSHKA (*opening the door, shouts*). Vasilisa Karp'vna! I'm no' 'fraid o' you . . . n-no' afraid! (*Ducks out.*)

(LUKA *laughs.*)

VASILISA. And who're you? . . .

LUKA. A traveler . . . passing through . . .

VASILISA. Spending a night or going to stay?

LUKA. I'll see . . .

VASILISA. Your passport!

LUKA. All right . . .

VASILISA. Give it to me!

LUKA. I'll bring it . . . bring it in to you.

VASILISA. Passing through! You ought to say: passing myself off . . . That'd be more like it . . .

LUKA (*with a sigh*). Ah, you don't make it very easy . . .

(VASILISA *goes toward the door to* PEPEL's *room.* ALYOSHKA *peeking out of the kitchen, whispers:* "*She gone? eh?*")

VASILISA (*turning around to him*). You still here?

(ALYOSHKA, *ducking back, whistles.* NASTYA *and* LUKA *laugh.*)

BUBNOV (*to* VASILISA). He's out . . .

VASILISA. Who?

BUBNOV. Vaska . . .

VASILISA. Did I ask you about him?

BUBNOV. I can see . . . you're looking around everywhere . . .

VASILISA. I'm looking around to see if things 're neat, understand? And how come you still haven't swept up? How many times did I tell you it's got to be clean here?

BUBNOV. It's the actor's turn . . .

VASILISA. It's none of my business whose turn! But if the sanitation department comes now and gives me a fine, why I'll . . . throw you out—all of you!

BUBNOV (*calmly*). Then what'll you live off?

VASILISA. And don't leave a speck anywhere! (*Goes to the kitchen. To* NASTYA.) What're you doing around here? How'd your face get all swollen? What're you just standing there for? Sweep the floor! Did you see . . . Natalya? Was she here?

NASTYA. Don't know . . . didn't see her . . .

VASILISA. Bubnov! Was my sister here?

BUBNOV. A . . . she came in with him . . .

VASILISA. He . . . was here?

BUBNOV. Vasily? He was . . . She was talking to Kleshch here, Natalya, I mean . . .

VASILISA. I'm not asking you who she was talking to! There's dirt everyplace . . . It's a pile of dirt! Oh, you . . . pigs! You clean it all up . . . you hear! (*Quickly goes out.*)

BUBNOV. What a beast, that damned woman!

LUKA. Pretty dead serious . . .

NASTYA. A life like that turns you into a beast . . . Tie any real person to a husband like hers . . .

BUBNOV. Now, she's not so tied . . .

LUKA. She always . . . explodes like that?

BUBNOV. Always . . . Came in to see her lover, see, but he was out . . .

LUKA. So she felt insulted. Oho-ho! All these different people directing things in this world . . . and scaring each other in all kinds of ways, and still there's no system in life . . . and nothing's clean . . .

BUBNOV. Everybody wants a system, but there aren't enough

brains for it. Got to sweep up, though . . . Nastya! . . . Get started.

NASTYA. Sure thing! You bet! I'm just your maid here . . . (*After a pause.*) I'm going to get drunk today . . . so drunk!

BUBNOV. At least that's doing something . . .

LUKA. How come now, girl, you want to drink? Just now you were crying, and now you're saying you're going to get drunk!

NASTYA (*defiantly*). I'll get drunk and I'll cry again . . . and that's that!

BUBNOV. It's not much . . .

LUKA. But why now, tell me. Now, even a pimple don't pop up without some reason . . .

(NASTYA *is silent, shaking her head.*)

LUKA. So . . . Ehe-he . . . Ladies and gents! What's to become of you? . . . Well, now, maybe I'll sweep up here. Where's your broom?

BUBNOV. Behind the door, in the entryway . . .

(LUKA *goes into the entryway.*)

BUBNOV. Nastenka!

NASTYA. What?

BUBNOV. Why'd Vasilisa go at Alyoshka?

NASTYA. He was saying about her that Vaska was fed up with her and that Vaska wanted to get rid of her . . . and take Natasha . . . I'm going to get out of here . . . go to another place.

BUBNOV. Why? Where?

NASTYA. I'm fed up . . . I'm one too many here . . .

BUBNOV (*tranquilly*). You're one too many everywhere . . . and everybody in the world is, too . . .

(NASTYA *shakes her head. She gets up, quietly goes out into the entryway.* MEDVEDEV *comes in, followed by* LUKA *with the broom.*)

MEDVEDEV. Don't think I know you . . .

LUKA. What about the others—you know them all?

MEDVEDEV. I've got to know everybody in my section . . . But you, now—I don't know you . . .

LUKA. That's because the whole world, now, didn't get put

into your section . . . Just a little bit got left outside . . . (*Goes out to the kitchen.*)

MEDVEDEV (*going up to* BUBNOV). It's true my section's not so big . . . though it's worse than any big one . . . Just now, before I came off duty, I took Alyoshka, the shoemaker, into the station house . . . He'd laid down, see, in the middle of the street, was playing his accordion and roaring away: don't want a thing, don't wish a thing! Horses are going up and down there, and in general there's traffic . . . could get run over by a wheel and so on . . . He's a wild fellow . . . So, I hauled him in just now. Likes to make a disturbance . . .

BUBNOV. You coming to play checkers tonight? . . .

MEDVEDEV. Sure. Hm—yes . . . And what about—ah—Vaska?

BUBNOV. All right . . . no change . . .

MEDVEDEV. Meaning . . . he's making out?

BUBNOV. Why shouldn't he? He can do all right . . .

MEDVEDEV (*doubtfully*). Can he? (LUKA *goes out into the entryway with a bucket in his hand.*) Hm—yes . . . Now—there's talk going round . . . about Vaska . . . you haven't heard?

BUBNOV. I hear a lot of things . . .

MEDVEDEV. About Vasilisa, seems . . . you haven't heard?

BUBNOV. What?

MEDVEDEV. Just . . . in general. Maybe you know, now, and are lying? Because everybody knows . . . (*Harshly.*) No lying now, m'friend . . .

BUBNOV. Why should I?

MEDVEDEV. What'd I tell you! Ah, the dogs! They're saying Vaska and Vasilisa . . . they're saying . . . but what's it to me? I'm not her father, I'm her uncle . . . What're they making fun of me for? . . . (KVASHNYA *enters.*) The kind of people you get nowadays . . . make fun of everything . . . Ah-ah! You're here . . .

KVASHNYA. My lovely general! Bubnov! He was pestering me in the market again about marrying him . . .

BUBNOV. Go ahead . . . Why not! He's got money and he's still a pretty sturdy cavalier . . .

MEDVEDEV. Who, me? Ho-ho!

KVASHNYA. Ah you, you ignoramus! No, don't you talk to me about that, not my sore spot! I've had all that, dearie; for a woman getting married is just the same as jumping through an ice hole in winter: I did it once—and I'll remember it the rest of my life.

MEDVEDEV. Just a minute, now . . . husbands—why, there're all different kinds.

KVASHNYA. But I'm just myself all the same! When my swell little man of a husband conked off—hope he rots in hell—I just sat all day by myself from joy: kept sitting there and just couldn't believe my good luck . . .

MEDVEDEV. If your husband was beating you—for no reason—you should have complained to the police . . .

KVASHNYA. I complained to God for eight years, and he did nothing!

MEDVEDEV. Now it's against the law to beat your wife . . . Now everything's got strictness and law in it—regular system! Can't beat anybody just for no reason . . . beat them to keep order . . .

LUKA (*leads* ANNA *in*). So, now we made it . . . eh, you! How can you walk around alone and you so weak? Where's your place?

ANNA (*pointing*). Thanks, grampa . . .

KVASHNYA. Here she is—the married woman . . . Just look at her!

LUKA. The woman's in a real bad way . . . Going along the entryway, holding on to the wall and—groaning . . . Why do you let her go around by herself?

KVASHNYA. Weren't watching, gramps, sorry. And her maid, I guess, went out for a walk, now . . .

LUKA. You're laughing at me there . . . But can a person just be thrown out like that? No matter what kind of fellow he is, he's always worth something . . .

MEDVEDEV. Got to have someone look after her! Suppose she ups and dies? There'll be a whole lot of red tape on account of that . . . Got to look after her!

LUKA. That's true, Mr. Sergeant . . .

MEDVEDEV. Hm—yes . . . though I'm not exactly a sergeant yet . . .

LUKA. Is that so? But your appearance is so heroic!

(*Noise and stamping in the entryway. **Muffled shouts.***)

MEDVEDEV. Seems there's a brawl?

BUBNOV. Sounds like it . . .

KVASHNYA. Might go have a look . . .

MEDVEDEV. And I've got to go . . . Ah, work and duty! And why separate people when they're fighting? They'll stop all by themselves . . . You get tired out fighting, you know . . . Just let them beat each other up freely, much as each of 'em can . . . they'll start fighting less, on account of they'll remember the beatings longer . . .

BUBNOV (*sliding off the bed*). You go have a little talk with the chief about that . . .

KOSTYLYOV (*flinging open the door, shouts*). Abram! Come . . . Vasilisa's . . . killing Natasha . . . Come!

(KVASHNYA, MEDVEDEV, BUBNOV *rush out into the entryway.* LUKA, *shaking his head, looks after them.*)

ANNA. Oh, Lord . . . Poor Natashenka!

LUKA. Who's fighting there?

ANNA. The landladies . . . sisters . . .

LUKA (*going over to* ANNA). Over what?

ANNA. Nothing. They're . . . both're stuffed full . . . healthy . . .

LUKA. And what's your name?

ANNA. Anna . . . I keep looking at you now . . . You look like my father . . . my old man . . . just as gentle . . . soft . . .

LUKA. I got mashed a lot, so that's why I'm soft . . . (*Laughs a jarring laugh.*)

(*Curtain*)

[Song—Act II]

ACT II

The same setting. Evening. On the beds around the stove, SATIN, *the* BARON, KRIVOI ZOB *and the* TARTAR *are playing cards.* KLESHCH *and the* ACTOR *are watching the game. On his bed* BUBNOV *is playing checkers with* MEDVEDEV. LUKA *is sitting on the stool by* ANNA'S *bed. The flophouse is lit by two lamps: one hangs on the wall near the cardplayers; the other, on* BUBNOV'S *bed.*

TARTAR. I'm playing once more, and no more . . .
BUBNOV. Zob! Sing something! (*Strikes up a tune.*)
  Sunlight rises, sinks at evening . . .
KRIVOI ZOB (*picking up the song*).
  But my cell is always dark . . .
TARTAR (*to* SATIN). Shuffle the cards! Shuffle them good! We know the sort of fellow y'are . . .
KRIVOI ZOB *and* BUBNOV (*together*).
  Day and night the men on sentry—yes, o-oh!
  Keep my window under guard . . .
ANNA. Beatings . . . insults . . . nothing else—I saw nothing else!
LUKA. Now, don't be sad!
MEDVEDEV. Where you moving? Be careful! . . .
BUBNOV. Ah-ha! Yes, yes, yes . . .
TARTAR (*threatening* SATIN *with his fist*). What're you trying to palm a card for? I see you . . . ah, you!
KRIVOI ZOB. Forget it, Asan! They're going to win by cheating on us anyway . . . Bubnov, start it again!
ANNA. Don't remember I ever had enough to eat . . . Grudged every little piece of bread . . . Shivered all my life . . . suffered . . . afraid I'd eat more than the next . . . Went around in rags all my life . . . all my miserable life . . . What for?
LUKA. There, now, my child! You tired? It's all right!
ACTOR (*to* KRIVOI ZOB). Play the jack . . . the jack, god damn it!
BARON. And we put on—the king.

KLESHCH. They always win.

SATIN. It's a habit we have.

MEDVEDEV. Give me a king!

BUBNOV. And me, too . . . no-ow . . .

ANNA. Dying like this . . .

KLESHCH. Look at it, how d'you like that! Prince,[1] quit playing! Give up, I tell you!

ACTOR. Without you he doesn't know what's happening?

BARON. You be careful, Andryushka, or I'll throw you to hell and gone!

TARTAR. Deal 'em out once more! The pitcher went out to get water, smashed itself up . . . and me, too!

KLESHCH (*shaking his head, goes over to* BUBNOV).

ANNA. I keep thinking: Lord! there isn't torments waiting for me in the next world, too, is there? Not there, too?

LUKA. Nothing like it! Lie down, now! Nothing at all! You'll get a good rest there! . . . Be patient yet. Everybody has to be, dear . . . everybody has to put up with life as he can. (*Gets up and goes out into the kitchen quickly.*)

BUBNOV (*starts singing*).

Keep it guarded as you want to . . .

KRIVOI ZOB.

I will never run away . . .

KRIVOI ZOB and BUBNOV (*together*).

How I want to get to freedom—yes, o-oh!
But I cannot break my chains.

TARTAR (*shouts*). Ah! You stuck a card up your sleeve!

BARON (*abashed*). Well . . . what d'you want me to do, stick it up your nose?

ACTOR (*persuasively*). Prince! You're wrong . . . Nobody, ever . . .

TARTAR. I saw him! The cheat! I won't play!

SATIN (*collecting the cards*). Cut the nagging, Asan . . . You know damned well we're cheats. So why did you play?

BARON. Lost forty kopeks, and you're making as much noise as if it was three rubles . . . and a prince besides!

TARTAR (*heatedly*). Y'got to play honest!

SATIN. Why so?

---

[1] A general nickname for Tartars in northern Russia because so many Tartars were princes in the south.

TARTAR. What d'you mean why so?

SATIN. Well . . . why?

TARTAR. Y'don't know?

SATIN. I don't. Do you?

(*The* TARTAR *spits, embittered. They all laugh at him.*)

KRIVOI ZOB (*kindly*). You're a strange one, Asan! Now you get this! If they're going to start living honest, they'll kick off in three days out of hunger . . .

TARTAR. What's that got to do with me! Y'got to live honest!

KRIVOI ZOB. The same tune! Let's go have some tea instead . . . Hey, Buben!

And, oh you chains, you chains of mine . . .

BUBNOV.

You iron watchmen guarding me . . .

KRIVOI ZOB. Let's go, Asanka! (*Goes out, singing.*)

I can't bust you, I can't break you . . .

(*The* TARTAR *threatens the* BARON *with his fist, and goes out after his friend.*)

SATIN (*to the* BARON, *laughingly*). Again, Your Youness,[2] you triumphantly got yourself into a mess. An educated man and yet you can't flip a card . . .

BARON (*throwing up his hands*). God knows how it . . .

ACTOR. You got no talent . . . no faith in yourself . . . and without that . . . you get nothing . . . never.

MEDVEDEV. I've got one king . . . and you've got two . . . hm—so!

BUBNOV. One won't be dead if he's got a head . . . Move.

KLESHCH. You've lost, Abram Ivanych!

MEDVEDEV. It's none of your business . . . see? And shut up . . .

SATIN. The winnings—fifty-three kopeks.

ACTOR. Three for me . . . But, what do I need three kopeks for?

LUKA (*coming out of the kitchen*). Well, you cleaned out the Tartar. You going to have some vodka?

BARON. Come on!

SATIN. Let's have a look at what you're like drunk.

LUKA. No better'n sober . . .

---

[2] A pun on his "old title" of Your Excellency.

ACTOR. Come on, old man . . . I'll recite you some couplets . . .
LUKA. What's that?
ACTOR. Verses. You understand?
LUKA. Ver-ses! And what'll I do with them, these verses!
ACTOR. They're entertaining. . . . But sometimes sad . . .
SATIN. Well, you night-club entertainer, you coming? (*Goes out with the* BARON.)
ACTOR. Coming . . . I'll catch up to you! Here now, old man, for example, some lines from a poem . . . I forget the beginning . . . I've forgotten it! (*Wipes his forehead.*)
BUBNOV. Jump! There goes your king . . . Your move!
MEDVEDEV. Made the wrong move . . . y'got him!
ACTOR. Before, when my organism wasn't poisoned with alcohol, I had a good memory, old man . . . But now . . . it's gone! Everything's gone for me. I always used to recite this poem with terrific success . . . lots of applause! You . . . don't know what applause is . . . It's like . . . vodka, boy! . . . I used to go out on stage and stand like this . . . (*Strikes a pose.*) Stand . . . and . . . (*Silence.*) Don't remember a thing . . . not a word . . . nothing! My favorite poem . . . It's not so good, old man, is it?
LUKA. What could be good about it, since it's your favorite you've forgotten? A man is all in what he likes best.
ACTOR. I've drunk myself to death, old man . . . I'm gone, friend . . . And why? Had no faith . . . I'm done for . . .
LUKA. Well, so what? You, now . . . get well! People get cured of drunkenness nowadays! Cured for free, boy . . . They've got a hospital just special for drunks . . . so's to cure them for nothing, I mean . . . Came 'round to saying, see, that a drunk's a man, too, and they're even glad when he wants to get cured! So, now, clear out! Go on . . .
ACTOR (*thoughtfully*). Where? Where's this?
LUKA. Why it's . . . in this town, now . . . what's it called? It's got a name . . . Now I'll tell you in just a minute! . . . Just you in the meantime get yourself ready. Lay off it! . . . Pull yourself together, and have patience . . . And then later you'll get cured . . . and you'll start living all over . . . That all over again's all right, isn't it? Well, make up your mind . . . in two stages.

ACTOR (*smiling*). All over again! . . . From the beginning . . . That's all right . . . Hm—yes . . . All over again. (*Laughs.*) Sure, now! I can do it! 'Cause I can, can't I?

LUKA. Why not? A man can do everything . . . just so long as he wants to . . .

ACTOR (*suddenly seeming to have awakened*). You're a queer one! So long for now! (*Whistles.*) Old man . . . 'bye. (*Goes out.*)

ANNA. Grampa!

LUKA. What, dear?

ANNA. Talk to me.

LUKA (*going over to her*). Sure, let's chat . . .

(KLESHCH *looks around, silently goes over to his wife, looks at her, and gestures with his arms and hands, as if wanting to say something.*)

LUKA. What is it, boy?

KLESHCH (*quietly*). Nothing . . . (*Slowly goes toward the door into the entrance, stands in front of it a few seconds, and—goes out.*)

LUKA (*having followed him with his eyes*). It's hard for your husband.

ANNA. I don't care about him.

LUKA. He used to beat you?

ANNA. And how! . . . It's on account of him, see, I've just withered away . . .

BUBNOV. My wife . . . had a lover; used to play really good checkers, the rat . . .

MEDVEDEV. Mm-mm . . .

ANNA. Grampa! Talk to me, honey . . . I feel so sick . . .

LUKA. It's all right! That's how it is before death, dear. It's all right! You just keep trusting . . . You'll die now, I mean, and have real peace . . . There'll be nothing more to be afraid of, nothing at all. Just peace, and quiet . . . Lie still now! Death—it sets everything at rest . . . it's sweet for us . . . You die and get a complete rest, they say . . . it's true, dear! 'cause where can a man rest up here?

(PEPEL *comes in. He is slightly drunk, dishevelled, and in a dismal mood. Sits down on a plank bed by the door and remains there silently, motionlessly.*)

ANNA. But what about up there—is there suffering, too?

LUKA. Nothing at all! Nothing like it! Now you believe me! Just peace and—nothing else! You'll get called up to the Lord and they'll tell him: "Lord, look here, here's your servant, Anna, come to you . . ."

MEDVEDEV (*harshly*). And how do you know what they'll say up there? Ah, you . . .

(*At the sound of* MEDVEDEV'S *voice,* PEPEL *raises his head and listens.*)

LUKA. I just do, Mr. Serg—

MEDVEDEV (*conciliatorily*). Mm . . . yes! Well . . . it's your business . . . Though . . . I'm not yet exactly . . . a serg—

BUBNOV. I jump two!

MEDVEDEV. Ah, you . . . Damn you . . .

LUKA. And the Lord'll look at you gently and lovingly and'll say: "I know this Anna, now!" So, he'll say, "Take her, Anna, now, up to heaven! Let her have peace . . . I know her life was mighty hard . . . she's weary . . . Give Anna peace . . ."

ANNA (*sighing*). Grampa . . . dear . . . if only that's true! If only . . . there's peace . . . and to feel nothing at all . . .

LUKA. You won't! There'll be nothing at all! You believe me now! You die joyfully, now, with no worry . . . Death—I tell you, it's the same for us as a mother for little children . . .

ANNA. But . . . maybe . . . maybe I'll get well?

LUKA (*smiling*). What for? To suffer again?

ANNA. Well . . . just a little longer . . . just to live . . . a little longer! If there's no suffering up there . . . then you can put up with it here a little . . . you can!

LUKA. There'll be nothing up there! . . . Just . . .

PEPEL (*getting up*). True enough . . . and, maybe, not true at all!

ANNA (*frightened*). O, Lord . . .

LUKA. Hey, handsome . . .

MEDVEDEV. Who's yelling?

PEPEL (*going over to him*). Me! What d'you want to make of it?

MEDVEDEV. You're yelling for nothing, that's what! A man's got to be very quiet . . .

PEPEL. Ah . . . you log of wood! . . . And an uncle besides . . . Ho-ho!

LUKA (*to* PEPEL *quietly*). Listen, don't shout! A woman's dying here . . . She already smells of the earth . . . don't disturb her!

PEPEL. For you, Grampa, sure—anything to please you! You're some fellow! Your lying's all right . . . you tell nice stories! Keep on. No matter . . . there's not much that's nice in this world!

BUBNOV. The woman's dying? Truly?

LUKA. Doesn't look as if she's joking . . .

BUBNOV. Means she'll stop coughing . . . She was coughing very restlessly . . . I jump two!

MEDVEDEV. Ah, y'ought to be shot through the heart!

PEPEL. Abram!

MEDVEDEV. I'm no Abram to you . . .

PEPEL. Abrashka! Natasha's—sick?

MEDVEDEV. And what do you care?

PEPEL. No, tell me: did Vasilisa beat her up bad?

MEDVEDEV. That's none of your business! It's a family matter . . . And who do you think you are, anyway?

PEPEL. Whoever I am . . . if just I want to, you'll never see little Natasha again!

MEDVEDEV (*quitting the game*). What's this you're saying? Who you talking about? My niece, now . . . ah, you thief!

PEPEL. A thief, but one you haven't caught . . .

MEDVEDEV. Just you wait! I'll get you . . . I'll soon . . .

PEPEL. And if you do it'll be the end of your whole little family. You think I'm going to keep my trap shut in front of the judge? You can sooner expect an elephant to fly! I'll get asked who started me off on being a thief and showed me where? Mishka Kostylyov and his wife! Who was the fence for you? Mishka Kostylyov and his wife!

MEDVEDEV. You're lying! They won't believe you!

PEPEL. They will, 'cause it's true! And I'll pull you in, too . . . ha! I'll fix you all, you rats, you'll see!

MEDVEDEV (*losing control*). You're lying! And . . . you're

lying! And . . . what wrong did I ever do you? You're a mad dog! . . .

PEPEL. And what did you ever do for me that was good?

LUKA. O-oh!

MEDVEDEV (*to* LUKA). You—what're you cawing about? What's this got to do with you? This is a family matter!

BUBNOV (*to* LUKA). Leave 'em alone! It's not you and me the noose's getting spliced for.

LUKA (*meekly*). I didn't mean nothing special! I was just saying that if somebody didn't do somebody something good, then he'd done him something wrong . . .

MEDVEDEV (*not understanding*). Aha! We here . . . we all of us know each other . . . but you—who are you, anyway? (*Snorting angrily, quickly goes out.*)

LUKA. The big knight got angry . . . Oho-ho, things are, I see, my boys—things here are mixed up!

PEPEL. He's run off to complain to Vasilisa . . .

BUBNOV. You're being a fool, Vasily. Somehow you've got up a lot of courage . . . Watch out. Courage is all right when you're off to the forest for mushrooms . . . but here it's got no point to it . . . You'll get your neck wrung real good.

PEPEL. No, come on now! You're not going to catch us Yaroslavl fellows with bare hands just like that . . . If there's a war, we'll fight . . .

LUKA. But in fact you ought to get out of here, boy, far as you can from here . . .

PEPEL. Where? Come on, out with it . . .

LUKA. Go . . . to Siberia!

PEPEL. Ha! No, I'll wait till I get shipped off to this Siberia of yours at government expense . . .

LUKA. Listen to me: you go, now! There you can make out all right . . . There they need fellows like you!

PEPEL. How I make out's already laid down for me! My old man spent his whole life sitting in jail and ordered it up for me, too . . . When I was little, even then I was called a thief, a thief's boy . . .

LUKA. But it's a good country, Siberia! A golden land! The man who's strong and got his wits about him can make out there like a cucumber in a hothouse.

PEPEL. Old man! What're you telling lies for all the time?

LUKA. Hunh?

PEPEL. He's gone deaf! What're you lying for, I'm asking you?

LUKA. Now what'm I lying about?

PEPEL. About everything . . . You keep saying it's good there, it's good here . . . see—you're lying! What for?

LUKA. Now, you just believe me; go on out and have a look for yourself . . . You'll say thanks . . . Why're you hanging around here? And . . . how come you need the truth so bad . . . Just think! It'll maybe—truth, I mean —'ll be like a blow on the head for you . . .

PEPEL. It's all the same to me! If it's a blow on the head, then that's what it is . . .

LUKA. You crazy fellow! What d'you want to kill yourself for?

BUBNOV. What're you two gassing about? I don't get it . . . What's this truth, Vaska, you need now? What for? You know the truth about yourself . . . and so does everybody else . . .

PEPEL. Hold on, don't start cawing! Let him tell me . . . Listen, old man: does God exist?

(LUKA *is silent, smiling.*)

BUBNOV. People all live . . . like chips of woods floating along a river . . . build themselves houses . . . and leave the chips to fall away . . .

PEPEL. Well? Does he? Out with it . . .

LUKA (*quietly*). If you believe, he does; if you don't, he doesn't. What you believe in, that's what exists . . .

(PEPEL, *silently and intently, surprised, looks at the old man.*)

BUBNOV. I'm going to have some tea . . . Want to go to the tavern? Hey!

LUKA (*to* PEPEL). Why you staring?

PEPEL. No reason . . . Wait a minute! That means . . .

BUBNOV. Well, I'm going by myself . . . (*Goes to the door and runs into* VASILISA.)

PEPEL. And so . . . you . . .

VASILISA (*to* BUBNOV). Nastasya's in?

BUBNOV. No . . . (*Goes out.*)

PEPEL. Ah . . . she's come . . .

VASILISA (*goes over to* ANNA). Still alive?

LUKA. Don't get her upset . . .

VASILISA. And you . . . why you hanging around here?
LUKA. I can clear out . . . if that's what . . .
VASILISA (*heading for the door into* PEPEL's *room*). Vasily! I've got something I want to talk to you about . . .
   (LUKA *goes up to the door into the entryway, opens it, and loudly slams it shut. He then carefully climbs onto a bed and up onto the stove.*)
VASILISA (*from* PEPEL's *room*). Vasya . . . come here!
PEPEL. I won't . . . don't want to . . .
VASILISA. But . . . what's wrong? What're you mad at?
PEPEL. I'm fed up . . . fed up with the whole damned business . . .
VASILISA. And . . . with me, too?
PEPEL. You, too . . .
   (VASILISA *pulls her kerchief tightly over her shoulders, pressing her hands against her breast. She goes to* ANNA's *bed, peers cautiously under the canopy, and goes back to* PEPEL.)
PEPEL. Well . . . out with it . . .
VASILISA. With what? I can't force you to be nice . . . and it's not in me to beg you for it . . . Thanks for letting me know the truth . . .
PEPEL. What truth?
VASILISA. That you're fed up with me . . . or isn't that true?
   (PEPEL *looks at her without speaking.*)
VASILISA (*moving closer to him*). Why're you staring? Don't you know me no more?
PEPEL (*sighing*). You're good-looking, Vaska . . . (*The woman puts her arm around his neck, but he shakes it off with a movement of his shoulder.*) but I never had a liking for you . . . I lived with you, and everything . . . but I never really liked you . . .
VASILISA (*softly*). O-oh . . . So, then . . .
PEPEL. So, we've got nothing to talk about! Nothing . . . Get away from me . . .
VASILISA. Somebody else caught your eye?
PEPEL. None of your business . . . And if she has, I wouldn't even ask you to be matchmaker . . .
VASILISA (*meaningfully*). You'd be making a mistake . . . Maybe I could arrange it . . .
PEPEL (*suspiciously*). With who?

VASILISA. You know . . . why pretend? Vasily . . . I'm a straightforward person . . . (*More softly.*) I won't hide anything . . . you've hurt me . . . For nothing at all, for no reason, you struck me down like with a whip . . . Used to say you loved me . . . and suddenly . . .

PEPEL. No suddenly about it . . . I long ago . . . You've got no heart, woman . . . A woman's got to have a heart . . . We're wild animals . . . we got to have . . . we got to be—trained . . . But you—what did you ever train me to? . . .

VASILISA. What's done is done . . . I know a man's not his own master . . . You don't love me any more . . . all right! That's the way it is . . .

PEPEL. So, now, that's it! Parted peaceably, without a lot of fuss . . . that's good!

VASILISA. No, wait a minute! Still . . . when I was living with you . . . I kept waiting all the time for you to help me get out of this slough . . . for you to free me from my husband, from my uncle . . . from this whole life . . . And maybe I didn't love you, Vasya, but . . . I loved my hope, loved this idea of mine in you . . . Y'understand? I kept waiting for you to pull me out . . .

PEPEL. You're no nail, and I'm no pincers . . . I kept thinking myself that you like a clever . . . 'Cause you are clever . . . You're—tricky!

VASILISA (*bending closer to him*). Vasya, let's . . . help each other . . .

PEPEL. How so?

VASILISA (*softly, forcefully*). You like . . . my sister, I know . . .

PEPEL. And on account of that you beat her up like hell! You watch out, Vaska! Don't you lay a hand on her . . .

VASILISA. Wait a minute. Don't get excited! Everything can be done quietly, and real good . . . Go ahead and marry her, y'want to. And I'll give you money, too . . . three hundred! If I get more, I'll give you more . . .

PEPEL (*drawing back*). Hold on . . . How come? For what?

VASILISA. Free me . . . from my husband! Take this noose off my neck . . .

PEPEL (*whistles softly*). That's i-it! Oho-ho! Now that's something—you thought up pretty tricky . . . means: the husband in the grave, the lover to hard labor, and yourself . . .

VASILISA. Vasya! Why hard labor? You don't—not yourself . . . one of your friends! And even if it's you yourself, who'll find out? Natalya! . . . Think of it. You'll have money . . . go away somewhere . . . Free me forever . . . and that there won't be a sister around me, that's a good thing for her. It's hard for me just to look at her . . . I get all spiteful against her on account of you . . . and I can't keep it in . . . I torment the girl, beat her . . . beat her so, that I'm in tears out of pity for her myself . . . But —I keep doing it. And—I will!

PEPEL. You beast! Look at her boasting about being a beast.

VASILISA. I'm not boasting, I'm telling the truth. Think about it, Vasya . . . You got stuck in jail twice on account of my husband . . . on account of his greediness . . . He's dug into me like a bedbug . . . sucking away at me four years now! And what kind of a husband is he for me? Rides Natasha all the time, makes fun of her—a beggar, he says! He's poison for everybody . . .

PEPEL. You spin it all pretty slyly . . .

VASILISA. What I'm saying's all clear . . . Only an idiot wouldn't understand what I want . . .

(KOSTYLYOV *comes in cautiously and steals forward.*)

PEPEL (*to* VASILISA). Now . . . go away!

VASILISA. Think it over. (*Sees her husband.*) What do you want? Looking for me?

(PEPEL *jumps up and wildly looks at* KOSTYLYOV.)

KOSTYLYOV. It's me . . . me! And you're here . . . alone? Ah-ha . . . You've—been talking? (*Suddenly stamps his feet and screams loudly.*) Vaska . . . witch . . . You bag . . . of begging bones! (*Frightened by his own shriek, he is met by silence and immobility.*) Forgive me, Lord . . . Again, Vasilisa, you made me sin . . . I've been looking for you all over . . . (*Shrieking.*) Time for bed! You forgot to put oil in the icon-lamps . . . Ah, you! Beggar! . . . you pig . . . (*Shakes his trembling hands at her.* VASILISA *slowly goes toward the door into the entryway, looking around at* PEPEL.)

PEPEL (*to* KOSTYLYOV). You! Get out . . . Clear out! . . .
KOSTYLYOV (*shouts*). I'm the landlord! Clear out yourself, yes! Thief . . .
PEPEL (*tonelessly*). Get out! Mishka . . .
KOSTYLYOV. Don't you dare! I'm the la- . . . I'll . . .
  (PEPEL *grabs him by the collar and shakes him. A loud rattle and a yowling yawning is heard on the stove.* PEPEL *lets* KOSTYLYOV *go, and the old man runs out into the entryway with a shout.*)
PEPEL (*having jumped up on the bed*). Who's that . . . Who's on the stove?
LUKA (*sticking his head over*). Hunh?
PEPEL. You!
LUKA (*calmly*). Me . . . me myself . . . Oh Lord a'mercy!
PEPEL (*shuts the door into the entryway, looks for the bolt, and does not find it*). Ah, god damn . . . Come on down, old man!
LUKA. Right awa-ay . . . coming . . .
PEPEL (*rudely*). What'd you get up on the stove for?
LUKA. And where should I have?
PEPEL. But . . . you went out in the entryway, didn't you?
LUKA. In the entryway, boy, it's cold for an old man like me . . .
PEPEL. Did you . . . hear?
LUKA. Why—sure! How couldn't I? Or you think—I'm deaf? Ah, my boy, you've got real luck coming . . . Real luck!
PEPEL (*suspiciously*). What luck? In what?
LUKA. Why, in that I climbed up on the stove.
PEPEL. But . . . what did you start making a fuss up there for?
LUKA. So's to, I mean—I got hot . . . on account of your orphan's luck . . . And then, too, I caught on, see? to how this boy didn't mess up . . . Just so's he don't strangle the old fellow . . .
PEPEL. Ye-es . . . I might . . . I hate . . .
LUKA. And no wonder! Not hard at all . . . People go wrong like that all the time . . .
PEPEL (*smiling*). What d'you mean? You went wrong yourself once?

LUKA. Boy, now you listen to what I'm going tell you: you got to get rid of this woman! Don't you give her a thing, and don't let her at you . . . She'll get her husband out of the way, all right, and a lot smarter than you would. Don't you listen to her, the devil . . . Just look at me. What do I look like? All bald . . . How come? On account of all these different damned women . . . Maybe I knew more of them, more of these women I mean, than I had hairs on my head . . . But this Vasilisa, now—she's . . . worse than a Hottentot!

PEPEL. I don't know . . . if I ought be thankful to you, or if you . . . too . . .

LUKA. Don't you say a thing! You won't say a thing better'n what I just said! You listen to me: the girl you like here, you go and take her by the arm, and off you go—hup! two! Go on! . . . Get out of here! . . .

PEPEL (*morosely*). Can't make people out! Who's good, who means trouble . . . Nothing makes sense . . .

LUKA. What's there to understand? People live all different . . . The way their heart lies, that's the way they live . . . good today, trouble tomorrow . . . But if this girl, now, 's really gotten a hold on you—real serious I mean—go off with her and that's that . . . Or else, go by yourself . . . You're young, you got plenty of time to get yourself a wife . . .

PEPEL (*takes him by the shoulder*). No. Now you tell me why you're saying all this . . .

LUKA. Hold on, let go of me . . . I want to look at Anna . . . For some reason she was wheezing bad . . . (*Goes to* ANNA'S *bed, opens the canopy, looks, touches her with his hand.* PEPEL, *pensive and perplexed, watches him.*) Most merciful Christ our Lord! Receive into Thy kingdom the soul of Thy newly-deceased servant, Anna . . .

PEPEL (*softly*). Dead? . . . (*Without going all the way over, he stretches up and looks at the bed.*)

LUKA (*softly*). She's finished suffering! . . . And where's her old man?

PEPEL. In the tavern, probably . . .

LUKA. Got to tell him.

PEPEL (*shuddering*). Don't like dead people . . .

LUKA (*goes to the door*). Why would anyone? . . . It's the living you got to love . . . the living . . .

PEPEL. I'm going with you . . .

LUKA. Scared?

PEPEL. I don't like . . .

(*They quickly go out. Emptiness and silence. On the other side of the door into the entryway one can hear a dull noise, uneven, incomprehensible. A moment later the* ACTOR *comes in.*)

ACTOR (*stops on the doorstep without shutting the door, and, holding on to the jamb with his hands, shouts*). Hey there, old man! Where are you? I—remembered it . . . Hey, listen. (*Staggering, takes two steps forward and, striking a pose, recites*):

Ladies and gentlemen! If the world
Can't find its way to the truth that's holy,
Then honor the madman who will furl
Mankind up in a dream of gold.

(NATASHA *appears in the doorway behind the* ACTOR.)
Old man! . . .
If our sun tomorrow would forget
To illuminate our earth in motion,
The world tomorrow would still be lit
By some unknown insane man's notion.

NATASHA (*laughing*). You booby! You're clobbered!

ACTOR (*turning around to her*). Ah-ah, it's you? But—where's the old man . . . that nice little old man? Nobody's here, I guess, seems like . . . Natasha, good-bye! Good-bye . . . truly!

NATASHA (*coming in*). You just said hello and here you are saying good-bye . . .

ACTOR (*barring her way*). I'm going away, going off . . . Spring'll come, and I'll be gone . . .

NATASHA. Let me by . . . Where're you going, now?

ACTOR. Going to find the city . . . get cured . . . You, too, go away . . . Ophelia . . . "get thee to a nunnery" . . . Y'understand, there's a hospital for organisms . . . for drunks . . . A magnificent hospital . . . Marble . . . marble floors! Light . . . clean, food . . . everything free!

And a marble floor, really! I'll find it, get cured, and . . .
once more I'll be . . . I'm on the road to rebirth . . .
as . . . King . . . Lear said, Natasha . . . My stage
name's Sverchkov-Zavolzhsky[3] . . . Nobody knows this,
nobody! Here I haven't got a name . . . Y'understand
how humiliating this is—to lose your name? Even dogs get
called something . . .

(NATASHA *walks carefully around the* ACTOR, *stops by* ANNA'S
bed, looks.)

ACTOR. Without a name you're not a man . . .

NATASHA. Look here . . . dear . . . I think she's dead . . .

ACTOR (*shaking his head*). Impossible . . .

NATASHA (*moving back*). Honest to God . . . You look!

BUBNOV (*in the doorway*). Look at what?

NATASHA. Anna's . . . dead!

BUBNOV. Means she's stopped coughing. (*Goes to* ANNA'S *bed,
looks, goes to his own place.*) Kleshch has got to be told . . .
it's his business . . .

ACTOR. I'll go . . . tell him . . . She lost her name! . . .
(*Goes out.*)

NATASHA (*in the middle of the room*). That's how I'll . . .
someday just like that . . . in a cellar . . . down and
out . . .

BUBNOV (*spreading some rags over his bed*). What? What're
you mumbling?

NATASHA. Nothing . . . just talking to myself . . .

BUBNOV. Waiting for Vaska? You watch out, Vaska'll break
your neck . . .

NATASHA. What's the difference who does it? I'd rather have
him . . .

BUBNOV (*lying down*). Well, it's your business . . .

NATASHA. But, you know . . . it's good she died . . . but
pitiful . . . O Lord! . . . What's the point of a man's
living?

BUBNOV. That's what everybody does: gets born, lives, and
dies. And I'll die . . . and you, too . . . What're you so
sorry about?

---

[3] If translated, the name would be "The Cricket from Beyond the Volga."

(*Enter* LUKA, *the* TARTAR, KRIVOI ZOB, *and* KLESHCH; KLESHCH *comes in behind everyone else, slowly, hunched up.*)

NATASHA. Sh-sh! Anna . . .

KRIVOI ZOB. We heard . . . God rest her soul, now she's dead . . .

TARTAR (*to* KLESHCH). Got to haul her out of here! Out in the entryway! Can't have a dead person here, the living got to sleep here . . .

KLESHCH (*quietly*). We'll do it . . .

(*Everyone goes over to the bed.* KLESHCH *looks at his wife over the others' shoulders.*)

KRIVOI ZOB (*to the* TARTAR). You think she's going to stink? There won't be none from her! . . . she got all dried up when she was still living . . .

NATASHA. O Lord! If someone'd just feel sorry . . . just say something about it! Ah, you . . .

LUKA. Now, child, don't take it to heart . . . It's no matter! How can they . . . how can we feel sorry for the dead? Eh, dear? We don't feel sorry for the living . . . don't even take pity on ourselves . . . how can we for her!

BUBNOV (*yawning*). And then, too, death doesn't care about talk . . . Sickness, now, is afraid of it, but death isn't!

TARTAR (*stepping back*). The police got to . . .

KRIVOI ZOB. The police—you got to do that! Kleshch! You notified the police?

KLESHCH. No . . . Got to bury her . . . and all I've got is forty kopeks . . .

KRIVOI ZOB. Well, in that case, y'got to borrow . . . or we'll take up a collection . . . One'll give five, another—what he can . . . But you notify the police . . . Hurry up! Or they'll think you killed the woman . . . or something . . .
(*Goes to the beds and gets ready to lie down beside the* TARTAR.)

NATASHA (*going over to* BUBNOV's *bed*). Now . . . I'm going to be dreaming about her . . . I always dream about people who've died . . . I'm afraid of going alone . . . it's dark in the entryway . . .

LUKA (*following her*). You steer clear of the living . . . that's what I'm telling you . . .

NATASHA. Walk me, Grampa . . .

LUKA. Let's go . . . let's go! All right! (*They go out. A pause.*)

KRIVOI ZOB. Oho-ho-ho! Asan! Soon it'll be spring, my friend . . . be warm for us again. Now the boys in the villages're fixing up their plows and harrows . . . getting set for the plowing . . . mm-yep! But us? . . . Asan? . . . Ah, already pounding it off, the damned Mohammedan! . . .

BUBNOV. The Tartars like sleeping . . .

KLESHCH (*stands in the middle of the flophouse and stares dully ahead*). What'll I do now?

KRIVOI ZOB. Go to sleep . . . that's all there is . . .

KLESHCH (*softly*). But . . . she . . . how can? . . .

(*Nobody answers him.* SATIN *and the* ACTOR *come in.*)

ACTOR (*shouting*). Old man! "Hither, my faithful Kent!"

SATIN. Here comes Miklukha-Maklai . . . ho-ho!

ACTOR. It's decided and done with! Old man, where's the city . . . where are you?

SATIN. Fata Morgana! The old man told you a good story . . . There's nothing at all! No cities, no people . . . nothing!

ACTOR. That's not true!

TARTAR (*jumping up*). Where's the landlord? I'm going to the landlord! Can't sleep, won't pay . . . Dead people . . . drunks . . . (*Quickly goes out.* SATIN *whistles after him.*)

BUBNOV (*in a sleepy voice*). Go to bed, boys, be quiet . . . at night y'got to sleep!

ACTOR. Yes, so! . . . Here—aha! A body . . . "Our nets brought forth a body from the deep" . . . 'S a poem . . . B-beranger!

SATIN (*shouting*). Bodies don't hear! Bodies don't feel! Shout . . . roar . . . bodies don't hear! . . .

(LUKA *appears in the doorway.*)

(*Curtain*)

ACT III

"The Wasteland," a yard littered with all kinds of rubbish and overgrown with tall weeds. Deep in it there is a high, brick, fireproof wall. It conceals the sky. Around it are elder bushes. On the right is the dark log wall of some yard building—a shed or stable. On the left is the bare grey wall, pieces of stucco still sticking to it, of the house where the Kostylyovs' flophouse is. It stands at an angle, so that its rear corner comes out almost to the middle of the empty lot. There is a narrow passage between it and the red wall. There are two windows in the grey wall: one on ground level, the other about two arshins [about 5 feet] higher, and closer to the fire-wall. A long, wide sled is lying by this wall, turned upside-down, and there is a log about four arshins long. On the right-hand side, near the wall, there is a pile of old planks and beams. It is evening; the sun is setting, throwing a reddish light over the fire-wall. It is early spring; the snow has recently melted. The black twigs of the elder bushes have no buds on them yet.
NATASHA *and* NASTYA *are sitting side by side on the log.* LUKA *and the* BARON *are on the sled.* KLESHCH *is lying on the pile of wood by the right-hand wall.* BUBNOV'S *mug sticks out of the ground-level window.*

NASTYA (*having closed her eyes, tells a singsong story, and nods her head in time to the words*). So he comes to the garden at night, to the pergola, as we had agreed . . . and I've been waiting for him a long time already and I'm trembling with fear and grief. He's all trembling, too, and—white as chalk, and in his hands he's got a gun . . .
NATASHA (*nibbling sunflower seeds*). Think of that! They're sure telling the truth when they say students are desperate . . .
NASTYA. And he says to me in a frightening voice: "My precious love . . ."
BUBNOV. Ho-ho! Precious?
BARON. Take it easy! If you don't like, y'don't have to listen, but nobody asked you to butt in . . . Go on!
NASTYA. "My darling love," he says! "My parents," he says,

"won't give their consent for us to get married . . . and're threatening to damn me forever on account of my love for you. So," he says, "on account of this I got to commit suicide." And the gun he's got is enormous and's loaded up with ten bullets . . . "Farewell," he says, "dear friend of my heart! I've resolved irrevocably . . . it's impossible for me to live without you." And I says to him: "My unforgettable friend . . . Raoul . . ."

BUBNOV (*surprised*). Wha-at? How's that? Controol?

BARON (*laughs*). Nastka! But you know . . . you know, last time he was Gaston!

NASTYA (*jumping up*). Shut up . . . you wretches! Ah . . . you homeless dogs! Can you . . . can you possibly understand . . . love? Real love? But mine was . . . mine was real! (*To the* BARON.) You! You good-for-nothing! . . . You educated man . . . Y'keep saying you used to drink coffee lying in bed . . .

LUKA. Now, you, hold on, there! Don't you go butting in! Got to show respect for a man . . . It's not what's said that matters, but why's it said—that's what matters! Go on with the story, child, it's all right!

BUBNOV. Go on with painting your feathers, y'old crow . . . go ahead!

BARON. Well—go on!

NATASHA. Don't pay attention to them . . . what do they count? They're just doing it out of envy . . . They got nothing to tell about themselves . . .

NASTYA (*sits down again*). I won't go on! . . . Won't say a word . . . If they aren't going to believe me . . . just going to laugh at me . . . (*Suddenly breaking off, she is silent for a few seconds, and, having again shut her eyes, she goes on ardently and loudly, waving her hand in time to the words as if listening to far-away music.*) And so—I says to him: "Joy of my life! Bright moon of mine! And it's absolutely impossible for me, too, to live in this world without you . . . on account of I love you so madly and am going to be loving you as long as the heart beats in my breast! But," I says to him, "don't kill yourself now so young . . . your life means so much to your dear parents, for who you're their whole joy and delight . . . Forget me! Better let me be done for . . . out of longing for you, my life . . . I'm all alone . . . I'm like that! Let me go ahead and perish, it makes no difference! I'm no good . . . and there's nothing for me . . . nothing at all . . ." (*Covers her face with her hands and cries soundlessly.*)

NATASHA (*turns aside, quietly*). Don't cry . . . don't!

(LUKA, *smiling, strokes* NASTYA's *head.*)

BUBNOV (*laughs*). Ah . . . you goddamned chicken!

BARON (*also laughs*). Grampa! You think that's all true? It's all out of that book, *Fatal Love* . . . It's all nonsense! Forget her! . . .

NATASHA. What's that to you? You! Shut up now . . . God's punished you enough.

NASTYA (*furiously*). You hopeless case! You hollow man! Where's your heart, now, where is it?

LUKA (*takes* NASTYA *by the hand*). Let's leave them, dear! It's nothing . . . don't be angry! I know . . . I believe! It's you is right, not them . . . 'Cause if you believe you had a real love . . . it means you did! You did! But don't get angry at him, at this fellow, now . . . He's . . . maybe laughing out of just plain envy . . . maybe he never had nothing real at all . . . nothing at all! Let's go! . . .

NASTYA (*tightly pressing her hands to her breast*). Grampa! Honest to God . . . it *was*! It all happened! . . . He was a student . . . a Frenchman . . . called Gastosha . . . with a little black beard . . . used to wear patent leathers . . . Cross my heart and hope to die! And he loved me so much . . . so much!

LUKA. I know! It's all right! I believe you! In patent leathers, you say? A-yai-ai! And—a-a—you also, loved him? (*They go out around the corner.*)

BARON. Oh, how stupid this girl is . . . kind, but stupid— unbearably stupid!

BUBNOV. How come . . . a man so much likes lying? It's always—like he was standing in front of the judge . . . really!

NATASHA. Guess lying, now . . . 's nicer than the truth . . . Me, too . . .

BARON. What d'you mean, "too?" Well?

NATASHA. I make things up . . . Make things up and—wait . . .

BARON. For what?

NATASHA (*smiling embarrassedly*). Just wait . . . Look, I think tomorrow . . . somebody'll come . . . just somebody . . . special . . . Or something'll happen . . . also unheard of . . . I've been waiting for days and days . . . always been waiting . . . But . . . actually—what's there to wait for? (*Pause.*)

BARON (*with a grin*). There's nothing to wait for . . . I'm not waiting for anything! Everything's already . . . been! It's gone . . . done with! . . . Now to go on!

NATASHA. But sometimes . . . I imagine to myself, that tomorrow I'll . . . die all of a sudden-like . . . And I get a terrible, frightened feeling . . . Y'can really imagine about death in summer . . . there're thunderstorms in summer . . . you can always get killed by a thunderstorm . . .

BARON. Your life's hard . . . This sister of yours . . . 's a real devil!

NATASHA. And who's life easy for? It's rotten for everybody . . . I can see . . .

KLESHCH (*until this moment motionless and apathetic, suddenly jumps up*). For everybody? That's not true! Not for everybody! If it was going to be for everybody . . . all right! Then it wouldn't hurt nobody . . . right!

BUBNOV. What the hell's got into you? Look at you, what a howl you've set up!

(KLESHCH *again lies down in his place and grumbles.*)

BARON. And . . . I've got to go make it up with Nastenka . . . if you don't she'll never give you anything for a drink.

BUBNOV. Hmm . . . People like lying . . . Nastka's . . . something clear and understandable! She's got used to painting up her mug . . . so she wants to do a little painting of the soul inside . . . put a little blush on it . . . But . . . the others—why? Now, Luka, for example . . . he lies a lot . . . and without it's being any use for himself . . . An old man at that . . . What's he do it for?

BARON (*smiling, walks away*). Everybody's got—greyish souls . . . Everbody wants to do a little touching up . . .

LUKA (*comes from behind the corner*). You, sir, what're you getting the girl all upset for? You oughtn't to be bothering her . . . Let her cry and do what she wants . . . 'Cause she's shedding tears for her own pleasure . . . how's that hurt you?

BARON. It's silly, old man! I'm fed up with her . . . Today Raoul, tomorrow Gaston . . . but always the same old story! Still—I'm off to make up with her . . . (*Goes out.*)

LUKA. You go, now, that's it . . . be nice! Never hurts nobody to be nice to a person . . .

NATASHA. You're good, Grampa . . . How come you're so— good?

LUKA. Good, you say? Well . . . all right, if you think so . . . all right. (*The sound of an accordion and singing come softly from behind the red wall.*) Y'got to be good to somebody, child . . . y'got to take pity on people! Christ, now, he took pity on everybody and told us to do that, too . . . I'll tell you now—y'take pity on a man at the right time . . . and good'll come of it! Now, for example, I used to be watchman at a summer house—this engineer's place near Tomsk . . . So! The house was standing in a forest, a lonely place . . . and winter'd come and I was all by myself, at this house, now . . . It was good—and nice! Only once, I hear this sound, see? people climbing in!

NATASHA. Robbers?

LUKA. It was. Trying to get in, sure enough! . . . I grab my gun, go outside . . . I look around—there's two of them . . . They're opening a window—and so busy with what they're doing they don't see me at all. I shout at them: hey you! . . . clear out! . . . But they, see, start at me with an axe . . . But I warn them: "Stop," I says, "or I'll shoot you!" And I keep pointing my gun at the one and then the other. They go down on their knees: "Let us go!" says they. But I'd already got real mad . . . on account of that axe, see! I says: "I was chasing you, you devils, you wouldn't go . . . and now," I says, "one of the two of you go break off some branches!" One went and broke some. "Now," I tells them, "one of you lie down and the other give him a good whipping!" And so they gave each other a good whipping, just like I ordered them to. And when they was done

... they says to me: "Grampa," they says, "give us some bread, for Christ's sake! We got nothing in our bellies," they says. There's robbers for you, dear ... (*Laughs.*) and with an axe, too, mind you! Sure ... Good peasants both of them ... I says to them: "Y'ought to have asked for bread right away, you devils." And they says: "We're sick and tired of it," they says, "You ask and ask and nobody gives you nothing. It gets you!" So they stayed with me the whole winter. The one of them, Stepan he was called, used to take the gun and head off for the forest ... But the other, Yakov he was, he kept being sick all the time, always coughing ... So the three of us together, see, did the watching of the house. Spring comes along, and they says to me: "Good-bye, grampa," they says! And off they went ... headed back to Russia ...

NATASHA. They were runaways? Convicts?

LUKA. Yep—really were—escaped convicts ... ran away from their settlement[4] ... Good peasants! ... If it wasn't that I'd took pity on them they'd have maybe killed me ... or something worse ... And then there'd be trial and prison and Siberia ... What's the point? Prison don't teach a man good, and Siberia don't, neither ... but a man does ... sure thing! A man can teach a man good ... very easy! (*Pause.*)

BUBNOV. Hmm—yes! ... Take me now, I don't know how to lie! What's the point? The way I see it, let the whole truth out, just as it comes! What's there to hold back?

KLESHCH (*suddenly jumping up again, as if singed, and shouting*). What truth? Where's the truth? (*With his hands pulling at the rags he has on.*) Here's the truth! No work, no strength! That's the truth! No place to go in ... no home of your own! You just kick the bucket ... that's it, that's the truth! Christ! What ... what's it to me, this—truth? Let me breathe ... give me air! What have I done wrong? What'll I do with this—truth? Y'can't live—goddamn it—y'can't live ... that's what the truth is! ...

BUBNOV. Listen to that ... he's really gone! ...

LUKA. Merciful Father! Listen, now, boy! You ...

[4] Convicts who had completed their term of hard labor had several years of forced residence in Siberia.

kleshch (*trembles in agitation*). Y'all here keep saying—tru-uth! You keep comforting everybody, old man . . . Let me tell you . . . I hate everybody! And that's truth, too . . . goddamned thing! Y'got me? Well, get it! Goddamn it! (*Runs off around the corner, looking back.*)

luka. Ai-yai-ai! The fellow got all upset . . . And where'd he run off to?

natasha. What's the difference, since he's nuts? . . .

bubnov. He really let go! Like as if he'd been playing theater . . . It happens like that, often . . . Hasn't got used to life yet . . .

pepel (*coming slowly from behind the corner*). Peace to this honest gathering! Well, Luka, you sly old devil, you still telling stories?

luka. Y'ought to have seen . . . how the fellow was shouting here!

pepel. Who? Kleshch, you mean? What happened to him? He was running like he'd been scalded . . .

luka. You'd run, too, if . . . your heart was as sore as his . . .

pepel (*sits down*). Don't like him . . . he's terribly vicious, and proud. (*Mimicking* kleshch.) "I'm a workingman." Like as if everybody else was beneath him . . . Go ahead and work if you like it . . . what's there to be so proud of about that? If you're going to judge people by their working . . . why then a horse is better than anybody . . . pulls away and—shuts up! Natasha! Family in?

natasha. Went to the cemetery . . . they were going to vespers . . .

pepel. Aha, that's why you're free, I see . . . It's not often!

luka (*pensively, to* bubnov). Now . . . you were talking—about truth . . . It's not always, this truth, I mean, it's not always good for what's ailing a man . . . y'won't always heal the heart with truth . . . Like for example there was this case; I knew a man who believed in a land of justice . . .

bubnov. In wha-at?

luka. In a land of justice. "Must be in the world," he'd say, "a land of justice . . . In this land," he says, "there're special people settling down . . . good people! Got respect for each other, keep helping each other all the time . . . and they got everything set up just fine and dandy!" And so this man's always figuring on going there . . . on finding this land of justice. He was a poor man, bad off . . . and when things would be getting so hard for him there was nothing to do but just lie down and die, he wouldn't give up but just keep right on grinning and saying: "No matter! I'll get through! Wait just a bit more and then I'll forget this whole life and I'll go off to the land of justice." That was the only delight he had—that land . . .

PEPEL. Well? Did he go?

BUBNOV. Where? Ho-ho!

LUKA. And so to this here place—this all happened in Siberia—this exile gets sent, a scholar fellow. He comes—this scholar fellow does—with books and maps and all kinds of things . . . The man goes up and says to this scholar fellow: "Show me now, if you don't mind," he says, "where's the land of justice lie and which is the road to it?" The scholar fellow gets his books out right away, opens up his maps . . . and looks and looks—there's no land of justice nowhere! Everything's right, all the lands are shown there, but there ain't the one of justice! . . .

PEPEL (*quietly*). So? There ain't one? (BUBNOV *laughs loudly*.)

NATASHA. You just wait . . . So, grampa?

LUKA. The man don't believe it. "It must be there," he says, "look some more! 'Cause," he says, "all these books and maps of yours are no good at all if there's no land of justice." The scholar fellow gets insulted. "My maps," he says, "are the best there is, but there just ain't no land of justice noplace, nohow." Well, at this point the man gets mad: "How can that be? I lived my whole life, put up with everything and waited, and believed all the time there is! And now it turns out on these maps there's nothing! It's robbery!" And he says to this scholar fellow: "Ah, you . . . you bastard! Scholar, ha! You're a dirty cheat!" and he hauls off and hits him on the ear—just like that! And again! . . . (*After a pause.*) And then, after that he goes home and—hangs himself! . . . (*Everyone is silent.* LUKA, *smiling, looks at* PEPEL *and* NATASHA.)

PEPEL (*quietly*). Go-od damn it . . . it's not a funny story . . .

NATASHA. Couldn't take being tricked . . .

BUBNOV (*sullenly*). It's all just a fairy story . . .

PEPEL. So . . . there's that land of justice for you . . . never showed up, it means . . .

NATASHA. I feel sorry . . . for that man . . .

BUBNOV. It's all made up . . . The whole thing! Ho-ho! A land of justice! I'll say! Ho-ho-ho! (*Disappears from the window.*)

LUKA (*nodding his head toward* BUBNOV's *window*). 'S laughing at it! Eheh-heh . . . (*A pause.*) Well, boys! . . . live and prosper. I'm leaving you soon . . .

PEPEL. Where you going now?

LUKA. Down to the Little Russians . . . Heard there's a new faith been started there . . . got to take a look . . . sure! . . . People're always looking, always wanting something better . . . Lord grant 'em the patience!

PEPEL. What do you think . . . they'll find it?

LUKA. People, you mean? Sure, they will! Who looks, finds . . . Who wants something bad enough, finds it!

NATASHA. If they'd just find anything . . . think up a better way of . . .

LUKA. They will! Only you got to help them, child . . . got to respect them . . .

NATASHA. How can I help? I'm . . . helpless myself . . .

PEPEL (*resolutely*). Again I . . . I want to talk to you again . . . Natasha . . . Right here, in front of him . . . he knows everything . . . Come away . . . with me!

NATASHA. Where? To jail?

PEPEL. I said I'm quitting being a thief! Honest to God—I'm quitting! And once I've said something I do it! I can read and write . . . I'll work . . . Here, he says I got to decide myself to go to Siberia . . . Let's go, all right? You think I'm not sick of this life of mine? Ah, Natasha! I know what it is . . . I see! . . . I keep telling myself it's all right, 'cause others steal more than me and get all kinds of honor and respect . . . only that doesn't help me! That's . . . not the trouble! I'm not repenting . . . don't believe in this conscience stuff . . . But there's one thing I feel—I got to live . . . different! Got to live better! Got to live so . . . so's I can have respect for myself! . . .

THE LOWER DEPTHS 137

LUKA. Right y'are, my boy! May the Lord help you . . . hope the Lord grants it to you! Right y'are: a man's got to respect himself . . .

PEPEL. I've been a thief—from the time I was little . . . everybody's always been calling me Vaska the thief, Vaska the thief's boy! Aha! Right? Oh, the hell with you! So there I am, a thief! Get me now: I'm a thief maybe on account of meanness, see? . . . maybe on account of nobody ever figured out another name for calling me . . . You find one . . . Natasha, all right?

NATASHA (*sadly*). Somehow I don't trust . . . words . . . I've got an uneasy feeling today . . . my heart aches . . . like as if I was waiting for something. You shouldn't have started up this talk today, Vasily . . .

PEPEL. Well, when then? It's not the first time I've said . . .

NATASHA. And what about my going with you? As for loving you . . . well . . . I don't, an awful lot . . . Sometimes —I like you . . . but other times, I'm disgusted just looking at you . . . It's clear I don't love you . . . When people love somebody—they don't see anything bad in him . . . but I see . . .

PEPEL. You'll get to love me—don't worry! I'll teach you to get used to me . . . just you agree! I've been watching you now more than a year . . . can see you're a strict young girl . . . a fine one . . . a real reliable person . . . gotten to love you a lot! . . .

(VASILISA, *dressed up, appears in the window and, leaning against the jamb, listens.*)

NATASHA. Maybe. You've gotten to love me, but my sister, now . . .

PEPEL (*confused*). Well, what about her? There's . . . all you want of that kind . . .

LUKA. Now you . . . pay no mind, child! If there's no bread, people eat goose-foot . . . if there's no bread, I mean . . .

PEPEL (*morosely*). You . . . be easy on me now! I live rough . . . a wolf's life—not much joy . . . like as if I was sinking in a bog . . . Whatever you get a hold on . . . it's all rotten . . . nothing holds . . . Your sister . . . I thought she . . . was different . . . If only she wasn't . . . so greedy for money, I'd have . . . done anything for her!

So long as she was all mine . . . Well, she's got to have somebody else . . . got to have money . . . and got to have freedom . . . freedom so's she can go off and have herself a time. She can't help me . . . But you're like a young fir: you prickle, but you hold . . .

LUKA. And I'm telling you, too—you take up with him, child, you do that! He's an all right fellow, he's good! Only you keep reminding him pretty often that he's a good fellow, so's he don't forget it, I mean! He'll believe you . . . You just say to him, Vasya, you say, you're a good man . . . Don't you forget that! Think, now, dear—what else're you going to do? That sister of yours is a spiteful creature, and that husband of hers—what can you say about him: he's a worse old man than anything you can think of saying . . . and this whole life here . . . where're you going? But this fellow's sturdy . . .

NATASHA. There's no place to go . . . I know . . . I've been thinking . . . Only, you see . . . there's nobody I trust . . . And I've got no place to go . . .

PEPEL. There's just one way . . . but I'm not going to let you go that way . . . Be better if I killed . . .

NATASHA (*smiling*). There . . . I'm not even your wife yet, and you're already wanting to kill me.

PEPEL (*embraces her*). Drop it, Natasha! What's the difference! . . .

NATASHA (*pressing against him*). Well . . . one thing I'll tell you, Vasily—and I'm swearing this and I mean it!—just the first time you lay a hand on me . . . or insult me some other way . . . I'm not going to spare myself . . . either I'll hang myself, or . . .

PEPEL. Let my hand dry up and fall off if I ever touch you!

LUKA. Never you mind, don't you worry, dear! He needs you more'n you need him . . .

VASILISA (*from the window*). Now there! they've got the marriage fixed up! Advice and love!

NATASHA. They're back! . . . O Lord! They saw . . . Oh, Vasily!

PEPEL. What're you scared of? Nobody is going dare touch you now!

VASILISA. Don't worry, Natalya! He's not going to beat you . . . He can't beat or love anyone . . . I know!

LUKA (*quietly*). Ah, that woman . . . poisonous snake! . . .

VASILISA. He just does a lot of big talking . . .

KOSTYLYOV (*comes out*). Natashka! What're you doing here, you sponger? Spinning out a lot of gossip? Making complaints about your family? And the samovar's not ready? And the table's not set?

NATASHA (*going out*). But you were going to go to church . . .

KOSTYLYOV. It's none of your business what we were going to do! You got to do your own business . . . what you're told to!

PEPEL. Shut up! She's not your servant no more . . . Natalya, don't go . . . don't do a thing! . . .

NATASHA. Don't you order me around . . . it's too early yet! (*Goes out.*)

PEPEL (*to* KOSTYLYOV). That's enough out of you! You had your time making fun of a person . . . it's finished! Now she's mine!

KOSTYLYOV. Yo-urs? When did you buy her? What did you pay?

VASILISA (*laughs loudly*).

LUKA. Vasya! Get out . . .

PEPEL. Look out . . . you big laughers! You'll be sorry!

VASILISA. Oh, how frightening! Oh, I'm scared!

LUKA. Vasily, get going! You see she's just egging you on, putting you up to it, y'understand?

PEPEL. Sure . . . She's lying . . . you're lying! Hope you never get what you want!

VASILISA. And what I don't want, never will happen, Vasya!

PEPEL (*threatens her with his fist*). We'll see . . . (*Goes out.*)

VASILISA (*disappearing from the window*). I'll fix you up a wedding, all right! . . .

KOSTYLYOV (*goes over to* LUKA). Well, old man?

LUKA. Not bad, old man! . . .

KOSTYLYOV. Yeh . . . I hear you're going?

LUKA. It's time . . .

KOSTYLYOV. Where to?

LUKA. Follow my nose . . .

KOSTYLYOV. Wandering, that means . . . Don't like living in one place, I guess?

LUKA. Help yourself, they say, and others'll help you . . .

KOSTYLYOV. How can you, wandering? A man's got to live in one place . . . It's no good, people living like cockroaches . . . Just crawling in wherever they want to . . . A man's got to attach himself to a place . . . and not go stumbling all over the earth for nothing . . .

LUKA. But supposing a fellow's got a place everywhere?

KOSTYLYOV. Means he's a bum . . . a no-good fellow . . . A man's got to have some sort of use to him, got to work . . .

LUKA. Well, now!

KOSTYLYOV. Sure. What else? . . . What's a . . . wanderer? A fellow that's gone wandering off in his head . . . different from everybody else . . . If he's a real wanderer, knows something . . . has found out something, now . . . something nobody needs . . . maybe he even found out the truth there . . . Well, nobody needs all the truth . . . that's for sure! Let him keep it to himself . . . and just be quiet. If he's a real . . . wanderer, now, why . . . that's what he does! Or else he'll talk so's nobody understands . . . And there's nothing he'll want, 'll never get in the way, doesn't bother people for nothing . . . How people get on is none of his business . . . He's got to lead a righteous life . . . got to live in the forest . . . in godforsaken places . . . where nobody can see him! And not bother nobody, and not criticize nobody . . . and pray for everybody . . . for all the sins of the world . . . for mine and yours . . . for all of 'em! That's why he runs away from all the fuss of the world . . . to pray. That's the way it is . . . (*A pause.*) But you . . . what kind of a wanderer are you? . . . Got no passport . . . A good man's got to have a passport . . . All good people got passports . . . sure! . . .

LUKA. There are people, and there are—others—pygmies,[5] too . . .

KOSTYLYOV. Don't you . . . go being wise! No riddles for

[5] The Russian is *cheloveki*, a sub-standard term meaning roughly "human critters."

me . . . I'm no dumber'n you. What's this—people and pygmies?

LUKA. Where's the riddle? I'm saying there's ground no good for sowing . . . and ground real good for growing . . . Whatever you put into it comes up . . . That's it, now . . .

KOSTYLYOV. So? What's the point?

LUKA. Well, take you, now . . . If the Lord Himself says to you: "Mikhailo! Be a man!" Makes no difference—nothing'll come of it at all . . . you're going to stay just like you are . . .

KOSTYLYOV. But . . . but—you know?—my wife's uncle's a policeman. And if I . . .

VASILISA (*comes in*). Mikhaila Ivanovich, come have tea.

KOSTYLYOV (*to* LUKA). You . . . I'll tell you something: get the hell out! out of this place! . . .

VASILISA. Yes, clear out, old man! . . . You got an awful long tongue . . . And besides who knows . . . maybe you're some kind of escaped convict . . .

KOSTYLYOV. And today, so's there's not a sign of you left! Or I'll . . . You watch out!

LUKA. Call your uncle? Call him . . . Caught a runaway, tell him . . . Your uncle might get a reward . . . maybe three kopeks . . .

BUBNOV (*in the window*). What're you selling? Three kopeks—for what?

LUKA. They're threatening to sell me now . . .

VASILISA (*to her husband*). Let's go . . .

BUBNOV. For three kopeks? You watch out, old man . . . They'll sell you for just one.

KOSTYLYOV (*to* BUBNOV) You . . . poked your nose out just like a goblin from under the stove! (*Moves off with his wife.*)

VASILISA. How many shady characters there are in the world . . . and various crooks! . . .

LUKA. Have a good meal! . . .

VASILISA (*turning around*). Keep your mouth shut . . . you stinking toadstool! . . . (*Goes around the corner with her husband.*)

LUKA. Tonight I'm taking off . . .

BUBNOV. It's better that way. It's always better to take off in time . . .

LUKA. You're right . . .

BUBNOV. I know. I got saved from hard labor, maybe, 'cause I took off in time.

LUKA. That so?

BUBNOV. Sure enough. It was like this: my wife took up with my foreman . . . The foreman's a good worker, all right . . . real expert at re-dyeing dog skins into raccoons—cats, too—into kangaroo fur . . . muskrat . . . anything you want. A clever fellow. So—my wife, now, takes up with him . . . and pretty soon they'd gone for each other so hard that I got to thinking, you watch out, boy, either you're going get poisoned or they'll bump you off somehow. I set in beating up my wife . . . and the foreman . . . Me . . . The fighting was fierce! Once he pulled out half my beard and busted a rib. Oh, and I got good and mad, too— once I clonked my wife on her bean with a iron poker . . . And, in general, there was a real war on! I see, though, that nothing's going to come of it all . . . they're getting the better of me! And so I started figuring out how I'd bump off my wife . . . really figured it out! But I caught hold of myself in time—and took off . . .

LUKA. It's better like that! Let 'em go ahead and make their 'coons out of dog skins there! . . .

BUBNOV. Only . . . the shop was in my wife's name . . . and I got left—you see how! Though, to tell the truth, I'd have drunk the shop away . . . I get a fit of hard drinking, see . . .

LUKA. A fit of hard drinking? Ah-ha!

BUBNOV. A terrible fit! Once I start filling my glass, I'll drink away everything I got, just the skin on me'll be left . . . And then, I'm lazy. It's terrible how I hate working!

(SATIN *and the* ACTOR *come in, arguing.*)

SATIN. Nonsense! You're not going anywhere . . . it's all just a lot of devilry! Old man! What kind of hot air did you blow into this left-over candle end?

ACTOR. It's not true! Grampa! Tell him he's lying! I'm going. I worked today, swept the street . . . and didn't drink any vodka! How's that? Here! Here's thirty kopeks, and I'm sober!

SATIN. It's all ridiculous, this! Give 'em to me, I'll drink 'em up . . . or bet 'em away . . .

ACTOR. Get the hell away! These are for my trip!

LUKA (*to* SATIN). And you—why're you trying to get him all confused?

SATIN. Tell me, you wonder-worker and favorite of the gods, what's going to become of me in life?[6] I've gone through everything I had, friend, smashed myself to pieces. Everything's not done for yet, grampa—there're cheats in the world still smarter than me!

LUKA. You're pretty cheerful, Kostyantin . . . Nice!

BUBNOV. Actor! Come over here!

(*The* ACTOR *goes over to the window and squats down in front of it. He talks to him in a low voice.*)

SATIN. You know, friend, when I was young I was pretty entertaining! I sure can remember! . . . An outgoing fellow . . . I danced terrificly, did some acting, liked to make people laugh . . . It was great!

LUKA. How come you went wrong, got off your way of going?

SATIN. What a nosy fellow you are, old man! You got to know everything—why?

LUKA. I'd like to understand the things people do . . . but I look at you, now—and I don't! You're mighty gallant, Kostyantin . . . no fool . . . and all of a sudden . . .

SATIN. Prison, grampa! I did four years seven months in it . . . and after prison—nothing works!

LUKA. Oho-ho! What put you in?

SATIN. A bastard! . . . lost my temper and killed the bastard in a fit of anger . . . It was in prison I learned how to play cards . . .

LUKA. You killed him—on account of a woman?

SATIN. On account of my own sister . . . But come on, now—leave me alone! I don't like to get asked questions . . . And . . . it was all long ago . . . My sister's dead . . . nine years now . . . have gone by . . . What a girl—oh, what a fine person that sister I had was! . . .

[6] Two lines from Pushkin's "The Lay of the Wise Oleg."

LUKA. You take life pretty easy! But it wasn't long ago, now . . . the locksmith here—how he yelled . . . a-ya-yai!
SATIN. Kleshch?
LUKA. Yeah. Got no work, he yells . . . got nothing!
SATIN. He'll get used to it . . . What's there for me to do about it?
LUKA (*softly*). Look out! Here he comes . . .
(KLESHCH *comes on slowly, his head hung low.*)
SATIN. Hey, widower! What're you dragging your tail for? What're you trying to work up?
KLESHCH. I'm thinking . . . about what'll I do? Got no tools . . . the funeral took everything!
SATIN. I'll give you some advice: do nothing! Just—burden the earth! . . .
KLESHCH. Sure . . . keep talking . . . I got some shame in front of people . . .
SATIN. Forget it! People aren't ashamed that you're worse off than a dog . . . Just think—you won't work, I won't work . . . hundreds of others . . . thousands, everybody! Get me? Everybody'll quit working! Nobody'll want to do anything—what'll happen then?
KLESHCH. Everybody'll all keel over from hunger . . .
LUKA (*to* SATIN). Y'ought to go join the Beguns[7] with talk like that . . . There are such people, Beguns they're called . . .
SATIN. I know . . . they're no fools, grampa!
(*From the* KOSTYLYOVS' *window comes* NATASHA's *shout: "What for? Stop . . . What fo-or?"*)
LUKA (*uneasily*). Natasha? Shouting? eh? Ah, you . . .
(*In the* KOSTYLYOVS' *apartment there is noise, a row, the sound of broken dishes, and* KOSTYLYOV's *shrill cry: "A-ah . . . damned heretic . . . bitch . . ."*)
VASILISA. Stop . . . wait . . . I'll show her . . . there . . .
NATASHA. They're beating me! Killing me! . . .
SATIN (*shouts in through the window*). Hey, you there!
LUKA (*fussing nervously*). Ought to . . . ought to call Vasily . . . call Vaska . . . O Lord! friends . . . boys . . .
ACTOR (*running out*). I'm off . . . Get him right away . . .
BUBNOV. Oh, they've started beating her a lot nowadays . . .
SATIN. Let's go, old man . . . we'll be witnesses!

[7] *Beguny*—a sect of Old Believers.

LUKA (*follows* SATIN). What kind of witness am I? What good . . . Better get Vasily in a hurry . . .

NATASHA. Sister . . . my own sister . . . Va-a-a . . .

BUBNOV. Gagged her . . . I'll go take a look . . .

(*The noise in the* KOSTYLYOVS' *apartment dies down, fading back, most likely, into the entry-way. The old man's shout is heard:* "*Stop!*" *The door slams loudly, and, like an axe, that sound cuts off all the noise. On stage it is quiet. Twilight.*)

KLESHCH (*sits indifferently on the sled, rubbing his hands hard. He begins to mutter something, at first inarticulately, and then—*). How so? . . . Got to live . . . (*Loudly.*) Got to have a place to come in to . . . Well? . . . There's none . . . there's nothing! Man's all by himself . . . all by himself, alone . . . Got no help . . .

(*Slowly, bent over, he goes out. A few seconds of portentous silence. Then somewhere in the passage a vague noise starts up. It becomes louder, a chaos of sounds, and draws nearer. Separate voices are heard.*)

VASILISA. I'm her sister! Let go . . .

KOSTYLYOV. What right have you got?

VASILISA. You convict! . . .

SATIN. Call Vaska! . . . Hurry up! . . . Zob—hit him!

(*A police whistle.*)

TARTAR (*runs out on stage. His right arm is in a sling*). What kind a law's this, killing in daytime?

KRIVOI ZOB (*behind him,* MEDVEDEV). Ah, I gave him one!

MEDVEDEV. You there, what d'you mean by fighting?

TARTAR. What about yourself? What kind of duty you got?

MEDVEDEV (*chasing the longshoreman*). Stop! Give me back my whistle . . .

KOSTYLYOV (*runs out on stage*). Abram! Grab him . . . get hold of him! He killed . . .

(KVASHNYA *and* NASTYA *come from around the corner. They hold* NATASHA *up by her arms; she is disheveled.* SATIN *backs off, pushing* VASILISA *who, flaying the air with her arms, tries to hit her sister. Near her,* ALYOSHKA, *like a raving lunatic, is jumping up and down and whistling into her ears, shouting and screaming. Several more tattered figures come in, both men and women.*)

SATIN (*to* VASILISA). Where you going? You goddamned hoot owl . . .

VASILISA. Get out of my way, you convict! I'll lose my life, but I'll tear her to pieces . . .

KVASHNYA (*taking* NATASHA *away*). Now, Karpovna, that's enough . . . Y'ought to be ashamed! What're you behaving like a brute for?

MEDVEDEV (*grabs* SATIN). Aha . . . got you!

SATIN. Zob! Skin 'em! . . . Vaska . . . Vaska! . . .

(*They all pile up together near the passage by the red wall.* NATASHA *is taken off to the right and sat down on the pile of lumber.*)

PEPEL (*bounding in from the little alley, silently with powerful movements pushes them all away*). Where's Natalya? You . . .

KOSTYLYOV (*ducking around the corner*). Abram! Grab Vaska! . . . Boys, help him lay hold of Vaska! He's a thief . . . a robber . . .

PEPEL. Ah, you . . . you old lech! (*Swinging hard, he hits the old man.* KOSTYLYOV *falls in such a way that only the upper half of his body can be seen from in front of the corner.* PEPEL *rushes to* NATASHA.)

VASILISA. Get Vaska! Boys . . . Hit the thief!

MEDVEDEV (*shouts at* SATIN). You can't . . . It's a family matter! They're all part of the family—and who're you?

PEPEL. What . . . what did she do to you? Pull a knife?

KVASHNYA. Look at it, the brutes! Scalded the girl's legs with boiling water . . .

NASTYA. Knocked over the samovar . . .

TARTAR. Maybe by accident . . . got to know for sure . . . no good just talking idle . . .

NATASHA (*almost fainting*). Vasily . . . take me . . . save me . . .

VASILISA. Merciful saints! Look here! Come look! He's dead! They killed him . . .

(*All rush over to the passageway, surround* KOSTYLYOV. BUBNOV *comes out of the crowd, goes to* VASILY.)

BUBNOV (*quietly*). Vaska! The old man . . . well . . . he's finished!

PEPEL (*looks at him as if not understanding*). Go . . . call 'em . . . got to get to the hospital . . . I'll settle with them!

BUBNOV. I'm telling you—somebody laid the old boy out . . . for keeps . . .

(*Noise on stage dies down, like a campfire on which water has been poured. Various low-voiced exclamations can be heard: "Really?" "I'll be!" "Ye-eh?" "Let's go, boy!" "Ah, God damn it!" "Now watch out!" "Let's clear out before the cops come!" The crowd thins out. People go out.* BUBNOV, *the* TARTAR, NASTYA, *and* KVASHNYA *rush to* KOSTYLYOV's *body.*)

VASILISA (*getting up from the ground, yells in a triumphant voice*). Killed him! Killed my husband . . . There's who did it! Vaska killed him! I saw it! Boys—I saw it! Well, Vasya? The police now?

PEPEL (*moves off from* NATASHA). Let me go . . . get away! (*Looks at the old man. To* VASILISA.) Well? You glad? (*Kicks the corpse with his foot.*) Died . . . the old son of a bitch! Came out the way you wanted it . . . And . . . why not clobber you, too? (*Rushes at her.* SATIN *and* KRIVOI ZOB *quickly grab him.* VASILISA *hides in the alley.*)

SATIN. Think what you're doing!

KRIVOI ZOB. Whoa! Where you jumping to?

VASILISA (*coming back*). So, Vasya, honey? There's no escaping fate . . . Police! Abram . . . blow your whistle!

MEDVEDEV. They pulled off my whistle, the devils . . .

ALYOSHKA. Here it is! (*Whistles.* MEDVEDEV *runs after him.*)

SATIN (*taking* PEPEL *over to* NATASHA). Vaska, don't be afraid! Killing a man in a fight . . . it's nothing! That doesn't mount up to a lot . . .

VASILISA. Hold Vaska! He killed him . . . I saw it!

SATIN. I hit the old boy, too, a couple of times . . . Didn't take much at all! You call me as witness, Vaska . . .

PEPEL. I . . . got no need to make excuses for myself . . . I just got to get Vasilisa into this . . . and I will! She wanted it . . . She was trying to persuade me to kill her husband . . . working me up to it! . . .

NATASHA (*suddenly, loudly*). Ah-ah . . . now I see! . . . That's how it was, Vasily? Good people! They're together in it! My sister and—him . . . they're together! They arranged it all! That's the way it was, Vasily? . . . That's what . . . you were talking to me for just now . . . so's she'd hear it all? Oh, kind people! She's his woman . . . you all know that . . . everybody knows it . . . they're together! She . . . It's she set him on to killing her husband . . . the husband got in their way . . . and I—I did, too . . . See—they've crippled me for life . . .

PEPEL. Natalya! What're you talking about . . . What're you talking about?

SATIN. Get a load of that . . . Jesus Christ!

VASILISA. You're lying! She's lying . . . I . . . he, Vaska, did it!

NATASHA. They're together! God damn you both! You both . . .

SATIN. Whew, what a deal! . . . Hang on, Vasily! They're going to sink you.

KRIVOI ZOB. No understanding it! . . . Ah, you . . . What a mess!

PEPEL. Natalya! You don't really . . . honest and truly? You really believe that I . . . and her . . .

SATIN. Honest to God, Natasha, just think a minute! . . .

VASILISA (*in the passageway*). Killed my husband . . . Your Excellency . . . Vaska Pepel, the thief . . . he did it . . . Chief! I saw it . . . everybody did . . .

NATASHA (*swaying and tossing almost unconscious*). Good people . . . my sister and Vaska did it! Listen, you police . . . that one there, my sister, she taught . . . persuaded . . . her lover . . . that's him, God damn him! They did it! Take 'em . . . try 'em . . . Take me, too . . . put me in prison! For Christ's sake . . . put me in prison! . . .

(*Curtain*)

ACT IV

The setting of Act I. But PEPEL's *room is gone; the partitions have been taken away. And in the place where* KLESHCH *used to sit, there is no little anvil. In the corner where* PEPEL's *room was, lies the* TARTAR, *fussing, and from time to time groaning.* KLESHCH *is sitting at the table; he is fixing an accordion, every so often trying out the stops. At the other end of the table are* SATIN, *the* BARON, *and* NASTYA. *In front them is a bottle of vodka, three bottles of beer, and a big chunk of dark bread. the* ACTOR *is tossing around and coughing on top of the stove. It is night. The stage is lit by a lamp standing in the middle of the table. Outside it is windy.*

KLESHCH. Sure . . . he cleared out during all that commotion . . .
BARON. Vanished from the police . . . like a puff of smoke up the chimney . . .
SATIN. "So flee sinners from the sight of the righteous!"
NASTYA. He was a nice old man! . . . But you're . . . not people . . . you're just rust spots!
BARON (*drinks*). To your health, m'lady!
SATIN. A curious little old man . . . true! Nastenka, here, fell in love with him . . .
NASTYA. I did . . . and I grew real fond of him! Sure! He saw everything . . . understood everything . . .
SATIN (*laughing*). And in general . . . was for a lot of us . . . like what the crumb is for those with no teeth . . .
BARON (*laughing*). Like what a plaster is for boils . . .
KLESHCH. He . . . could feel sorry for people . . . Now, you all . . . can't at all . . .
SATIN. What good is it to you if I feel sorry for you? . . .
KLESHCH. You can . . . well, I don't mean that you can feel sorry . . . you know how not to insult people . . .
TARTAR (*sits down on the bed and rocks his lame arm like a child*). Was a good old man . . . Had law in his heart! Who's got law in his heart is good! Who's lost the law is done for! . . .

BARON. What law, Prince?

TARTAR. The one . . . There's different . . . You know which one . . .

BARON. Go on!

TARTAR. Don't hurt a man: that's the law!

SATIN. That's called the Code of Penal and Correctional Punishments . . .

BARON. And then there's the Statutes of Penalties to be Imposed by Justices of the Peace . . .

TARTAR. It's called Koran . . . Your Koran must be the law . . . the heart must be the Koran . . . so!

KLESHCH (*trying out the accordian*). It's wheezing, damn it! The Prince is talking right . . . got to live according to the law . . . according to the Gospels . . .

SATIN. Go ahead . . .

BARON. Try it . . .

TARTAR. Mohammed gave Koran, said: "Here is the law! Do as it's written down here! Later'll come a time, the Koran won't be enough . . . the time'll give its own law, new law." Every time gives its own law . . .

SATIN. Why sure . . . the time came and gave the Penal Code . . . It's a tough law . . . you won't wear it out so soon!

NASTYA (*striking the table with her glass*). And why . . . why am I living here . . . with you all? I'm going to leave . . . go somewhere . . . to the end of the world!

BARON. Without shoes, m'lady?

NASTYA. Naked! I'll crawl on all fours!

BARON. That'll be quite a picture, m'lady . . . on all fours . . .

NASTYA. Yes, and I'll do it! Just so I don't see your ugly mug any more . . . Ah, I'm sick of it all! This whole life . . . everybody! . . .

SATIN. If you're going take the Actor along with you . . . He was figuring on going there, too . . . He's been informed that just half a verst from the end of the world there's a hospital for organons . . .

ACTOR (*poking his head out from the top of the stove*). For or-ga-ni-sms, you idiot!

SATIN. For organons poisoned by alcohol . . .

ACTOR. Indeed! He's going away! He's going away . . . you'll see!

BARON. Who's that, sir?

ACTOR. Me!

BARON. *Merci*, votary of the goddess . . . what's her name? Goddess of drama, of tragedy . . . What's she called?

ACTOR. The Muse, you thickhead! Not a goddess, but the Muse!

SATIN. Lachesis . . . Hera . . . Aphrodite . . . Atropos . . . Who the hell knows! It's all the old man's doing . . . got the Actor all worked up . . . you understand, Baron?

BARON. The old man's a fool . . .

ACTOR. Ignoramuses! You savages! Mel-po-me-ne! Heartless creatures! You'll see—he's going away! "Glut yourselves, you dark and dreary minds . . ." poem by Beranger . . . right! He'll find himself a place . . . where there's no . . . no . . .

BARON. Nothing, sir?

ACTOR. Right! Nothing! "This pit . . . will be a grave for me . . . I die, worn out by infirmity!" What're you living for? What for?

BARON. You! Kean, or The Genius and Dissipation! Don't shout!

ACTOR. Nonsense! I will!

NASTYA (*raising her head from the table, waves her hands*). Go ahead! Let them listen!

BARON. What's the idea, lady?

SATIN. Leave 'em alone, Baron! The hell with them! . . . Let 'em shout . . . they'll bust their heads . . . let 'em! There's point to it! . . . Don't get in a man's way, as the old fellow used to say . . . In fact, it was he, the old bag of yeast, who soured all the rest of us living here . . .

KLESHCH. Lured them off somewhere . . . but himself didn't tell them how to go . . .

BARON. The old man's a fake . . .

NASTYA. Nonsense! You yourself are a fake!

BARON. Shut your face, m'lady!

KLESHCH. The old man, now . . . didn't like the truth much . . . Rose up against it a lot . . . that's what you got to! Sure—what truth's here? And without it you can't breathe

... Take the prince there ... smashed his hand working ... will have to have it sawed right off, y'hear ... There's your truth for you!

SATIN (*striking the table with his fist*). Shut up! You're—all of you—pigs! You woodenheads! ... Shut up about the old man! (*More calmly.*) You, Baron, you're the worst of the lot! ... You understand nothing ... and keep talking nonsense! The old man was no fake. What's truth? Man. That's truth! He understood that ... you don't! You've all got bricks in your heads ... I understand the old man ... yes! He was lying ... but out of pity for you, God damn you! There're lots of people who lie out of pity for their neighbors ... I know! I've read about it! Lie handsomely, inspiredly, excitingly! ... There's such a thing as a comforting lie, a reconciling lie ... A lie explains away the weight that has crushed a workingman's hand ... and indicts people dying of hunger ... I know what a lie is! Whoever's weak inside ... and whoever sucks his life from others—they need lies ... A lie holds some of them up, others screen themselves behind it ... But whoever's his own master ... whoever's independent and doesn't live off somebody else, what's he want a lie for? Lying is the religion of slaves and masters ... Truth's the god of the free man!

BARON. Bravo! Beautifully said! I agree! You talk ... like an honest man!

SATIN. Why can't a cheat sometimes talk well, since honest people ... talk like cheats? Sure ... I've forgot a lot, but I still know some things! The old man? He's a very clever fellow! ... He ... worked on me like acid on an old and dirty coin ... Let's drink to his health! Fill 'em up! ...

(NASTYA *fills a glass of beer and gives it to* SATIN.)

SATIN (*smiling*). The old man lives in himself ... he sees everything his own way. Once I asked him: "Grampa, what're people living for?" (*Trying to talk with* LUKA's *voice and imitating his manner.*) "Why, people, now, are living for something better, my boy! Like, say, there are carpenter-joiners and everything—trash—the people ... And now, out of them gets born this joiner—a joiner such as the world's never seen before; he does better than everybody else and there's not a joiner equal to him. Puts his stamp on the whole trade of joinery . . . and right away moves the whole thing twenty years ahead . . . And so all the rest, too . . . the locksmiths, now . . . shoemakers and other working people . . . and all the peasants . . . and even the gentry—everybody's living for something better! Each thinks he's living for himself, but turns out it's for something better! About a hundred years . . . and, maybe, there'll be even more living for a better man!"

(NASTYA *looks intently in* SATIN's *face.* KLESHCH *stops working on the accordion and listens, also. The* BARON, *his head lowered, softly taps the table with his fingers. The* ACTOR, *peering out over the stove, tries carefully to slide down onto the bed.*)

"Everybody, my boy, everybody there is, lives for something better! That's why we got to respect every man . . . 'cause we got no way of knowing who he is, how come he got born, and what he can do . . . Maybe he got born for our good luck . . . for some special good for us? . . . 'Specially got to respect little children . . . the little ones! The little ones got to have room! Don't get in the way of little children's living . . . Be good to 'em!" (*A pause.*)

BARON (*thoughtfully*). Hmm—yes . . . for something better? That . . . reminds me of our family . . . An ancient name . . . from the time of Catherine . . . nobility . . . soldier-heroes! . . . Frenchmen by birth . . . Joined the service, worked up higher and higher . . . Under Nicholas I, my grandfather, Gustave deBille . . . had a high position . . . wealth . . . hundreds of serfs . . . horses . . . cooks . . .

NASTYA. Bull! No such thing!

BARON (*jumping up*). Wha-at? We-ell . . . what else!

NASTYA. No such thing!

BARON (*shouts*). A house in Moscow! A house in Petersburg! Carriages . . . carriages with coats of arms on them!

(KLESHCH *takes the accordion, gets up and moves over to one side, from where he carefully follows the scene.*)

NASTYA. There weren't!

BARON. Shut up! I'm telling you . . . there were dozens of footmen! . . .

NASTYA (*with relish*). The-ere weren't!

BARON. I'll kill you!

NASTYA (*getting ready to run*). There were no carriages!

SATIN. Drop it, Nastenka! Don't get him irritated . . .

BARON. Just you wait . . . you piece of trash! My grandfather . . .

NASTYA. You had no grandfather! There was nothing! (SATIN *bursts out laughing*.)

BARON (*tired from anger, sits down on the bench*). Satin, tell her . . . the slut . . . You—you're laughing, too? You . . . too—don't believe me? (*Shouts in despair, pounding the table with his fists.*) It all was real, God damn you all!!

NASTYA (*triumphant*). So-o, now you've set up a howl? Y'understand now what it's like for a person when nobody'll believe him?

KLESHCH (*coming back to the table*). I was thinking there'd be a fight . . .

TARTAR. Ah, people are stupid! It's no good!

BARON. I . . . can't allow people to make fun of me! I have proofs . . . my papers, damn you!

SATIN. Forget them! And forget about your grandpa's carriages. You're not going to go anywhere in a carriage of the past . . .

BARON. But how can she dare! . . .

NASTYA. You tell me! How I do!

SATIN. See? she does! How's she any worse than you? Though for sure her past has not only no carriages and no grandpa in it, but not even a mother and father . . .

BARON (*calming down*). God damn you . . . You . . . know how to talk about things without getting worked up . . . But it seems . . . I've got no will of my own . . .

SATIN. Get yourself some. It's a useful thing . . . (*A pause.*) Nastya! You going to the hospital?

NASTYA. What for?

SATIN. To see Natasha.

NASTYA. *Now* you think of her! She left long ago . . . left and—disappeared! She's nowheres around . . .

SATIN. Means—she's done for . . .

KLESHCH. Be interesting to see who sinks who deeper? Vaska Vasilisa, or her him?

NASTYA. Vasilisa'll get out of it! She's tricky. And Vaska'll get sent off to hard labor . . .

SATIN. For killing in a fight you only get prison . . .

NASTYA. Too bad. Ought to be hard labor . . . Hard labor . . . for all of you . . . sweep you right away, like trash . . . into some big pit!

SATIN (*with surprise*). What's eating you? You off your rocker?

BARON. Here, I'll give her a good one right on the ear . . . for being so cheeky!

NASTYA. Just you try! Just touch me!

BARON. I will!

SATIN. Cut it out! Don't . . . don't insult a person! I can't get him out of my head . . . that old man! (*Guffaws.*) Don't insult a person! . . . But if once upon a time I got insulted—so I'd never forget it the rest of my life! What do you do? Forgive? Nothing. Nobody . . .

BARON (*to* NASTYA). You've got to understand that I'm not to be compared to you! You . . . stinking wretch!

NASTYA. Ah, you dog! Why, you live off me like a worm off an apple!

(*A sudden burst of laughter from the men.*)

KLESHCH. Ah . . . the idiot! An apple!

BARON. Can't even . . . get angry . . . she's such a little fool!

NASTYA. You laughing? Like hell you are! There's nothing funny about it for you!

ACTOR (*gloomily*). Let 'em have it!

NASTYA. If only I . . . could! I'd . . . (*Takes a cup from the table and throws it on the floor.*) do that to you!

TARTAR. Why smash the dishes? Eh-eh . . . dummy! . . .

BARON (*getting up*). I'll teach her manners . . . right this minute!

NASTYA (*running away*). Go to hell!

SATIN (*after her*). Hey! That'll do! Who you scaring? What's it all about, anyway?

NASTYA. Wolves! Hope you drop dead! You wolves! (*Runs out.*)

ACTOR (*gloomily*). Amen!

TARTAR. Oo-ooh! Wicked woman—Russian woman! Cheeky

... wants her own way! Tartar girl's not like that! Tartar girl knows what's right!

KLESHCH. Ought to give her a good, sound thrashing ...

BARON. Di-irty bitch!

KLESHCH (*trying out the accordion*). Fixed! But its owner still isn't back ... The boy's burning himself up ...

SATIN. Now—bottoms up!

KLESHCH. Thanks! And I guess it's time to turn in ...

SATIN. Getting used to us?

KLESHCH (*having emptied the glass, goes over to his bed in the corner*). It's all right ... There're people all over ... In the beginning you don't see this ... then you take a closer look, and it turns out everybody's ... all right! (*The* TARTAR *spreads something out on his bed, kneels, and prays.*)

BARON (*pointing the* TARTAR *out to* SATIN). Look!

SATIN. Leave him alone. He's a good fellow ... don't bother him! (*Bursts out laughing.*) I'm being nice today ... for some goddamned reason! ...

BARON. You're always nice when you've had too much ... And smart ...

SATIN. When I'm drunk ... I like everything ... Sure ... He's praying? Splendid! A man can believe or not believe ... that's his business! A man's free ... He pays for everything himself: for faith, for lack of faith, for love, for intelligence. A man pays for everything himself and that's why he's free! ... Man—that's the truth for you! What's man? ... It's not you, or me, or them ... no! It's you, me, them, the old man, Napoleon, Mohammed ... all in one! (*With his finger, outlines a figure of a man in the air.*) You get it? It's pretty clever! All the beginnings and ends are in it ... Everything's in man, everything's for man! Just man exists, and everything else is what he does with his hands and his brains! Ma-an! It's colossal! It sounds ... majestic! M-a-n! Got to respect man! No feeling sorry ... no humiliating him with pity ... got to respect him! Let's drink to man, Baron! (*Gets up.*) This is all right—this feeling yourself a man! I'm a prisoner, a murderer, a sharper—all right! When I'm going along the street, people look at me like I was a crook ... and step aside and turn around . . . and often say to me, "You dirty dog! You fake! Go to work!" Work? What for? To fill my belly? (*Guffaws.*) I've always hated people who worry too much about getting their belly full. That's not the question, Baron! That's not the question! Man's above that! Man's above just being full!

BARON (*shaking his head*). You think things out . . . That's good . . . I suppose it makes you feel good inside . . . I haven't got that . . . don't know how. (*Looks around, and then softly, cautiously, speaks.*) I'm afraid . . . sometimes. You understand? I get all scared . . . Because—what's there ahead?

SATIN (*pacing*). Don't be silly! Who's there for a man to be afraid of?

BARON. You know . . . for as long as I can remember . . . there's been some kind of a fog floating around in my head. I never could understand a thing. I feel . . . sort of awkward . . . I feel as if all my life I've just been changing my clothes . . . But why? I don't understand! I studied—wore the uniform of the Institute for Sons of the Nobility . . . but what did I study? I don't remember . . . I got married—put on a tail-coat, then a dressing-gown . . . but chose a nasty wife, and—why? I don't understand . . . Went through everything I had—wore some grey coat and rust-colored trousers . . . but how did I ruin myself? I didn't notice . . . Served in a government bureau . . . had a uniform, a cap with a cockade . . . embezzled government funds—they put prisoner's overalls on me . . . and then I put this on . . . Everything's . . . like in a dream . . . isn't it? It's . . . absurd . . .

SATIN. Not very . . . it's more stupid . . .

BARON. Sure . . . I think so, too: stupid . . . But . . . there was some reason I got born . . . wasn't there?

SATIN (*laughing*). Probably . . . Man gets born for something better! (*Nodding his head.*) That's . . . pretty good!

BARON. That . . . Nastka! . . . Ran off . . . where? I'll go have a look . . . where she is. All the same . . . she . . . (*Goes out. A pause.*)

ACTOR. Tartar! (*A pause.*) Prince!

(*The* TARTAR *turns his head around.*)

ACTOR. Say a prayer . . . for me . . .
TARTAR. What?
ACTOR (*more softly*). Say a prayer . . . for me! . . .
TARTAR (*after a pause*). Do it yourself . . .
ACTOR (*quickly climbs down from the stove, goes over to the table, pours some vodka with a trembling hand, drinks, and practically runs out into the entryway*). I'm off for good!
SATIN. Hey, you, you Sicambrian! Where you going? (*Whistles. In comes* MEDVEDEV, *in a woman's quilted jacket, and* BUBNOV; *both are tight, but not very. In one hand* BUBNOV *has a bunch of pretzels, and in the other, several smoked Caspian roach; under his arm is a bottle of vodka, and in the pocket of his jacket, another.*)
MEDVEDEV. A camel—that's something like an ass! Only's got no ears . . .
BUBNOV. Cut it out! You're something like an ass yourself.
MEDVEDEV. A camel's got no ears at all . . . It hears through its nostrils . . .
BUBNOV (*to* SATIN). Old friend! I was looking all over for you in all the taverns! Take the bottle, I got all my hands full!
SATIN. Put the pretzels on the table and then one hand'll be free . . .
BUBNOV. Right y'are! Ah you . . . Y'copper, look at that! Some fellow, isn't he? Real clever.
MEDVEDEV. Crooks're all smart . . . I know! Can't make out unless they are. A good man, now he's all right being stupid; but a bad one's absolutely got to have brains. But about camels, now, you got it wrong . . . it's a draught animal . . . got no horns . . . and no teeth . . .
BUBNOV. Where's everybody? How come nobody's here? Hey, come on out . . . this is on me! Who's there in the corner?
SATIN. You going to drink everything up soon? Stuffed idiot!
BUBNOV. Me? . . . soon! This time I got just a very little capital together . . . Zob! Where's Zob?
KLESHCH (*coming to the table*). He's out . . .
BUBNOV. Uu-uu-rrrr! Bulldog! Gobble, gobble, gobble! A turkey! No barking, no growling! Drink, have a good time, and be cheerful . . . For everybody—it's all on me! Boy, I sure like to treat you all! If only I was rich . . . I'd . . . set up a free tavern! Honest to god! With music and a choir

of singers . . . Come on in, drink, eat, listen to the singing . . . unburden your heart! Hey! you poor man . . . come on into my free tavern! Satin! . . . For you I'd . . . Take half of all my capital! There!

SATIN. Give it all to me right now . . .

BUBNOV. All my capital? Right now? Ok! There's a ruble . . . some more . . . a twenty-kopek piece . . . some fives . . . some sunflower seeds . . . that's everything!

SATIN. Good enough! It'll be safer with me . . . I'll do a little playing with it . . .

MEDVEDEV. I'm a witness . . . money given into safe-keeping . . . how much there?

BUBNOV. You? You're a camel . . . We don't need witnesses . . .

ALYOSHKA (*comes in barefoot*). Boys! Got my feet wet!

BUBNOV. Come on, wet your whistle . . . That's all there is to it. You're nice . . . you sing and play . . . that's really fine! But—you're drinking—that's no good! That's bad for you, boy . . . drinking's bad for you! . . .

ALYOSHKA. I go by you! Only when you're drunk are you like a man . . . Kleshch! You fixed the accordion? (*Sings, hopping around.*)
Oh, if I didn't have
A pretty handsome mug,
My little babe, my love,
Would never give me a hug!
I'm frozen stiff, boys! It's c-c-old!

MEDVEDEV. Hmm—and may one ask who's this babe?

BUBNOV. Get off it! You just keep your mouth shut now, boy! You're no cop . . . it's all over! No cop, and no uncle . . .

ALYOSHKA. But just auntie's husband!

BUBNOV. One of your nieces is in prison, the other's dying . . .

MEDVEDEV (*haughtily*). Nonsense! She's not dying: she just dropped out of sight on me!

(SATIN *guffaws.*)

BUBNOV. Makes no difference, boy! a man without nieces is no uncle!

ALYOSHKA. Your Excellency! A poor wayfaring stranger![8]

[8] In Russian, *otstavnoi kozy barabanshchik*, meaning an insignificant man who has lost his social position, and derived from

My little girl's got money,
I haven't got a thing!
But I'm a cheerful guy,
So I'm all right—and sing!

It's cold!

(ZOB *comes in, and then—until the end of the act—several other figures, men and women. They undress, lie down on the plank beds, grumble.*)

KRIVOI ZOB. Bubnov! What did you run off for?

BUBNOV. Come here! Sit down . . . let's sing together, boy! My favorite . . . all right?

TARTAR. Night, got to sleep! Singing got to do by day!

SATIN. Come on, it doesn't matter, Prince! You—come over here!

TARTAR. What do you mean—doesn't matter? Be a lot of noise . . . When singing's done always makes noise . . .

BUBNOV (*having gone over to him*). Prince! What's with your hand? Did they cut it off on you?

TARTAR. What for? Got to wait . . . Maybe won't be having to . . . A hand's not iron, it's not long in the cutting . . .

KRIVOI ZOB. Loading's your business, Asanka! Without a hand you're good for nothing! We count according to what our hands can do and our back can lift . . . Having no hand is as good as being no man! You're done for! . . . Go on, have some vodka . . . and that's it!

KVASHNYA (*comes in*). Ah, all you lovely residents of mine! What it's like outside, what it's like! Cold, slushy . . . My little cop here?

MEDVEDEV. Here!

KVASHNYA. You wearing my jacket again? And seems you're . . . a little gone, eh? What's the big idea?

MEDVEDEV. On account of it's . . . Bubnov's name day . . . and it's cold . . . slushy!

KVASHNYA. Don't try that on me—slushy! No tricks . . . Go to bed . . .

MEDVEDEV (*goes out into the kitchen*). Sleep now . . . all right . . . want to . . . it's time!

SATIN. How come you're . . . so damned strict with him?

the old custom of a man dressed as a goat and of a drummer accompanying the itinerant bear-leader (*vozhak medvedya*).

KVASHNYA. Can't do it different, dear. Got to keep a man like that under a tight hand. I took him in to live with me: I figured he'll be some good to me . . . since he's a military man, and you're all wild people . . . my business is just a woman's . . . But there he's off drinking! That does me no good at all!

SATIN. You didn't do so good picking yourself a helpmate . . .

KVASHNYA. No, did just fine . . . You're not going to want to live with me . . . you got such airs! And if you ever did, a week wouldn't be gone . . . before you'd have gone through me and all my junk with your card-playing!

SATIN (*bursts out laughing*). That's for sure, little missus! I'd lose . . .

KVASHNYA. Didn't I tell you! Alyoshka!

ALYOSHKA. Here he is—myself!

KVASHNYA. What's all this you're blabbing about me?

ALYOSHKA. Me? Everything! Everything, honestly. There's a woman for you, I tell them! Amazing! Flesh, fat, bones—got ten poods' worth,[9] but brains—not an ounce!

KVASHNYA. Ah, you're just making that up! I even got a lot of brains . . . No, why do you tell people I beat my little cop?

ALYOSHKA. I thought you did, when you were pulling him by the hair . . .

KVASHNYA (*laughing*). Idiot! As if you don't see nothing. Why wash your dirty linen in public? . . . And on top of that, it's humiliating to him . . . On account of what you said he started drinking . . .

ALYOSHKA. Means they're telling the truth when they say even a chicken'll drink!

(SATIN *and* KLESHCH *burst out laughing*.)

KVASHNYA. Oh, you big joker! And what sort of fellow are you, Alyoshka?

ALYOSHKA. The very best sort! Can do anything! I follow my nose wherever it leads me!

BUBNOV (*by the* TARTAR's *bed*). Let's go! Makes no difference—we're letting nobody sleep! We're going to sing . . . all night! Zob!

KRIVOI ZOB. Sing? All right . . .

[9] A pood is about 36 pounds.

ALYOSHKA. And I'll play for you!

SATIN. We'll listen!

TARTAR (*smiling*). All right, Bubnov, y'devil . . . bring the liquor! We'll drink, we'll have a good time, then when death's here, we'll be dying!

BUBNOV. Fill him a glass, Satin! Zob, sit down! Hey, boys! Does a fellow need a lot? Look at me—I've had a drop—and I'm glad! Zob! . . . Start her up . . . my favorite! I'll sing some . . . and I'll cry! . . .

KRIVOI ZOB (*starts singing*).

Su-unlight rises, sinks at e-ve-ning . . .

BUBNOV (*joining in*).

Bu-ut my cell is always da-ark!

(*The door is suddenly opened.*)

BARON (*standing on the threshold, shouts*). Hey . . . you! Come on . . . come here! To the Wasteland . . . there . . . the Actor's . . . hung himself!

(*Silence. Everybody looks at the* BARON. NASTYA *appears from behind him and slowly, her eyes wide open, goes toward the table.*)

SATIN (*quietly*). Ah . . . spoiled the song . . . Id-iot!

(*Curtain*)

The Puppet Show

Aleksandr Aleksandrovich Blok

dedicated to
VSEVOLOD EMILYEVICH
MEYERHOLD

A NOTE ON THE PLAY

Written in 1906, this one-act play, or "fairy show" as Blok later called it, was the first play of his to be performed. The actors of Vera Kommissarzhevskaya's theater in St. Petersburg, directed by Vsevolod Meyerhold, who also played the lead, presented it in December 1906, to mixed reviews. M. A. Kuzmin wrote incidental music for it; N. N. Sapunov designed the setting. In a review of the Symbolist theater in 1907, Andrei Bely used the play and the performances as an excuse for asserting the impossibility of Symbolist theater that did not become entirely mime, a play of marionettes.

After having seen one of the final rehearsals of the play, Blok wrote Meyerhold a long letter, on December 22, 1906, explaining what he had discovered in, or noticed about, his play. Blok makes clear that he means, by the use of set figures, to reach that vitality and permanence he believes lies behind the mask of this world: "*Every* piece of buffoonery wants to become a battering ram to smash right through all the dead stuff; . . . at this point *the hour of mystery must strike:* the substance has become numb, powerless, and submissive; in this sense I *accept the world*—the whole world with its stupidity, obliqueness, dead and dry colors—only in order to fool this old bony witch and make her young again. In the embraces of the Fool and the Buffoon the old world brightens up, becomes young, and its eyes become translucent, depthless."

He had a clear idea of how each actor was to play: Columbine was to be "all the time profoundly still, . . . all one music—her voice, her golden braid, and plain white clothing"; the Chairman of the Meeting was to speak "with a pious (although asinine) anxiety"; Harlequin, though profound in his own way, "is eternally youthful"; the Author is a light joke, a man "who doesn't understand the central point, that the piece of buffoonery fools the old witch, and by deception overcomes the substance it deals with." Blok knew that to express the seriousness of what he understood, he had to make his characters appear temporarily absurd, as Pierrot's last line clearly indicates.

Too *avant garde* for its time to be successful theater, this short play remains one of the important and best examples of a new idea of the theater that arose in Russia even at the time of Chekhov and Gorky's dramatic successes, and one which developed during the ensuing twenty years.

The present translation is made from the text in *Sobranie sochinenii*, Volume VI, Leningrad, 1933, which is also the final text published by Blok during his lifetime. The stylization of the play lies not only in the musical accompaniment and stage gestures but also in the rhymed verse, the puns, and the game of figures.

DRAMATIS PERSONAE

Columbine
Pierrot
Harlequin
Mystics of both sexes in frock coats and the latest style dresses, but later masked and in masquerade costume.
The Chairman of the Meeting of the Mystics
Three couples in love
A clown
The author

An ordinary room on stage with three walls, a window and a door. MYSTICS *of both sexes, in frock coats and the latest style dresses, are sitting around a lighted table in expressions of deep concentration. A little to one side, by the window, sits* PIERROT *in a loose white overall—dreamy, distraught, pale, without whiskers or eyebrows, like all Pierrots. The* MYSTICS *are silent for a while.*

FIRST MYSTIC. You listening?
SECOND MYSTIC.   Yes.
THIRD MYSTIC.   Something will happen.
PIERROT. Oh, endless horror, endless dark!
FIRST MYSTIC. You waiting?
SECOND MYSTIC.   I am.
THIRD MYSTIC.   The coming is near:
  The wind outside has made the sign.
PIERROT. Unfaithful! Where are you? Through sleepy streets
  There stretches out a chain of lamps,
  And two by two the lovers meet,
  Each warmed inside by his love's light.
  Where are you? The last two gone, why can't
  We enter the appointed circle?
  I'll go and strum my sad guitar
  Beneath the window where you dance!
  I'll rouge my pale and moonlit face,
  I'll pencil eyebrows, glue on a moustache.
  You hear, Columbine, how my poor heart

Is sweetly singing its sad song?

(PIERROT *brightens up and then falls to brooding. But the anxious* AUTHOR *slips out from behind the curtains on one side.*)

AUTHOR. What's he saying? My dear ladies and gentlemen! I hasten to assert that this actor is cruelly mocking my author's rights. The action takes place in Petersburg in winter. Where did he get the window and the guitar? I didn't write my drama for a puppet show . . . I assure you . . . (*Suddenly embarrassed at his own unexpected appearance, he hides behind the curtain again.*)

PIERROT (*has paid no attention to the* AUTHOR. *Sits and sighs dreamily*). Columbine!

FIRST MYSTIC. You listening?

SECOND MYSTIC. Yes.

THIRD MYSTIC. A maid is coming from a distant land.

FIRST MYSTIC. Oh, her features—like marble!

SECOND MYSTIC. Oh, her eyes—such a void!

THIRD MYSTIC. Oh, how pure she is—how terribly white!

FIRST MYSTIC. She'll come—and at once all voices will die.

SECOND MYSTIC. Yes. Silence will fall.

THIRD MYSTIC. Very long?

FIRST MYSTIC. Yes.

SECOND MYSTIC. All white, like snow.

THIRD MYSTIC. On her shoulder, a scythe.

FIRST MYSTIC. Who is she?

SECOND MYSTIC (*leans over and whispers something in the ear of the* FIRST). You won't give me away?

FIRST MYSTIC (*in genuine horror.*) Never!

(*The* AUTHOR *sticks his head out again in fright but quickly disappears, as if someone had pulled him back by his coattails.*)

PIERROT (*dreamily, as before*). Columbine! Come!

FIRST MYSTIC. Quiet! You hear the footsteps!

SECOND MYSTIC. I hear rustling and sighs.

THIRD MYSTIC. Oh, who's among us?

FIRST MYSTIC. Who's at the window?

SECOND MYSTIC. Who's at the door?

THIRD MYSTIC. Can't see a thing.

FIRST MYSTIC. Shine the light. Isn't it she that's come at this hour?

(*The* SECOND MYSTIC *holds up the candles. Completely unexpectedly and impossible to tell where from, an extraordinarily beautiful girl with a plain and tranquil face of a dull whiteness appears at the table. She is in white. Her calm eyes look out with equanimity. A plaited braid falls down her back. The girl stands motionless. Ecstatic* PIERROT *prayerfully falls on his knees. He is visibly choked with tears. For him everything is unsaid. In horror the* MYSTICS *fall back in their chairs. One helplessly swings his foot. Another makes strange movements with his hand. A third rolls his eyes.*)

THE MYSTICS (*coming to after a while, loudly whisper*). She came!
How white her clothing is!
The void that's in her eyes!
Her features pale as marble!
On her shoulder, a scythe!
It's—death!

PIERROT (*hears this. Slowly rising, he goes over to the girl, takes her by the hand, and leads her center stage. He speaks in a resonant and joyful voice, like the first clap of a bell*). Ladies and gentlemen! You're wrong! This is Columbine! This is my fiancée!

(*General horror. Hands are clasped. The tails of the frock coats fly.*)

THE CHAIRMAN OF THE MEETING (*goes solemnly up to* PIERROT). You're out of your mind. All evening we waited for things to happen. Something did. She came to us—our serene savior. Death has called on us.

PIERROT (*in a resonant, childlike voice*). I don't pay attention to fairy tales: I'm a simple man. You won't fool me. This is Columbine. This is my fiancée.

CHAIRMAN. Ladies and Gentlemen! Our poor friend has gone out of his mind from fright. He never gave any thought to what we've spent our whole lives getting ready for. He hasn't plumbed the depths and hasn't prepared himself humbly to meet the Pale Lady in his final hour. Let's magnanimously forgive the simple fool. (*Turns to* PIERROT.) Friend, you can't stay here. You're interfering with our final evening. But, please, take one more good look at her features: you see how white her clothing is, what paleness there is all about her; oh, she's white like the mountain snows! Her eyes reflect the glassy void. Don't you see the scythe[1] on her shoulder? Don't you recognize death?

PIERROT (*a distraught smile runs across his pale face*). I'm going. Either you're right, and I'm an unhappy madman, or you've lost your mind, and I'm a lonely, misunderstood dreamer. Carry me, snowstorm, through the streets! Oh, endless horror! Endless dark!

COLUMBINE (*follows* PIERROT *to the exit*). I won't leave you. (PIERROT *stops, confused.*)

CHAIRMAN (*imploringly clasps his hands*). Airy phantom! We've waited for you all our lives! Don't abandon us! (*A handsome youth in* HARLEQUIN *dress comes in. Little bells on him ring in silvery tones.*)

HARLEQUIN (*goes up to* COLUMBINE). I'm waiting for you at the crossroads,
In the twilight of a winter day!
My snowstorm sings around you, Friend,
With bells to ring you on your way.
(*He puts his hand on* PIERROT'S *shoulder.* PIERROT *falls prostrate and lies motionless in his loose white overall.* HARLEQUIN *leads* COLUMBINE *off by the hand. She gives him a smile. General loss of heart. All are draped lifelessly in their chairs. The sleeves of the frock coats have fallen down and cover the hands, as if there were no hands. Heads have shrunk into collars. It seems as if empty frock coats are draped over the chairs. Suddenly* PIERROT *jumps up and runs out. The curtain closes. At that moment the ruffled and agitated* AUTHOR *jumps out in front of the footlights.*)

AUTHOR. Dear Ladies and Gentlemen! I deeply beg your pardon, but I decline all responsibility! They're playing tricks on me! I wrote a really real play, the essence of which I consider it my duty to explain to you in a few words: it's about mutual love between two young hearts! A third person bars their way: but the barriers finally fall, and the lovers are united forever in wedlock! I never decked my heroes out in clown's clothing! They're acting out some old legend without my knowledge! I don't accept legends, myths, or other such vulgarities! Especially allegoric play-

---

[1] In Russian, *kosà* means both "braid" and "scythe." The visual ambivalence is dependent on the verbal pun.

ing with words: it's indecent to call a woman's braid the scythe of death! It slanders womankind! Dear ladies and gent . . .

(*A hand, protruding from the curtain, snatches the* AUTHOR *by the back of his neck. With a shriek, he disappears into the wings. The curtain quickly opens. A ball. Maskers go round and round to the quiet sounds of dance music. Other maskers, knights, ladies, clowns, wander among them. Sad* PIERROT *sits in the middle of the stage on the same bench where Venus and Tannhäuser usually kiss.*)

PIERROT. I stood between two streetlamps
And listened to what they said,
How they whispered under their mantles,
And the night kept kissing their eyes.

A silvery snowstorm spun
Them the needed wedding ring.
And I saw in the night how the girl
Smiled straight—kept smiling—at him.

But then he seated my girl
In a regular hired sleigh!
I walked through the freezing fog
And watched them far away.

He caught her up in his nets
And, laughing, jingled his bells!
But when he wrapped her up tight—
Ah, the girl fainted and fell!

He didn't offend her at all,
But the girl fell into the snow!
Sitting, she couldn't hold up! . . .
I couldn't hold back a laugh! . . .

To the dance of the frozen icicles
Around my dear little cardboard girl,
He jangled and jumped in the air,
And, behind, I danced round the sleigh!

And we sang on the sleepy street:
"Ah, what misfortune has struck,"

And high over the cardboard girl
A star shone green in the sky.

All night through the snow-covered streets
We wandered—Harlequin and Pierrot . . .
He drew close to me with affection,
And with a feather tickled my nose!

He whispered to me: "My friend,
We're together for many a day . . .
Let's both be sorry about
Your cardboard, your dear, fiancée!"

(PIERROT *sadly moves off. After a while a* COUPLE IN LOVE *appears on the same bench. He is in blue; she, in pink; their masks are the colors of their clothes. They imagine themselves in church and look up into the cupola.*)

SHE. Darling, you whisper, "Lean back . . ."
Now I'm looking into the cupola.
HE. I gaze at an endless height—
There where the cupola has caught the sunset.
SHE. How the gilt up high has faded.
How the icons flicker up above.
HE. Our sleepy story is quiet now.
You've innocently closed your eyes. (*A kiss.*)
SHE. . . . Someone dark is standing by the column
And winking his evil eye!
My lover, I'm afraid of you!
Let me cover myself with your cape. (*Silence.*)
HE. Look how peaceful the candles are,
How the sunset has caught in the cupolas.
SHE. Yes. Our times together are sweet.
Let me be all given up to you. (*Squeezes close to him.*)
(*The quiet dance of the Maskers and clowns hides the* FIRST COUPLE *from the audience. A second* COUPLE IN LOVE *bursts out in the middle of the dance. In front—*SHE, *wearing a black mask and a swirling red cape. Behind—*HE, *all in black, supple, wearing a red mask and a black cape. Their movements are headlong.* HE *rushes after her, sometimes catching up to her, sometimes going past her. A whirlwind of capes.*)
HE. Leave me alone! Don't torture, don't haunt me!

Don't prophesy me a pitch-black fate!
You're being exultant about having won!
Will you take off your mask? Plunge into the night?

SHE. Come follow me! Reach me! Catch up!
I'm more sad and more passionate than your fiancée!
Put your lithe arm around me, embrace me!
Drink my dark cup dry to the lees!

HE. I swore true love to someone else!
You flashed your fiery eyes at me,
You led me to a dark back alley,
And with a deadly venom poisoned me!

SHE. It wasn't me—it was my cape
Flew up behind me like a storm!
Yourself, you chose to step
Inside my magic line!

HE. Be careful, witch! I will unmask!
And you'll find out I have no face!
You swept my features into the dark
Where my black double bowed his head.

SHE. I'm a free maiden! My path leads to conquest!
Follow me now wherever I lead!
Oh, you will come down my fiery trail
And will live in delirium with me!

HE. I go, obeying my harsh fate.
Oh, mantle, spin a wire of flame!
But three'll go down the evil road:
You—and I—and this double of mine!

(*They vanish in a whirlwind of capes. It seems as if a third man bursts out of the crowd behind them, someone exactly like the lover, completely like a supple tongue of black flame. Amid the dancers a third* COUPLE IN LOVE *appears. They sit down in the middle of the stage. The Middle Ages. Bending pensively,* SHE *follows his movements with her eyes.* HE—*all in severe, straight lines, big and pensive, in a cardboard helmet—traces a circle on the floor in front of her with a huge wooden sword.*)

HE. Do you understand the play in which we're playing a not unimportant role?

SHE (*like a quiet and audible echo*). Role.

HE. Do you know that the maskers made our meeting today marvellous?

SHE. Marvellous.

HE. So you believe me? Oh, today you're more beautiful than ever.

SHE. Ever.

HE. You know everything that has been and will be. You understand the meaning of the circle drawn here.

SHE. Here.

HE. Oh, how charmingly you talk! Diviner of my soul! How much your words tell my heart!

SHE. Heart.

HE. Oh, Eternal Happiness! Eternal Happiness!

SHE. Happiness.

HE (*with a sigh of relief and triumph*). It's nearly dawn. This foul night is almost gone.

SHE. Gone.

(*At this moment, one of the* CLOWNS *decides to pull a trick. He runs up to the lover and sticks out his tongue. The lover swats the* CLOWN *on the head with his heavy wooden sword. The* CLOWN *folds up over the footlights and hangs there. A stream of cranberry juice spurts from his head.*)

CLOWN (*shouts piercingly*). Help! The cranberry juice is running out of me!

(*Having dangled there a moment, he goes off. Noise. Confusion. Happy shouts: "Torches! Torches! A torchlight procession!" A* CHORUS *appears with torches. The* MASKERS *crowd together, laugh, jump up and down.*)

CHORUS. Into the twilight drop by drop
    The resin lightly falls!
Faces shrouded in dark clouds
    Shine with a sheen that has dulled!
Drop after drop, spark after spark!
    A pure and resinous rain!
Where are you, shimmering, nimble
    Leader aflame?

(HARLEQUIN *comes out of the* CHORUS *like a Corybant.*)

HARLEQUIN. I dragged a fool behind me
Through sleepy, snowy streets!

The world opened to rebellious eyes,
The snow-wind sang high over me!
Oh, how I wished in my young breast
To deeply sigh and see the world!
To finish in an empty waste
My springtime and lighthearted feast!
Here no one dares to understand
That spring flows by high up above!
Here nobody knows how to love!
Here people live a mournful dream!
Greetings, world! You're with me again!
Your soul has long been close to mine!
I go to breathe the spring
Through your golden window frame!

(*He jumps through the window. The distance, visible through the window, turns out to have been painted on paper. The paper bursts.* HARLEQUIN *flies head over heels into nothingness. Only the sky becoming light can be seen through the hole in the paper. The night runs out; morning hovers. Against the background of the bustling dawn stands Death, slightly swaying in the morning breeze, in long, white sheets, with a lusterless, feminine face and a scythe on her shoulder. The blade shines silvery, like an overturned moon dying in the morning light. Everyone rushes in opposite directions in terror. The knight trips over his wooden sword. The ladies drop flowers all over the stage. The Maskers motionlessly huddled together as if crucified on the walls, seem dolls from an anthropology museum. The mistresses hide their faces in their lovers' capes. The profile of the light blue Masker is subtly outlined against the morning sky. At his feet, the frightened, kneeling pink Masker presses her lips to his hand. As if having risen from the ground,* PIERROT *slowly crosses the stage, reaching his arms out toward Death. As he comes closer, her features begin to come alive. A blush plays across the dullness of her cheeks. The silver scythe is lost in the spreading morning fog. Against the red glow of the sun, in the window niche, there stands a beautiful girl with a tranquil smile on her calm face—* COLUMBINE. *At that moment, as* PIERROT *comes up and is about to touch her hand with his own, the triumphant head of the* AUTHOR *pokes out between him and* COLUMBINE.)

AUTHOR. My dear ladies and gentlemen! My work hasn't been wasted! My rights are supported! You see, the barriers fell! This gentleman fell out the window! Now you are to witness the happy reunion of the two loved ones after long separation. They may, indeed, have spent great effort on overcoming obstacles—but now they're being united forever! (*The* AUTHOR *starts to join the hands of* PIERROT *and* COLUMBINE. *But suddenly all the scenery rolls up, and flies up. The Maskers run away. The* AUTHOR *turns out to be bent over only* PIERROT, *who lies helplessly on an empty stage in his loose white overall with red buttons. Having realized his situation, the* AUTHOR *runs off headlong.*)

PIERROT (*raises himself up and speaks plaintively and dreamily*). Where have you led me? How can I guess?
You've left me to a wretched fate.
Poor, poor Pierrot, stop lying around;
Get up and find yourself a fiancée.

(*After a pause.*)
Ah, how radiant she was who's gone—
Her jangling friend took her away.
She did fall down—she was made of cardboard.
And I came on to laugh at her.

She lay prostrate on the floor, all white.
Ah, our dance together was so gay!
But she could not get up again.
She was a cardboard fiancée.

So now I'm here, with my pale face,
But it's a sin to laugh at me:
What can I do? She did fall down . . .
I'm very sad. You think it funny?

(PIERROT *pensively pulls a little reed pipe from his pocket and starts playing a song about his own pale face, about his hard life, and about his fiancée,* COLUMBINE.)

(*Curtain*)

He Who Gets Slapped

A DRAMATIC PRESENTATION

IN FOUR ACTS

Leonid Nikolayevich Andreyev

dedicated with deep affection
to my friend
SERGEI SERGEYEVICH
GOLOUSHEV

A NOTE ON THE PLAY

Born in Oryol in 1871, Andreyev became widely recognized following the appearance of his first book, a collection of short stories published in 1901. Mikhailovsky highly praised the book. Andreyev became associated with the *Znanie*[1] group and was closely connected with Gorky. Chekhov encouraged him. Both Andreyev's realistic and Symbolist works are shot through with a special horror and dread, with a sense that something terrible lurks behind life.

Tolstoy thought Andreyev's work, especially the plays, artificial and pretentious, untrue to life and dependent for their success on the performers' abilities. Once he quipped that Andreyev's work reminded him of the story of one little boy talking to another: " 'I was out taking a walk and suddenly I see this wolf running at me . . . You scared? . . . You scared?' And so Andreyev is always asking me," Tolstoy went on, " 'You scared?' I'm not in the least scared."

Chekhov, on the other hand, who disapproved of the Symbolists and Decadents, whose attitudes toward art Andreyev partly shared, felt that Andreyev "would remain in literary history." Andreyev, Gorky and Kuprin, Chekhov said, would "be read for ages."

By no means is all of Andreyev's work still read—he wrote more than two dozen plays, in addition to many stories and novels—but what remains is haunting and important. His protest against war, *The Red Laugh*, and his protest against capital punishment, *The Seven Who Were Hanged*, are outstanding literary works, in which Andreyev's skill in characterization transforms a single, topical theme into material of permanent significance.

Almost all of Andreyev's work is dominated by some central idea. He said, as if following Maeterlinck, that the most

[1] *Znanie*—a Petersburg publishing house, founded in 1898, of which Gorky became a member in 1900. It soon became a co-operative venture, issuing separate volumes and anthologies (almanacs) of its members' work. Gorky and Andreyev were its most famous members. It represented a quasi-realistic school of writing.

dramatic of all material is thought. Usually it is elaborated in a series of symbolic references. When the symbols lean heavily toward allegory, as in *The Life of Man*, or toward fantasy, as in *The Black Maskers*, we now find the work less appealing than when the symbols are made to inform on an external and realistic plot, as in *He Who Gets Slapped*.

This play is a narrative of the lives and loves of a circus troupe and, equally, a bitter and ironic attack on the world which laughs at the clown, HE. Whether or not the story be read as autobiography—like HE, Andreyev felt his ideas had been stolen and betrayed—or as actualization of a transcendental symbolism—Andreyev wrote F. A. Korsh that the play had "a touch of symbolism"—the meaning of the story patently lies beyond the mere consequences of events. Yet all the stage events conspire, so to speak, to one end. The whole play is a symbol: one of the most powerful and original modern dramas.

First published in 1916 in volume twenty-four of the almanac *Shipovnik* (*The Sweetbrier*), the play was dedicated to Andreyev's close friend, Sergei Goloushev, a doctor, liberal journalist and theater critic. Goloushev kept a diary in which he noted psychological observations of his own about Andreyev, including the fact that the figure of the clown, HE, and his revolt against self-satisfied bourgeois manners and values, closely represents Andreyev himself and presents many thoughts and ideas which Andreyev deeply believed.

In the early part of June, 1915, Andreyev wrote A. A. Kipen that in the fall he would compose a sensational drama, the heroine of which would be an animal tamer. A letter to his friend Goloushev on September 10, 1915, indicates that the play was already finished. On October 23, it was given a private reading in the apartment of L. G. Mundstein, the editor of the magazine *Rampa i zhizn* (*The Footlights and Life*). In the November first issue Andreyev described what he understood by drama: "Right now in the contemporary theater we have the triumph of drama. Drama is the lower middle-class's and the Philistines' favorite form of stage art. For drama, which is the complete opposite to tragedy and comedy, has always served to express their feelings and experiences." Andreyev's "drama," though it preserved the outer forms of conventional drama, was directed against such then-popular plays as Artsybashev's *Jealousy* and Surguchov's *The Violins of Fall*. Consuelo, Andreyev wrote, was the heart of his play: "In appearance, she must be a *goddess*—in the precise meaning of the laws of classic beauty. . . . As for her character, her psyche, C[onsuelo] is noble, pure and unconsciously *tragic*. . . . And it's not the external dramatic nature of magnificent Zinida, but the true and profound *tragedy* created by the contradiction between Consuelo's divine essence and its *fortuitous* external expression. . . ."

The play was first performed on October 27, 1915, in the Moscow Dramatic Theater, of which I. F. Schmidt was the managing director. Polevitskaya played Consuelo, a role written for her. The play opened in the Aleksandrinsky Theater in Petersburg on February 2, 1916, and was a great success; Andreyev even received a laurel wreath at the end of the third act. At the end of April, 1916, a film, based on the play, was released with the director and some of the cast from the original Moscow production. The play was widely translated; it first appeared on the New York stage in 1922, and even served as the subject for the opera *Pantaloon*, written by Robert Ward and first performed at the Juilliard School of Music in 1956 and at the New York City Center in 1959 as *He Who Gets Slapped*.

Andreyev died in 1919, in his house at Kuokkala, then in Finland, about forty minutes north of Leningrad by train.

This translation was made from the text in Volume XVII ("*Ironic Stories*") of Andreyev's *Sochineniya* (*Works*), Moscow, 1917. The text may also be found in the recent volume Leonid Andreyev, *Pesy* (*Plays*), Moscow, 1959.

DRAMATIS PERSONAE

Consuelo, a bareback rider; advertised as "The Queen of the Tango on Horseback"
Count Mancini, Consuelo's father
He, a clown in Briquet's circus; advertised as "He Who Gets Slapped"
Briquet ["Papa Briquet"], the circus manager
Zinida, a lion tamer, Briquet's wife
Alfred Bezano, a rider
A Gentleman
Baron Regnart
Jackson, a clown; "The Sun of Jackson"
Tili }
Poli } musical clowns
Thomas, Angelica, and other performers in Briquet's circus.

The action takes place in one of the large cities of France.

ACT I

In the Circus—a large, indeed enormous, dirty room with plaster walls. In the left wall, in an arcaded niche, the single window leads outside somewhere—the light is limpid and weak, so that even by day the electricity has to be on. On the back wall, at the very top, there is a row of little windows with smoky glass—these windows lead into the circus somewhere, and in the evenings, during performances, are brightly lit, but are dark by day. In this same wall, above two stone steps, there is a big door hammered tightly shut and whitewashed. In the right-hand wall, virtually in the corner, a high, wide door, without a frame and arched on top, leads to the stables and the arena: by day, it is rather dark; in the evening, dimly lit. This room serves various needs. Here is the office of the circus manager, PAPA BRIQUET; *here is his little desk; here, too, is the dressing room for some of the performers and the place they get together during the performances and rehearsals. Old junk has collected here, too: some half-broken gilded chairs from some pantomime set, all kinds of odds-and-ends of circus life. Bright posters cover the walls. It is morning. Rehearsals are going on in the circus, preparations for the evening's performance. As the curtain rises, the cracking of a whip and the shouts of the horse trainer from the arena. The stage is empty for a few moments, then the two musical clowns,* TILI *and* POLI, *come on, practicing a new march. Playing on little flutes, they go from the darkened door to the window. The sounds are pleasant but light, and the performers' little steps are both mincing and clownishly pompous. They are dressed in jackets; their shaved faces and their height make them look alike. The younger,* TILI, *has a knitted scarf around his neck. Both have derbies on the backs of their heads. Having reached the window,* TILI *glances to see what is outside; the clowns turn around and march back.*

POLI (*stops*). Stop! You're off again. Listen to me. (*Plays a solo on the flute right in* TILI'S *face;* TILI *listens absent-mindedly, rubbing his nose.*) Like that. All right?

(*Both play and march on. In the doorway they meet the*

Manager and MANCINI; *the latter, chewing on the gilt head of a cane, is behind.* COUNT MANCINI *is lean and spare, all his seams worn shiny, tightly buttoned up—and he carries himself with the utmost dignity. He likes to flourish his cane aristocratically and strike dazzling poses, laughs often, at which times his whole lean, pointed face takes on a satiric expression. The Manager,* PAPA BRIQUET, *is a short, fat, calm man with a slightly hesitant walk. The clowns make way; the Manager stares quizzically at the elder.*)

POLI (*distorting his speech*). Our music. The March of the Ants. For the pantomime.

BRIQUET. Ah! . . .

(*They part. The clowns start playing, but* POLI *stops and goes back. The younger follows.*)

POLI. Papa Briquet, Jacques is working bad today.

BRIQUET. Why?

POLI. He's got a sore throat. Take a look what's wrong with him.

BRIQUET. Come over here. All right, open wider, wider! (*Puts the clown under the light by the window and, frowning, peers down his throat.*) Paint it with iodine.

POLI. I said it was nothing. Well?

(*Playing, they go out with the same little mincing and pompous steps. The Manager sits down; Mancini has struck a pose by the wall and smiles derisively.*)

MANCINI. You doctor them, too? Be careful, Papa Briquet, you have no degree.

BRIQUET. In little things. They're all worried about themselves.

MANCINI. He simply burned his throat on absinthe: the pair of them get drunk every night. Papa Briquet, I'm surprised at you, how little you're concerned with propriety! (*Laughs.*)

BRIQUET. I'm fed up with you, Mancini.

MANCINI. *Count* Mancini, at your service.

BRIQUET. I'm fed up with you, *Count* Mancini. You butt in everywhere and interfere with the performers' working. Someday they'll let you have it, and I won't try to stop them.

MANCINI. As a man of a different background and social standing, I can't treat your performers as equals. What fancy of yours is this, Briquet? I honor you, too, just by talking to you like this, intimately and quite simply . . .

BRIQUET. Cut it out! . . .

MANCINI. I'm joking. But, in fact, if they ever think of attacking me—well, you've seen this, haven't you? (*Pulls a stiletto out of his cane. Admires it himself.*) A very useful thing! But do you know what a girl I found yesterday just outside town! (*Laughs.*) All right, all right—agreed you don't like it, every man has his own taste. But listen! You have to give me a hundred francs.

BRIQUET. Not a centime.

MANCINI. Then I'm taking Consuelo. Everything's finished!

BRIQUET. You say this every day.

MANCINI. Now, I'm saying it now! And you'd say it, too, if you were in such shameful need as I. No, listen to me—don't I have to keep up the honor of my name? Right? Why, you know that if the misfortunes of my family led to my having to make my daughter, Countess Veronica, a bareback rider . . . for a piece of bread! For a piece of bread, do you understand me, you lunkhead! . . .

BRIQUET. You throw away too much on girls. You'll end up in jail, Mancini!

MANCINI. In jail! No, but don't I have to keep up the honor of my family? (*Laughs.*) The Mancinis were known all over Italy for loving girls—only young girls. Why, is it my fault that I have to spend mad amounts of money for what my ancestors got free? You're an ass, a *parvenu;* you don't understand what family tradition is. I don't drink, I quit playing cards completely after that incident—all right, all right, no smirking!—and if I give up girls, too, why, what will be left of the Mancinis? Merely a coat of arms! Now listen, just for tradition's sake—give me a hundred francs!

BRIQUET. I said I wouldn't, and I won't.

MANCINI. But you know I give Consuelo a whole half of her pay. Or do you think I don't love my child, my only daughter, the last fond memory of her blessed mother still remaining to me? What cruelty! (*Pretends to cry and wipes his eyes with a dirty lace handkerchief embroidered with a crown.*)

BRIQUET. You ought to say instead, she's such a damned

fool she gives you half of what she earns. I'm fed up with you!

(*Zinida, the wild-animal tamer, enters, a strikingly beautiful, self-possessed woman with calmly imperative movements, which at first glance seem even lackadaisical. She is the common-law wife of Manager* BRIQUET.)

ZINIDA (*to* MANCINI). H'lo.

MANCINI. Madame Zinida! Let this barbarian, this vulgar soul, run me through with his dagger, but even in his presence I cannot restrain the outburst of my love. (*Clownishly falls on his knees.*) Madame, Count Mancini begs the honor of taking you to wife!

ZINIDA (*to* BRIQUET). Wants money?

BRIQUET. Yeh.

ZINIDA. Don't give it to him. (*Languidly sits down in a corner of the torn sofa and shuts her eyes.* MANCINI *gets up and dusts off his knees.*)

MANCINI. Duchess! be not so cruel. I am no lion, I am no tiger, no wild beast like those you are accustomed to taming. I am simply a humble domestic animal who wants . . . to ah-h, to ah-h, to taste a little green grass.

ZINIDA (*without opening her eyes*). Jim told me you've got a teacher for Consuelo. What's that for?

MANCINI. A father's care, Duchess; the care and tireless concern of an adoring heart. The extreme misfortunes of my family also left certain gaps in her upbringing. My dear friends! Count Mancini's daughter, the Countess Veronica, is practically illiterate. Is this tolerable? And you, Briquet, you vulgar thing, you ask why I need money?

ZINIDA. He's being foxy.

BRIQUET. What're you teaching her?

MANCINI. Everything. A student used to come to instruct her, but I fired him yesterday: he fell in love with Consuelo and was mewing away behind the door like a tomcat. Everything, Briquet, you don't know. Literature, mythology, spelling . . .

(*Two youngish girl performers come in with fur jackets on over their costumes, and wearily sit down side by side in the corner.*)

I don't wish my daughter to . . .

ZINIDA. He's being foxy.

BRIQUET. You're stupid, Mancini. What're you doing this for? (*Lecturing.*) You're terribly stupid, Mancini. What does she want to know things for? Since she's here, she doesn't have to know a thing about all that, understand? What's this geography? Anybody'll tell you it's nonsense. Why, I'd be twice as happy if I didn't know geography. If I were president, I'd completely forbid all performers to read books: let them read the posters and nothing else! . . . (*During* BRIQUET'S *speech both clowns and another performer come in; they sit down quietly and wearily.*)

BRIQUET. Right now your Consuelo's a first-class performer, but after you've taught her mythology and she's started reading, she'll be rotten, a loose girl, and then she'll poison herself. I know their books; I read them myself; they teach only vice and then how to kill yourself.

FIRST GIRL PERFORMER. But I love the novels you read in the papers.

BRIQUET. So you're another fool, and you'll fall, too. Believe me, my friends: we must completely forget about whatever's out there. Can we really ever understand what's going on out there?

MANCINI. You're against education! You're an obscurantist, Briquet!

BRIQUET. And you're stupid. Say, you're just the one to ask, you're from out there: what did you learn?

(*The performers laugh.*)

But if you'd been born in the circus, like me, you'd know something. Education—that's just a lot of nonsense and nothing else. Ask Zinida now; she knows everything they know outside, including geography and mythology, and did that make her any happier? Tell them, dear.

ZINIDA. Leave me alone, Louis.

MANCINI (*angrily*). Oh, after all, go to hell! When I hear your asinine philosophy, I feel like skinning you out of not a hundred francs, but two hundred, a thousand! My god, what an ass, even if you are the manager. I'll say it again, right in front of them all: you pay very little, you miser, you must give Consuelo a hundred francs more. Listen, you honest vagabonds: who fills up the circus every evening?

You, you two musical asses? The tigers and lions? Little
anybody needs those hungry cats . . .

ZINIDA. Leave the tigers alone.

MANCINI. Forgive me, Zinida, I don't mean to offend you—
on my honor. I myself am enraptured by your wild daring
and gracefulness. I kiss your sweet hands, my heroine, but
what do *they* understand of heroism?

(*In the arena a small orchestra strums a tango.*)

(*Excitedly.*) There it is, there it is! You hear it? So tell me,
honest vagabonds, isn't it Consuelo and Bezano who draw
the crowds? Their tango on horseback is, you know . . .
you know, is . . . God damn it, even His Holiness the
Pope himself would break down!

POLI. That's true. The number's famous everywhere. But I
think the idea was Bezano's?

MANCINI. The idea, the idea! The boy's in love, like a tomcat,
that's all the idea he has. And what's an idea without a
woman? A lot you'll dance with just your idea. Isn't that
so, Papa Briquet?

BRIQUET. There's the contract.

MANCINI. What base formality!

ZINIDA. Give the count ten francs and let him clear out.

MANCINI. Ten? Not on your life! Fifteen! Come, stop being
stubborn, Papa, for the sake of family tradition—twenty,
all right? On my honor, I can't do with less. (BRIQUET *gives
him twenty francs. Nonchalantly*). Merci.

ZINIDA. Get some from your Baron.

MANCINI (*raising his eyebrows, in noble indignation*). From the
Baron? Woman, who do you think I am? That I should
become indebted to a stranger who . . .

ZINIDA. You're up to some trick, some kind of real trick.
I still don't know you well, but I bet you're really no good.

MANCINI (*laughs*). An insult from two lovely lips.

(*A performer comes in; by build, a* WRESTLER.)

WRESTLER. Papa Briquet, some gent from the other world
has come to see you.

GIRL PERFORMER. A ghost?

WRESTLER. No, seems alive. You ever seen ghosts drunk?

BRIQUET. If he's drunk, send him away, Thomas. He wants
me, or the Count?

WRESTLER. You. Maybe he's not drunk, after all, but is simply a ghost.

MANCINI (*primping himself*). A man from the social world?

WRESTLER. Right. I'll send him in, Papa Briquet, and go on. Good-bye.

(*In the arena, the cracking of a whip, shouts; the sounds of a tango alternately fade out completely and sound loud and close. On stage, silence.*)

BRIQUET (*touching* ZINIDA's *hand*). Tired?

ZINIDA (*removing his hand*). No.

POLI. Your red lion is restless today, Zinida.

ZINIDA. You shouldn't tease him.

POLI. I played him a piece from *Traviata*. And he joined in singing fine. What about putting that on as a number, Papa Briquet?

(THOMAS *shows a* GENTLEMAN *in and points out: there's the manager. He himself goes out staggering heavily. The* GENTLEMAN *is a man no longer young, with a hideous but lively, audacious and rather strange face. He is dressed in an expensive fitted overcoat with a fur collar, holds his hat and his gloves in his hand.*)

GENTLEMAN (*bowing and smiling*). Have I the pleasure of meeting the manager?

BRIQUET. Yes. Sit down. Get a chair, Tili.

GENTLEMAN. Oh, don't bother. (*Looks around.*) These are your performers? How do you do.

MANCINI (*adjusting his coat and slightly bowing his head*). Count Mancini.

GENTLEMAN (*surprised*). Count?

BRIQUET (*vaguely*). Yes, Count . . . And whom have I the honor of? . . .

GENTLEMAN. I myself don't know yet. You all choose names for yourselves, don't you? But I haven't yet. You'll advise me later. I've already thought of some but, you know, it always comes out too . . . literary!

BRIQUET. Literary?

GENTLEMAN. Yes. It seems too made up.

(*They look at him in surprise.*)

I think these two gentlemen are clowns. I'm so glad . . .

Let me shake your hands. (*Gets up and with a pleasant smile shakes the clowns' hands. They make an idiotic face.*)

BRIQUET. But, please . . . what can I do for you?

GENTLEMAN (*still with the same pleasant and trusting smile*). It's not you for me, but I for you! I want to work for you, Papa Briquet.

BRIQUET. Papa Briquet? But you don't at all look like . . .

GENTLEMAN (*reassuringly*). That'll pass. I will. Here, these gentlemen just now made a remarkable face . . . Would you like me to repeat it? Like this. (*He makes an idiotic face, precisely copying the clowns.*)

BRIQUET. Right. (*Involuntarily.*) You're not drunk, sir?

GENTLEMAN. No. I don't drink at all. Why, do I look like a drunk?

POLI. Some are like that.

GENTLEMAN. No, I don't drink. This is simply the peculiarity . . . of my talent!

BRIQUET. Where were you working before? A juggler?

GENTLEMAN. No, but I'm delighted you feel I'm one of you, Papa Briquet. Unfortunately, I'm not a juggler, and . . . I've never worked. I just do it.

MANCINI. But you have the look of a man from the social world.

GENTLEMAN. Oh, you're flattering me, Count! It's just the way I am.

BRIQUET. What do you . . .?[2] you want? Can't help but tell you that everything's filled up here.

GENTLEMAN. That doesn't matter. I want to be a clown, if I may.

(*Some smile.* BRIQUET *begins to become angry.*)

BRIQUET. What can you do? You know that's a lot to want. Well, what can you do?

GENTLEMAN. Nothing. Isn't that absurd: to be able to do nothing?

BRIQUET. Not absurd at all. Any loafer can do as much.

GENTLEMAN (*helplessly, but still smiling; looks around*). I can think up something . . .

---

[2] BRIQUET here switches to the singular, familiar form and then corrects himself. After his next speech he uses the singular until shown HE's identification paper.

BRIQUET (*ironically*). Literary?

(*The clown* JACKSON *comes in quietly and, unnoticed, stops in back of the* GENTLEMAN.)

GENTLEMAN. Yes, even something literary. For example, what would you say to a short but really good speech . . . well, on religion, say? A little debate between two clowns.

BRIQUET. A debate? Cut it out, boy, this is no academy.

GENTLEMAN (*grieved*). What a shame! Something of that sort— a light joke about the creation of the world or about how it's run?

BRIQUET. And the Commissioner? It won't work.

JACKSON (*coming forward*). About how it's run? You don't like it? I don't either. Shake.

BRIQUET (*introducing them*). Our leading clown, the famous Jackson.

GENTLEMAN (*in delight*). My god, really you? Let me shake your hand warmly; you've given me such pleasure by your extraordinary . . .

JACKSON. Very pleased.

BRIQUET (*shrugging his shoulders*). This guy wants to be a clown; take a look at him, Jim.

(*At a sign from* JACKSON, *the* GENTLEMAN *hurriedly takes off his coat and throws it on a chair. He is ready to be looked over.* JACKSON, *moving around him, critically looks him over.*)

JACKSON. To be a clown, hm! Turn around. Hm! For a clown . . . yes . . . smile, now wider, wider! Is that a smile! So. I suppose the makings are there, all right, but to develop fully . . . (*In vexation.*) You probably can't even do a somersault?

GENTLEMAN (*sighing*). No.

JACKSON. How old are you?

GENTLEMAN. Thirty-nine. Too old?

(JACKSON, *whistling, moves away.*)

BRIQUET (*coldly*). We don't need your services, sir.

(*Silence.*)

ZINIDA (*softly*). Take him.

BRIQUET (*angrily*). But what the hell, what'll I do with him, since he can't do anything. He's just drunk!

GENTLEMAN. On my word of honor, I'm not. Thank you for

your support, madam. You're not the famous Madame Zinida, Lion Tamer, whose regal beauty and daring? . . .

ZINIDA. Yes, but I don't like to be flattered.

GENTLEMAN. That wasn't flattery!

MANCINI. You're simply not accustomed to people from the social world, my dear. Flattery! The gentleman was expressing his delight sincerely and handsomely, and you . . . that's your ignorance, Zinida. As for me . . .

(CONSUELO *and* BEZANO *come in in costume.*)

CONSUELO. You here, Papa?

MANCINI. Yes, my child. You're not tired? (*Kisses her on the forehead.*) My daughter, sir, the Countess Veronica, professionally known as the world-famous Consuelo, Queen of the Tango on Horseback. Did you ever see her?

GENTLEMAN (*bowing*). I was enraptured. Amazing!

MANCINI. Yes, everyone says so. How do you like her name? Consuelo! I took it from one of Madame George Sand's novels; it means "consolation."

GENTLEMAN. What brilliant erudition!

MANCINI. Oh, it's nothing. Despite your eccentric desire, I see, sir, that you're a man of my sort, and I must tell you that only the catastrophic misfortunes of an ancient line . . . *Sic transit gloria mundi*, sir!

CONSUELO. Everyone's heard it, Papa. Where's my kerchief, Alfred?

BEZANO. Here you are.

CONSUELO (*to the* GENTLEMAN). It's real Venetian. Do you like it?

GENTLEMAN (*again bowing to* CONSUELO). My eyes are blinded. What beauty! No, Papa Briquet, the more I see, the more I want to stay with you. (*Makes the blank face of a simpleton.*) On the one hand—a count, on the other . . .

JACKSON (*approvingly*). That's not bad. Listen, put your thinking cap on and figure out who you can be. Here everybody does his own thinking.

(*Silence. The* GENTLEMAN *thinks, his finger pressed to his forehead.*)

GENTLEMAN. Thinking, thinking . . . Eureka!

POLI. That means he got it. Well?

GENTLEMAN. Eureka! Here, with you, I'll be HE Who Gets Slapped.

(*General laughter; even* BRIQUET *smiles.*)

GENTLEMAN (*looking at everyone and smiling*). You see: you all really laughed. Now, is that easy?

(*All become serious.* TILI *the clown sighs.*)

TILI. No, it isn't. Did you laugh, Poli?

POLI. A lot. Did you?

TILI. Me, too. (*Plays a comic-serious little tune on his lips, imitating musical instruments.*)

JACKSON. HE Who Gets Slapped? That's not bad.

GENTLEMAN. It isn't, is it? I like it very much myself. It fits my special abilities perfectly. You know, friends: I thought up a name for myself, too . . . I'll be called HE. All right?

JACKSON (*reflectively*). HE? Not bad.

CONSUELO (*singingly*). How silly he is! "HE—like a dog. Papa, are there dogs like that?

(*Suddenly* JACKSON *pretends to slap* GENTLEMAN *across the face. He staggers back and turns pale.*)

GENTLEMAN. What!

(*General guffawing muffles his words.*)

JACKSON. HE Who Gets All the Slaps in the Face! Or didn't you?

POLI (*distorting his speech*). He says that's not enough.

(*The* GENTLEMAN *smiles, rubbing his cheek.*)

GENTLEMAN. So unexpected—and suddenly getting down to business . . . But it's strange: you didn't hurt me, and yet my cheek burns!

(*Laughter again. The clowns shout like ducks, like cocks; they bark and bare their teeth.* ZINIDA *goes out after having said something to* BRIQUET *and having glanced at* BEZANO. MANCINI *assumes the air of someone bored and looks at his watch. Both girl performers go out.*)

JACKSON. Take him, Papa Briquet, he'll keep us on our toes.

MANCINI (*looking at his watch*). But don't forget that Papa Briquet is as miserly as Harpagon. And if you're thinking of straightening out your affairs, you'll find you're much mistaken . . . (*Laughs.*) A slap in the face—what's a slap in the face? Here, it's just pocket money, a franc-and-a-half a dozen. Go back to the social world; you'll earn much more there. My friend, the Marquis Justi, for one slap in the face —just imagine!—for only one little box on the ear, received fifty thousand lire!

BRIQUET. Keep out of this, Mancini. Will you look after him, Jackson?

JACKSON. All right.

POLI. Do you like music? For example, a Beethoven sonata on a broom or Mozart on bottles?

HE. Alas, no! But I'll be endlessly grateful if you'll teach me. A clown! This has been my dream since childhood. When my schoolmates were deeply absorbed, some in Plutarch's heroes and others in science and study, I dreamed of being a clown. Beethoven on a broom! Mozart on bottles! This is just what I've been looking for all my life. But a costume? Oh, my friends, I need a costume right away.

JACKSON. Obviously you don't understand a thing. A costume, see (*presses his finger to his forehead*), is something you have to think about for a long time. You noticed the sun on me here? (*Slaps himself behind.*) I was looking for that for two years!

HE (*delightedly*). I will look!

MANCINI. Well, it's time for us to go. Consuelo, my child, you must get dressed. (*To* HE.) We're having lunch at Baron Regnart's—my friend, the banker.

CONSUELO. I'm not going, Papa. Alfred said I still have to work some more today.

MANCINI (*raising his hands in horror*). But, my child! What position are you putting me in? I promised the Baron, the Baron will be waiting for us . . . No, that's out of the question! I'm even perspiring.

CONSUELO. Alfred says . . .

BEZANO (*dryly*). She has to work a little more. You all rested? Let's go.

MANCINI. But that's—God knows what! Listen, you, Bezano, you jockey, are you mad? In the interests of art I've let you take up with my daughter a bit, but . . .

CONSUELO. Stop it, Papa. How stupid you are. We have to

work. Have lunch by yourself with your Baron. Ah, Papa, again you didn't take a clean handkerchief? I washed two for you yesterday. What did you do with them?

MANCINI (*blushing for shame*). The washerwoman does my laundry, and you still play dolls, Consuelo. That's silly! You chatter away without thinking, but these . . . Lord knows what these gentlemen might imagine. Ridiculous! I'm going.

CONSUELO. Want me to write him a note?

MANCINI (*spitefully*). A note! Even a horse would laugh at your notes! Good-bye!

(*Goes out, angrily twirling his cane. The musical clowns follow him respectfully, strumming a funeral march.* HE *and* JACKSON *laugh. The performers gradually leave.*)

CONSUELO (*laughing*). Do I really write so badly? And I like it so much—writing little notes. Did you like the little letter, Alfred, or did you laugh, too?

BEZANO (*blushing*). No, I didn't laugh. Let's go, Consuelo. (*They both go out, meeting* ZINIDA *in the doorway.*)

ZINIDA. You want to work more, Bezano?

BEZANO (*politely*). Yes. Somehow it's a bad day today. How are your lions, Zinida? The weather seems to me to be bothering them.

CONSUELO (*from off stage*). Alfred!

ZINIDA. Yes. You're being called. Go on. (BEZANO *goes out.*) Well, all finished?

BRIQUET. Finishing now.

JACKSON (*leaving*). Until tonight. Think about your costume, HE, and I will, too. And be here tomorrow at ten. Don't be late, or you'll get an extra slap. I'll take care of you.

HE. I won't be late. (*Watches him go.*) Probably a very good man? What fine people you have with you, Papa Briquet. And this handsome rider, most likely, is in love with Consuelo, isn't that right? (*Laughs.*)

ZINIDA. What's that to you? For a starter, you're already poking your nose into other people's business too much. How much does he want, Papa?

BRIQUET. Wait a minute. Listen, HE, I'm not going to draw up a contract with you . . .

HE. Oh, sure, that's fine, anything you want. And you know

what? We're not going to talk about money, either, right now! You're a fine, honest man, Briquet; you yourself will see my work and then . . .

BRIQUET (*with pleasure*). That's extremely decent of you. See, he really can't do anything, can he, Zinida?

ZINIDA. If that's the way he wants it. Has to be registered. Give me the book.

BRIQUET. Here. (*To* HE.) I don't like writing. We register all the performers in this, for the police, you know. Somebody can get killed, or . . .

(*Sounds of a tango and shouts again come from the arena.*)

ZINIDA. What's your name?

HE (*smiling*). HE. I've already chosen it. Or don't you like it?

BRIQUET. We like it, but we need your real name. You have a passport?

HE (*confused*). A passport? I haven't. More accurately, I do have something of that sort, but I didn't think you were so strict. Why do you need it?

(ZINIDA *and* BRIQUET *look at each other silently;* ZINIDA *pushes the book away.*)

ZINIDA. Then we can't take you. We can't get into trouble with the police just because of you.

BRIQUET. This is my wife, you didn't know that. She's right. A horse can kick you, or you might think up something like that yourself, who knows what you're like. It makes no difference to me, but out there, see, they look at it differently. A dead man's just a dead man to me; I don't ask him questions and leave it all up to God or the devil, but they're very curious. They need it for some regulation, probably, I don't know. You have a card with your name on it?

HE (*rubs his forehead in hesitation*). What'll I do? I have a card, but . . . (*Smiles.*) You understand that I very much don't want my name known.

BRIQUET. Some trouble?

HE. Yes, something like that . . . Why can't one imagine that I simply have no name at all? Couldn't I lose my name like a hat? Or say that it was changed on me? When a stray dog comes to you, you don't ask it its name but give it a new one. Let me be a dog like that. (*Laughs.*) The Dog HE!

ZINIDA. You can tell the two of us. Nobody else will find out—unless, of course, you decide to break your neck.

HE (*hesitant*). Your word of honor?

(ZINIDA *shrugs her shoulders.*)

BRIQUET. Where people are honest, every word's a word of honor. It's clear you come from outside.

HE. All right. Here. Please don't be surprised. (*Hands the card to* ZINIDA. *She looks at it and hands it to* BRIQUET. *Then they both look at* HE.)

BRIQUET. If this is true, sir, and you are what's written here . . .

HE. For God's sake, for God's sake! That's finished, that's gone long ago; it's simply a receipt for an old hat! I beg you, forget it, as I have. I am HE Who Gets Slapped and nothing else.

(*Silence.*)

BRIQUET. Please excuse me if I just once more ask you most respectfully: you're not drunk, sir? There's something in your eyes that . . .

HE. No. I'm HE Who Gets Slapped. And since when have you and I stopped *tutoyering* each other, Papa Briquet? You make me feel hurt.

ZINIDA. In short, it's his business, Briquet. (*Puts the card away.*) But you're a very strange gent, that's for sure. (*Smiling.*) And you've already noticed that Bezano's in love with the bareback rider? And that I love my Briquet—can you see that?

HE (*also smiling*). Oh, yes! You worship him.

ZINIDA. I worship him. Take him out, Briquet, and show him arena and the stables. I'll put something down here.

HE. Yes, yes! Please. I'm so happy at last—because you've taken me on. That's true, isn't it? You're not fooling? The arena! The sand of the arena! The ring I'll be running in, getting my slaps! Yes, yes, let's go, Briquet. Until I feel the sand under my feet, I can't believe it all.

BRIQUET. All right, let's go. (*Kisses* ZINIDA.) Come on. (*They head for the door.*)

ZINIDA. Wait—HE! Answer me one question. I have a man who cleans the cages, oh, just a regular worker nobody knows. He cleans the cages. And you know: he always goes into the lions, just whenever he wants to, doesn't even look at them, feels right at home. Why is this? And nobody knows him, but everybody knows who I am, and when I go in, they're all scared to death, but . . . He's such a fool; you'll see him! (*Laughs.*) But don't you decide to go in, HE—my Rusty will give you such a slap!

BRIQUET (*displeased*). You're at it again, Zinida. Drop it.

ZINIDA (*laughing*). Yes, go on, go on. Ah, yes: send Bezano in, Louis, I have to settle accounts with him.

(HE *and the Manager go out.* ZINIDA *glances at the card once more and puts it away. She gets up and paces the room briskly, stops and listens to the sounds of the tango. The music suddenly breaks off.* ZINIDA *stands waiting, without moving, looking straight into the dark doorway.*)

BEZANO (*coming in*). You called me, Zinida? Hurry, tell me what's up, I have no time.

(ZINIDA *looks at him silently. Flushing and frowning,* BEZANO *just as silently turns to the door.*)

ZINIDA. Bezano?

BEZANO (*stopping, without looking up*). What d'you want? I'm in a hurry.

ZINIDA. Bezano! For days I've been hearing that you're in love with Consuelo. Is that true?

BEZANO (*shrugging his shoulders*). She and I work together.

ZINIDA (*taking a step forward*). No, tell me: is it true you love her, Alfred?

BEZANO (*blushes like a boy but looks straight into* ZINIDA'S *eyes. Proudly*). I don't love anybody. How could I? I don't love anybody. Today Consuelo's here; tomorrow her father'll take her away. Who am I? An acrobat, a shoemaker's son from Milan. And she? I don't even know how to talk, I haven't got the words, like my horse. Who am I to fall in love?

ZINIDA. But you love me . . . a little?

BEZANO. No. I already said that.

ZINIDA. Still no? Just a little? No?

BEZANO (*after a pause*). I'm afraid of you.

(ZINIDA *is about to shout something angry but keeps control of herself, lowers her eyes, and seemingly extinguishes their gleam. She turns pale.*)

ZINIDA. Am I really so . . . terrifying?

BEZANO. You're beautiful, like a queen. You're almost as beautiful as Consuelo. But I don't like your eyes. Your eyes order me to love you, but I can't when I'm ordered. I'm afraid of you.

ZINIDA. Do I really order you? No, Bezano—I'm only asking.

BEZANO. But why don't you look at me? There, I caught you: you yourself know your eyes don't know how to ask. (*Laughs.*) Your lions have spoiled you.

ZINIDA. My Rusty loves me.

BEZANO. No. If he does, then why is he so dull?

ZINIDA. Yesterday he licked my hand like a dog.

BEZANO. And all this morning he's been looking and looking for you with his eyes to gobble you up. He sticks his mug out and looks as if he sees just you. He's afraid of you and hates you. Or do you want me, too, to lick your hand like a dog?

ZINIDA. No. It's me, me, Alfred, who wants to kiss yours. (*In a frenzy.*) Let me kiss your hand!

BEZANO (*sternly*). The way you talk I'm ashamed to hear you.

ZINIDA (*restraining herself*). A person can't be tortured the way you torture me! Alfred, I love you! No, I'm not ordering you: look me in the eye. I love you!

(*Silence.* BEZANO *turns toward the exit.*)

BEZANO. Good-bye.

ZINIDA. Alfred! . . .

(HE *appears in the door and stops.*)

BEZANO. And please don't ever say you love me. I don't want to hear it, or I'll leave here. You say, "I love you," as if you were beating me with a whip. You know—it's disgusting!

(*Spins sharply and goes out. They both catch sight of* HE. BEZANO, *frowning, quickly passes by;* ZINIDA *turns back to her place at the table with an expression of haughty indifference.*)

HE (*coming closer*). Excuse me, I . . .

ZINIDA. Sticking your nose in again, HE? You want a slap that much?

HE (*laughing*). No, I just forgot my coat. I didn't hear a thing.

ZINIDA. It doesn't matter to me whether you did or didn't.

HE. May I get my coat?

ZINIDA. Go ahead, if it's yours. Sit down, HE.
HE. I will.
ZINIDA. Answer me. Could you fall in love with me, HE?
HE. Me? (*Laughing.*) Me and love? Take a look at me, Zinida: have you ever seen a lover with such a face?
ZINIDA. With a face like that you can have a lot of success.
HE. That's because I feel good! That's because I lost my hat! That's because I'm drunk. Or am I not? But everything's spinning around in front of me, as in front of a young girl at a dance. How good it is here! Hurry up and slap me, I want to act. Maybe it will even arouse love in me. Love! (*As if listening to something in his heart. With exaggerated horror.*) You know what? I feel it!
(*The sounds of the tango come again from the arena.*)
ZINIDA (*listening*). For me?
HE. No. I don't know yet. For everybody! (*Listens.*) Yes, they're dancing. How lovely Consuelo is! And how handsome the young man is; he has the body of a Greek god, as if Praxiteles had sculpted him. Love! Love!
(*Silence. Music.*)
ZINIDA. Tell me, HE . . .
HE. What would you have, Queen?
ZINIDA. HE! What can I do to make my animals love me?

(*Curtain*)

ACT II

The same room, evening, during the performance. Bits and scraps of music, shouts, and the roar of applause come in from outside. The upper windows are lit. CONSUELO *and* BARON REGNART *are on stage.* CONSUELO, *wearing her riding costume, sits with her feet on the sofa, a shawl over her shoulders.* BARON REGNART *is in front of her, a tall, heavy-set gentleman in a dress coat, a rose in his buttonhole. His legs set wide and vulgarly apart, he looks at* CONSUELO *thickly with motionless, bulging, spidery eyes.*

BARON. Is it true that your papa . . . that the Count introduced you to this Marquis Justi, a very rich man?

CONSUELO (*surprised*). No! He's joking. He often talks about some Marquis Justi or other, but I've never seen him.

BARON. But you know that your father is simply a fraud?

CONSUELO. Oh, no, he's so nice!

BARON. Did you like the diamonds?

CONSUELO. Yes. Very much! I was awfully sorry Papa made me give them back to you. He said it wasn't decent. I even cried a little.

BARON. Your father's a pauper and a fraud.

CONSUELO. Oh, no, don't say such things about him! He's so fond of you.

BARON. Let me kiss your hand.

CONSUELO. The idea! That's never done! You can kiss someone when you meet and when you say good-bye, but not in-between.

BARON. Everybody's in love with you, and that's why you and your father pretend you're so important. Who's this new clown you have, this HE? I don't like him—a clever rascal. Is he in love with you, too? I saw the way he looked at you.

CONSUELO (*laughs*). Oh, really! He's so funny. Yesterday he got fifty-two slaps; we counted. Just think: fifty-two slaps in the face! Papa said: if only he could get money for them!

BARON. Consuelo! But you like Bezano?

CONSUELO. Yes, very much. He's so handsome! HE said—I

mean HE, the clown—that we're the most beautiful couple in the world. HE calls him Adam and me, Eve . . . But isn't that probably indecent? HE is so indecent.

BARON. Does HE often talk to you?

CONSUELO. Often, but I don't understand him. He always seems drunk.

BARON. Good Lord! Consuelo—in Spanish that means "consolation." Your father's an ass. Consuelo, I love you.

CONSUELO. Talk to Papa.

BARON (*angrily*). Your father's a swindler and a blackmailer, who ought to be carried off to the Commissioner. Don't you understand that I can't marry you?

CONSUELO. Papa says you can.

BARON. No, I can't. And what if I shoot myself? Consuelo, sweet stupid, I love you unbearably. Unbearably, understand? I've probably gone mad and should be taken to the doctor, dragged along by the scruff of my neck and beaten with sticks. Why do I love you so?

CONSUELO. Then you'd better get married.

BARON. I've had hundreds of women, real beauties, but I never saw them. You're the first one I've seen—and I see nothing else. Who overwhelms man by love—God or the devil? The devil's overwhelmed me. Let me kiss your hand.

CONSUELO. No. (*She becomes pensive and sighs.*)

BARON. Do you ever think, really? What are you thinking about, Consuelo?

CONSUELO (*sighs*). I'm somehow sorry for Bezano. (*Sighs.*) He's so kind when he's teaching me, and his room is so tiny . . .

BARON (*furiously*). You were there?

CONSUELO. No, I heard from HE. (*Smiling.*) Listen, you hear the noise out there? That's him getting his slaps in the face. Poor man! Though it doesn't hurt at all, and it's only on purpose. The intermission comes soon.

(*The* BARON *throws away his cigar, takes two steps and falls on his knees before the girl.*)

BARON. Consuelo! . . .

CONSUELO. Oh, no, get up, get up. Let go of my hand!

BARON. Consuelo!

CONSUELO (*in disgust*). Get up now; I'm disgusted. You're so fat!

(*The* BARON *rises. The sound of voices and people comes through the door—the intermission. Chattering happily, excited, the clowns come in. The first is* HE, *dressed as a clown, with blackened eyebrows and a white nose, applauded by the rest. Voices of the performers: "Bravo,* HE!" *Girl performers, horseback riders, acrobats—all are in their appropriate costumes.* ZINIDA *is missing. Then* PAPA BRIQUET *appears.*)

POLI. A hundred slaps! Bravo, HE!

JACKSON. Not bad, not bad! You'll go far.

TILI. Today he was a teacher, and we were the pupils. Once more, now; make it a hundred and one!

(*Jokingly strikes* HE. *Laughter. They greet the* BARON. *He is polite but rude, fed up with these vagabonds and taciturn, to which all have become accustomed.* MANCINI *goes up to him, the same as ever, with the same cane.*)

MANCINI (*greeting him*). What a success, Baron! And to think how the public loves slaps in the face . . . (*In a whisper.*) Your knees are dirty, Baron, brush them off. The floor here is very dirty. (*Aloud.*) Consuelo, my child! How do you feel? (*Goes over to his daughter. There is gay noise and talking. Waiters from the buffet bring in soda and drinks.*)

CONSUELO. But where's Bezano?

HE (*bowing to the* BARON, *intimately*). You don't recognize me, Baron?

BARON. Yes, I do. You're the clown HE.

HE. Yes. I am HE Who Gets Slapped. May I ask, Baron, if you received the diamonds?

BARON. What do you mean!

HE. I was asked to return some diamonds to you, and I just wondered . . . (*The* BARON *turns his back on him.* HE *laughs loudly.*)

JACKSON. Whiskey and soda! Believe me, ladies and gentlemen, he'll go far; I'm an old clown and I know the audience. Today he eclipsed even me, and my sun was clouded over! (*Slaps himself behind.*) They don't like puzzles; they need slaps in the face, which they pine for and dream about at home. Your health, HE! Another whiskey and soda! Today he got enough slaps in the face to take care of the whole parquet . . .

TILI. No, there weren't! I'll bet you!

POLI. It's a bet! Shake! I'll go count the ugly mugs in the parquet.

A VOICE. The parquet didn't laugh.

JACKSON. Because it was getting slapped. But the balcony did, because it was watching how the parquet got slapped. Your health, HE!

HE. And yours, Jim! But why didn't you let me finish my speech, I was all set!

JACKSON (*with an air of importance*). Because it was blasphemous, old friend. Politics are all right; manners—all you want; but leave Providence alone. And believe me, I shut your mouth just in time. Isn't that right, Papa Briquet?

BRIQUET (*coming over*). It was too literary; this is no academy. You keep forgetting, HE!

TILI. But to slap a man's mouth shut—phew!

BRIQUET (*lecturing*). No matter when you shut a man's mouth for him, it's always in time. If only when he's drinking . . . Hey, whiskey and soda!

VOICES. Whiskey and soda for the manager!

MANCINI. But that's obscurantism! You philosophizing again, Briquet?

BRIQUET. I'm dissatisfied with you today, HE. Why tease them? They don't like that. Your health! A good slap in the face has to be pure, like crystal—pow! pow! right, left—and that's it. They like it, and they laugh and love you. But in your slaps there's a flavor of something else, you understand, some sort of smell!

HE. But they laughed!

BRIQUET. But without delight, without delight, HE! You pay, but right away charge it up to them. It's not the right way to do it; they won't like you.

JACKSON. That's just what I keep telling him. He's already begun to make them angry.

BEZANO (*coming in*). Consuelo, where are you? I've been looking for you. Let's go. (*They both go out. The* BARON *slowly follows them;* MANCINI *respectfully accompanies him to the door.*)

HE. Ah, friends, you don't understand! You've simply grown old and lost your knack for the stage.

JACKSON. Oho! Just who's grown so old, young man?

HE. Don't be angry, Jim. But it's—a way of playing, do you see? I become happy when I go out in the arena and hear the music. I have a mask on, and it seems absurd to me, as in a dream. I have a mask on, and I act. I can say everything, like a drunk, you understand? Yesterday, with that stupid face, when I was playing a great man, a philosopher! ... (*Having adopted a haughty and statuesque air,* HE *repeats his acting of the day before, to general laughter.*) And was walking like this—and was saying how great and wise and incomparable I was—what divinity there was dwelling in me—and how high I was above the earth—and how glory was radiant around my head! (*Changing his voice, in a patter.*)—and you, Jim, hit me the first time—and I asked: What's that? Am I being applauded?—and when at the tenth slap I said, "I think I'm being sent for from the Academy." (*Acting, he looks around with an air of invincible arrogance and grandeur. Laughter.* JACKSON *slaps* HE *in the face.*) What for?

JACKSON. For playing for nothing, you fool. *Garçon*, the check. (*Laughter. In the distance, a bell rings, summoning them to the arena. The performers quickly scatter, some running. The waiters are hurriedly paid.*)

BRIQUET (*in a chant*). To the arena! To the arena!

MANCINI. I must have a word with you, HE. You're not going on yet?

HE. No, I've got a break now.

BRIQUET. To the arena! To the arena!

(*The clowns go out singing piercingly. Gradually, all are gone. The sounds of a fanfare.* HE *stretches out on the sofa, yawns.*)

MANCINI. HE, you have what my family never did: money. Shall I order a bottle? Waiter, bring us one.

(*The waiter, who cleared the dishes, brings in a bottle of wine and glasses. He goes out.*)

HE. For some reason, you're depressed, Mancini. (*Stretching.*) No, at my age a hundred slaps in the face isn't easy. For some reason, you're depressed. How are you getting on with the girl?

MANCINI. Shhh! Badly. Complications. Her parents. (*Shudders*.) Ah!

HE. Jail?

MANCINI (*laughs*). Jail! One must keep up the luster of one's name. Ah, HE, I'm joking, but it's worse than hell for me! You're the only one who understands me. But listen—what kind of a passion is this? Explain it to me. It'll give me grey hair, put me in jail, drive me to my grave—I'm a tragic man, HE. (*Wipes away tears with a dirty handkerchief*.) Why don't I love what's allowed? Why every moment, even in moments of ecstasy, must I think about some . . . law? It's stupid, HE. I'm becoming an anarchist! My god! Count Mancini an anarchist, that's all that was needed!

HE. But can't you settle?

MANCINI. And the money?

HE. But the Baron? . . .

MANCINI. Of course, that's all he's waiting for, that vampire. And he'll wait till he wins! He'll wait till I give him Consuelo for ten thousand francs! For five!

HE. That's cheap.

MANCINI. But did I say it wasn't cheap, or that that's what I want? But if these petty bourgeois are going to strangle me, choking my throat—like this! Ah, HE, it's absolutely clear that you're a man from the world of society. You understand me. I showed you the diamonds which I sent back to him? Damned honesty, it didn't even let me substitute fake stones!

HE. Why not?

MANCINI. Because then I would have spoiled the whole game. You imagine he didn't weigh them afterwards?

HE. He won't get married.

MANCINI. Yes, he will. You don't understand him. (*Laughs*.) He's a man who half his life had only desire, and now love has come. If he doesn't get Consuelo, he's finished, like . . . like a withered daffodil. God damn him and his automobile! Have you seen it?

HE. I have. Give the girl to the horseback rider.

MANCINI. Bezano? (*Laughs*.) Now look what we've talked ourselves into! Oh, yes—that joke of yours about Adam and Eve. Don't, please . . . It's witty but it compromises the girl. She told me.

HE. Or to me.

MANCINI. But do you have a billion? (*Laughs.*) Ah, HE, I'm not up to your clown's jokes. They say the prisons here are most repulsive, no difference is made between people of our level and plain riffraff. Why are you looking at me like that? Are you laughing?

HE. No.

MANCINI (*angrily*). I'll never grow used to these faces! You're so vilely painted up . . .

HE. He won't marry. You're too ambitious and proud, Mancini, but he won't marry. What's Consuelo? She's uneducated; when she's not on her horse, any maid from a good house has better manners and talks more cleverly . . . (*Casually.*) She's not stupid?

MANCINI. She's not stupid, but, HE, you're a fool. What's this about intelligence in a woman? You amaze me, HE! Consuelo is still an uncut diamond, and only a real ass can't see her radiance. Do you know that, at one point, I started giving her shape?

HE. You hired a teacher? Well, so?

MANCINI (*nodding his head, mysteriously*). And I was frightened—it took hold so fast! I let him go. I was even frightened. Another month or two and she would have chased me out. (*Laughs.*) The wise old jewelers in Amsterdam used to keep their stones uncut—on account of thieves. My father told me.

HE. That's a diamond's dream. Then it sleeps. No, you're clever, Mancini!

MANCINI. You know what blood flows in an Italian woman's veins? She has the blood of Hannibal and Corsini, of Borgia and some dirty Lombard or Moor. Oh, she's not a woman of an inferior race with only peasant or gypsy stock behind her! An Italian woman has in her all possibilities, all forms, just like our wonderful marble. You understand, you lunkhead? Strike her here—and she's a kitchen maid whom you'll throw out for being dirty and raucous as a crow, a cheap kept woman. But carefully—gently! touch her on this side—and she's a queen, a goddess, a Venus of the

Capitol! And she sings like a Stradivarius, and you weep—you lout! An Italian woman . . .

HE. Why, you're a poet, Mancini! But what will the Baron make her?

MANCINI. What do you mean "what?" Why . . . a baroness, you lunkhead! What strikes you funny? I don't understand. It's simply great luck that this pig-in-love isn't a duke or a prince: he'd make her a princess, and then I'd be in for it! In a year they wouldn't let me into the kitchen! (*Laughs.*) Me! And I'm Count Mancini, and she's just a simple . . .

HE (*rising*). What are you mumbling? You're not her father? Mancini!

MANCINI. Shh! God damn it, I'm all upset today. And who am I? Good heavens! Of course, her father! (*Twists his face in laughter.*) You lunkhead, or don't you see the family resemblance? Just look: the nose—so! the eyes! (*Suddenly sighs deeply.*) Ah, HE, I'm so unhappy. And just think: at the same time that a man is perishing here in his struggle for the honor of his ancient line, out there, in the parquet, sits that pig, that elephant with spider eyes looking at Consuelo, and . . .

HE. True, he has the motionless stare of a spider. You're right.

MANCINI. And didn't I say that? A spider! Yet I'll make him marry her. You'll see! (*Walks back and forth excitedly, swinging his cane.*) You'll see! All my life I've been getting ready for this battle. (*Paces. Silence and stillness.*)

HE (*listening*). Why is it so quiet out there? A strange stillness.

MANCINI (*squeamishly*). I don't know! There it's quiet, but here (*touches his cane to his forehead*) there's a real storm and whirlwind! (*Bends toward the clown.*) HE, shall I tell you something amazing? An event of a most unusual quirk of nature? (*Laughs and, with an important expression, goes on.*) For three centuries now the Counts Mancini have been absolutely childless! (*Laughs.*)

HE. Really! But then how do you get born?

MANCINI. Shhh! That's the secret of our holy mothers! Heh-heh. We're too ancient, too elegant, after all, to be bothered with such vulgar business, in which any and every peasant is stronger than we.

(*A circus attendant comes in.*)

Look here, what do you want? The manager's out in the arena.

ATTENDANT (*bowing*). I know. Baron Regnart asked me to deliver this letter to you.

MANCINI. The Baron? He's there?

ATTENDANT. The Baron has left. He doesn't expect an answer.

MANCINI (*opening the little envelope with trembling hands*). God damn it! God damn it!

(*The attendant moves to go out.*)

HE. Wait. Why isn't the music playing? Why is it so quiet?

ATTENDANT. It's Madame Zinida's number with the lions.

(*He goes out.* MANCINI *rereads the little note.*)

HE. Well, what is it, Mancini? You're beaming like the sun of Jackson.

MANCINI. What? You asked me, I think, "What is it?" Here, this is what! (*Balancing his cane, he pirouettes.*)

HE. Mancini! . . .

(*A coquettish expression on his face and in his eyes,* MANCINI *continues dancing.*)

But tell me, you dog!

MANCINI (*putting out his hand*). Give me ten francs! Give me ten francs right away! Ah, HE! Give me them! (*Quickly and mechanically puts the money in his vest pocket.*) HE! If I don't have an automobile in a month, you can give me one of your slaps!

HE. What? He'll marry her? He's decided?

MANCINI. What does that mean, "decided?" (*Laughs.*) A man has the noose around his neck, and you're asking how does he feel? The Baron . . . (*Stops still, astounded.*) Look there, HE! . . .

(*Stumbling, as if heavily drunk or sick, his eyes covered with his hand,* BRIQUET *enters.*)

HE (*going up to him and putting his arm around his shoulder*). What's wrong? Papa Briquet!

BRIQUET (*moaning*). A-a-a-ah . . . I can't! . . . A-ah!

HE. Did something happen? Are you sick? Say something.

BRIQUET. I couldn't look! (*Takes his hand down and opens his staring eyes wide.*) What's she doing? Ah, what she's doing! Must get her. She's gone mad! I couldn't look! (*Shudders.*) She'll be torn to pieces, HE! The lions will tear her to pieces.

MANCINI. Not at all, Briquet! She's always like that. Why, look at you, like a child; you ought to be ashamed of yourself.

BRIQUET. No. Today she's out of her mind. What's happened to the crowd! It's as if they'd all died; they don't breathe. I couldn't look! Listen—what's that?!

(*They all listen, but outside there is the same stillness.*)

MANCINI (*agitated*). I'll take a look.

BRIQUET (*shouting*). No! You mustn't! Ah, the damned work! Don't go! You might set it off . . . All the eyes looking at her . . . at the beasts . . . No, it's impossible! It's blasphemy! I had to leave. HE, she'll be torn to pieces!

HE (*trying to be cheerful*). Now, calm down, Briquet! I had no idea you were such a coward! Aren't you ashamed! Drink some wine. Mancini, give him some wine.

BRIQUET. Don't want any. Lord, if only it were over!

(*They listen.*)

I've seen a lot in my life, but this! . . . She's out of her mind.

(*They listen. Suddenly the silence is broken as if a huge stone wall had fallen: outside there is the thunder of applause, shouts, music, and the roar of voices neither quite those of beasts nor of humans. On stage, joyful excitement;* BRIQUET, *beside himself, sinks onto a chair.*)

MANCINI (*excited*). You see! You see, you lunkhead!

BRIQUET (*laughing and sobbing*). I'll never again let . . .

HE. Here she is!

(ZINIDA *comes in alone. She looks like a drunken Bacchante or a madwoman. Her hair is all disheveled; her dress is completely off one shoulder. She walks without seeing where she's going, her eyes shining. She's like a living statue of a mad victory. Behind her comes a performer with a pale face; then two clowns; then* CONSUELO *and* BEZANO *all pale. All look at* ZINIDA *in fear, as if afraid to be touched by her or to be looked at by those huge eyes.*)

BRIQUET (*shouting*). You've gone crazy! Ah, you idiot!

ZINIDA. Me? No. Did you see, did you see? Well—what did you think?! (*Stands smiling, enjoying her mad victory.*)

TILI (*plaintively*). Stop now, Zinida! The hell with you!

ZINIDA. But did you see? Well—what did you think?

BRIQUET. Go home! Go home! All you here do what you want. Zinida, let's go home!

POLI. You can't, Papa. There's still your number.

ZINIDA (*exchanging looks with* BEZANO). Ah, Bezano! (*Laughs long and happily.*) Bezano . . . Alfred! You saw it: my animals love me!

(*Without answering,* BEZANO *goes out.* ZINIDA *seems to have been put out like a flame: her smile fades, her eyes dull, her face pales.*)

BRIQUET (*suffering, bent toward her, looks at her and speaks softly*). A chair. (ZINIDA *sits down. Her head lies weakly on her shoulder, her arms hang. She starts shivering, and shivers more and more, her teeth chattering.*)

ZINIDA (*whispering*). Cognac.

(*A performer runs off for cognac.*)

BRIQUET (*helplessly*). What's the matter with you, Zinida? My darling!

MANCINI (*fussing*). She must calm down. Well, go on, go on, you vagabonds. I'll take care of everything, Papa Briquet. Her coat! Where's her fur coat? She's cold.

(*A clown passes the fur coat. They wrap her up.*)

TILI (*meekly*). Don't you need some music?

MANCINI (*giving her the cognac*). Drink, Duchess! Drink—drink it all. That's it.

(ZINIDA *drinks it like water, apparently not tasting it; she shivers. The clowns quietly go out. With a sudden deft movement,* CONSUELO *throws herself on her knees in front of* ZINIDA *and kisses her hands, warms them.*)

CONSUELO. Sweet, sweet one . . . are you cold? Your soft little hands . . . sweet one . . . good . . . my love . . .

ZINIDA (*lightly pushing her back*). Ho-home! It'll pass in a minute, it's nothing. I'm very, very . . . Home! You stay here, Briquet, they still need you. No, it's nothing.

CONSUELO. Are you cold? Take my shawl.

ZINIDA. No. Leave me alone.

(CONSUELO *gets up and moves away.*)

BRIQUET. It's all your books, Zinida! Mythology! Tell me now: what did you have to have those animals love you for? Beasts! You understand, HE? You come from there, too; she'll sooner listen to you, so explain it to her! Well, who can these creatures love, these hairy monsters with their diabolic eyes?

HE (*agreeably*). I think only those like them. You're right, Papa Briquet: it has to be the same breed!

BRIQUET. Why, of course! This is all stupidity, literature! You tell her, HE.

HE (*putting on the air of a man pondering*). Yes. You're right, Briquet.

BRIQUET. You see, you little fool? Everybody says so.

MANCINI. Pooh, how fed up I am with you, Briquet! You're an absolute despot, a real tyrant!

ZINIDA (*Smiling wanly and holding her hand out to* BRIQUET *to be kissed*). Relax, Louis. It's all over with. I'm going. (*Gets up, stumbling, still shivering.*)

BRIQUET. But how can you by yourself? Darling . . .

MANCINI. Lunkhead! And have you ever seen Count Mancini abandon a woman when she needed assistance? I'll take her back, rest assured, you lout, I'll take her back. Thomas, run get the automobile! And don't you push, Briquet, you're as clumsy as a rhinoceros! That's right, that's right! (*Supporting* ZINIDA, *they slowly escort her to the exit—* MANCINI *and* BRIQUET. CONSUELO, *her chin resting on her hand in an involuntarily arty pose, looks after them.*)

MANCINI (*turning around*). I'll come back for you, my child! (*Only* HE *and* CONSUELO *remain. In the arena there is music again, shouting, laughter.*)

HE. Consuelo!

CONSUELO. Is that you, dear HE?

HE. Where did you get such a pose? I've seen it only in marble. You look like Psyche.

CONSUELO. I don't know, HE. (*Sighs and sits down on the sofa, retaining in her pose the same artificiality and beauty.*) How sad it is here today, HE. Do you feel sorry for Zinida?

HE. What did she do?

CONSUELO. I didn't see. Once I shut my eyes I didn't open them again. Alfred says she's evil, but that's not true. Her eyes were so kind . . . but her little hands so cold! Like a dead person's. Why does she do this? Alfred says you have to be bold, beautiful and calm, but this is disgusting . . . what she does. Isn't that right, HE?

HE. She loves Alfred.

CONSUELO. Alfred? My Bezano? (*Shrugs her shoulders, surprised.*) How does she love him? The way everybody does?

HE. Yes, like that, the way everybody does. Or even more.

CONSUELO. Bezano, Bezano . . . No, that's absurd!

(*Silence.*)

What a lovely costume you have, HE! Did you think it up yourself?

HE. Jim helped me.

CONSUELO. Jim's so kind. All clowns are.

HE. I'm wicked.

CONSUELO (*laughing*). You? You're the kindest of all! Oh, God! two whole parts more. It's the second now, and Alfred and I are in the third. Will you watch me?

HE. I always watch you, my beauty. How beautiful you are, Consuelo!

CONSUELO. Like Eve? (*Smiles.*)

HE. Yes. Consuelo! If the Baron asks you to marry him, will you?

CONSUELO. Of course, HE! That's all Papa and I are waiting for. Yesterday Papa said he couldn't wait much longer. I don't love him, of course, but I'll be his true and faithful wife. Papa wants to teach me how to play the piano.

HE. Are those your words about the "true and faithful wife"?

CONSUELO. Mine; why, who else's? He loves me so, poor man. HE, what is love? Everybody says: love, love . . . Take Zinida, the poor thing. And what a dull evening this is! HE, did you draw the laugh on your face yourself?

HE. Myself, little Consuelo.

CONSUELO. Where did you learn how? Once I tried to draw my own, but nothing came out. Why aren't women clowns? But you're not saying anything, HE; even you are dull today!

HE. No. Today I'm happy. Give me your hand, Consuelo, I want to tell your fortune.

CONSUELO. But do you know how? How clever you are! There. Only don't lie, like a gypsy.

(HE *has fallen on one knee and taken her hand. Both, bent over, study it.*)

Am I lucky?

HE. Yes, lucky. But wait a minute . . . this line . . . that's strange. Ah, Consuelo, the things that are said here! (*Acts.*) I shudder, my eyes can hardly dare make out these strange letters, these fatal signs . . . Consuelo!

CONSUELO. Is that what the stars say?

HE. That's what they say. Their voice is remote and terrible; their rays are pale and their shadows slide by like the ghosts of dead maidens. Their spell is on you. Consuelo, beautiful Consuelo, you stand at the gates of Eternity!

CONSUELO. I don't understand. Will I live long?

HE. This line . . . how far it goes. That's what's strange! You'll live forever, Consuelo!

CONSUELO. There, HE, now you've lied, just like a gypsy!

HE. But that's the way it's traced here, silly! But here . . . No, think only what the stars say. Here you have everlasting life, love and fame, though here . . . Listen to what Jupiter says. He says: Goddess, you must not belong to a son of earth! And if you—think of marrying the Baron—you'll perish—you'll die, Consuelo!

CONSUELO (*laughing*). Will he eat me?

HE. No. You'll die before he can.

CONSUELO. And what will Papa do then? Isn't that said there, HE? (*Laughing, she softly sings a waltz motif, repeating the far-off and quiet sounds of the orchestra.*)

HE. Don't make fun of the voice of the stars, Consuelo! They're far away, their rays are pale and soft, and their shadows slide by almost unnoticed, but their spell is dark and terrible. You're at the gates of Eternity, Consuelo. Your fate is laid out ahead of time; you're predestined. And your Alfred, whom your heart loves and your mind doesn't know—your Alfred won't save you. He himself is an alien on earth. He himself is deep in a dark dream. He himself is an errant god who never, never, Consuelo, will find the road to heaven. Forget Bezano!

CONSUELO. I don't understand a thing! Do gods really exist? The teacher used to tell me they did, but I thought it was all a fairy tale. (*Laughs.*) And my Bezano is a god?

HE. Forget Bezano! Consuelo, you know who can save you? The only one who can save you? Me!

CONSUELO (*laughing*). You, HE?

HE. Yes, don't laugh! Look: you see the letter H here? That's me, now, yes, me: HE.

CONSUELO. HE Who Gets Slapped? And is that there, too?

HE. And that's there, too; the stars know everything. But look what's said about him farther on! Consuelo, welcome him! HE—he's an old god in new clothing who came down to earth for love of you. Of you, silly Consuelo!

CONSUELO (*laughing and humming*). A fine god!

HE. Don't laugh! The gods don't like empty laughter, when the lips are beautiful. And gods languish and die when they aren't recognized. Oh, Consuelo, oh great joy and love, recognize the god and take him! Think: suddenly, just once a god has gone out of his mind!

CONSUELO. Do gods, also, go out of their minds?

HE. Yes—when they are half man. Then they often go out of their minds. He suddenly saw his own grandeur—and he shuddered in horror from infinite loneliness, from superhuman melancholy. It's horrible when melancholy touches a god's soul!

CONSUELO. I don't like this. What language are you talking? I don't understand you.

HE. The language of your awakening! Consuelo, recognize and accept a god thrown down from on high, like a stone! Accept a god descended to your hand to live, to act his part, to be endlessly and joyfully drunk! Behold him, goddess!

CONSUELO (*suffering*). I don't understand, HE! Don't touch my hand.

HE (*gets up*). Go to sleep—and awake anew, Consuelo! And once awake, remember the time you rose from the azure sea with the sea's foam! Remember that sky—and the soft east wind—and the murmuring of the foam at your marble feet.

CONSUELO (*her eyes shut*). I think . . . wait . . . I'm remembering something. Remind me more.

HE (*bent over* CONSUELO, *his arms raised, speaks softly but imperatively, as if invoking*). You see how the waves play? Remember what the Sirens then were singing—remember their world of unclouded joy, their white bodies half blue in the blue water . . . Or is it the sun singing? Like the strings of a divine harp, the golden rays stretch out—don't you see the hand of God giving the world harmony, light and love? Aren't the mountains blue with smoke, endlessly praising him? Remember the prayer of the mountains, remember the prayer of the sea, Consuelo!

(*Silence.*)

(*Imperatively.*) Remember now, Consuelo!

CONSUELO (*opening her eyes*). No! Ah, HE, it was so nice . . . and now suddenly I've forgotten everything. But in my heart there's still something . . . Help me, HE! Remind me! It's painful for me. I hear a lot of voices and they're all singing "Consuelo! Consuelo!" But what's next?

(*Silence.*)

But what's next? . . . It's painful for me. Remind me, HE! (*Silence. Outside, in the arena, the music suddenly bursts out in a wild circus gallop. Silence.*)

HE . . . (*Opens her eyes and smiles.*) That's Alfred galloping. Do you recognize his music?

HE (*angrily*). Pay no attention to the boy! (*Suddenly falls on his knees in front of* CONSUELO.) I love you—Consuelo! My heart's discovery, the light of my nights—I love you, Consuelo! (*Looks at her in ecstasy and tears—and gets a slap in the face. Stumbling back*). What's that!

CONSUELO. A slap in the face! Did you forget who you are? (*With angry eyes, rising.*) You're HE Who Gets Slapped. You forgot? A fine god who has such a mug—a beaten-up mug! You didn't get driven out of heaven by slaps in the face, did you, god?

HE. Wait, don't get up. I . . . I haven't finished playing my role yet!

CONSUELO (*sitting down*). Oh, you're just playing?

HE. Wait! Just a minute! Consuelo!

CONSUELO. You tricked me. Why did you play so that I'd believe you?

HE. I'm HE Who Gets Slapped.

CONSUELO. You're not angry that I hit you? I didn't mean to. But you were so disgusting! But now you're funny HE again. How talented you are! Or are you drunk?

HE. Hit me again.

CONSUELO. No!

HE. It's necessary for my role. Hit me!

CONSUELO (*laughing, touches his cheek with the tips of her fingers*). There you are!

HE. Didn't you understand that you're the Queen and I'm the court fool who's in love with the Queen? Consuelo!—or don't you know that every queen has a fool and he's always in love with her and everybody beats him for that? HE Who Gets Slapped.

CONSUELO. No, I didn't know.

HE. Every queen has! There's one for beauty, there's one for wisdom—oh, how many fools she has! Her court is filled with fools in love, and the sound of the slaps doesn't stop even at night. But I've never gotten such a good slap in the face as the one from you, my little Queen!

(*Footsteps; someone appears at the door.* HE *notices, and goes on with his acting, making faces all the more.*)

There can be no rivals to HE, the clown! Who could withstand such a hail of slaps in the face, such a cats-and-dogs rain, without getting wet? I adore you, beauty incomparable! (*Weeps feignedly loud.*) Have pity on me, a poor fool! (*Two people come in: a performer dressed as a horseback rider and some gentleman from the audience. Very courteous, reserved, in black, his hat in his hand.*)

CONSUELO (*laughing, confused*). Somebody has come, HE. Stop now!

HE (*rising*). Who? Who has dared burst into the chambers of my queen?

(*Suddenly falls silent.* CONSUELO, *laughing, jumps up and runs out, casting a quick glance at the gentleman.*)

CONSUELO. You've cheered me up, HE. Good-bye! (*From the door.*) Tomorrow you'll get a little note.

HORSEBACK RIDER (*laughing*). A merry fellow, sir. Did you happen to see him? Here he is. HE, the gentleman wishes to see you.

HE (*dully*). What can I do for you?

(*The rider, smiling and having bowed, goes out. The two take a step toward each other.*)

GENTLEMAN. Is that . . . you?

HE. Yes, it's me. And it's . . . you?

(*Silence.*)

GENTLEMAN. Can I believe my eyes? So that's you . . .

HE (*angrily*). Here I'm called HE! I have no other name, you hear! HE Who Gets Slapped. And if you[3] intend to remain, please take note of it!

GENTLEMAN. *You?* But as far as I remember . . .

HE. Here everybody is addressed in the singular, and you . . . (*scornfully*) you're not worthy of anything better anyplace!

GENTLEMAN (*humbly*). You haven't forgiven me . . . HE?
(*Silence.*)

HE. Are you here with my wife? Is she in the circus?

GENTLEMAN (*hastily*). Oh, no. I'm alone. She stayed there.

HE. You haven't dropped her?

GENTLEMAN (*humbly*). No. We have . . . a son. When you so unexpectedly and mysteriously disappeared, leaving that strange and . . . insulting letter . . .

HE (*laughing*). Insulting? Can you still be insulted? Why are you here? Did you look for me, or was it just by chance?

GENTLEMAN. I've been looking for you for half a year in every country. And suddenly today, absolutely by chance . . . I know nobody here, and I went to the circus . . . We must talk things out . . . HE! I beg you!
(*Silence.*)

HE. That's the shadow I can't shake off! Talk things out—you suggest we still have to talk things out? All right. Leave your address with the doorman, I'll let you know when you can see me. But now—get out. (*Arrogantly.*) I'm busy!

(*Having bowed, the* GENTLEMAN *goes out.* HE, *not having answered the bow, stands with his hand outstretched like a great noble who has just shown out a tiresome petitioner.*)

(*Curtain*)

[3] *He* uses the second person singular; the Gentleman keeps to the polite form.

ACT III

The setting is the same. Morning, before rehearsal begins. HE, *lost in thought, paces the room in big steps. He is wearing a wide, colorful plaid jacket, has a gay necktie on; his bowler is on the back of his head. His bumpy face is smooth-shaven, like an actor's. His brows are blackened, his lips tightly drawn—a harsh and morose expression. With the* GENTLEMAN'S *arrival his expression changes; his face becomes clownishly mobile, like a living mask.*

The GENTLEMAN *appears in the doorway. He is dressed in black, completely proper, and his thin face is shot through with sickly yellow. In moments of excitement he often blinks his dull, colorless eyes.* HE *does not notice him.*

GENTLEMAN. Good morning, sir.

HE (*turning around and peering absent-mindedly*). Ah—it's you!

GENTLEMAN. I'm not late? . . . But you look as if you hadn't expected me. I'm not interfering? You yourself, though, set this time, and so I took it upon myself . . .

HE. Never mind the formalities! What do you want from me? Out with it; I've no time to waste.

GENTLEMAN (*looking around squeamishly*). I assumed that you would invite me to go someplace else—to your house . . .

HE. I have no other place. This is my home.

GENTLEMAN. But we can be interrupted here.

HE. So much the worse for you: speak to the point.

(*Silence.*)

GENTLEMAN. May I sit down?

HE. Do. Careful, that chair is broken!

(*The* GENTLEMAN *pushes the chair away in fright and helplessly looks around: everything here seems dangerous and strange to him. He chooses a seemingly sturdy little gilt sofa and sits down, sets his top hat down, slowly pulls off his tight-fitting gloves.* HE *watches him indifferently.*)

GENTLEMAN. With that costume and that face you make an

even stranger impression. If yesterday this all seemed only
a dream, today you . . .

HE. You've forgotten my name? I'm called HE.

GENTLEMAN. You absolutely insist on speaking to me so—
familiarly?[4]

HE. Absolutely. But you're squandering time like a millionaire. Hurry up!

GENTLEMAN. Really, I don't know . . . Everything here amazes me so—these posters, the horses and the animals I walked past looking for you—and finally, you! A clown in a circus! (*Politely smiles a little.*) Could I have expected it? True, when everybody there decided you were dead, I alone protested; I felt that you were still alive. But to find you in such circumstances—that's beyond my understanding!

HE. You said you had a son. He doesn't look like me?

GENTLEMAN. I don't understand!

HE. But don't you know that widows or divorced women often have children by their new husband who look like the old one? You've never had such a piece of bad luck? (*Laughs.*) And your book, too, is successful, I've heard?

GENTLEMAN. You want to insult me again?

HE (*laughing*). What a touchy and uneasy swindler! Sit back, don't worry—that's the way people talk here. Why were you looking for me?

GENTLEMAN. My conscience . . .

HE. You have none. Or else you were worried you hadn't robbed me completely and came for the rest? But what else can you take from me? My fool's cap with its rattles? You'll never take that: it's too big for your bald head! Crawl back where you came from, you bookworm.

GENTLEMAN. You can't forgive the fact that your wife . . .

HE. The hell with my wife!

(*The* GENTLEMAN *is astounded and raises his eyebrows.* HE *laughs.*)

GENTLEMAN. Really, I don't know . . . But what language! I'm really having a hard time of it trying to express my ideas—in this atmosphere. But if you're so—indifferent to

[4] *He* addresses the Gentleman in the familiar singular; the Gentleman uses the formal plural.

your wife, who—let me emphasize this—once loved you and considered you a saintly man . . . (HE *laughs*.) then what led you to such a . . . a step as this? Or can't you forgive me my success? To be sure, not wholly deserved. And by your humiliation you seem to take revenge on me and the others who don't understand you. But you were always so indifferent to fame! Or else your indifference was simply a mask, and when a more fortunate rival . . .

HE (*bursts out laughing*). Rival! You—my rival?

GENTLEMAN (*paling*). But my book!

HE. You can talk about your book? To me?

(*The* GENTLEMAN *blanches.* HE *looks at him with curiosity and a slightly sardonic smile.*)

GENTLEMAN (*raising his eyes.*) I'm a very—unhappy—man.

HE. Why?

GENTLEMAN. I'm a very unhappy man. You must forgive me. I'm deeply—I'm incorrigibly and infinitely unhappy.

HE. But after all, why? Tell me. (*Walks up and down.*) You yourself said your book's having a stunning success, you're praised, you're famous. There's isn't a cheap newspaper which doesn't use your name—and your ideas. Who knew me? Who had any use for my ponderous nonsense in which you couldn't discover any meaning? You—you great defiler —you made my ideas accessible even to horses! With all the art of a great profaner, a costumer of ideas, you set my Apollo out as a hairdresser, turned my Venus into a whore, pinned donkey ears on my bright hero—and your career was made, as Jackson says. Wherever I go, the whole street grins at me with a thousand ugly mugs in which—oh, the mockery of it all!—I recognize the features of my own children. Oh, how hideous your son must be who looks like me! So why are you miserable—you miserable wretch?

(*The* GENTLEMAN *lowers his head, pulling at his gloves.*) Because the police haven't caught you yet, have they? What am I babbling on about? Can you be caught at all? You're always within the law. And you're still tormented by the fact that you aren't married to my wife: your thefts are always witnessed by some notary. Why torture yourself, my friend? Get married! I'm dead. Or isn't my wife enough for you? Take my fame, also—it's yours! Take my ideas!

Exercise your rights, legal heir! I'm dead! And dying (*makes a stupidly reverential face*) forgave you. (*Bursts out laughing.*)

(*The* GENTLEMAN *raises his head and, bending forward, fixes his dulled glance straight on* HE'S *eyes.*)

GENTLEMAN. But pride?

HE. You're—proud?

(*The* GENTLEMAN *straightens up and silently nods.*)

Now really! And please move back; I find this unpleasant. And to think that once I somewhat liked you and even thought you talented! You—my pancake-flat shadow!

GENTLEMAN (*nodding*). I am your shadow.

(HE *paces the room and, smiling, looks at the* GENTLEMAN *over his shoulder.*)

HE. No—you're enchanting. But what a farce! What a heart-rending farce! Listen, tell me straightforwardly and frankly, if you can: do you genuinely hate me?

GENTLEMAN. Yes. With all the hatred there is on earth. Sit here.

HE. Are you ordering me?

GENTLEMAN. Sit here. Thank you. (*Bending over.*) I'm respected, and I have fame—right? I have a wife and son—right? (*Laughs quietly.*) But my wife loves you: our favorite conversation is about your genius. She thinks you're a genius. She and I love you even in bed. Shh! I have to be devious about it. My son—yes, he'll be like you. And when I go to my desk, to get away from everything that isn't mine, to my inkwell, to my books—there, too, I run up against you. Always you, everywhere you—I'm never alone, never myself and alone. And when at night—understand this, sir!—I retreat to my lonely thoughts, to my sleepless night's reflections—there, too, in my head, in my wretched brain I find your image—your damned, your hateful image!

(*Silence. The* GENTLEMAN *leans back and blinks.*)

HE (*mumbling*). What a farce the way everything's marvellously turned upside-down in this world: the robbed turns out to be the robber; the robber complains of thievery, and curses! (*Laughs.*) Listen: you're not my shadow, I was wrong. You're a crowd. Living my life, you hate me. Breathing the air I breathe, you're being suffocated by spite. And suffocating from spite, hating me and loathing me, you drag yourself along on the tail end of my ideas. But backwards! Backwards, old friend! Oh, what a wonderful farce! (*Walks back and forth, smiling. Silence.*) Listen: wouldn't it be easier for you if I . . . really died?

GENTLEMAN. Yes. I think so. Death effects a separation and dulls the memory. Death . . . reconciles. But you don't look like a man who . . .

HE. Yes, yes . . . Death! Of course!

GENTLEMAN. Sit here.

HE. I'm listening. Well?

GENTLEMAN. Of course, I dare not ask you . . . (*Twists his mouth.*) ask you to die, but tell me: you're never going to go back there? No, don't laugh. I'll kiss your hand if you want me to. No, you needn't make a face. Would I have kissed your hand, now, if it had been . . . dead?

HE (*softly*). Get away—you toad!

(TILI *and* POLI *come in with little steps, playing, as in the first scene, and for long do not notice the two in conversation.*)

HE. Jacques!

TILI. Oh, hello, HE. We're studying. You know, it's very hard; Jacques has as much music in him as my pig.

HE (*casually*). This is my friend . . . For the benefit performance?

(*The clowns, in greeting, make an idiotic face.*)

POLI. Yes. What are you working up? You're a sly one, HE. Consuelo said that you were getting something ready for her benefit. She's leaving soon, did you know that?

HE. Really?

TILI. Zinida said so. Or else would they be giving her a benefit? But she's a fine girl.

POLI (*taking his flute*). Well? And don't walk like that—as if you were an elephant. You're an ant! Well? (*Playing, they go out.*)

GENTLEMAN (*smiling*). Those your new friends? How strange they are!

HE. Everything's strange here.

GENTLEMAN. This costume of yours—black used to suit you so—it dazzles the eyes.

HE (*looking himself over*). No, it's handsome. The rehearsal has begun, you'll have to go. You're in the way.

GENTLEMAN. But you didn't answer my question!

(*In the arena: the soft sounds of a tango from a little orchestra.*)

HE (*listening to the music, absent-mindedly*). Which one?

GENTLEMAN (*not hearing the music*). I beg you to tell me: will you ever go back there or not?

HE (*listening to the music*). Never . . . never, never.

GENTLEMAN (*getting up*). Thank you, I'm going now.

HE. Never, never, never . . . Yes, go on—and don't come back. There, you were at least bearable and useful for something, but here you're superfluous.

GENTLEMAN. But if something happens to you? You're a healthy man, but the surroundings are such here, the people . . . How will I find out? No one here knows your name?

HE. No one here knows my name, but you'll find out. Well, anything else?

GENTLEMAN. I may rest assured? You give me your word of honor? Of course—relatively assured.

HE. Yes, you may be relatively assured. Never! (*They go toward the door. The* GENTLEMAN *stops.*)

GENTLEMAN. And may I come to the circus? Will you let me?

HE. Of course! Why, you're part of the audience! (*Laughs.*) But I won't give you a pass. But why should you come here? Do you like the circus that much? Since when?

GENTLEMAN. I'd like to watch you some more and, perhaps, understand . . . What a metamorphosis! Knowing you, I can't imagine that here, too, you aren't working out some idea. But what? (*Peers at* HE *closely.* HE *makes a face and in clownish fashion pulls a long nose.*) What's that?

HE. My idea! I have the honor of paying you my respects, Prince! My regards to your noble spouse and to Your Excellency's cha-arming son!

(MANCINI *enters.*)

MANCINI. You really live in the circus, HE. No matter when I come, you're always here. He's a fanatic in his work, sir.

HE (*introducing them*). Prince Poniatowski! Count Mancini!

MANCINI (*primping himself*). Very, very pleased. You, too, Prince, know my odd friend? What a great face! Isn't that true? (*Patronizingly touches* HE's *shoulder with his cane.*)

GENTLEMAN (*awkwardly*). Yes, I have had the pleasure, since . . . I have the honor, Count . . .

MANCINI. The honor is mine, Prince.

HE (*showing him out*). Be careful, Your Excellency, in the dark passageways: there are sudden steps here. Unfortunately, it's not possible for me to escort you to the street myself . . .

GENTLEMAN (*stopping, softly*). You won't shake my hand in farewell? We're parting forever.

HE. Unnecessary, Prince. I still have hope of meeting you in the Kingdom of Heaven. You'll be there, too, won't you?

GENTLEMAN (*squeamishly*). When did you manage it all? There's so much of the clown in you.

HE. I'm HE Who Gets Slapped. Good-bye, Prince! (*They take one more step.*)

GENTLEMAN (*pensively staring into* HE'S *eyes; in a very soft voice*). You—haven't gone mad?

HE (*just as softly, opening his eyes wide*). I'm afraid . . . I'm afraid you're right, Prince. (*Still more softly.*) Ass! You've never expressed yourself so accurately: I've gone mad! (*Miming, he outlines a flight of steps—from his head to the floor. Laughing.*) Gone mad! Prince—good-bye!

(*The* GENTLEMAN *goes out.* HE, *coming back, does a* pas *and spins into a pose.*)

HE. Mancini, let's dance a tango! Mancini, I worship you!

MANCINI (*sitting down, relaxed, and playing with his cane*). Now there, don't forget yourself, HE. But you're hiding something, you lunkhead. I always said you came from the world of society. It's so easy with you! who's this Prince of yours—a real one?

HE. Real to the highest degree. Just like you!

MANCINI. A likeable face, though for some reason I immediately took him for a gravedigger come to take an order. Oh, HE! When will I finally part with these dirty walls, with Papa Briquet, with the stupid posters, the vulgar riders!

HE. Soon now, Mancini.

MANCINI. Yes, soon now. Oh, HE—I'm simply worn out in this environment. I'm beginning to feel like a horse. You're from the world of society, but you still don't know what high society is! At last, to dress properly, to attend receptions, to make a brilliant display of wit, once in a while play a little baccarat (*Laughs.*) without resorting to magic tricks and juggling . . .

HE. And in the evening make your way to the suburbs where you're thought of as an honest papa who loves little children, and . . .

MANCINI. And hook something, right! (*Laughs.*) I'll wear a silk mask, and two footmen will walk along behind me so this foul mob doesn't insult me. Oh, HE, the blood of my ancestors seethes in me! Take a look at this stiletto. What do you think, was it ever bloodied?

HE. You frighten me, Count!

MANCINI (*laughing and sheathing the stiletto*). Lunkhead!

HE. How are things with the girl?

MANCINI. Shh! The bourgeois are completely satisfied and sing praises to my name. (*Laughs.*) In general, the luster of my name burns with unparalleled vigor! By the way, you don't happen to know which automobile company is considered the best? Money is no object. (*Laughs.*) Ah, Papa Briquet!

(BRIQUET *comes in, dressed in his coat and top hat. They exchange greetings.*)

BRIQUET. Well, now, so you've gotten a benefit for your Consuelo, Mancini! By the way, let me tell you that if it hadn't been for Zinida . . .

MANCINI. Now listen, Briquet, you're an absolute ass. What are you complaining for? For Consuelo's benefit performance the Baron's taking the whole parquet; isn't that enough for you, you tightwad?

BRIQUET. I love your daughter, Mancini, and I'm sorry to let her go. What doesn't she have here? Honest work, great friends—and the atmosphere?

MANCINI. It's not what she doesn't have, it's what I don't— understand? (*Laughs.*) I asked you, Harpagon, to add something on, but now—will you change a thousand francs for me, Mr. Manager?

BRIQUET (*with a sigh*). Hand it over.

MANCINI (*casually*). Tomorrow. I left it home. (*All three laugh.*) Laugh, laugh! But today we're going with the

Baron to his villa in the suburbs. They say it's not a bad one . . .

HE. What for?

MANCINI. Well, you know the whims of these millionaires, HE. Wants to show Consuelo some sort of winter roses, and me, his cellar. He's coming for us here . . . What's the matter, little Consuelo?

(CONSUELO *comes in, almost in tears.*)

CONSUELO. I can't, Papa, you tell him! What right has he to shout at me? He just about hit me with his whip.

MANCINI (*straightening up*). Briquet! I ask you, as the Manager, what sort of a stable is this? Hit my daughter—with a whip? I'll give it to that boy! A nobody jockey—no, God knows what this is! God knows what this is, I swear!

CONSUELO. Papa . . .

BRIQUET. Yes, I'll tell . . .

CONSUELO. No, don't! Alfred didn't hit me at all, it was stupid of me. What have you made up now? He himself is so sorry . . .

BRIQUET. Still, I'll tell him, that . . . .

CONSUELO. Don't you dare! You don't have to say anything. He did nothing!

MANCINI (*still more angry*). He has to say he's sorry, that boy.

CONSUELO. Oh, but he did. How stupid you all are! I just can't get it right today; I got all upset; it's nothing. He excused himself so, silly fool, and I didn't want to forgive him. Hello, HE, dear; I didn't notice you. How well that tie suits you. Where you going, Briquet? To Alfred?

BRIQUET. No; on my way. I'm going home. Zinida asked me to say hello to you for her. She won't be in today, either. (*Goes out.*)

CONSUELO. How dear Zinida is, how good! Papa, why does everybody here seem so dear to me now? I suppose because I'll soon be leaving. HE, you didn't happen to hear the march Tili and Poli are going to play? (*Laughs.*) It's so gay.

HE. Yes, I heard it. Your benefit will be wonderful.

CONSUELO. I think so, too, myself. Papa, I want to eat something. Get me a sandwich.

HE. I'll go, my Queen!

CONSUELO. Run, HE. (*Shouts.*) Only no cheese.

(MANCINI *and* CONSUELO *alone.* MANCINI, *spread out in an armchair, looks his daughter over critically.*)

MANCINI. There's something special about you today, my child. I don't know whether it's good or bad. You were crying?

CONSUELO. Yes, a little. Oh, how I want to eat something!

MANCINI. But you had breakfast . . .

CONSUELO. Actually, no. Today again you forgot to leave any money, and without money . . .

MANCINI. Oh, God damn it! What a memory! (*Laughs.*) But we're going to have a good meal today; don't fill yourself up on sandwiches. No, I really do like you. You ought to cry more often, my child, it washes away your superfluous naïveté; makes you more of a woman.

CONSUELO. Am I so naïve, Papa?

MANCINI. Very! Too much so! I like it in others, but in you . . . and besides, the Baron . . .

CONSUELO. Nonsense. I'm not naïve. But you know, Bezano swore at me so, why even you would have cried. God knows what all!

MANCINI. Shh! Never say "God knows what all." It's indecent.

CONSUELO. I'm only talking to you.

MANCINI. Even when you're talking to me, you shouldn't— I know anyway. (*Laughs.*)

(*Sounds of unusually wild and headlong circus gallop, sharp shouts, the cracking of a whip.*)

CONSUELO. Oh, listen, Papa! That's Alfred's new number. He makes such a jump! Jim says that he'll definitely break his neck. Poor dear!

MANCINI (*indifferently*). Or legs or back—they all break something. (*Laughs.*) Fragile toys!

CONSUELO (*listening to the music*). I'll be sad without them. Papa, the Baron promised to make me a ring which I can gallop around as much as I want . . . He's not lying?

MANCINI. A ring? (*Laughs.*) No, he's not lying! By the way, my child, about barons you say, "He's not telling the truth" and not, "He's lying."

CONSUELO. It's all the same. It's good to be rich, Papa; you can do everything.

MANCINI (*excitedly*). Everything! Everything, my child! Ah, today our fate is decided; pray to the God of mercy, Consuelo: the Baron hangs by a thread.

CONSUELO (*indifferently*). Really?

MANCINI (*gesturing with his fingers*). By the finest silk thread. I'm practically convinced that he'll propose today. (*Laughs.*) Winter roses and a spider web among the roses so that my little bug . . . He's such a spider!

CONSUELO (*indifferently*). Yes, a terrible spider. Papa, I still shouldn't let him kiss my hand?

MANCINI. Under no conditions. You don't know these men yet, my child.

CONSUELO. Alfred never kisses.

MANCINI. Alfred! Your Alfred is a boy and doesn't dare. But these men—extreme restraint is essential with them, my child. Today he'll kiss your little fingers; tomorrow, your wrist; and the day after, you'll be in his lap!

CONSUELO. Phew, Papa, what you're saying! You ought to be ashamed!

MANCINI. But I know . . .

CONSUELO. Don't you dare! I don't want to hear such stuff! I'll give the Baron such a slap in the face—worse than HE gets. Just let him try.

MANCINI (*grievously throwing up his hands*). But all men are like that, my child.

CONSUELO. That's not true. Alfred's not! Oh, but where's HE? He said he'd run, but he still isn't back.

MANCINI. The buffet is closed, and he *had* to get it. Consuelo, as your father, I want to warn you again about HE: don't trust him. There's something about him, you know . . . (*Makes circles with his fingers near his head.*) He doesn't act straight!

CONSUELO. You say that about everybody. I know HE: he's so sweet and he loves me!

MANCINI. Believe me: there's something about him.

CONSUELO. Papa, I'm fed up with your advice! Ah, HE, *merci.*

HE (*somewhat out of breath, hands her the sandwiches*). Eat, Consuelo.

CONSUELO. It's still warm—you ran all the way, HE? Thank you so much! (*Eats.*) HE, do you love me?

HE. I do, my Queen. I'm your court fool.

CONSUELO (*eating*). But when I leave, will you get yourself another queen?

HE (*bowing low*). I'll follow you, my incomparable one. I'll carry your white train and wipe away my tears with it. (*Pretends to cry.*)

MANCINI. Lunkhead! (*Laughs.*) But how sad, HE, that gone are those marvellous times when dozens of motley fools would show their tricks in the Mancini court, and get money sometimes, and sometimes kicked. Now Mancini must go to a filthy circus to see a proper fool; and besides—whose is he? Mine? Not at all; anybody's who pays a franc. With all this democracy we soon won't be able to breathe, HE. It, too, needs fools. Just think, HE, what unprecedented impudence!

HE. We serve who pays, what can you do, Count?

MANCINI. But isn't it saddening? But now you just imagine: we're sitting in my castle, I'm sipping wine by the fireplace, and at my feet you're babbling your nonsense, ringing your little bells and amusing me. You even nettle me a little once in a while; that's sanctioned by tradition and essential for the circulation of the blood. Then afterward I get tired of you, I want the next—and so I give you a kick . . . HE, how splendid that would be!

HE. It would be divine, Mancini!

MANCINI. Indeed! And you would be getting gold, those enchanting little yellow pieces. Yes, when I get rich I'll hire you—that's decided.

CONSUELO. Do, Papa.

HE. And when the Count, wearied by my idle chatter, gives me a kick with his noble foot, I'll lie at the feet of my Queen and . . .

CONSUELO (*laughing*). Wait for the same? Well, I've finished. Give me a handkerchief, Papa, to wipe my hands; you have another one in your other pocket. Oh, Lord, I still have to work!

MANCINI (*anxiously*). But don't forget, my child!

CONSUELO. No, today I won't. You go ahead.

MANCINI (*looking at his watch*). Yes, it's already time. He asked me to call for him when you're ready. Before I get back

... you still have to dress. (*Laughs.*) *Signori! Miei complimenti!*

(*Flourishing his cane, he goes off.* CONSUELO *sits down in a corner of the sofa, wrapped in her shawl.*)

CONSUELO. Well, HE, lie down at my feet and tell me something silly. You know, you're handsomer when your laugh is painted on, but even just as you are you're very, very dear! So—HE? Why don't you lie down?

HE. Consuelo! Are you going to marry the Baron?

CONSUELO (*indifferently*). I think so. The Baron hangs by a thread. HE, there's one sandwich left in the paper there; eat it.

HE. Thank you, my Queen. (*Eats.*) You remember my prediction?

CONSUELO. Which? How quickly you swallow it! Well, was it good?

HE. It was. That if you marry the Baron, then ...

CONSUELO. Oh, that! But you were just joking then, weren't you?

HE. Who knows, my Queen? Sometimes a man jokes, and suddenly it turns out he's been telling the truth: the stars don't ever speak pointlessly. If it's hard even for a man sometimes to open his mouth and get a word out, think what it's like for a star!

CONSUELO (*Laughs.*) I should think so—what a mouth!

HE. No, little one, if I were you I'd think it over deeply. You might suddenly die! Don't marry the Baron, Consuelo!

CONSUELO (*thinking*). What is it—death?

HE. I don't know, my Queen; nobody does. The same as love! But your little hands will go cold and your eyes will close. You'll leave here—and the music will play without you, and wild Bezano will gallop around without you, and Tili and Poli will play on their little flutes without you: tili-tili poli-poli ...

CONSUELO. Don't! I'm sad enough anyway, HE dear. Tili-tili, poli-poli ...

(*Silence.* HE *looks at* CONSUELO *closely.*)

HE. You were crying, little Consuelo?

CONSUELO. Yes, a little; Alfred upset me. But really is it my fault that I can't get anything right today? I was trying, but if I just can't!

HE. Why not?

CONSUELO. I don't know. I feel something here (*puts her hand on her heart*) I don't know. I suppose I'm sick, HE. What is sickness? Is it very painful?

HE. It's not sickness. It's the enchantment of the far-away stars, Consuelo! It's the voice of your fate, my sweet little Queen!

CONSUELO. Don't talk nonsense, please. What have the stars to do with me? I'm so tiny. That's nonsense, HE! Tell me instead some other story you know: about the deep, blue sea and those gods—you know?—who are so beautiful. Have they all died already?

HE. They're alive, but they keep in hiding, goddess.

CONSUELO. In the woods and the mountains? Can you run into them? Ah, HE, just think: suddenly I'd run into a god and he'd look at me! I'd run away. (*Laughs.*) And this morning, when there was no breakfast, suddenly I was so depressed, everything was so loathsome, I thought: if only a god would come and feed me! And just as soon as the thought crossed my mind, I suddenly heard . . . word of honor, honestly! I heard, "Consuelo." Someone was calling. (*Angrily.*) Please don't laugh!

HE. But am I?

CONSUELO. Word of honor, honestly. Oh, HE, but he didn't come, you know. He just called me and then hid; try and find him! But it became so painful for me, and it still hurts right to this minute. Why did you remind me of my childhood? I had forgotten it completely. There, there was the sea . . . and something else . . . a lot, a lot . . . (*Closes her eyes, smiles.*)

HE. Remember it, Consuelo!

CONSUELO. No. (*Opening her eyes.*) I've forgotten it all! (*Glances around the room.*) HE, you see the kind of poster that will be up for my benefit performance? Papa thought it up himself, and the Baron likes it; he laughed.
(*Silence.*)

HE (*softly*). Consuelo, my Queen! Don't go to the Baron's today!

CONSUELO. Why not? (*After a pause.*) How impudent you are, though, HE.

HE (*lowering his head; softly*). I don't want you to.

CONSUELO (*rising*). What's this? You don't want me to!

HE (*putting his head farther down*). I don't want you to marry the Baron. (*Imploring.*) I . . . won't let you . . . I . . . beg you!

CONSUELO. Who, then, would you have me marry? Not yourself, surely, you court fool? (*Laughs maliciously.*) Have you gone crazy, honey? I won't let you . . . That's what he said! He won't let me! No, this is simply intolerable! What have you to do with me? (*Paces the room, looking angrily over her shoulder at* HE.) A fool, a clown who'll be turned out of here tomorrow! I'm fed up with all your idiotic stories. Or do you so like to be slapped in the face? An idiot who couldn't think up anything better—slaps in the face!

HE (*without looking up*). Forgive me, my Queen.

CONSUELO. Delighted when people laugh at him . . . A god, too! No, I won't forgive you. I know you: up here (*pointing to her head*) you've got something going on! He laughs . . . so sweet . . . keeps playing away, and then suddenly, plop! He says: do what he says! You got your fingers burned, honey, didn't pick the right girl! Here, carry my train, that's your job . . . fool!

HE. I'll carry your train, my Queen. Forgive me; let me again see the image of my gracious and beautiful goddess.

CONSUELO (*calming down*). You're playing again?

HE. I am.

CONSUELO. There, you see! (*Laughing, sits down.*) Silly HE.

HE. I see everything, my Queen. I see how beautiful you are— and I see how low your poor fool lies beneath your feet. His foolish little bells tinkle somewhere in an abyss. On his knees he begs that you forgive him and have pity on him, divine lady. He was too impudent and arrogant; he was playing so merrily, he overplayed—and lost his tiny bit of reason, his last little store of judgment. Forgive him!

CONSUELO. Well, I will. (*Laughs.*) And now will you let me marry the Baron?

HE (*also laughing*). But I still won't let you marry the Baron.

But what does it matter to the Queen whether or not she has the permission of the fool who is in love with her?

CONSUELO. Well, get up, you're forgiven. But do you know why? You think because of what you said? You're a tricky rascal, HE! No, because of the sandwiches, that's why! You were so sweet and so out of breath when you brought them—poor little HE. Starting tomorrow, you can lie at my feet again. Just as soon as I whistle for you: *ici* . . .

HE. Then I'll lie right down at your feet, Consuelo—it's decided. But today all my little bells have flown away and . . .

(BEZANO *enters, he is embarrassed.*)

CONSUELO. Alfred? You want me?

BEZANO. Yes. Are you going to work some more, Consuelo?

CONSUELO. Of course I am. As much as you want! But I thought that you were angry at me, Alfred. I'll pay attention now.

BEZANO. Oh, you did! Don't be offended that I shouted the way I did . . . really, I . . . But you know, when you have to teach something, and the person . . .

CONSUELO. Lord—do you think I don't understand! You're still too kind, unbearably kind, that you keep on agreeing to teach such a silly idiot as myself. Don't I know that? Let's go!

BEZANO. Let's! We haven't seen each other yet today, HE. Hello.

HE. Hello, Bezano. No, no, wait a minute, just a minute. Stay like that! Right.

(CONSUELO *and* BEZANO *stand side by side; the rider frowns,* CONSUELO *laughs and blushes.*)

BEZANO (*displeased*). What have you thought up now, HE?

CONSUELO (*blushing*). Like Adam and Eve? How silly you are. It's dreadful! (*Moves to go.*) I'll just change my shoes, Alfred . . .

HE. Consuelo, what about your father and the Baron? They'll be here for you in a minute.

CONSUELO. Well, let them. They can wait, they're not such big shots! (*Runs out.* BEZANO *hesitatingly follows her.*)

HE. Wait just a moment, Bezano. Sit down.

BEZANO. What more do you want? I've no time to fuss around with nonsense.

HE. Or stand up—as you like! Bezano, do you love her? (*Silence.*)

BEZANO. I don't let anybody interfere in my business. You go too far, HE. I don't know you; you came in off the street—and why should I trust you?

HE. And you think you know the Baron? Listen, it's hard for me to say this—but she loves you. Save her from the spider! Or are you blind and don't see the webs woven here in all the dark corners? Break out of your enchanted circle in which you go rushing around like a blind man. Whisk her away, abduct her, do what you want . . . even kill her and take her to Heaven or to hell—but don't give her to that man! He's a profaner of love. And if you're timid, if you're terrified of laying a hand on her, then kill the Baron. Kill him!

BEZANO (*smiling*). And who will kill the others after him?

HE. She loves you!

BEZANO. She herself said so?

HE. What petty, foolish, human pride! And you a god—god, young man! Why don't you want to believe me? Or does the street I came in from put you off? But look at me yourself, look me in the eye: do eyes like these not tell the truth? Yes, my face is hideous, I grimace and make faces, and I'm surrounded by laughter—but don't you see behind it a god, just such as you are? Now look, look at me!

(BEZANO *bursts out laughing.*)

What are you doing—boy!

BEZANO. You . . . were just now exactly like in the arena . . . remember? When you're a great man and you're sent for from the Academy, whack! HE Who Gets Slapped.

HE (*also bursts out laughing*). Yes, yes—just like that, Bezano! Very much so! (*Plays with tormented tenseness, striking a pose.*) I think they've sent for me from the Academy?

BEZANO (*frowning*). But I don't like this playing. Stick your own face out, if you want to, but don't touch me. (*Goes to the door.*)

HE. Bezano! . . .

BEZANO (*turning around*). And don't let me ever hear about

Consuelo and about . . . my being a god, don't you dare! You know—it's disgusting! (*Goes out, angrily striking his riding-boots with his whip.*)

(HE *is alone. Angrily, with a distorted face, he takes a step after the rider, stops—and soundlessly laughs, his head thrown back.* MANCINI *and the* BARON *find him in that position.*)

MANCINI (*laughing*). What a joker you are, HE! You even laugh alone.

(HE *loudly guffaws.*)

Now stop, fool! How it gets hold of you.

HE (*bowing low and sweepingly*). Good morning, Baron. My deepest respects, Count. I beg you to forgive me, Count, but you came upon the clown at work—so to speak, in the midst of his daily enjoyments, Baron.

MANCINI (*raising his eyebrows*). Shh! But you're a clever fellow, HE. I'll ask Papa Briquet to give you a benefit. You want me to, HE?

HE. Do me the favor, Count.

MANCINI. Now, now, not too much. Be simpler, HE. (*Laughs.*) But how many slaps in the face will you get during your benefit if on regular days your face gets rung like a gong! A strange occupation, isn't it, Baron?

BARON. Very strange. But where's the young Countess?

MANCINI. Yes, yes . . . I'll go get her at once. The child, she's so carried away by her benefit and the work—she calls her leaps and jumps work, Baron!

BARON. I can wait. (*Sits down, his top hat on his head.*)

MANCINI. No, why? I'll hurry her up. I'll be right back. And you, HE, take charge and entertain our dear guest. You won't be bored with him, Baron.

(*Goes out.* HE *paces sweepingly through the room, smiling and glancing at the* BARON. *The* BARON *sits with his legs placed wide apart and his chin on his cane. The top hat is on his head.* HE *is at ease.*)

HE. How would you wish to be entertained, Baron?

BARON. Nohow. I don't like clowns.

HE. And I, barons.

(*Silence.* HE *puts his derby on his head, with broad gestures takes a chair and noisily puts it in front of the* BARON. HE *sits down straddling it, imitating the* BARON'S *pose and looks straight at him. Silence.*)

HE. Can you keep quiet for a long time?

BARON. Very long.

(*Silence.* HE *taps the floor with his foot.*)

HE. Can you wait for a long time?

BARON. Very long.

HE. Until you get what you want?

BARON. Until I get what I want. And you?

HE. Me, too.

(*Silently, having moved their heads, they look at each other. From the arena come sounds of a tango.*)

(Curtain)

ACT IV

The benefit performance for CONSUELO. *In the arena, music. In the circus room, more disorder than usual. The clothes of the performers are hung up or lying around in the corners. Thrown carelessly on the table, a large bouquet of fire-red roses.*

Three horseback riders smoke and chat in the arched doorway—second-rate performers whose job is to ride horseback. Their combed-down hair is parted alike; two have mustaches, the third is clean-shaven with a face like a bulldog.

FIRST (*clean-shaven*). Stop, Henri. Ten thousand francs! That's too much even for a Baron!

SECOND. How much are roses now?

CLEAN-SHAVEN. I don't know. In winter they're more, of course, but all the same Henri is talking nonsense. Ten thousand!

SECOND. The Baron has his own greenhouses; it doesn't cost him anything.

HENRI (*throwing away the cigar which has burned the ends of his fingers*). No, you're unbearable, Grab! Listen, it's a whole wagonful! It smells of roses a mile away. So as to strew the whole arena . . .

CLEAN-SHAVEN. Just the ring.

HENRI. Makes no difference. To cover over the ring they need thousands and thousands of roses and rosebuds! You'll see what it'll amount to when they're laid out like a carpet. He ordered a carpet, Grab, you understand?

SECOND. What a Baron-like whim! Isn't it our time?

HENRI. Not yet, we'll make it. I like this: a fire-red tango on a fire-red carpet of winter roses!

CLEAN-SHAVEN. Consuelo will gallop over the roses, but Bezano?

SECOND. But Bezano, over the thorns. (*Smiles.*)

CLEAN-SHAVEN. The boy has no self-respect; I'd have refused!

HENRI. But it's his job, he has to, Grab. (*Laughs.*) You talk to him about self-respect: he's as wicked and proud as a little devil.

SECOND. No, it's a wonderful benefit, don't talk like that. It's nice to look at the crowd; they're so excited . . .

HENRI. Psst!

(*All three, like schoolboys caught in the act, throw away their cigars and cigarettes and make way for* ZINIDA, *who comes in with* HE.)

ZINIDA (*sternly*). Why are you here, gentlemen? Your place is at the barrier.

HENRI (*smiling, respectfully*). We just stopped for a minute, Madame Zinida, we're on our way. What a successful evening, isn't it? And what celebrity for Papa Briquet!

ZINIDA. Yes. Go on now and, please, don't leave your places. (*The riders go out.* ZINIDA *opens the table and puts some papers away. She is in her lion tamer's costume.*) What were you doing near the animals, HE? You frightened me.

HE. Nothing, Duchess. I just wanted to hear what the animals were saying about the benefit. They're prowling back and forth in their cages and snarling.

ZINIDA. The music annoys them. Well, HE? Sit down. The evening's splendid—and I'm very glad that Consuelo's leaving us! You hear about the Baron's roses?

HE. Everybody's talking about them. The roses of Hymen!

ZINIDA. Here are some more. (*Pushing a bouquet away.*) They've been thrown around everywhere! Yes, I'm glad. She's extra here and gets in the way of our work. It's a real misfortune for a troupe when such a girl . . . too beautiful and—too easily gotten at—gets set up in it.

HE. But you know it's a legitimate marriage, Duchess.

ZINIDA. That makes no difference to me.

HE. Even spiders, you know, need to improve their species! What charming little spiders will come forth from that pair! Can you imagine, Zinida? Looking like Consuelo-the-mother and with an inside like Baron-the-father, they'll be adornments to any arena.

ZINIDA. You're malicious today, HE—and morose.

HE. I'm laughing.

ZINIDA. But not cheerfully. Why have you no make-up?

HE. I'm in the third part; I still have time. And what does Bezano think of the evening? Is he pleased, too?

ZINIDA. I haven't talked to Bezano. But you know what I think, my friend: you're extra here, too!
(*Silence.*)

HE. How would you have me understand that, Zinida?

ZINIDA. The way it was said. In essence, Consuelo sold herself for nothing: what's the Baron and his miserable millions? They say about you that you're very clever, maybe, perhaps even too much so—so now think and tell me: how much would I go for?

HE (*as if fixing the price*). Only for a crown.

ZINIDA. A baroness'?

HE. No, a queen's.

ZINIDA. Why, you're not stupid at all. But did you guess that Consuelo isn't Mancini's own daughter?

HE (*astounded*). What do you mean! And does she know?

ZINIDA. Hardly, and why should she? Yes, she's an orphan girl from Corso whom he preferred to put in circulation, rather than . . . But she's legally his daughter—Countess Veronica Mancini.

HE. It's good when everything is done legally, isn't it, Zinida? Curious, she's more of a blue blood than Mancini himself. One might think that it was she picked *him* up on the street and turned him into father and count. Count Mancini!
(*Laughs.*)

ZINIDA. Yes, you're sullen. HE, I've changed my mind: stay here.

HE. I won't be extra?

ZINIDA. When she's gone, you won't be . . . Oh, you still don't know how good it is here, how easy on soul and body. I understand you, I'm also clever. Just like you, I brought with me from out there the habit of needing chains, and for a long time fettered myself . . . to whatever turned up, just so long as I could hold on.

HE. Bezano?

ZINIDA. Bezano and others; there were a lot, and there'll be lots more. My red lion, the one I'm hopelessly in love with, is more terrible and worse than any Bezano. But that's all nothing—bad habits you're sorry to get rid of, like old servants who steal small change. Forget Consuelo; she has her own road ahead of her.

HE. An automobile or diamonds?

ZINIDA. And where have you ever seen a beautiful girl in just gingham? If he doesn't buy one thing, he'll buy another—they'll buy everything beautiful, for sure. Of course I know that for ten years she'll be a sad and lonely beauty looked on by paupers from the sidewalk; then she'll start touching up her eyes and smiling, and then take . . .

HE. The driver or the footman on the box as a lover? You foresee things pretty well, Zinida!

ZINIDA. But isn't it so? I don't want to break in on your confidence, but today I feel sorry for you, HE! What can you do against fate? Don't be offended, my friend, at what a woman says. I like you, but you're neither handsome nor young nor rich, and your place . . .

HE. Is on the sidewalk, from which beautiful girls are looked at? (*Laughs.*) But if I don't want it?

ZINIDA. What has your "I want" or "don't want" to do with it? I'm sorry for you, poor friend, but if you have any strength and are a man . . . But you seem to me the sort who has only one road: to forget it all.

HE (*laughing*). Does that mean being strong to you? Is that like you, Queen Zinida, who wants to arouse love even in a lion's heart? For even one instant of false possession you're ready to pay with your life, yet you advise me . . . to forget! Give me your strong hand, my beautiful, and see what strength there is in my handshake . . . and don't be sorry for me!

(BRIQUET *and* MANCINI *come in. The latter is dry and pompous, dressed in new clothes but with the same cane and the same silent satiric laugh.*)

ZINIDA (*whispers*). You'll stay?

HE. Yes, I won't go.

MANCINI. How're we doing, my dear? Why, you're blinding, I swear, you're blinding! Your lion's an ass if he doesn't kiss your little hand, even as I take the liberty . . . (*Kisses her hand.*)

ZINIDA. May I congratulate you, Count?

MANCINI. Yes. *Merci.* (*To* HE.) Hello, my good man!

HE. I have the honor to pay my respects, Count.

BRIQUET. Zinida, the Count wants to pay the forfeit on

Consuelo's contract right away . . . on the Countess's.
You don't happen to remember, Mama, according to the
contract, how much it is?

ZINIDA. I'll take a look right away, Papa.

MANCINI. Yes, please. Consuelo won't be back here again;
we're leaving tomorrow.

(ZINIDA *and* BRIQUET *look through the papers.* HE *takes*
MANCINI *by the elbow rather roughly and leads him aside.*)

HE (*softly*). And how are your girls, Mancini?

MANCINI. What girls? What is this: nonsense or blackmail?
Look out, my good man, be careful: the Commissioner is
not far off.

HE. You're too harsh, Mancini! I thought that confidentially . . .

MANCINI. Now listen: what kind of "confidentially" can there
be between a clown and me? (*Laughs.*) You're absurd, HE:
you should have proposed something and not asked!

BRIQUET. Three thousand francs, Count.

MANCINI. Is that all? For Consuelo? All right, I'll tell the
Baron.

ZINIDA. And you also took . . .

BRIQUET. Never mind, Mama, forget it!

ZINIDA. And you also took some in advance, Count; I have
it written down here: eighty francs and twenty centimes.
Would you include this money also?

MANCINI. Of course, of course, what a question! You'll get
three thousand, one hundred. (*Laughs.*) Twenty centimes!
I never thought I could be so accurate: twenty centimes!
(*Seriously.*) Ah, and besides that, my friends! Consuelo, the
Countess, my daughter, and the Baron expressed their
desire of taking leave of the company . . .

HE. The Baron also?

MANCINI. Yes, Auguste also. They want to do this during the
intermission. And so I ask you to assemble here—the most
decent of you—but without pushing and shoving, without
pushing and shoving! HE, my dear man, be so good as to
run into the buffet and tell them to bring in a basket of
champagne and glasses right away. You hear me?

HE. Certainly, Count.

MANCINI. Wait! Not so fast. What's that, a new costume?
You're all on fire, like a devil in hell!

HE. You do me too much honor, Count: how am I a devil? I am only a poor sinner whom the devils singe. (*Goes out, bowing clownishly.*)

MANCINI. A talented fellow, all right, but a real pusher!

BRIQUET. That's the colors of the tango, in honor of your daughter, Count. He needs it for a new skit which he doesn't want to reveal. Wouldn't you like to sit down, Count?

MANCINI. Auguste is waiting for me, but, however . . . (*Sits down.*) Still, I'm sorry to be leaving you, my friends! Yes, high society, of course, prerogatives, the palaces of the nobility—but where will I find such freedom and . . . such simplicity? And then, these posters, these fiery announcements which take your breath away in the morning—there was something beckoning, emboldening in them. I'll get old there, my friends!

BRIQUET. But the higher pleasures, Count . . . Why don't you say anything, Zinida?

ZINIDA. I'm listening.

MANCINI. By the way, my dear: how do you like my suit? You have wonderful taste. (*Straightens his lace necktie and lace cuffs.*)

ZINIDA. I like it. You're like a noble of old times, Count.

MANCINI. Yes—but it isn't too much, is it? Who wears lace and satin nowadays? This foul democracy will soon dress us all out in burlap—and what then? (*With a sigh.*) Auguste says that this jabot isn't quite appropriate.

ZINIDA. The Baron is too severe.

MANCINI. Well, yes! But still it seems to me that he's right: I've been somewhat affected here by your make-believe.

(HE *comes in. Behind him, two servants pull a basket of champagne and glasses. They get things ready on the table.*)

MANCINI. Aha. *Merci*, HE. Only, please, no bourgeois popping of corks; quietly and modestly. The bill is for Baron Regnart. So we'll meet here, Briquet; I'm off now.

ZINIDA (*looking at her watch*). Yes, the act is finishing now.

MANCINI. My god! (*Hurriedly goes out.*)

BRIQUET. God damn him to hell!

ZINIDA (*pointing to the servants*). Take it easy, Louis.

BRIQUET. No, God damn him to hell! And you couldn't support me, Mama. Left it up to me to talk to him. High society, higher pleasures! The swindler!

(HE *and* ZINIDA *laugh; the servants smile.*)

BRIQUET (*to the servants*). There's nothing to laugh at. Get out! We'll take care of things ourselves. Whiskey and soda, Jean! (*Snarls.*) Champagne!

(JACKSON *comes in in costume.*)

JACKSON. Whiskey and soda for me, too! At least I hear laughter from you—those idiots have completely forgotten how. My sun has come up and gone down today, crawled all around the arena—if only there'd been a smile! They look at my ass like into a mirror—excuse me, Zinida! But you're not bad, HE—well, look out for your cheeks today —I hate good-looking boys.

BRIQUET. A benefit audience!

JACKSON (*looking at his face in a little mirror*). The parquet is filled with some sort of barons and Egyptian mummies; my stomach's all sick with fear. I'm an honest clown; I can't stand their looking at me like that, as if I'd stolen somebody's handkerchief. Give them some good slaps in the face, HE.

HE. Don't worry, Jim, I'll get even with them. (*Goes out.*)

ZINIDA. And Bezano?

JACKSON (*growling*). Bezano! Crazy success, of course. But he's gone mad himself; he'll break his neck tomorrow. Why does he take such risks? Or has he wings like a god? The hell with him; he's disgusting to look at—that's not real work.

BRIQUET. You're right, Jim; it isn't real work! Your health, old friend!

JACKSON. And yours, Louis!

BRIQUET. It's no work any more when all kinds of barons show up here! There they are laughing, but I'm mad at them, mad at them, Jim. What have they got to do here, these barons? Let them steal chickens in somebody else's coop, but leave us alone. Ah, if I were the Minister I'd put up an iron fence between us and those gents.

JACKSON. I'm very sorry for little Consuelo, too . . . I'm disgusted. And somehow I think that all of us, today, are more like swindlers than honest performers. Don't you think so, Zinida?

ZINIDA. Everybody does what he wants to. It's Consuelo's business and her father's.

BRIQUET. Stop it, Mama, that's not true! Everybody's far from doing what he wants to; it just comes out like that . . . God knows why!

(ANGELICA *and* THOMAS, *the acrobat, come in, in costume.*)

ANGELICA. Is there going to be champagne here?

BRIQUET. And you're already delighted?

THOMAS. There it is. Oho, so much!

ANGELICA. The Count told me to come in. I met him . . .

BRIQUET (*angrily*). If he said so, all right, come in, but there's nothing here to be glad about! Look out, Angelica, you'll end up badly; I see right through you . . . How's she doing, Thomas?

THOMAS. All right.

ANGELICA (*softly*). Ooo, how angry you are today, Papa Briquet!

(HE, TILI *and* POLI *come in; another performer behind them. All in costume.*)

TILI. Poli, do you really want some champagne?

POLI. No, not at all. Do you, Tili?

TILI. I don't at all, either. HE, did you see how the Count walks? (*Walks, mimicking* MANCINI. *Laughter.*)

POLI. And I'll be the Baron; take my arm. Easy, you ass, you stepped on my family tree.

ANGELICA. It'll be over in a minute; Consuelo is galloping now —this is her waltz. What success she has!

(*All listen to the waltz in the arena.* TILI *and* POLI *pick up the tune.*)

ANGELICA. But she's so lovely! Are these her flowers?

(*They listen. Suddenly it seems the wall is coming down: the thunder of applause, shouts, roaring. Much movement on stage. The performers pour champagne. Others come in, laughing and talking. They become quiet at the sight of the Manager and the champagne.*)

VOICES. They're coming now! What success! I should think so, when the whole parquet . . . And what about the tango? Don't be envious, Alfonsinka!

BRIQUET. Easy, no pushing. Zinida, don't be so silent . . . High society!

HE WHO GETS SLAPPED

(CONSUELO *comes in arm-in-arm with the solid-stepping* BARON. *She is radiant.* MANCINI *is self-important and happy. Behind them are riders, performers—both men and girls. The* BARON *has a fire-red rose in his buttonhole. All applaud:* "*Bravo! Bravo!*")

CONSUELO. Ladies and gentlemen . . . my dears . . . Papa, I can't. (*Throws herself on* MANCINI *and buries her face in his shoulder.*)

(MANCINI *with a smile looks over her head at the* BARON. *The* BARON, *too, smiles slightly. But in general he is stern and motionless. A new burst of applause.*)

BRIQUET. Enough, enough, boys and girls!

MANCINI. Now, calm down, calm down, my child. How much they all love you! (*Stepping forward a little.*) Ladies and gentlemen! Baron Regnart did me the honor yesterday of asking for the hand of my daughter, Countess Veronica, whom you all know by the name of Consuelo. Please take your glasses . . .

CONSUELO. No, I'm Consuelo today, and I'll always be Consuelo. Zinida, darling! (*Throws herself on* ZINIDA'S *neck. Fresh applause.*)

BRIQUET. Stop now. Quiet! Take your glasses and . . . well take them! You've come here, so take them!

TILI (*trembling*). They're very afraid. Pick your own up first, Papa, and we'll follow you.

(*They raise their glasses.* CONSUELO *is beside the* BARON, *with her left hand holding on to the sleeve of his frock coat, in her right hand a glass, out of which the wine is spilling.*

BARON. Your wine is spilling, Consuelo.

CONSUELO. Ah!—it doesn't matter. I'm scared, too. Are you, Papa?

MANCINI. Little silly . . . (*An awkward silence.*)

BRIQUET (*stepping forward*). Countess! As the Manager of this circus . . . having had the honor of repeatedly . . . observing . . . your successes . . .

CONSUELO. Not like that, Papa Briquet. I'm Consuelo. What are you all doing to me? I'm going to cry. I don't want to be Countess; kiss me, Briquet!

BRIQUET. Ah, books have ruined you, Consuelo! (*With tears in his eyes, kisses* CONSUELO.)

(*Laughter, applause; the clowns cackle, bark and in all kinds of other ways express their excitement and ecstasy. The motley crowd of clowns, costumed for a performers' pantomime, begins to take on life. The* BARON *is motionless, surrounded by space; people clink glasses with him quickly and respectfully and immediately go away. They clink cheerfully and eagerly with* CONSUELO; *she exchanges kisses with the women.*)

JACKSON. Quiet! Consuelo! After today, I'm putting out my sun: let dark night fall with your going away. You were a great friend and co-worker. We've all loved you and we'll go on loving the traces of your little feet in the sand. Now we have nothing else left!

CONSUELO. You're so good—so good, Jim, there's nobody better! And your sun is better than all other suns; I laughed at it so much! Alfred, my darling—why don't you come closer? I've been looking for you.

BEZANO. My congratulations, Countess.

CONSUELO. Alfred! I'm Consuelo!

BEZANO. On horseback, but here . . . My congratulations, Countess.

(*Moves off, having hardly taken a sip.* CONSUELO *is still holding hers.* MANCINI *glances at the* BARON *with a smile—the* BARON *is motionless.*)

BRIQUET. Nonsense, Bezano! You're making Consuelo angry. She's a good friend.

CONSUELO. No, it's nothing.

ANGELICA. You'll still do the tango with her; what sort of Countess is she?

TILI. And can I drink to you, Consuelo? You know, Poli's already kicked the bucket from melancholy, and soon I will, too. I've got such a weak stomach!

(*Laughter. The* BARON *frowns, unnoticed. Movement.*)

MANCINI. Enough, enough, my friends! The intermission will soon be over.

CONSUELO. So soon! I feel so good here.

BRIQUET. I order it made longer, they can sit and wait a bit. Tell them, Thomas!

MANCINI. Auguste, the musicians, too, ask permission to congratulate you and Consuelo. How do you feel about it?

BARON. Of course, of course.

(*The musicians come in in a crowd. The* CONDUCTOR, *an old Italian, solemnly raises his glass—without looking at the* BARON.)

CONDUCTOR. Consuelo! Here you're called Countess, but for me you were and still are Consuelo . . .

CONSUELO. Yes, of course!

CONDUCTOR. Consuelo! My violins and bassoons, my trumpets and kettledrums drink to your health. Be happy, my child, as you were happy here. And we will always keep in our hearts the bright memory of the light-winged fairy who so long bent our bow. I have finished! Greet our beautiful Italy for me, Consuelo.

(*Applause, greetings. The musicians, having toasted, one after another go out into the corridor.* CONSUELO *is practically in tears.*)

MANCINI. Now don't get upset, my child, it's not done. If I'd known that you'd take all this comedy like this—Auguste, just look how this little tender heart is all upset!

BARON. Calm down, Consuelo.

CONSUELO. I'm all right. Ah, Papa, listen!

(*In the corridor, sounds of a tango. Exclamations.*)

MANCINI. There, you see: they're doing that for you.

CONSUELO. How kind they are. My tango! I want to dance— well, who will dance with me? (*With her eyes, looks for* BEZANO. BEZANO *turns away. Sadly.*) Well, who then?

VOICES. The Baron! Let the Baron. The Baron!

BARON. Very well. (*Takes* CONSUELO *by the hand and stands in the middle of a cleared circle.*) I don't know how to tango, but I will hold you tightly. Dance, Consuelo! (*He stands heavily and stolidly, his legs apart, like a man of iron. Very serious, he holds* CONSUELO'S *hand tightly.*)

MANCINI (*clapping*). Bravo! Bravo!

(CONSUELO *makes several movements—and pulls her hand away.*)

CONSUELO. No, I can't do it like that. How silly! Let me go! (*She goes over to* ZINIDA *and embraces her as if hiding by her. The music continues. The* BARON *calmly moves off to one side. A hostile silence among the performers. They shrug their shoulders.*)

MANCINI (*alone*). Bravo, bravo! That's enchanting, charming!
JACKSON. Well, not really, Count.

(TILI *and* POLI, *imitating the* BARON *and* CONSUELO, *dance without moving from the spot.*)

TILI (*whining*). Let me go!
POLI. No, you won't get away from me! Dance!

(*The music breaks off. General, too loud laughter; the clowns bark and roar.* PAPA BRIQUET, *by gestures, tries to install peace. The* BARON *seems as indifferent as before.*)

MANCINI. When all's said and done, these honest vagabonds are too free and easy. (*Shrugs his shoulders.*) The smell of the stables, what can you do, Auguste!
BARON. Don't worry, Count.

(HE, *glass in hand, goes up to the* BARON.)

HE. Baron! Will you allow me to drink a toast to you?
BARON. Do.
HE. To your dancing!

(*In the crowd, light laughter.*)

BARON. I don't dance.
HE. Then a different one. Baron! Let's drink to those who can wait the longest until they get what they want!
BARON. I don't accept toasts the meanings of which are incomprehensible to me. Speak . . . more simply.

(*A woman's voice: "Bravo,* HE!" *Light laughter.* MANCINI *nervously says something to* PAPA BRIQUET, *who throws up his arms.* JACKSON *takes* HE *by the arm.*)

JACKSON. Leave off, HE. The Baron doesn't like jokes.
HE. But I want to drink with the Baron! What is simpler? Simpler? Baron—let's drink to the little distance which always remains between—the cup and the lip! (*Throws out the wine and laughs.*)

(*The* BARON *indifferently turns his back. In the arena, music and the ring of a bell calling for the start.*)

BRIQUET (*relieved*). Now, there! To the arena, ladies and gentlemen, to the arena! To the arena!

(*The performers run out; the crowd thins. Laughter and the sound of voices.*)

MANCINI (*excited, whispers to the* BARON). Auguste, Auguste!
BRIQUET (*to* ZINIDA). Thank God, the start! Ah, Mama, I asked you; you'd really like a scandal; you always . . .

ZINIDA. Drop it, Louis.

(HE *goes up to* CONSUELO, *who is standing alone.*)

CONSUELO. HE, darling, what are you doing? I thought you didn't even want to come near me. (*Softly.*) You saw how Bezano was?

HE. I was waiting my turn, my Queen. It's so hard to get through the crowd to you.

CONSUELO. To me? (*Smiling sadly.*) I'm standing alone . . . Well, what do you want, Papa?

MANCINI. My child, Auguste . . .

CONSUELO (*tearing her hand away*). Leave me alone! I'll be there in a minute . . . Come over here, HE. What did you say to him? They all laughed. I didn't hear it. What was it?

HE. I made a joke, Consuelo.

CONSUELO. Don't, please, HE, don't! Don't make him angry; he's so frightening. You saw how he squeezed my hand! I almost cried out. (*With tears in her eyes.*) He hurt me!

HE. Refuse him—it's still not too late.

CONSUELO. It is, HE. Be quiet!

HE. You want me to—I'll take you away.

CONSUELO. Where? (*Laughs.*) Ah, my sweet silly little boy, where could you take me? Be quiet, be quiet. How pale you are; do you love me, too? Don't, HE, please don't. What do they love me for?

HE. You are so beautiful!

CONSUELO. No, no, that's not true. They shouldn't love me. I still felt a little cheerful, but when they started saying . . . such tender things . . . and about Italy . . . saying good-bye to me as if I were dying . . . I thought I'd scream! Be quiet, be quiet. Instead drink to . . . my happiness . . . (*Smiles sadly.*) To my happiness, HE. What are you doing?

HE. Throwing out the glass from which you drank with everybody. I'll get you another. Wait for me. (*Goes off to pour some champagne.* CONSUELO *walks in deep reflection. Almost everyone has gone; only the main characters are here.*)

MANCINI (*coming up*). But this is simply indecent, Veronica! Auguste is so kind and is waiting for you, and you and this clown . . . are exchanging some absurd secrets. People are looking at you; it's becoming ridiculous! It's time, Veronica, that you lost the habit of . . .

CONSUELO (*loudly*). Leave me alone, Papa. This is what I want, and I'll do it. They're all my friends . . . you hear? Leave me alone!

BARON. Stop now, Count. Please, Consuelo, talk to anyone you want as much as you want. Wouldn't you like a cigar, Count? Briquet, my good man, have them extend the intermission a little longer.

BRIQUET. Certainly, Baron; the parquet may become somewhat annoyed . . . (*Goes out and soon returns.* HE *gives* CONSUELO *a glass.*)

HE. Here's your glass. To your happiness, to your freedom, Consuelo!

CONSUELO (*taking the glass*). And where's yours? We must drink to each other.

HE. You'll leave me half.

CONSUELO. I have to drink that much? I'll be drunk, HE. I still have to gallop.

HE. No, you won't be drunk. My little girl, have you forgotten that I'm your sorcerer and your fairy tale? Drink peacefully; I enchanted the wine, there's a spell in it. Drink, goddess.

CONSUELO (*lingering*). How kind your eyes are. But why are you so pale?

HE. Because I love you. Look into my kind eyes and drink. Give yourself up to my charms, goddess! You'll fall asleep and awaken again, as before—remember?—and you'll see your own country, the sky . . .

CONSUELO (*raising the glass to her lips*). I'll see it; is that true?

HE (*growing still paler*). Yes! Wake up, then, goddess—and remember the time when you rose on the foam from the azure sea. Remember that sky—and the soft wind from the east—and the whispers of the foam around your marble feet . . .

CONSUELO (*drinking*). There. Look: exactly half! Take it. But what's the matter with you? Are you laughing or crying, HE?

MANCINI (*lightly pushing* HE *back*). That'll do, Countess, my patience has run out! Auguste may be so kind and permit this, but I, your father . . . your hand, Countess! Step aside, my good man!

CONSUELO. I'm tired.

MANCINI. You're not tired of chatting away and drinking wine with a mountebank, but when duty calls you . . . Briquet, have them ring the bell; it's time.

CONSUELO. I'm tired, Papa.

ZINIDA. Listen, Count, this is cruel: don't you see how pale she's become . . .

BARON. What's the matter with you, Consuelo?

CONSUELO. Nothing, I'm all right.

ZINIDA. She simply needs rest, Baron; why, she hasn't even sat down . . . and such excitement . . . Sit down here, dear, cover up, rest a little. Men are so cruel!

CONSUELO. I still have to work. (*Closing her eyes.*) Are the roses ready yet?

ZINIDA. They are, they are. You'll have such an extraordinary carpet, you'll go along as if through the air. Rest now.

POLI. You want some music? We'll play you a little song; you want us to?

CONSUELO (*smiling, her eyes closed*). I do.

(*The clowns play a quiet and simple little song: tili-tili, poli-poli. Everyone is silent.* HE *sits in a corner, his back turned;* JACKSON, *leaning against him, lazily drinks wine. The* BARON, *in his usual pose, his legs set wide and heavily apart, looks at* CONSUELO'S *pale face with bulging, motionless eyes.*)

CONSUELO (*suddenly shouting*). Aii! It hurts.

ZINIDA. What's wrong? Consuelo!

MANCINI. My child! Are you ill? Do calm down.

BARON (*paling*). Wait . . . she's overexcited. Consuelo!

(CONSUELO *rises and stares straight forward with wide-open eyes, as if listening to what is going on inside herself.*)

CONSUELO. Aii! It hurts. Here, by the heart. Papa, what is it? I'm afraid. What is it? And my legs . . . what's happened to my legs? I can't stand up. (*Falls onto the sofa, her eyes wide open.*)

MANCINI (*bustling about*). A doctor! Ah, my god, this is terrible. Auguste, Baron . . . this never happened to her before! It's nerves, your nerves, relax, my child . . .

BRIQUET. A doctor!

(*Someone runs out for a doctor.*)

JACKSON (*frightened*). HE, what is this! HE!

HE. It's death, Consuelo. My sweet little Queen, I've killed you. You are—dying! (*Cries wildly.*)

(CONSUELO *screams and, having closed her eyes, calms down. Everyone is in confusion. The* BARON *motionless, looks only at* CONSUELO.)

MANCINI (*hissing*). You're not telling the truth—you swindler! You damned comedian, what did you give her? You poisoned her—you robber! A doctor!

HE. A doctor won't help. You're dying, my sweet little Queen. Consuelo! Consuelo!

(BEZANO *runs in quickly: "The Manager!"—falls silent and looks on in horror. Someone else comes in. Briquet waves his hand: "The door!"*)

CONSUELO (*in a weak and far-away voice*). You're joking, HE? Don't scare me; I'm so afraid. Is this death? I don't want it. Aii . . . Dear HE, my darling little HE, tell me you're joking, I'm afraid . . . HE, my darling!

(HE *imperatively pushes the* BARON *away and stands in his place over* CONSUELO. *The* BARON *stands as before, looking only at* CONSUELO.)

HE. Yes, I'm joking. Don't you hear my laughter, Consuelo? Everybody here is laughing at you—little silly! Don't, Jim, she's tired and wants to sleep. How can you laugh, Jim! Go to sleep, my dear, go to sleep, dear heart, go to sleep, my love!

CONSUELO. Yes, it doesn't hurt now. Why did you joke like that and scare me so? Now I think it's funny. You yourself used to say that I . . . will . . . live forever . . .

HE. Yes, Consuelo! You will, forever. Go to sleep! Be calm! (*Raising his arms, he puts all his effort into it and seems to raise her soul higher and higher.*) How easy now for you, how bright, how many lights shine all around you . . . You can be blinded by the light!!

CONSUELO. Yes, it's bright. Is this the arena?

HE. No, it's the sea and the sun . . . what a sun! Don't you feel that you're the foam—the white sea foam, and you're flying toward the sun. How light you feel—you have no body—you're flying! Higher, still higher, my love!

CONSUELO. I'm flying. I'm the sea foam, and that's the sun, it's shining so . . . I'm all right. (*Dies. Silence.*)

(HE *still stands with upraised arms, glances at her—and drops his arms down. Stumbling, he moves back. He stands for a moment more, then sits down, dropping his head onto his arms, by himself fighting off the numbness of approaching death.*)

BRIQUET (*softly*). Is she asleep, Mama?

ZINIDA (*letting go of her dead hand*). I'm afraid not . . . Go away, Louis. Baron, you better go. Baron, you don't hear me! (*Cries.*) Louis, she's dead.

(BRIQUET *and the clowns weep*, MANCINI *is overwhelmed; the* BARON *and* HE *are motionless—each in his place.*)

JACKSON (*taking out a huge, colored clown's handkerchief and wiping away his tears*). Withered, like a flower . . . Sleep, little Consuelo. Only the traces of your little feet on the sand are left now. (*Cries.*) Ah, what have you done, what have you done, HE! It would have been better if you'd never come here.

(*In the arena, music.*)

BRIQUET (waving his hand). The music, stop the music. They've gone mad out there. What a terrible thing!

(*Someone runs out.* ZINIDA *goes up to the weeping* BEZANO *and strokes him on his bowed, pomaded head. Glancing at her, he grabs her hand and draws close to her with his eyes. The* BARON, *pulling the rose out of his buttonhole, silently pulls its petals off and drops them, grinding them under his foot. Pale, frightened faces peer in the door—the same costumed crowd.*)

ZINIDA (*over* BEZANO's *head*). You have to get the Commissioner, Louis.

MANCINI (*coming out of his stupor, shouts*). The police, call the police. It's murder. I'm Count Mancini! I'm Count Mancini! They'll chop off your head, you robber, you damned comedian, you thief! I'll kill you myself, you swindler! Ah, you!

(*With effort,* HE *raises his heavy head.*)

HE. Cut off my head—and then what . . . your Excellency?

BRIQUET. Sir, listen to me, sir; I'm going for the Commissioner . . . sir! Stop!

(*The* BARON *suddenly takes a step forward and, looking* HE *in the eye, speaks hoarsely, holding his throat and coughing.*)

BARON. I'm a witness. I saw it. I'm a witness. I saw how he sprinkled poison. I . . .

(*He goes out just as suddenly, with the same direct and heavy steps. Everyone steps aside from him in fear.* HE *again drops his head; a shudder every so often runs over his body.*)

JACKSON (*throwing up his hands*). So it's really true? Poisoned her? Ah, HE, what a bastard you are! Is that the way to play a role? Now wait for one more—for the last slap from the executioner! (*Draws his hand across his neck, indicating the guillotine.* TILI *and* POLI *involuntarily repeat his gesture.*)

ZINIDA. Leave his soul in peace, Jim. He was a man and loved her. Lucky Consuelo!

(*A shot in the corridor.* THOMAS *runs in frightened and points to his head.*)

THOMAS. The Baron . . . The Baron . . . skull! Shot himself!

BRIQUET (*raising his arms*). God, what's this? The Baron? What a terrible thing for our circus!

MANCINI. The Baron? The Baron? It can't be! What do you mean? Ah . . .

BRIQUET. Calm down, Count! And who would have thought? Such an . . . important gentleman.

HE (*with effort raising his head, barely able to make things out with his beclouded eyes*). What now? . . . What happened?

THOMAS. The Baron shot himself. Word of honor: right here! Is lying there.

HE (*understanding*). The Baron? (*Laughs.*) So the Baron . . . burst?

JACKSON. Stop! It's shameful. A man died, and you . . . But what's the matter with you, HE?

(HE *gets up, raised to his feet by the last flood of consciousness and life; speaks forcefully and angrily.*)

HE. You loved her so, Baron? You loved her so? My Consuelo? And you want to get ahead of me there, too? No! I'm coming! And we shall still fight it out there, you and I—whose she is for ever.

(*Seizing his throat, he falls prostrate. People rush to him. Confusion.*)

(*Curtain*)

The Days of the Turbins

A PLAY IN
FOUR ACTS

Mikhail Afanasyevich Bulgakov

A NOTE ON THE PLAY

Though Aleksandr Blok's poem, *The Twelve*, is often celebrated as *the* poem of the Russian Revolution, its basically apolitical subject includes mainly one side of the political struggle. In many ways, Bulgakov's play, *The Days of the Turbins*, seems the most profound depiction of the motives and morality behind both Reds and Whites. Though the Turbins and their friends are Whites at the beginning of the play, by the end they all, except for Studzinsky, have joined the Reds. The play dramatizes the change in their allegiance and focuses on the reasons for it.

Bulgakov, born in Kiev in 1891, where he received his medical degree in 1916, published a novel called *The White Guard* in the magazine *Russia*, in 1925. He immediately set to dramatizing his own novel. By 1919 he had given up medicine for journalism, and in the early years of the new government, following the civil war, he lived abroad (1921–23). Following its premiere at the Moscow Art Theater in Moscow, in 1926, the play was attacked for being too sympathetic to the Whites, for not being "revolutionary" enough, and, for some time, it was out of favor. Bulgakov wrote other plays—including a dramatization of the end of Pushkin's life, *The Last Days*, presented by the Moscow Art Theater in 1943—and prose, including a "continuation" of Chichikov's journeys, begun in Gogol's *Dead Souls*, to satirize contemporary bureaucracy. *The Days of the Turbins* became part of the repertoire of the K. S. Stanislavsky Theater in Moscow in 1954. In 1955, along with the play about Pushkin, it was published in a separate volume, from which this translation was made. Bulgakov died on March 10, 1940.

DRAMATIS PERSONAE

Turbin, Aleksei Vasilyevich, an artillery Colonel, 30 years old
Turbin, Nikolai [Nikolka], his brother, 18 years old
Talberg, Elena Vasilyevna, their sister, 24 years old
Talberg, Vladimir Robertovich, a Colonel on the General Staff, her husband, 38 years old
Myshlayevsky, Viktor Viktorovich, a First Lieutenant in the artillery, 38 years old
Shervinsky, Leonid Yurevich, a Second Lieutenant, the Hetman's personal aide
Studzinsky, Aleksandr Bronislavovich, a Captain, 29 years old
Lariosik, a cousin from Zhitomir, 21 years old
The Hetman for the whole Ukraine
Bolbotun, the Commander of Petlura's 1st Cavalry Division
Galanba, a Cossack Lieutenant and follower of Petlura, formerly a Captain of Uhlans
Uragan
Kirpaty
von Schratt, a German General
von Dust, a German Major
A German army doctor
A deserter, a man from the Sech
A man with a basket
A valet
Maksim, Supervisor of students in a *gimnaziya*,[1] 60 years old
A telephone operator in the Cossack (Petlura) cavalry
First officer
Second officer
Third officer
First cadet
Second cadet
Third cadet
Cadets and Cossack (Petlura) cavalrymen

The first, second, and third acts take place in the winter of 1918; the fourth act, in the beginning of 1919.
The scene is the city of Kiev.

[1] A school, roughly equivalent to junior high school and high school combined.

ACT I

SCENE 1

The TURBINS' *apartment. Evening. There is a fire in the fireplace. As the curtain rises, a clock strikes nine times and tenderly plays a minuet by Boccherini.* ALEKSEI *is bent over some papers.*
NIKOLKA (*plays a guitar and sings*).

The news is worse and worse.
Petlura's coming close.
We loaded the machine guns,
Fired at Petlura's bums.
The guns went rat-a-tat-tat tat-tat tat-tat.
The boys were at it at-at-at.
Hey, you saved us, fellows, hey!

ALEKSEI. What the hell are you singing! Some scullery songs. Sing something decent.

NIKOLKA. What do you mean, scullery? I made it up myself, Alyosha. (*Sings.*)

Sing or not—you make the choice,
You haven't got that good a voice!
Some people have a voice that can
Make your hair stand up on end . . .

ALEKSEI. That has to do with your voice, precisely.

NIKOLKA. Alyosha, that's unfair of you, honestly! My voice isn't like Shervinsky's, true, but still it's more or less all right. A dramatic voice, probably really a baritone. Lenochka, oh Lenochka! What do you think, do I have a voice?

ELENA (*from her room*). Who? You? Not the slightest.

NIKOLKA. She's all upset, that's why she says that. But, by the way, Alyosha, my singing teacher told me: "You could have sung in the opera, actually, Nikolai Vasilyevich," he says, "if it weren't for the Revolution."

ALEKSEI. Your singing teacher is an idiot.

NIKOLKA. I knew it! Complete nervous upset in the Turbin house! The singing teacher's an idiot. I have no voice, though yesterday I still did, and a pessimistic tone in general. But by my nature I tend more toward optimism. (*Plucks the strings.*) Though you know, Alyosha, I'm beginning to get worried myself. It's already nine, and he said he'd be here in the morning. Maybe something's happened to him?

ALEKSEI. You keep your voice down. Understand?

NIKOLKA. Lord, what a job to be the brother of a married sister.

ELENA (*from her room*). What time does the clock in the dining room say?

NIKOLKA. A-a . . . nine. Our clock's fast, Lenochka.

ELENA (*from her room*). Don't pretend, please.

NIKOLKA. See, she's upset. (*Sings.*) Hazy . . . Ah, it's all so hazy! . . .

ALEKSEI. Don't break my heart, please. Sing something cheerful.

NIKOLKA (*sings*).
Hello there, summer boys!
Hello there, summer girls!
The summer season started long ago . . .
Hey, song of mine! . . . My darling! . . .
Glug-glug-glug you bottle
Of fine old Russian stuff!! . . .
Grand little peakless caps,
Riding boots of fashion,
Here comes the Guard's cadets . . .
(*Suddenly the electricity goes off. A detachment of soldiers passes by outside the windows, singing.*)

ALEKSEI. What the hell is this! It keeps going out every minute. Lenochka, bring a candle, please.

ELENA (*from her room*). All right! . . . All right! . . .
(ELENA, *coming from her room with a candle, stops and listens. A distant explosion of a cannon shell.*)

NIKOLKA. How close! Makes you think they're shooting near Svyatoshino. It'd be interesting to know what's going on there. Alyosha, maybe you'd send me to find out what's happening at headquarters? I could ride there and back.

ALEKSEI. Sure, that's all we need from you. Sit still, please.

NIKOLKA. Yes, sir, Colonel . . . Actually, I . . . because, you know, doing nothing . . . makes me feel a bit ashamed

... Men are fighting there ... if only our division were ready sooner.

ALEKSEI. When I need your advice in getting up a division, I'll tell you. Understand?

NIKOLKA. I understand. Sorry, Colonel, sir.

(*The electricity goes on.*)

ELENA. Alyosha, where's my husband?

ALEKSEI. He'll come, Lenochka.

ELENA. But what's happening? He said he'd come in the morning, but it's already nine, and he isn't here yet. Something hasn't happened to him, has it?

ALEKSEI. Lenochka, come, of course that's impossible. You know that the line to the west is defended by the Germans.

ELENA. But then why isn't he here yet?

ALEKSEI. Well, I guess they're stopping at every station.

NIKOLKA. Revolutionary traveling, Lenochka. You ride an hour and stand still for two.

(*The doorbell rings.*)

Well, there he is, what did I tell you! (*Rushes to open the door.*) Who's there?

MYSHLAYEVSKY'S VOICE. Open up, for God's sake, hurry!

NIKOLKA (*lets* MYSHLAYEVSKY *into the front hall*). But it's you, Vitenka?

MYSHLAYEVSKY. Well, of course it's me, big as life! Nikol, take my rifle, please, and my coat. What a hell of a mess!

ELENA. Viktor, where've you come from?

MYSHLAYEVSKY. From near Krasny Traktir. Hang it up carefully, Nikol. There's a bottle of vodka in the pocket. Don't break it. Let me spend the night, please, Lena; I won't make it home, I'm completely frozen.

ELENA. Oh, my Lord, of course! Hurry and get close to the fire. (*They go over to the fireplace.*)

MYSHLAYEVSKY. Oh ... oh ... oh ...

ALEKSEI. What, they couldn't give you any felt boots, was that it?

MYSHLAYEVSKY. "Felt boots!" Those bastards! (*Crowds close to the fire.*)

ELENA. I tell you what: water for the bathtub is heating in there now; you hurry and get him undressed and I'll get him some underclothes and a shirt. (*Goes out.*)

MYSHLAYEVSKY. Pull 'em off, my boy, pull, pull . . .

NIKOLKA. Just a minute, just a minute. (*Pulls off* MYSHLAYEVSKY'S *boots.*)

MYSHLAYEVSKY. Easy, boy, oh, easy there! Wouldn't mind some vodka, a little drink of vodka.

ALEKSEI. I'll get it right away.

NIKOLKA. Alyosha, his toes are frozen.

MYSHLAYEVSKY. My toes've gone to hell, gone to hell, that's for sure.

ALEKSEI. What're you talking about! They'll be all right. Nikolka, rub his feet with vodka.

MYSHLAYEVSKY. You think I'd let him use vodka to rub my feet! (*Drinks.*) Rub with your hand. Ouch! . . . It hurts! . . . Easy.

NIKOLKA. Oh-oh-oh! . . . How the Lieutenant's frozen!

ELENA (*appears with wrapper and slippers*). Into the tub with him right away. Off with you!

MYSHLAYEVSKY. God keep you well, Lenochka. Let me have just a little more vodka. (*Drinks.*)

(ELENA *goes out.*)

NIKOLKA. Well, you warmed up, Lieutenant?

MYSHLAYEVSKY. Feels better. (*Lights a cigarette.*)

NIKOLKA. You tell us, now, what's going on down by Traktir?

MYSHLAYEVSKY. There's a snowstorm by Traktir. That's what's there. And I'd send that snowstorm, and the cold, and the German bastards, and Petlura, you know where! . . .

ALEKSEI. I don't understand, though, why did they drive you down to Traktir?

MYSHLAYEVSKY. There are these peasants down there by Traktir. Those same damned God-bearers Mr. Dostoyevsky wrote up.

NIKOLKA. What do you mean? In the papers it says the peasants are on the side of the Hetman . . .

MYSHLAYEVSKY. What're you poking newspapers at me for, you cadet? I'd hang your whole damned newspaper riffraff from the one branch! Out scouting this morning I personally ran into one old man and I asked him, "Where're your boys?" The village was just like it was empty. And his sight being poor he didn't notice I had shoulder loops sticking out under my hood and he answers, "The men are all gone off to Petlura."

NIKOLKA. Oh-oh-oh-oh . . .

MYSHLAYEVSKY. Just exactly "oh-oh-oh-oh." I grabbed this old God-bearing grumbler by his shirt front and said, "The men are all gone off to Petlura? I'll shoot you right on the spot, you old . . . I'll show you how fellows run off to Petlura. I'll help you run right off to the Kingdom of Heaven."

ALEKSEI. How did you wind up in town then?

MYSHLAYEVSKY. Got relieved today, thank the good Lord! Some infantry troops arrived. I made a row at headquarters on guard duty. It was terrible! They're sitting there, drinking cognac in the car. I says to them, you, I says, are sitting with the Hetman in the palace, but the artillery officers have been kicked out into the cold in their riding boots to trade shots with the peasants! They didn't know how to get rid of me. We assign you, Lieutenant, they says, according to your speciality, to any artillery detachment. Go into town . . . Alyosha, take me on.

ALEKSEI. With pleasure. I was meaning to call you up myself. I'll give you the first battery.

MYSHLAYEVSKI. Benefactor! . . .

NIKOLKA. Hurrah! . . . We'll all be together. Studzinsky as senior officer . . . Great! . . .

MYSHLAYEVSKY. Where are you stationed?

NIKOLKA. We've taken over the Aleksandrovskaya School. Tomorrow or the next day we can set out.

MYSHLAYEVSKY. You waiting on tenterhooks for Petlura to clonk you on the back of the head?

NIKOLKA. Well, we'll see who clonks whom!

ELENA (*appears with some sheet toweling*). Come, Viktor, get going, get going. Go on, wash up. Here's a towel.

MYSHLAYEVSKY. Lena serene, let me hug you and kiss you for all your bother. What do you think, Lenochka, shall I drink some vodka now or afterward, right with supper?

ELENA. I think afterward, right with supper. Viktor! You didn't see my husband? My husband's lost.

MYSHLAYEVSKY. What do you mean, Lenochka, he'll show up.

He'll be here right away. (*Goes out.*)

(*The bell rings continuously.*)

NIKOLKA. There he is! There he is! (*Runs into the hall.*)

ALEKSEI. Lord, what way is that to ring a bell?

(NIKOLKA *opens the door.* LARIOSIK *appears in the doorway with a suitcase and a bundle.*)

LARIOSIK. So here I am. I did something to your bell.

NIKOLKA. You pushed the button in too far. (*Runs out the door onto the stairs.*)

LARIOSIK. Oh, my God! Forgive me, for God's sake! (*Goes into the room.*) So here I am. How do you do, dear Elena Vasilyevna. I recognized you right away from your pictures. Mama asked me to give you her warmest regards.

(*The bell stops.* NIKOLKA *comes in.*)

And also to Aleksei Vasilyevich.

ALEKSEI. Mine to her.

LARIOSIK. How do you do, Nikolai Vasilyevich. I've heard so much about you. (*To everyone.*) You're surprised, I see? Let me give you a letter; it'll explain everything to you. Mama told me to give you the letter to read even before I took off my things.

ELENA. What an illegible hand!

LARIOSIK. Yes, dreadful! If you like, maybe I'd better read it myself. Mama has such a handwriting that sometimes she writes something and then later can't make out herself what she wrote. I have a handwriting like that, too. It's something we inherited. (*Reads.*) "Dearest, dearest Lenochka! I'm sending you my little boy just straight off, as one of the family; warm him and shelter him, as only you know how to do. After all, you have such a big apartment . . ." Mama's very fond of you and has a lot of respect for you, and equally for Aleksei Vasilyevich. (*To* NIKOLKA.) And for you, too. (*Reads.*) "The little boy is headed for Kiev University. With his abilities"—oh, that's Mama for you!—"he just can't sit in Zhitomir and waste time. I'll send the cost of his keep to you punctually. I wouldn't like it for the little fellow, used to living in the family, to live with strangers. But I'm in a great rush, the hospital train is leaving now; he'll tell you everything himself . . ." Hm—that's all.

ALEKSEI. May I ask with whom I have the honor of talking?

LARIOSIK. What do you mean with whom? You don't know me?

ALEKSEI. Unfortunately, I haven't the pleasure.

LARIOSIK. My God! And you, Elena Vasilyevna?

ELENA. I don't know, either.

LARIOSIK. My God, this is real witchcraft! Mama, you know, sent you a telegram which was supposed to explain everything to you. She sent you a sixty-three word telegram.

NIKOLKA. Sixty-three words! Oh . . . oh . . . oh . . .

ELENA. We never got any telegram.

LARIOSIK. Didn't get it? My God! Forgive me, please. I thought you were expecting me, and right away, without taking my things off . . . Excuse me . . . I, I think I smashed something . . . I'm a terribly unlucky person!

ALEKSEI. Now, you be good enough to tell us your name.

LARIOSIK. Larion Larionovich Surzhansky.

ELENA. It's Lariosik! Our cousin from Zhitomir?

LARIOSIK. Well, yes.

ELENA. And you . . . you've come to stay with us?

LARIOSIK. Yes. But, you see, I thought you were expecting me . . . Forgive me, please, I've tracked up your floor . . . I thought you were expecting me, but seeing how it is, I'll go to some hotel . . .

ELENA. Now just what hotel! Wait, first of all you take off your things.

ALEKSEI. Sure, nobody's after you; take off your coat, please.

LARIOSIK. I'm sincerely grateful to you.

NIKOLKA. Over here, please. You can hang your coat up in the hall.

LARIOSIK. I'm sincerely grateful to you. How nice it is in your apartment!

ELENA (*in a whisper*). Alyosha, what are we going to do with him? He's a nice boy. Let's put him in the library; the room's empty anyway.

ALEKSEI. Sure, go ahead, tell him.

ELENA. I'll tell you what, Larion Larionovich, first of all, a bath . . . Someone's already there—Lieutenant Myshlayevsky . . . But you know, after a train ride . . .

LARIOSIK. Yes, yes, dreadful! . . . Dreadful! . . . Why it

took me eleven days to get from Zhitomir to Kiev . . .

NIKOLKA. Eleven days! . . . Oh-oh-oh! . . .

LARIOSIK. It's terrible, terrible! . . . Such a nightmare!

ELENA. Now, please!

LARIOSIK. I'm sincerely . . . Oh, excuse me, Elena Vasilyevna, I can't take a bath.

ALEKSEI. Why can't you?

LARIOSIK. Excuse me, please. Some scoundrels on the hospital train stole my suitcase with the underclothes in it. The suitcase with books and manuscripts was left, but the underclothes all disappeared.

ELENA. Well, that's something we can fix.

NIKOLKA. I'll give him some; I will!

LARIOSIK (*intimately, to* NIKOLKA). I think I have a shirt, though, at least. I wrapped Chekhov's collected works up in it. But would you be good enough to let me have some underpants?

NIKOLKA. Sure. They'll be too big for you, but we'll take them in with safety pins.

LARIOSIK. I'm sincerely grateful to you.

ELENA. Larion Larionovich, we'll put you in the library. Nikolka, show him where!

NIKOLKA. Follow me, please. (LARIOSIK *and* NIKOLKA *go out.*)

ALEKSEI. There's a character for you! I'd give him a haircut first thing. Well, Lenochka, give me a light; I'll go into my own room. I have a lot of things to do, and I keep getting interrupted here. (*Goes out.*)

(*The bell rings.*)

ELENA. Who's there?

TALBERG'S VOICE. Me, me. Open up, please.

ELENA. Thank God! Where've you been? I was so worried!

TALBERG (*entering*). Don't kiss me. I'm coming in from outdoors, and you might catch a cold.

ELENA. Where've you been?

TALBERG. We were held up at the German headquarters. Important business.

ELENA. Well, come on, come on, hurry up and get warm. We'll have some tea right away.

TALBERG. Don't want any tea, Lena; later. If you please, whose field jacket's that?

ELENA. Myshlayevsky's. He's just come in from the front line, completely frozen.

TALBERG. Still, you could put it away.

ELENA. I'll do it right away. (*Hangs the jacket up behind the door.*) You know, we have news. My cousin from Zhitomir has just come unexpectedly, the famous Lariosik. Aleksei has put him up in the library.

TALBERG. I knew it! One *señor* Myshlayevsky's not enough. On top of that some Zhitomir cousins have to show up. This isn't a house but a public inn. I absolutely don't understand Aleksei.

ELENA. Volodya, you're just tired and in a bad mood. Why don't you like Myshlayevsky? He's a very good man.

TALBERG. Remarkably good! An old habitué of inns.

ELENA. Volodya!

TALBERG. However, now's not the time for Myshlayevsky. Lena, shut the door . . . Lena, something terrible has happened.

ELENA. What?

TALBERG. The Germans are leaving the Hetman to the mercy of fate.

ELENA. Volodya, what do you mean! How do you know?

TALBERG. Just found out, absolutely hush-hush, at German headquarters. Nobody knows, not even the Hetman.

ELENA. What'll happen now?

TALBERG. What'll happen now . . . Hm . . . Nine-thirty. So . . . What'll happen now? . . . Lena!

ELENA. What did you say?

TALBERG. I said "Lena!"

ELENA. Well, what about "Lena?"

TALBERG. Lena, I have to run now.

ELENA. Run? Where?

TALBERG. Germany, to Berlin. Hm . . . My dearest, you can imagine what'll happen to me if the Russian army doesn't crush Petlura and he takes Kiev?

ELENA. You could be hidden.

TALBERG. My sweet, how could I be hidden! I'm not a needle. There's not a man in town who wouldn't know me. Hide the assistant to the Minister of War! I can't sit in somebody else's apartment without my service jacket like *señor* Myshlayevsky. I'd be most excellently found.

ELENA. Wait! I don't understand . . . That means we both have to run?

TALBERG. That's the point, we don't. The whole terrible picture has just been clarified. The city is surrounded on all sides, and the only way of getting out is on the train of the German staff. They aren't taking women. They gave me one place because of my connections.

ELENA. In other words, you want to go alone?

TALBERG. My dearest, I don't "want to," there's nothing else I can do! Understand it, it's a catastrophe! The train's leaving in an hour and a half. Make up your mind, and as quickly as possible.

ELENA. In an hour and a half? As quickly as possible? Then I've made it up—go ahead.

TALBERG. You're a clever girl. I always said that. What else was I going to say? Yes, that you're a clever girl! However, I've already said that.

ELENA. How long are we separating for?

TALBERG. For a month or two, I think. I'll just wait out all this mess in Berlin, and when the Hetman comes back . . .

ELENA. But if he doesn't at all?

TALBERG. That's impossible. Even if the Germans quit the Ukraine, the Entente will take it and restore the Hetman. Europe needs a Ukraine with a Hetman, as a buffer between it and the Moscow Bolsheviks. You see, I've figured it all out.

ELENA. Yes, I see, but let me say this: the Hetman is still here, and they're drawing up their troops. So how can you suddenly run off in front of everybody? Will that be so clever?

TALBERG. Darling, that's naïve of you. I'm telling just you secretly, "I'm running," because I know you'll never tell anybody. Colonels on the General Staff don't run. They travel on assignment. I have a paper in my pocket from the Hetman's ministry assigning me to Berlin. Not bad, eh?

ELENA. Not bad at all. But what'll happen to them, to the rest?

TALBERG. Let me thank you for comparing me to the rest. I'm not "the rest."

ELENA. Let my brothers know about this.

TALBERG. Of course, of course. I'm even partly glad I'm going alone for such a long time. Somehow, you'll still manage to keep our rooms for us.

ELENA. Vladimir Robertovich, it's my brothers that are here! Do you really think they're crowding us out? You haven't got the right . . .

TALBERG. Oh no, no, no . . . Of course not . . . But you know the saying: *Qui va à la chasse, perd sa place.* Now, I have a favor to ask, the last one. While I'm gone, hm . . . of course . . . that Shervinsky'll be coming here . . .

ELENA. He's been coming while you were here.

TALBERG. Unfortunately. You see, my dearest, I don't like him.

ELENA. Why, if I may ask?

TALBERG. His courting of you has become too importunate, and I should very much like . . . hm . . .

ELENA. What would you very much like?

TALBERG. I can't tell you what. You're an intelligent woman and splendidly brought up. You know superbly how to behave in order not to reflect badly on the Talberg name.

ELENA. All right . . . I won't reflect badly on the Talberg name.

TALBERG. Why do you answer me so dryly? After all, I'm not talking to you about the possibility of your cuckolding me. I know very well that that's impossible.

ELENA. Why do you presume, Vladimir Robertovich, that that's impossible?

TALBERG. Elena, Elena, Elena! I don't recognize you. There's the result of dealing with Myshlayevsky! A married woman, to betray me! . . . A quarter to ten! I'll be late!

ELENA. I'll pack your things right away . . .

TALBERG. Darling, don't, don't, just the little suitcase, there's some linen in it. Only, for God's sake, hurry up. I give you one minute.

ELENA. Nevertheless, you go say good-bye to my brothers.

TALBERG. Of course, absolutely, only don't forget, I'm going off on an assignment.

ELENA. Alyosha! Alyosha! (*Runs out.*)
ALEKSEI (*coming in*). Yes, yes . . . Ah, hello, Volodya.
TALBERG. Hello, Alyosha.
ALEKSEI. What's all the fuss about?
TALBERG. Well, you see, I have some important news for you. Tonight the Hetman's position became very serious.
ALEKSEI. How so?
TALBERG. Extremely serious.
ALEKSEI. What's up?
TALBERG. It's very possible that the Germans won't help and he'll have to push Petlura back with his own forces.
ALEKSEI. What do you mean!
TALBERG. It's very possible.
ALEKSEI. There's something dirty here . . . Thanks for having told me.
TALBERG. And now the other thing. Since I'm leaving now on an assignment . . .
ALEKSEI. Where, if it's not a secret?
TALBERG. For Berlin.
ALEKSEI. Where? Berlin?
TALBERG. Yes. No matter how I threw my weight around, I couldn't get out of it. Such an outrage!
ALEKSEI. For long, may I ask?
TALBERG. For two months.
ALEKSEI. Ah, so.
TALBERG. And so, let me wish you all the best. Take care of Elena. (*Holds out his hand.*)
  (ALEKSEI *puts his hand behind his back.*)
What does that mean?
ALEKSEI. It means that I don't much like your assignment.
TALBERG. Colonel Turbin!
ALEKSEI. Yes, sir, Colonel Talberg.
TALBERG. You'll have to answer to me for that, Mr. Brother of my wife!
ALEKSEI. When would you like me to, Mr. Talberg?
TALBERG. When . . . Five to ten . . . When I come back.
ALEKSEI. God knows what'll have happened by the time you're back!
TALBERG. You . . . you . . . I've been meaning to have a talk with you for a long time.

ALEKSEI. Don't dare upset your wife, Mr. Talberg!
ELENA (*coming in*). What were you talking about?
ALEKSEI. Nothing, nothing, Lenochka!
TALBERG. Nothing, nothing at all, dearest! Well, good-bye, Alyosha!
ALEKSEI. Good-bye, Volodya!
ELENA. Nikolka! Nikolka!
NIKOLKA (*coming in*). Here he is, myself. Oh, he's here? . . .
ELENA. Volodya's going off on an assignment. Say good-bye to him.
TALBERG. Good-bye, Nikol.
NIKOLKA. Have a good trip, Colonel.
TALBERG. Elena, here's some money for you. I'll send some from Berlin right away. My regards to you all. (*Rushes into the hall.*) Don't see me off, darling, you'll catch cold. (*Goes out.* ELENA *follows him.*)
ALEKSEI (*in an unpleasant voice*). Elena, you'll catch cold. (*A pause.*)
NIKOLKA. Alyosha, how come he just left like that? Where to?
ALEKSEI. Berlin.
NIKOLKA. Berlin . . . At a moment like this . . . (*Looking out the window.*) Haggling with the cab driver. (*Philosophically.*) Alyosha, you know, I've noticed he looks like a rat.
ALEKSEI (*mechanically*). Absolutely right, Nikol. And our house—like a ship. Well, go join the guests. Go on, go on.
   (NIKOLKA *goes out.*)
The division's done for, down to the last. "Very serious." "Extremely serious." The rat! (*Goes out.*)
ELENA (*returns from the hall. Looks out the window*). He's gone . . .

SCENE 2

The table is set for supper.

ELENA (*at the piano, plays one and the same chord*). He's gone. So he's gone . . .
SHERVINSKY (*suddenly appears on the threshold*). Who's gone?

ELENA. My God! How you scared me, Shervinsky! How did you get in without ringing?

SHERVINSKY. Why, your door's open—wide open. Greetings and salutations, Elena Vasilyevna. (*Takes a huge bouquet out of its wrapper.*)

ELENA. How many times have I asked you, Leonid Yuryevich, not to do this. It makes me uncomfortable that you're spending so much money.

SHERVINSKY. Money exists to be spent, as Karl Marx said. May I take off my cloak?

ELENA. And if I said no?

SHERVINSKY. I'd sit in it all night, at your feet.

ELENA. Oh, Shervinsky, that's a soldier's compliment.

SHERVINSKY. Sorry, a guardsman's. (*Takes his felt cloak off in the hall; keeps on a very splendid Circassian caftan.*) I'm so glad to see you! I haven't seen you for so long!

ELENA. If memory doesn't deceive me, you were here yesterday.

SHERVINSKY. Ah, Elena Vasilyevna, what's "yesterday" nowadays! So, who's gone?

ELENA. Vladimir Robertovich.

SHERVINSKY. He was supposed to come back today!

ELENA. Yes, he did . . . and again went away.

SHERVINSKY. Where?

ELENA. What marvelous roses! . . .

SHERVINSKY. Where?

ELENA. Berlin.

SHERVINSKY. Berlin? For long, if I may ask?

ELENA. For a month or two.

SHERVINSKY. For two months! What are you saying! . . . That's too bad, too bad, too bad . . . I'm so upset, so upset! . . .

ELENA. Shervinsky, you're kissing my hand for the fifth time.

SHERVINSKY. I'm overwhelmed, if I may say so . . . My God, this is everything! Hurrah! Hurrah!

NIKOLKA'S VOICE. Shervinsky! *The Demon!*[2]

ELENA. Why are you so wildly happy?

---

[2] He is asking for the aria from Rubinstein's opera *The Demon*, based on the text of the Lermontov poem.

SHERVINSKY. I'm delighted that . . . Ah, Elena Vasilyevna, you wouldn't understand! . . .

ELENA. You're not a man of the world, Shervinsky.

SHERVINSKY. I'm not? Why not, now? . . . No, I am . . . I'm just upset, you know . . . And so, therefore, he's gone, but you're staying.

ELENA. As you see. How's your voice?

SHERVINSKY (*at the piano*). Ma-ma . . . mia . . . mi . . . He's far away, he's far . . . he's far away, he won't know . . . Yes . . . In incomparable voice. Came here in a cab, thought even my voice was gone, but I get here—and it turns out my voice is fine.

ELENA. Did you bring the music?

SHERVINSKY. Why of course, of course . . . You're an absolute goddess!

ELENA. The only thing that's good about you is your voice, and the thing you ought to be doing, really, is having an operatic career.

SHERVINSKY. There's something to that. You know, Elena Vasilyevna, once I sang the epithalamion in *Zhmerinka*. It has a high F, as you know, but I hit A and held it for nine beats.

ELENA. For how many?

SHERVINSKY. For seven. It's not fair of you not to believe me. Honestly. Countess Gendrikova was there . . . She fell in love with me after that A . . .

ELENA. And then what happened?

SHERVINSKY. Poisoned herself. Potassium cyanide.

ELENA. Ah, Shervinsky! It's really a disease with you, honestly. Gentlemen! Shervinsky! Supper's on the table!
(ALEKSEI, STUDZINSKY, *and* MYSHLAYEVSKY *come in.*)

ALEKSEI. Hello, Leonid Yuryevich. Welcome.

SHERVINSKY. Viktor! You're alive! Well, thank God. Why do you have a turban on?

MYSHLAYEVSKY (*in a turban of toweling*). Hello, Adjutant.

SHERVINSKY (*to* STUDZINSKY). Greetings, Captain.

(LARIOSIK *and* NIKOLKA *come in.*)

MYSHLAYEVSKY. Let me introduce you. The senior officer of our division Captain Studzinsky, and this is *M'sieur* Surzhansky. He and I had a bath together

NIKOLKA. Our cousin from Zhitomir.

STUDZINSKY. Very pleased.

LARIOSIK. Sincerely glad to meet you.

SHERVINSKY. Lieutenant in the Uhlan Regiment of His Imperial Majesty's Palace Guards and Personal Aide to the Hetman, Shervinsky.

LARIOSIK. Larion Surzhansky. Sincerely glad to meet you.

MYSHLAYEVSKY. Don't you feel so overwhelmed. Of the former palace, of the former guards, of the former regiment . . .

ELENA. Gentlemen, come to the table.

ALEKSEI. Yes, do, please, for it's already twelve, and we must get up early tomorrow.

SHERVINSKY. Oh, what splendor! What's the occasion for the feast, if I may ask?

NIKOLKA. The division's last supper. Tomorrow we set out, Lieutenant . . .

SHERVINSKY. Aha . . .

STUDZINSKY. Where would you like me, Colonel?

SHERVINSKY. Where would you like me?

ALEKSEI. Wherever you want, wherever you want. Please! Lenochka, be hostess. (*They sit down.*)

SHERVINSKY. So, that means, he's gone and you've stayed?

ELENA. Shervinsky, keep quiet.

MYSHLAYEVSKY. Lenochka, will you drink some vodka?

ELENA. No, no, no! . . .

MYSHLAYEVSKY. Well, some white wine, then.

STUDZINSKY. May I pour you some, Colonel?

ALEKSEI. *Merci*. And yourself, please.

MYSHLAYEVSKY. Your glass.

LARIOSIK. Actually, I don't drink vodka.

MYSHLAYEVSKY. Heavens, I don't, either. But just one little glass. How'll you eat the salt herring without vodka? I absolutely can't understand.

LARIOSIK. I'm sincerely grateful to you.

MYSHLAYEVSKY. I haven't had any vodka for a long, long time.

SHERVINSKY. Gentlemen! To Elena Vasilyevna's health! Hurrah!

STUDZINSKY.
MYSHLAYEVSKY. } Hurrah! . . .
LARIOSIK.

ELENA. Shh! What're you doing, gentlemen! You'll wake up the whole street. As it is, they keep saying that we have a drinking bout here every day.

MYSHLAYEVSKY. Oh, it's fine! Vodka refreshes you. Isn't that so?

LARIOSIK. Yes, very!

MYSHLAYEVSKY. I beg you, just one more little glass apiece. Colonel . . .

ALEKSEI. Take it easy, Viktor, we have to set out tomorrow.

NIKOLKA. And we will!

ELENA. What about the Hetman? Tell me.

STUDZINSKY. Yes, what about the Hetman?

SHERVINSKY. Everything's fine. What a supper there was yesterday in the palace! . . . For two hundred guests. Grouse . . . And the Hetman in national costume . . .

ELENA. But they say the Germans are leaving us to the mercy of fate?

SHERVINSKY. Don't believe any of the rumors, Elena Vasilyevna.

LARIOSIK. Thank you very much, Viktor Viktorovich, sir. You know, actually, I don't drink vodka.

MYSHLAYEVSKY (*drinking*). Shame on you, Larion!

SHERVINSKY. } Shame on you!
NIKOLKA.

LARIOSIK. I humbly thank you.

ALEKSEI. Nikol, don't you work on that vodka too hard.

NIKOLKA. Yes, sir, Colonel! I'll have some white wine.

LARIOSIK. How cleverly you down it, Viktor Viktorovich.

MYSHLAYEVSKY. Comes with practice.

ALEKSEI. Thanks, Captain. Some salad?

STUDZINSKY. Many thanks.

MYSHLAYEVSKY. Lena precious! Drink the white wine. Joy of my life! Redheaded Lena, I know why you're so upset. Forget it! It's all for the best.

SHERVINSKY. All for the best.

MYSHLAYEVSKY. No, no, bottoms up, Lenochka, bottoms up!

NIKOLKA (*picks up his guitar, sings*).
> *One will drain the cup, another will be wise . . .*
> *to drain the cup . . .*

ALL (*sing*). *All happiness to Elena Vasilyevna!*
—*Lenochka, drink up!*
—*Drink up . . . drink up . . .*
  (ELENA *drinks*.)
—Bravo!!! (*They clap*.)
MYSHLAYEVSKY. You look wonderful today. Honestly. And that robe suits you, I swear. Gentlemen, just look, what a fine robe, perfectly green!
ELENA. It's a dress, Vitenka, and it's not green, but grey.
MYSHLAYEVSKY. Oh, so much the worse. It's all the same. Gentlemen, look here, isn't she a beautiful woman? Wouldn't you say so?
STUDZINSKY. Elena Vasilyevna is very beautiful. To your health!
MYSHLAYEVSKY. Lena serene, let me hug you and kiss you.
SHERVINSKY. Now, now, Viktor, Viktor! . . .
MYSHLAYEVSKY. Leonid, get back. Step back from a married woman, from somebody else's wife!
SHERVINSKY. If you please . . .
MYSHLAYEVSKY. I can, I'm a childhood friend.
SHERVINSKY. You're a pig, no childhood friend . . .
NIKOLKA (*rising*). Gentlemen, to the health of the Divisional Commander!
  (STUDZINSKY, SHERVINSKY, *and* MYSHLAYEVSKY *rise*.)
LARIOSIK. Hurrah! . . . I beg your pardon, gentlemen, I'm not in the army.
MYSHLAYEVSKY. No matter, no matter, Larion! You did right!
LARIOSIK. Good Elena Vasilyevna! I can't express how fine it is for me here with you . . .
ELENA. I'm very glad.
LARIOSIK. Good Aleksei Vasilyevich! . . . I can't express how fine it is for me here with you! . . .
ALEKSEI. I'm very glad.
LARIOSIK. Gentlemen, cream-colored shades . . . your whole soul is at ease behind them . . . you forget all the horrors of the civil war. And don't our wounded souls so thirst for peace . . .
MYSHLAYEVSKY. Do you, if I may ask, write poetry?
LARIOSIK. Me? Yes . . . I do.

MYSHLAYEVSKY. Thought so. Sorry I interrupted you. Go on.

LARIOSIK. It's all right . . . Cream-colored shades . . . They separate us from the entire world . . . However, I'm not in the army . . . Ah! . . . Pour me just another little glassful.

MYSHLAYEVSKY. Bravo, Larion! Look at you, you old fox, and you said you didn't drink. You're a nice fellow, Larion, but you deliver a speech like a real clod.

LARIOSIK. No, don't say that, Viktor Viktorovich; I've delivered speeches before, and not just once . . . among my dead Papa's co-workers . . . in Zhitomir . . . Well, there were tax assessors there . . . They also . . . Oh, how they criticized me!

MYSHLAYEVSKY. Tax assessors are famous brutes.

SHERVINSKY. Drink, Lena, drink something, my dear!

ELENA. You want to get me drunk? Oh, what an awful man!

NIKOLKA (*at the piano, sings*).

Tell me now, wizard, you pet of the gods,
What is to happen to me in life?
To the enemy's joy will I soon be dead
And buried deep in a grave in the earth?

LARIOSIK (*sings*).

Now louder, you music, play us the victory.

ALL (*sing*).

We are the victors; the enemy flees.
Now to . . .

LARIOSIK. The Tsar! . . .[3]

ALEKSEI. What do you mean, what do you mean!

ALL (*sing a phrase without words*).

. . . .
We shout out a loud Hurrah! Hurrah! Hurrah!

NIKOLKA (*sings*).

Coming to meet him from the dark woods . . .
(*All sing.*)

LARIOSIK. Oh! How gay it is at your place, Elena Vasilyevna, my dear! Lights! . . . Hurrah!

---

[3] This soldiers' song, adapted from a poem by Pushkin ("The Wise Oleg") had different words after 1917; the "People's Commissars" replaced "The Tsar, Russia, and Faith."

SHERVINSKY. Gentlemen! The health of His Eminence the Hetman of the Whole Ukraine. Hurrah! (*A pause.*)

STUDZINSKY. Sorry, I'm going to go fight tomorrow, but I won't drink that toast and I urge other officers not to.

SHERVINSKY. Captain!

LARIOSIK. Something completely unexpected.

MYSHLAYEVSKY (*drunk*). On account of him, the devil, I got my feet frozen off. (*Drinks.*)

STUDZINSKY. Colonel, do you approve of the toast?

ALEKSEI. No, I don't.

SHERVINSKY. Colonel, let me, I'll make another!

STUDZINSKY. No, let me, I will!

LARIOSIK. No, let me, I will. To the health of Elena Vasilyevna and equally to that of her good husband who has departed for Berlin!

MYSHLAYEVSKY. There y'are! You guessed it, Larion! Couldn't have done better!

NIKOLKA (*sings*).

Tell me the whole truth, don't be afraid . . .

LARIOSIK. I'm sorry, Elena Vasilyevna, I'm not in the army.

ELENA. It doesn't matter, doesn't matter, Larion. You're sincere, a good man. Come over here.

LARIOSIK. Elena Vasilyevna! Ah, my God, the red wine! . . .

NIKOLKA. Salt, we'll put salt on it . . . It doesn't matter.

STUDZINSKY. This Hetman of yours! . . .

ALEKSEI. Just a minute, gentlemen! . . . What's it all about, in fact? Have we given ourselves over to him to be made fun of, is that it? If your Hetman, instead of playing away at this damned comedy of establishing a separate Ukraine, began forming an officer corps, why, there wouldn't be hide or hair of Petlura here in Little Russia. And on top of it we'd slap down the Bolsheviks in Moscow like flies. And just in time! They're eating cats there, they say. And he, the bastard, would save Russia!

SHERVINSKY. The Germans haven't permitted the formation of an army; they're afraid of it.

ALEKSEI. It's a mistake. The Germans ought to have had it explained to them that we're no danger for them. It's all over! We lost the war. We now have something much more terrible than the war, than the Germans, than anything else in the world: we have the Bolsheviks. We ought to have said to the Germans: "What do you want? Need bread, sugar? Here, take it, bust, choke on it, but at least help us so our peasants don't catch the Moscow disease." But now it's too late; now our officers have all turned into café habitués. A café army! Go round them up. They'll sure go fight for you. They, the bastards, have foreign money in their pockets. Just sit there, in a café on Kreshchatik, along with the whole headquarters crowd from the Guards. My, it's just splendid! Colonel Turbin got a division: fly off, hurry up, get it together, set out, Petlura's coming! . . . Great! Just yesterday I took a look at them and, I give you my word of honor, for the first time in my life my heart shuddered.

MYSHLAYEVSKY. Alyosha, that's my little commander for you! You got a real artilleryman's heart! I drink to your health!

ALEKSEI. Shuddered, because for a hundred cadets there were a hundred and twenty students, and holding a rifle like a spade. And then yesterday in the square . . . It was snowing, there was a fog in the distance . . . It all seemed to me, you know, like a coffin . . .

ELENA. Alyosha, why are you saying such gloomy things? Don't you dare!

NIKOLKA. Don't get upset, Commander, we won't give up.

ALEKSEI. Why, gentlemen, here I sit among you, and have only one constant thought. Ah! If only we could have foreseen all this before! You know what this Petlura of yours is? It's a myth, an empty fog. He doesn't exist at all. Look out the window; see what's there. There, there's a snowstorm, some shadows . . . In Russia, gentlemen, there are two powers: the Bolsheviks and us. We'll meet yet. I see more terrible times ahead. I see . . . Oh, all right! We won't put Petlura down. But, you know, he won't have come for long. And after him the Bolsheviks will come. It's because of that that I'm going! Against the impossible, but I'm going! Because, when we meet up with them, things'll go more cheerfully. Either we'll bury them or, more likely, they'll bury us. I drink to the encounter, gentlemen!

LARIOSIK (*at the piano, sings*).
  A longing to meet,
  To promise, to talk—
  All in this world
  Doesn't matter a straw . . .
NIKOLKA. Well done, Larion! (*Sings.*)
  A longing to meet,
  To promise, to talk . . .
  (*All sing in confusion.* LARIOSIK *suddenly bursts into tears.*)
ELENA. Lariosik, what's wrong?
NIKOLKA. Larion!
MYSHLAYEVSKY. What're you doing, Larion, who's hurt you?
LARIOSIK (*drunk*). I got scared.
MYSHLAYEVSKY. Of who? The Bolsheviks? Well, we'll show 'em right away! (*Takes his Mauser.*)
ELENA. Viktor, what're you doing!
MYSHLAYEVSKY. Going to go shoot the commissars. Who of you is a commissar?
SHERVINSKY. The Mauser's loaded, gentlemen!
STUDZINSKY. Lieutenant, sit down this instant!
ELENA. Gentlemen, get it away from him!
  (*They take away the Mauser.* LARIOSIK *goes out.*)
ALEKSEI. What's wrong with you, you mad? Sit down this instant! It's my fault, gentlemen.
MYSHLAYEVSKY. Means I wound up in a group of Bolsheviks. Very nice. How you doing, Comrades! We'll drink to the health of the commissars. They're such nice fellows!
ELENA. Viktor, don't drink any more!
MYSHLAYEVSKY. Shut up, you lady commissar!
SHERVINSKY. Lord, how drunk he is!
ALEKSEI. Gentlemen, it's all my fault. Pay no attention to what I said. My nerves are simply all tense.
STUDZINSKY. Oh no, Colonel. Believe me, we understand and agree with everything you said. We will always defend the Russian Empire!
NIKOLKA. Long live Russia!
SHERVINSKY. Let me say something! You misunderstood me! The Hetman will do what you suppose. Then when we have managed to free ourselves of Petlura and the Allies will have helped us crush the Bolsheviks, then the Hetman will lay

the Ukraine at the feet of His Imperial Majesty the Sovereign Emperor Nikolai Aleksandrovich . . .

MYSHLAYEVSKY. What Aleksandrovich? And he says I'm drunk.

NIKOLKA. The Emperor was killed . . .

SHERVINSKY. Gentlemen! The news of the death of His Imperial Majesty . . .

MYSHLAYEVSKY. Is somewhat exaggerated.

STUDZINSKY. Viktor, you're an officer!

ELENA. Let him finish, gentlemen!

SHERVINSKY. . . . was thought up by the Bolsheviks. You know what happened in the palace of Emperor Wilhelm when the Hetman's retinue was presented to him? Emperor Wilhelm said: "But about what happens later you will be addressed by . . ." and the doors opened and our sovereign walked out.

(LARIOSIK *enters*.)

He said: "Gentlemen of the officer corps, go to the Ukraine and assemble your detachments. When the time comes, I will personally lead you into the heart of Russia, to Moscow!" And he burst into tears.

STUDZINSKY. He's been killed!

ELENA. Shervinsky! Is this true?

SHERVINSKY. Elena Vasilyevna!

ALEKSEI. Lieutenant, it's a legend! I've already heard the story.

NIKOLKA. Makes no difference. The Emperor's dead, long live the Emperor! Hurrah! . . . The anthem! Shervinsky! The anthem! (*Sings.*) *God save our tsar!* . . .

SHERVINSKY.
STUDZINSKY. } *God save our tsar!*
MYSHLAYEVSKY.

LARIOSIK (*sings*). *Mighty, triumphant* . . .

NIKOLKA.
STUDZINSKY. } *Reign on* . . .
SHERVINSKY.

ELENA.
ALEKSEI. } Gentlemen, what is this! Shouldn't do this!

MYSHLAYEVSKY (*weeps*). Alyosha, is this a people! You know they're bandits. A trade union of murderers of tsars. Pyotr the Third . . . Now, what did he do to them? Just what? And they shout: "No war!" Great . . . He stopped the war. And then? One of his own courtiers smashed a bottle in his puss! . . . A prince let Pavel Petrovich have it on the ear with a cigar case . . . And this . . . I forget, what's his name . . . with the sideburns, nice fellow, figures, I'll do something nice for the peasants, set 'em free, damned devils. So that's what they threw the bomb at him for? Ought to give 'em a real thrashing, the no-gooders. Alyosha! Oh, I don't feel so good, boys . . .

ELENA. He's sick!

NIKOLKA. The Lieutenant's sick!

ALEKSEI. Into the tub with him.

(STUDZINSKY, NIKOLKA, *and* ALEKSEI *lift* MYSHLAYEVSKY *up and carry him out.*)

ELENA. I'll go see what's wrong with him.

SHERVINSKY (*blocking the door*). Don't, Lena!

ELENA. Gentlemen, gentlemen, but I must . . . It's a mess . . . Full of tobacco smoke . . . Lariosik, Lariosik! . . .

SHERVINSKY. What are you doing, what are you doing, don't wake him!

ELENA. On account of you I'm a little high myself. Lord, my legs won't move.

SHERVINSKY. Here, over here . . . Will you let me . . . beside you?

ELENA. Sit down . . . Shervinsky, what's going to happen to us? How's this all going to end? Ah? . . . I had a bad dream. In general, recently, everything's getting worse and worse all around.

SHERVINSKY. Elena Vasilyevna! Everything will be fine, and don't you believe dreams . . .

ELENA. No, no, my dream was prophetic. It seemed we all were on a ship going to America and sitting in the hold. And then there was a storm. The wind was howling. It was cold, so cold. Huge waves. And we're in the hold. The water comes up to our feet . . . We crawl up onto some kind of planking. And suddenly there are rats. Such loathsome things, so huge. It was so terrible I woke up.

SHERVINSKY. But you know what, Elena Vasilyevna? He won't come back.

ELENA. Who?

SHERVINSKY. Your husband.

ELENA. Leonid Yuryevich, that's plain impudence. What business is it of yours? He'll come back, or he won't.

SHERVINSKY. It makes all the difference to me. I love you.

ELENA. I've heard that before. You just keep on making things up.

SHERVINSKY. Honest to God, I love you.

ELENA. Well, but do it to yourself.

SHERVINSKY. I don't want to, I'm tired of that.

ELENA. Wait, wait. Why did you think of my husband when I told you about the rats?

SHERVINSKY. Because he's like one.

ELENA. All the same, what a pig you are, Leonid! First of all, he's not in the least like one.

SHERVINSKY. Like two peas in a pod. Pince-nez, a little pointed nose . . .

ELENA. Very, very nice! To say foul things about someone who's absent, and to his wife at that!

SHERVINSKY. What sort of wife of his are you?

ELENA. What do you mean?

SHERVINSKY. Take a look at yourself in the mirror. You're beautiful, clever, as they say, intellectually sophisticated. In general, a woman to a T. You accompany on the piano splendidly. But beside you he's a coat hanger, a careerist, a mere feature of the headquarters staff.

ELENA. Behind his back, now! Excellent! (*Puts her hand over his mouth.*)

SHERVINSKY. I'll tell him that to his face, too. I've long wanted to. I'll tell him and challenge him to a duel. You're miserable with him.

ELENA. And who will I be happy with?

SHERVINSKY. Me.

ELENA. You won't do.

SHERVINSKY. Oh-ho! . . . Why not?

ELENA. What's good about you?

SHERVINSKY. Look closely.

ELENA. Well, your aide's insignia, and you're as handsome as a cherub. And your voice. And that's all.

SHERVINSKY. I knew it! What bad luck! Everybody says the same thing: Shervinsky's an aide, Shervinsky's a singer, the one or the other . . . But that Shervinsky has a heart—that's something nobody notices. And so Shervinsky lives like a homeless dog, and Shervinsky has nobody on whose breast he can lay his head.

ELENA (*pushing his head away*). What a vile Lovelace! I know all your adventures. You tell everybody the same thing. Including that little skinny one of yours. Fie, with the rouged lips . . .

SHERVINSKY. She's not skinny. She's a mezzo-soprano. Elena Vasilyevna, honest to God, I've never told her anything like this and never will. It's wrong of you, for your part, to talk like this, Lena. It's very wrong of you, Lena.

ELENA. I'm not Lena to you!

SHERVINSKY. Well, it's wrong of you, Elena Vasilyevna. In general, you have no feeling at all for me.

ELENA. Unfortunately, I like you very much.

SHERVINSKY. Aha! You do. But you don't love your husband.

ELENA. No, I do.

SHERVINSKY. Lena, don't lie. A woman who loves her husband doesn't have eyes like that. I've seen women's eyes. You can see everything in them.

ELENA. Certainly, you're experienced, of course.

SHERVINSKY. How could he go!

ELENA. And you'd have done the same.

SHERVINSKY. Me? Never! It's shameful. Admit that you don't love him!

ELENA. Oh, all right: I don't love him and don't respect him. I don't. You satisfied? But nothing follows from this. Take your hands away.

SHERVINSKY. But why did you kiss me then?

ELENA. You're lying! I've never kissed you. A liar in aiguillettes!

SHERVINSKY. Me lie? . . . And at the piano? I was singing "Almighty God" . . . and we were alone. And I'll even tell you when—November eighth. We were alone, and you kissed me on my lips.

ELENA. I kissed you for your voice. Understand? For your voice. Kissed you as a mother would. Because you have a marvellous voice. And that's all.

SHERVINSKY. All?

ELENA. This is torture. Word of honor! The dishes are dirty. These are all drunk. My husband's gone off somewhere. All around the lights . . .

SHERVINSKY. We'll get rid of the light. (*Puts out the upper light.*) All right like that? Listen, Lena, I love you very much. You know, no matter what I won't let you go. You'll be my wife.

ELENA. Pushed his way in like a serpent . . . like a serpent.

SHERVINSKY. What kind of serpent am I?

ELENA. Takes advantage of every opportunity and tempts. You won't get anywhere. Anywhere. No matter what he may be like, I'm not going to ruin my life on account of you. Maybe wou'll turn out to be even worse.

SHERVINSKY. Lena, how lovely you are!

ELENA. Go away! I'm drunk. You yourself got me drunk on purpose. You're a famous rascal. Our whole life is crumbling. Everything'll be lost, ruined.

SHERVINSKY. Elena, don't you fear, I won't leave you at such a moment. I'll be beside you, Lena.

ELENA. Let me go. I'm afraid of reflecting badly on the Talberg name.

SHERVINSKY. Lena, forget him completely and marry me . . . Lena! (*They kiss.*) Will you get a divorce? (*They kiss.*)

LARIOSIK (*suddenly*). Don't kiss or else I'll be sick.

ELENA. Let me go! My God! (*Runs out.*)

LARIOSIK. Oh!

SHERVINSKY. Young man, you didn't see a thing!

LARIOSIK (*dimly*). No, I did.

SHERVINSKY. What do you mean?

LARIOSIK. If you have a king, play the king, but don't touch the queens! . . . Don't touch 'em! . . . Oh! . . .

SHERVINSKY. I wasn't playing with you.

LARIOSIK. No, you were.

SHERVINSKY. Lord, he's dead drunk!

LARIOSIK. We'll see what Mama tells you when I die. I said

I wasn't in the army, couldn't have so much vodka. (*Falls onto* SHERVINSKY's *chest.*)

SHERVINSKY. He's all done in!

(*The clock strikes three and plays a minuet.*)

(*Curtain*)

ACT II

SCENE 1

The HETMAN's office in the palace. An enormous desk; telephones on it. There is a separate field telephone. On the wall is a huge map in a frame. Night. The office is brightly lit. The door opens and a VALET admits SHERVINSKY.

SHERVINSKY. Hello, Fyodor.

VALET. Good day, Lieutenant, sir.

SHERVINSKY. What's this! Nobody here? But which of the aides is on duty at the phones?

VALET. His Excellency, Prince Novozhiltsev.

SHERVINSKY. But where is he?

VALET. I have no idea. He left half an hour ago.

SHERVINSKY. How can that be? And there was no one on duty at the phones for a half hour?

VALET. No one called. I was at the door the whole time.

SHERVINSKY. As if it mattered that no one did! What if someone had? At such a moment! God knows what's going on!

VALET. I'd have taken a message. That's what I was told to do, until you came, to take a message.

SHERVINSKY. You? To take down a message from the field! What's happened to him, his brain gone soft? Ah, I know, I know! He fell sick?

VALET. Not a bit. He left the palace entirely.

SHERVINSKY. What do you mean—entirely? You're joking, Fyodor, my good man. Without handing over duty he left the palace? You mean he went off to the madhouse?

VALET. I don't know. Only he collected his toothbrush, towel and soap from the aides' room. I even gave him a newspaper.

SHERVINSKY. What do you mean, a newspaper?

VALET. I'm giving you the report, Lieutenant; he wrapped his soap up in yesterday's newspaper.

SHERVINSKY. But look, his sword's still there!

VALET. Yes, he left in civilian clothes.

SHERVINSKY. Either I'm mad, or you are. He left me some kind of a note at least? Told you to give me anything?

VALET. To give you his respects.

SHERVINSKY. You're excused, Fyodor.

VALET. Yes, sir. May I add, sir?

SHERVINSKY. Well?

VALET. He received some bad news.

SHERVINSKY. From where, from home?

VALET. Not a bit. On the field phone. And started hurrying right away. And his face changed a lot, too, when he'd heard it.

SHERVINSKY. Fyodor, I hope that you're not concerned with the hue of the faces of His Eminence's aides. You're talking too much.

VALET. Please excuse me, Lieutenant. (*Goes out.*)

SHERVINSKY (*talks into the telephone on the* HETMAN'*s desk*). Twelve–twenty-three . . . *Merci* . . . This Prince Novozhiltsev's appartment? . . . Ask Sergei Nikolayevich . . . What? In the palace? He's not in the palace. I'm talking from the palace myself . . . Wait, Seryozha, why it's your own voice! . . . Ser . . . Please . . .

(*The telephone rings off.*)

What boorishness! I heard perfectly well that it was he himself. (*A pause.*) Shervinsky, Shervinsky . . . (*Calls up on the field phone, the phone whines.*) Headquarters of the Svyatoshino force? . . . Let me have the staff commander . . . What—he's not there? His deputy . . . Staff of the Svyatoshino force? . . . What kind of devil's play is this? . . . (*Sits down at the desk, rings telephone.*)

(*The* VALET *comes in.*)

(*Makes a note.*) Fyodor, give this note to a messenger right away. Have him go to my apartment right away, on Lvovskaya Street, where, when he shows this note, they'll give him a package. Have him bring it back here at once. Here are two karbovanetses[4] for him for the cab. Here's a note to the commander's office to let him through.

VALET. Yes, sir. (*Goes out.*)

SHERVINSKY (*rubs his side whiskers reflectively*). What kind of devil's play is this, my word!

[4] Karbovanets—in the Ukraine, a ruble.

(The telephone on the desk rings.)

Hello . . . Yes . . . His Eminence's personal aide, Lieutenant Shervinsky . . . Your health, Your Excellency . . . What, sir? *(A pause.)* Bolbotun! . . . What, with the whole staff? . . . Yes, sir! . . . Right, sir, I'll tell him . . . Yes, Your Excellency . . . His Eminence is supposed to be here at twelve o'clock tonight. *(Hangs up the receiver.)*

(The telephone rings off. A pause.)

I've had it, gentlemen! *(Whistles.)*

(Backstage the muffled command: "Attention!" then the many-voiced shout of the men on watch: "Your health, Your Eminence!")

VALET *(opens both halves of the door)*. His Eminence!

(The HETMAN *comes in. He is in a very splendid Circassian caftan, raspberry-colored wide breeches and boots of the Caucasian sort without heels and without spurs. The bright shoulder loops of a general. A short-cropped, greying mustache, a smoothly-shaved head; about forty-five years old.)*

HETMAN. Hello, Lieutenant.

SHERVINSKY. Your health, Your Eminence.

HETMAN. Have they come?

SHERVINSKY. May I ask who?

HETMAN. What do you mean, who? I called a conference here for a quarter to twelve. The commander of the Russian army is supposed to be here, the head of the garrison, and representatives of the German command. Where are they?

SHERVINSKY. I have no idea. No one has come.

HETMAN. They're always late. Give me the report for the last hour. Quickly!

SHERVINSKY. I wish to inform Your Eminence that I have only just come on duty. Cornet Prince Novozhiltsev, who was on duty before me . . .

HETMAN. I've long been meaning to point out to you and the other aides that you ought to speak Ukrainian. It's a disgrace, after all! Not one of my officers speaks the language of the country, and this has a very negative affect on the Ukrainian detachments. Please be so gud.[5]

---

[5] Ukrainian, though a separate Eastern Slavic language, has many terms and features very similar to Russian; hence, Shervinsky's brief attempt at it by distorting Russian.

SHERVINSKY. Ay, sir, Your Eminence. The aide on duty Cornet . . . Prince . . . (*Aside.*) God damned if I know what "Prince" is in Ukrainian! . . . Damn it! (*Aloud.*) Novozhiltsev, temporarily acting for . . . I think . . . thunk . . . therunk . . .

HETMAN. Speak Russian!

SHERVINSKY. Yes, sir, Your Eminence! Cornet Prince Novozhiltsev, who was on duty before me, apparently fell ill suddenly and left for home even before I had arrived . . .

HETMAN. What's that you're saying? Left his post? What about yourself, now? You have your wits about you? How's this possible—left his post? Means he deserted his duty? What's going on here with you all, after all? (*Calls up on the phone.*) The commander's office? . . . Send a detail at once . . . You must listen to the voice and know who's speaking. A detail to the apartment of my aide, Cornet Novozhiltsev, arrest him and take him into your office. Immediately.

SHERVINSKY (*aside*). That's what he deserves! He'll learn not to talk over the phone with a make-believe voice. The cad!

HETMAN (*on the telephone*). This minute! (*To* SHERVINSKY.) Well, did he leave a record?

SHERVINSKY. Yes, indeed. But there's nothing on the tape.

HETMAN. Now, what's he up to? Did he go off his head? Lose his mind? Why, I'll shoot him right away, right here, by the palace wall. I'll show you all! Get in touch at once with the headquarters of the Commander. Ask him here immediately! And the same for the head of the garrison and all the Regimental Commanders. Quickly!

SHERVINSKY. I wish to inform Your Eminence of some news of extraordinary importance.

HETMAN. What more news have you there?

SHERVINSKY. Five minutes ago they called in from the headquarters of the Commander and said that the Commander of the volunteer army under Your Eminence had suddenly fallen ill and, with his entire staff, had left for Germany on the German train. (*A pause.*)

HETMAN. You in your right mind? Your eyes look as if you were sick . . . You have any idea what you've just reported to me? What's happened? A catastrophe, is that it?

They ran away? Why don't you say anything? Well! . . .

SHERVINSKY. Exactly so, Your Eminence, a catastrophe. At ten this evening Petlura's forces broke the front lines of the city and Bolbotun's cavalry went through the opening . . .

HETMAN. Bolbotun's? . . . Where? . . .

SHERVINSKY. Beyond Slobodka, ten versts.

HETMAN. Wait . . . wait . . . so . . . what now? . . . Ah, yes . . . In any case, you're an excellent, efficient officer. I noticed that long ago. Here's what. Get in touch with the German headquarters at once and ask the command's representatives to come over here this minute. Quickly, dear boy, quickly!

SHERVINSKY. Yes, sir. (*On the telephone.*) Number three. *Seien Sie bitte so liebenswürdig, Herrn Major von Dust an den Apparat zu bitten.*

(*A knock on the door.*)

Ja . . . Ja . . .

HETMAN. Come in.

VALET. The representatives of the German command, General von Schratt and Major von Dust, ask to see you.

HETMAN. Show them in at once. (*To* SHERVINSKY.) Never mind.

(*The* VALET *admits* VON SCHRATT *and* VON DUST. *Both are in grey uniform.* SCHRATT *is long-faced, grey-haired.* DUST *has a purplish face. Both wear monocles.*)

SCHRATT. *Wir haben die Ehre, Euer Durchlaucht zu begrüssen.*

HETMAN. *Sehr erfreut, Sie zu sehen, meine Herren. Bitte nehmen Sie Platz.*

(*The Germans sit down.*)

Ich habe eben die Nachricht von der schwierigen Lage unserer Armee erhalten.

SCHRATT. *Das ist uns schon längere Zeit bekannt.*

HETMAN (*to* SHERVINSKY). Please take minutes of the conference.

SHERVINSKY. May I take them in Russian, Your Eminence?

HETMAN. General, may I ask you to speak Russian?

SCHRATT (*with a heavy accent*). Oh yes! Mit great pleasure.

HETMAN. I have just now learned that Petlura's cavalry has broken the city's front line.

(SHERVINSKY *writes.*)

Besides, I have some very improbable news from the headquarters of the Russian command. The Russian headquarters staff has shamefully run away! *Das ist ja unerhört!* (*A pause.*) Through you I now turn to the German government . . . with the following statement: Mortal danger threatens the Ukraine. Petlura's bands threaten to seize the capital. In the event that that happens, anarchy would overcome the capital. Therefore, I beg the German High Command to send troops at once to repel the bands which have burst through this far, and to restore order in the Ukraine, so friendly to Germany.

SCHRATT. Unforchunly de Cherman command can't do dis.

HETMAN. How so? Tell me, General, why not?

SCHRATT. *Physisch unmöglich!* Physically is dis impossible. *Erstens*, in de first, cordink to our information, de Petlura hass two hundert tousant troops splendidly ekvipped. *Und* in de mean vile de Cherman command iss gadderink all de divisions und takink dem to Chermany.

SHERVINSKY (*aside*). Bastards!

SCHRATT. Dus, at our command ve haven't got enough of de forces. *Zweitens*, in de second, de whole Ukraine is showink up on de side of de Petlura.

HETMAN. Lieutenant, strike that sentence from the record.

SHERVINSKY. Yes, sir.

SCHRATT. Haf nodinks gainst dat. Strikes it. Dus, de stoppink of de Petlura is dis impossible.

HETMAN. That means that the German command is suddenly leaving me, the army and the government to the mercy of fate?

SCHRATT. No-o, we haf de orders to take measures for de rescue of Your Eminence.

HETMAN. What measures does the command propose?

SCHRATT. De immediate evacuations of Your Eminence. Right into de train *und nach* Chermany.

HETMAN. Forgive me, I don't understand anything . . . How can this be done? Sorry. Perhaps it was the German command that evacuated Prince Belorukov?

SCHRATT. Exactly so.

HETMAN. Without getting my approval? (*Becoming nervous.*) I don't agree. I'm going to send the German government a protest against such actions. I still have the chance of gathering an army together in the city and defending Kiev myself. But responsibility for the destruction of the capital will fall on the German command. And I think that the governments of England and France . . .

SCHRATT. De governments of Enkland! De governments of France! . . . De Cherman governments feels enough strengd in itself not to give over de destruction of de capitals.

HETMAN. Is that a threat, General?

SCHRATT. Is a varnink, Your Eminence. At de command of Your Eminence dere is no troops. De position is catastrophical . . .

DUST (*quietly, to* SCHRATT). *Mein General, wir haben gar keine Zeit. Wir müssen . . .*

SCHRATT. *Ja, ja* . . . Your Eminence, let me say vun last vord: ve chust now got de information dat de Petlura's cavalry is eight versts from Kiev. Und tomorrow mornings it vill come in . . .

HETMAN. I'm the last to find this out!

SCHRATT. Your Eminence, you know vat vill be mit you in cases dey make you captured? Dere's a chudchment on Your Eminence. It's a very sad vun.

HETMAN. What sort of judgment?

SCHRATT. Beggink Your Eminence's pardon. (*A pause.*) Hangkink. (*A pause.*) Your Eminence, I must ask for de reply from you right avay. Dere's only ten little minutes vich I haf at my disposals, after dat I take off all de responsibilities for Your Eminence life. (*A long pause.*)

HETMAN. I'll go!

SCHRATT. Ah, you vill? (*To* DUST.) Pe so good as to do it secretly und mit no noises.

DUST. Oh, no noise! (*Shoots from his revolver into the ceiling twice.*)

(SHERVINSKY *is beside himself.*)

HETMAN (*putting his hand on his revolver*). What's this mean?

SCHRATT. Oh, pe reassured, Your Eminence. (*Disappears through the portiere of the right-hand door.*)

(*Backstage commotion, shouting:* "Guard, to arms!" *The sound of heavy footsteps.*)

DUST (*opening the middle door*). Ruhig! Calm down! General von Schratt caught de revolver in his trousers und py mistake got a vound in de head.

(*Voices backstage: "The Hetman! Where's the Hetman?"*) De Hetman is very well. Your Eminence, please pe so good as to show yourself . . . De guard . . .

HETMAN (*in the center doorway*). All is calm, cease the alarm.

DUST (*in the doorway*). Please let trough de doctor mit de instruments.

(*The alarm dies down. A German army* DOCTOR *comes in with a box and a bag of medicines.* DUST *shuts and locks the center door.*)

SCHRATT (*coming out from behind the portiere*). Your Eminence, please redress yourself into de Cherman uniform, like you vas me, und I'm a vounded vun. Ve'll take you out of de city secretly so's nobody knows, so's de guard don't get demselfs upset.

HETMAN. Do as you wish.

(*The field phone rings.*)

Lieutenant, answer that!

SHERVINSKY. His Eminence's office . . . What? . . . What? . . . (*To the* HETMAN.) Your Eminence, two regiments of Cossack infantry have gone over to Petlura . . . In the exposed sector, the enemy's cavalry has appeared. Your Eminence, what do you want me to tell them?

HETMAN. What to tell them? Tell them to hold the cavalry back if they can, even just half an hour! I have to go! I'll give them armored cars!

SHERVINSKY (*into the telephone*). You there? . . . Hold them back even just half an hour! His Eminence will give you some armored cars!

DUST (*taking a German uniform out of the box*). Your Eminence! Ver vould you like to?

HETMAN. In the bedroom.

(*The* HETMAN *and* DUST *go out right.*)

SHERVINSKY (*downstage, on the apron*). To run away, perhaps? Will Elena go or not? (*Decisively, to* SCHRATT.) Your Excellency, I humbly ask you to take me with the Hetman; I'm his personal aide. Besides, I have with me . . . my . . . fiancée . . .

SCHRATT. Unforchunly, Lieutenant, I can't take mit me neider both you und your fiancée. If you are vantink to go, go to de station to our headkvarters train. I varn you ahead of de time dere is no places dere, is already dere de personal aide.

SHERVINSKY. Who?

SCHRATT. Vat's his name . . . Prince Novozhiltsev.

SHERVINSKY. Novozhiltsev! But when did he manage to do that?

SCHRATT. Ven dere is de catastroph, every vun becomes very kvick. He vas chust ofer at de headkvarters now.

SHERVINSKY. And there, in Berlin, he'll serve under the Hetman?

SCHRATT. Ah, no-o! De Hetman vill pe alone. No sveet at all. Ve only take chust to de border dose who vould like to safe de necks from de peasants of yours, but dere every vun does vat he likes.

SHERVINSKY. Oh, humbly grateful. I'll manage to save my own neck here, too . . .

SCHRATT. Right, Lieutenant. Vun should never leaf vun's homeland. *Heimat ist Heimat.*

(*The* HETMAN *and* DUST *enter. The* HETMAN *has changed into the uniform of a German general. He is confused, smokes.*)

HETMAN. Lieutenant, burn all the documents here.

DUST. *Herr Doktor, seien Sie liebenswürdig.* Your Eminence, pe seated.

(*They seat the* HETMAN. *The doctor bandages his head up tight.*)

DOCTOR. *Fertig.*

SCHRATT (*to* DUST). De car!

DUST. *Sogleich.*

SCHRATT. Your Eminence, lie down.

HETMAN. But this must be announced to the people . . . A manifesto? . . .

SCHRATT. De manifesto! . . . Go ahead . . .

HETMAN (*dully*). Lieutenant, take this down . . . God did not grant me the strength . . . and I . . .

DUST. Manifesto . . . Dere's no time for de manifesto . . . Send de telegram from de trains . . .

HETMAN. Never mind!

DUST. Your Eminence, lie down.

(*The* HETMAN *is put on a stretcher.* SCHRATT *hides. They open the center door, the* VALET *appears.* DUST, *the* DOCTOR *and the* VALET *carry the* HETMAN *out the left door.* SHERVINSKY *helps them to the door, comes back.* SCHRATT *comes in.*)

SCHRATT. All is in order. (*Looks at his wrist watch.*) Vun o'clock in de mornink. (*Puts on a kepi and a cloak.*) Goot-pye, Lieutenant. I advise you not to keep sittink around here. You can perfectly kvietly disperse. Take off de shoulders loops. (*Listens.*) Hear?

SHERVINSKY. Running fire.

SCHRATT. Precisely. A pun! "Runnink!" You haf a pass for de side door?

SHERVINSKY. I do.

SCHRATT. *Auf Wiedersehen!* Pe kvick! (*Goes out.*)

SHERVINSKY (*crushed*). A pure German bit of work. (*Suddenly perks up.*) Well, come on, now, there's no time to lose. No time, no time . . . no time . . . (*At the desk.*) Oh, the cigarette case! Gold! The Hetman forgot it. Leave it here? Impossible, the servants'll steal it. Oho! Must weigh a pound. A historical thing of value. (*Puts it in his pocket.*) Come on, now . . . (*Behind the desk.*) We'll not burn any of the documents and papers, except for this list of the aides. (*Burns the papers.*) Am I a pig or not? No, I'm not. (*On the telephone.*) Fourteen–fifty-three . . . Yes . . . The division? . . . Call the commander to the phone! This minute! . . . Wake him up! (*A pause.*) Colonel Turbin? . . . Shervinsky speaking. Listen, Aleksei Vasilyevich, carefully: the Hetman's turned tail . . . Beat it! . . . I'm telling you seriously . . . No, there's time before dawn . . . Tell Elena Vasilyevna not to leave the house tomorrow no matter what . . . I'll come in the morning to hide. Good-bye. (*Rings off.*) And my conscience is clean and at rest . . . Fyodor!

(*The* VALET *comes in.*)

Did the messenger bring the package?

VALET. Yes, sir.

SHERVINSKY. Hurry, bring it here!

(*The* VALET *goes out, then returns with a bundle.*)

VALET (*confused*). May I ask where His Eminence is?

SHERVINSKY. What kind of question is that? The Hetman wishes to rest. And, in general, keep your mouth shut. You're a good man, Fyodor. In your face there's something . . . I don't know . . . attractive . . . proletarian . . .

VALET. Yes, sir.

SHERVINSKY. Fyodor, bring me my towel, razor and soap from the aides' room.

VALET. Yes, sir. And a newspaper?

SHERVINSKY. Right you are. And a newspaper.

(*The* VALET *goes out the left-hand door. While he is gone,* SHERVINSKY *puts on a civilian overcoat and hat, takes off his spurs. He ties his sword and Novozhiltsev's into a bundle. The* VALET *appears.*)

SHERVINSKY. This hat look good on me?

VALET. Indeed, sir. Will you put the razor in your pocket?

SHERVINSKY. The razor in the pocket . . . So . . . Fyodor, good man, let me leave you fifty karbovanetses as a keepsake.

VALET. Humbly grateful.

SHERVINSKY. Let me shake your honest, working hand. Don't be surprised, I'm democratic by nature. Fyodor! I've never been in the palace, never served as an aide.

VALET. I understand.

SHERVINSKY. I don't know you. In general, I'm an opera singer . . .

VALET. He didn't move on?

SHERVINSKY. Cleared out.

VALET. Ah, the rascal!

SHERVINSKY. Unspeakable bandit!

VALET. And left us all, that means, to the mercy of fate?

SHERVINSKY. As you see. It's not so terrible for you, but what about me?

(*The telephone rings.*)

Hello . . . Ah! Captain! . . . Yes! Throw everything to hell and run . . . Means I know what I'm talking about . . . Shervinsky . . . The best of luck. Good-bye! . . . Fyodor, good man, pleasant as it is for me to chat away with you, you yourself see I've no time left at all . . . Fyodor, while I have the authority I give you this office. What are you looking at me like that for? You funny man!

Just think what a blanket can be made out of that portiere. (*Disappears.*)
(*A pause. The telephone rings.*)

VALET. Hello . . . What can I do for you? . . . You know what? Throw everything to hell and run . . . Fyodor speaking . . . Fyodor!

SCENE 2

A bare, gloomy room. A sign over the door: "Headquarters First Cavalry Division." [6] *A light blue and yellow standard. A kerosene lamp by the entrance. Evening. From outside the windows, from time to time, comes the sound of horses' hoofs. An accordion softly plays familiar airs.*

TELEPHONE OPERATOR (*into the phone*). This is me, Franko, calling the field again . . . The field, I want! . . . Y'hear? . . . This is headquarters, Cavalry Division.
(*The telephone rings its signals. There is commotion backstage.* URAGAN *and* KIRPATY *bring in a* DESERTER *from the Sech. His face is bloody.*)
BOLBOTUN. What's this?
URAGAN. Caught a deserter, Colonel.
BOLBOTUN. Which regiment? (*Silence.*) Which regiment, I'm asking you? (*Silence.*)
TELEPHONE OPERATOR. This is still me! Me from headquarters, Franko, calling the field! This is headquarters, cavalry division! . . . Y'hear? . . . Oh, God damn you! . . .
BOLBOTUN. What you up to, God damn your mother! Ha? What you up to? . . . In a time when every honest Cossack's goin' out to defend the Ukrainian republic 'gainst the White Guards an' the Communist Yids, in a time when every peasant's joined the ranks of the Ukrainian Army, what you up to slipping away in the bushes? You know

---

[6] Much of this scene, set in the insurgent Cossack camp, is in Ukrainian.

what the Hetman's officers are doing with our peasants, or the commissars there? Burying 'em alive in the earth! Eh? That's how'll I dig you up a grave myself! Myself! Sotnik[7] Galanba!

(*Voice backstage: "The Colonel's calling the Sotnik!" Commotion.*)

Where did you take him? . . .

KIRPATY. Out back of the stacks, the son of a bitch, running off, slipping away! . . .

BOLBOTUN. Ah, you, dirty dog, dirty dog!

(GALANBA *comes in, cold, black, with a black peasant hat.*) Sotnik, question the deserter . . . Franko, the disposition! Don't pick at the phone!

TELEPHONE OPERATOR. Right away, Colonel, right away! What can you do with him? "Don't pick . . ."

GALANBA (*with a cold expression*). Which regiment? (*Silence.*) Which regiment?

DESERTER (*weeping*). I'm no deserter. Mercy, Sotnik! I was staggering to sick bay. My feet are completely frozen.

TELEPHONE OPERATOR (*into the phone*). Where's the disposition lying? . . . Please be so good. The commander of the cavalry division asks for the disposition . . . Y'hear? . . . What can you do with this phone!

GALANBA. Feet frozen? And so why didn't you get a paper saying so from the headquarters of your regiment? Ha? Which regiment? (*Threatens him.*)

(*Horses can be heard going across the timbered bridge.*)

DESERTER. The Second Sech.

GALANBA. We know you, you boys from the Sech. All nogoods. Traitors. Bolsheviks. Take off your boots, take 'em off. And if you didn't freeze 'em, but are lying, why I'll shoot you dead right here. Boys! A light!

TELEPHONE OPERATOR (*into the phone*). Send us a messenger for reconnoitering . . . Into the outskirts! . . . Yes! Yes! . . . I hear! . . . Hurry! Have this messenger take the disposition for our headquarters. Good? . . . Colonel, the disposition'll be here right away . . .

BOLBOTUN. Good . . .

GALANBA (*taking out his Mauser*). And here's your terms: feet

[7] A Cossack lieutenant.

all right—I'll have you off in the other world. You all step back so's I don't get somebody else.

(*The* DESERTER *sits down on the floor, takes off his boots. Silence.*)

BOLBOTUN. This is right. So's the others get a lesson.

(*They shine a light on the* DESERTER.)

KIRPATY (*with a sigh*). Frozen . . . He was telling the truth.

GALANBA. You should have got a paper. A paper, scum! And not go running from the regiment . . .

DESERTER. Wasn't nobody to get a paper from. Ain't no medic in the regiment. Ain't nobody. (*Weeps.*)

GALANBA. Arrest him! And take him arrested to the sick bay! When the medic's bandaged his leg, see him back here to headquarters and give 'im fifteen with a ramrod, so's he knows what it means, running from his regiment with no papers.

URAGAN (*taking him out*). Go on, get goin'!

(*An accordion backstage. A voice languidly sings: "Oh, little apple, where you rolling, the Cossack boys won't let you home . . ." Excited voices outside the window: "Grab 'em! Grab 'em! Over the bridge! Run over the ice . . ."*)

GALANBA (*out the window*). Boys, what's up? What's going on?

A VOICE. Some Yids, Sotnik, took off over the bridge over the ice from Slobodka.

GALANBA. Boys! Scout 'em out! To horse! To horse! Into your saddles! Kirpaty! Come, go after 'em! Only, take 'em alive! Alive!

BOLBOTUN. Franko, get the connection!

TELEPHONE OPERATOR. Got it, Colonel, just got it!

(*Heavy footsteps backstage.* URAGAN *appears, brings in the* MAN WITH A BASKET.)

MAN WITH A BASKET. Boys, don't mind me. Whatcha doing! I'm just a artisan . . .

GALANBA. What did you find on him?

MAN WITH A BASKET. Have mercy, Comrade Officer . . .

GALANBA. What's that? Comrade? Who's comrade to you here?

MAN WITH A BASKET. 'Scuse me, Mr. Officer.

GALANBA. I ain't no mister to you. The misters're all with the Hetman over in town right now. And we're going to be cleaning out the guts of these misters of yours a bit. Boy, give it to him, you're closest. Cut this mister off at the neck. You going to say now there's misters here? Y'see?

MAN WITH A BASKET. I see.

GALANBA. Put the light on him, boys! Seems to me this here's a Communist.

MAN WITH A BASKET. What're you doing! What're you up to, have mercy! I'm a shoemaker, just look at me.

BOLBOTUN. He talks too much like one of those Moscow boys.

MAN WITH A BASKET. We're Kalugans, your worship. From Kaluga province. And we're not happy that we've come down here, down to your Ukraine. I'm a shoemaker.

GALANBA. Your papers!

MAN WITH A BASKET. My passport? Right away. My passport's all straight, might say.

GALANBA. What's in the basket? Where you headed?

MAN WITH A BASKET. There are boots in the basket, your . . . exc . . . yo . . . little boots . . . b . . . We do work for the store. Live in Slobodka ourselves, and carry the boots into town.

GALANBA. Why at night?

MAN WITH A BASKET. Just exactly the right time, so's to be in town by morning.

BOLBOTUN. Boots . . . Oho-ho . . . This is good!

(URAGAN *uncovers the basket.*)

MAN WITH A BASKET. 'Scuse me, honorable Citizen, they aren't mine, they're my master's goods.

BOLBOTUN. Your master's? This is better. Masters' goods is good goods. Boys, help yourselves to a pair of masters' goods.

(*They pick out boots.*)

MAN WITH A BASKET. Citizen Minister of War! I'm done for without those boots. Just go straight right into my grave! There's two thousand rubles' worth here . . . It's my master's . . .

BOLBOTUN. We'll give you a receipt.

MAN WITH A BASKET. Have mercy on me, what'll I do with a receipt? *Throws himself at* BOLBOTUN, *who strikes him a blow on the ear. He throws himself at* GALANBA.) Mister

Cavalry Officer! Two thousand rubles' worth. The thing is, if I was a bourgeois or, say, a Bolshevik . . .

(GALANBA *hits him on the ear.*)

(*Sits down on the floor, confused and lost.*) What's going on? Oh, never mind, take them! Means it's for supplying the army? . . . Only then let me add a little pair to go with them. (Begins taking off his boots.)

TELEPHONE OPERATOR. Just look, Colonel, what's he doing there?

BOLBOTUN. What you doing, there? Laughing, are you, you louse egg? Get back there, away from the basket. How long you going to hang around underfoot? How long? My patience is worn out, get going. Boys, step back. (*Takes his revolver.*)

MAN WITH A BASKET. What're you doing! What're you doing! What're you doing! . . .

BOLBOTUN. Get the hell out!

(*The* MAN WITH A BASKET *rushes for the door.*)

ALL. Thank you very much, Colonel!

TELEPHONE OPERATOR (*into the phone*). I hear! . . . I hear! . . . Glory! Praise! Colonel! Colonel! The men of two of the Hetman's Cossack infantry have just come into headquarters. Batko's talking things over with them about coming over to our side.

BOLBOTUN. Great glory! If these regiments are with us, then Kiev's ours.

TELEPHONE OPERATOR (*on the phone*). Gritsko! We got some new boots! . . . Yes . . . yes . . . I hear you, I hear . . . Glory! . . . Praise be, Colonel, please come to the phone.

BOLBOTUN (*on the phone*). Commander of the First Cavalry Division, Colonel Bolbotun . . . I'm listening . . . Yes . . . yes . . . I'll ride out right away. (*To* GALANBA.) Sotnik, have them all come, all four regiments of cavalry! They've taken the approaches to the city! Glory! Praise!

URAGAN.
KIRPATY. } Glory! To the attack!

(*Commotion.*)

GALANBA (*out the window*). Saddle up! Saddle up! To horse!

(*Outside the window, a din:* "*Hurrah!*" GALANBA *runs out.*)
BOLBOTUN. Undo the phone! Give me a horse!
(*The* TELEPHONE OPERATOR *unplugs the phone. Commotion.*)
URAGAN. A horse for the commander!
VOICES. First column at a gallop, march!—Second column at a gallop, march! . . .
(*Outside the window, hoofbeats, whistling. All run out offstage. Then an accordion thunders, flying past . . .*)

(*Curtain*)

ACT III

SCENE 1

The entrance hall of the Aleksandrovskaya gimnaziya. Stacks of rifles. Boxes, machine guns. A huge stairway. Up above, a portrait of Aleksandr I. Through the glass of the windows, dawn. Backstage, a thunderous noise: the division is marching along the corridors of the gimnaziya to the sound of music.

NIKOLKA (*backstage sings to the ridiculous tune of a soldiers' song*).
The night breathed heavily the ecstasy of passion,
With worry and with hazy thoughts all filled.
(*A whistle.*)
CADETS (*sing deafeningly*).
I waited for you with a wild, desired happiness,
I waited by the window for you, thrilled.
(*A whistle.*)
NIKOLKA (*sings*).
I decked our little place all out in flowers . . .
STUDZINSKY (*on the landing of the stairs*). Division, halt!
   (*Backstage, the division halts with a clatter.*)
   As you were! Lieutenant!
MYSHLAYEVSKY. First battery! Stand to! Forward march!
(*The division marches backstage.*)
STUDZINSKY. Left-right! Left-right!
MYSHLAYEVSKY. Hut! Hut! Hut! First battery, halt!
FIRST OFFICER. Second battery, halt!
(*The division stops.*)
MYSHLAYEVSKY. Battery, you may smoke! At ease!
(*Backstage, din and talking.*)
FIRST OFFICER (*to* MYSHLAYEVSKY). I'm short five in the platoon, Lieutenant. Ran off, apparently. No-good students!
SECOND OFFICER. A piggish, dirty mess in general. Y'can't make any of it out.
FIRST OFFICER. Why isn't the commander coming? We were supposed to set out at six, and now it's a quarter to seven.

MYSHLAYEVSKY. Quiet, Lieutenant, he was called up to the palace. He'll be right here. (*To the* CADETS.) What, you frozen?

FIRST CADET. Exactly so, Lieutenant, it's sort of cold.

MYSHLAYEVSKY. Why're you standing still? You're as blue as a corpse. Stamp up and down, get warmed up. After the command "at ease" you're not a statue. Every man's his own stove. Liven up! Hey, second platoon, bust up the desks in the classrooms, heat the stoves! Snap to it!

CADETS (*shouts*). Boys, pile into the classroom!—Bust the desks, heat up the stoves!

(*Noise, commotion.*)

MAKSIM (*appears from the closet, in horror*). Your Excellency, what're you doing? Heating the stoves with the desks! What kind of abuse is this! I was told by the director . . .

FIRST OFFICER. This is his fourteenth time . . .

MYSHLAYEVSKY. And what are we going to heat the stoves with, old man?

MAKSIM. With firewood, sir, firewood.

MYSHLAYEVSKY. And where's your firewood?

MAKSIM. We haven't any.

MYSHLAYEVSKY. So, clear out, old man, go to hell! Hey, second platoon, what the hell you doing? . . .

MAKSIM. Lord Almighty, saints protect us! What's happening here! Tartars, absolute Tartars. There've been a lot of soldiers . . . (*Goes out. Shouts backstage.*) Officers, what are you doing!

CADETS (*break up the desks, saw them up, feed the stoves. They sing*).

Ah, you boys and pretty babes of mine! . . . (*Mournfully.*)
Have mercy on us, Lord, this final time . . .

(*A sudden explosion nearby. A pause. Commotion.*)

FIRST OFFICER. A shell.

MYSHLAYEVSKY. Burst somewhere close by.

FIRST CADET. That was meant for us, Lieutenant, I bet.

MYSHLAYEVSKY. Nonsense! That was Petlura spitting.

(*The singing dies down.*)

FIRST OFFICER. I think, Lieutenant, we'll have the chance of getting a look at Petlura today. Interesting to know what he looks like.

SECOND OFFICER (*gloomy*). You'll find out, don't rush.

MYSHLAYEVSKY. That's not up to us. If the orders say so, we'll see him. (*To the* CADETS.) Cadets, what the hell are you doing? What're you moping there for? Get a move on!

CADETS (*sing*).

And when we're taken up to heaven,
Up along the whitened stairs . . .

SECOND CADET (*rushes up to* STUDZINSKY). The Divisional Commander!

STUDZINSKY. Fall in! Division, attention! Dress center! Officers! Officers!

MYSHLAYEVSKY. First battery, attention!

(ALEKSEI *enters.*)

ALEKSEI (*to* STUDZINSKY). The roll! How many missing?

STUDZINSKY (*quietly*). Twenty-two men.

ALEKSEI (*tears up the roll*). Our pickets at Demiyevka?

STUDZINSKY. Yes, sir!

ALEKSEI. Call them in!

STUDZINSKY (*to the* SECOND CADET). Call in the pickets!

SECOND CADET. Yes, sir. (*Runs out.*)

ALEKSEI. I order the officers and men of the division to pay close attention to what I'm going to tell them. Listen—remember. With it in mind, do it. (*Silence.*)

During the night there occurred sharp and sudden changes in our position, in the position of the entire Russian army, I would say, in the position of the Ukrainian government . . . Therefore I make the announcement to you that I am disbanding the division. (*Dead silence.*)

The fight against Petlura is over. I order you all, including the officers, immediately to take off your shoulder loops, all medals and insignia of honor, and immediately run off and conceal yourselves in your houses. (*A pause.*)

I've finished. Do as you are ordered!

STUDZINSKY. Colonel! Aleksei Vasilyevich!

FIRST OFFICER. Colonel! Aleksei Vasilyevich!

SECOND OFFICER. What's this mean?

ALEKSEI. Be quiet! Don't argue! Do what you've been ordered! Be quick!

THIRD OFFICER. What does this mean, Colonel? Arrest him! (*Noise and confusion.*)

CADETS. Arrest him! . . .
  We don't understand a thing! . . .
  What d'you mean, arrest him?! . . . What are you, mad? . . .
  Petlura's broken through! . . .
  Isn't that nice! I knew he would! . . .
  Shhh!
FIRST OFFICER. What's this mean, Colonel?
THIRD OFFICER. Hey, first platoon, follow me!
  (*Confused* CADETS *run in with their rifles.*)
NIKOLKA. What do you mean by this, gentlemen, what are you doing?
SECOND OFFICER. Arrest him! He's gone over to Petlura!
THIRD OFFICER. Colonel, you're under arrest!
MYSHLAYEVSKY (*holding the* THIRD OFFICER *back*). Stop, Lieutenant!
THIRD OFFICER. Let me go, Lieutenant, hands off! Cadets, grab him!
MYSHLAYEVSKY. Cadets, get back!
STUDZINSKY. Aleksei Vasilyevich, look what's happening.
NIKOLKA. Get back!
STUDZINSKY. Get back, I tell you! Don't obey the junior officers!
FIRST OFFICER. Gentlemen, what is this?
SECOND OFFICER. Gentlemen!
  (*Confusion. The officers have revolvers in their hands.*)
THIRD OFFICER. Don't obey your senior officers!
FIRST CADET. Mutiny in the division!
FIRST OFFICER. What are you doing?
STUDZINSKY. Quiet down! Attention!
THIRD OFFICER. Seize him!
ALEKSEI. Quiet! I have more to say!
CADETS. There's nothing more to say!
  We don't want to hear it!
  We don't want to hear it!
  Line up behind the Commander of the second battery!
NIKOLKA. Let him speak!
THIRD OFFICER. Shh, cadets, quiet down! Let him say what he wants, we won't let him out of here!
MYSHLAYEVSKY. Pull your cadets back this instant.

FIRST OFFICER. Attention! Stand to!

CADETS. Attention! Attention! Attention!

ALEKSEI. Sure . . . I'd be just a fine fellow if I went into battle with such a staff, which the Lord God's sent me in the form of you. But, gentlemen, what's excusable in a boy-volunteer is inexcusable (*To the* THIRD OFFICER) in you, Lieutenant! I thought that all of you would understand that a real misfortune has happened, that your commander doesn't waggle his tongue to tell you shameful things. But you're slow-witted. Whom do you want to defend? Answer me. (*Silence.*)

Answer when your commander asks you! Whom?

THIRD OFFICER. We promised to defend the Hetman.

ALEKSEI. The Hetman? Splendid! This morning at three o'clock the Hetman, leaving the army to the mercy of fate, ran off, disguised as a German officer, on a German train headed for Germany. So that at the very time the Lieutenant's figuring on defending the Hetman, he's been long gone. He's safely on his way to Berlin.

CADETS. To Berlin?—What's he talking about!—We don't want to hear it!

FIRST CADET. Gentlemen, what're you listening to him for?

STUDZINSKY. Shut up!

(*A din. Dawn is reflected through the windows.*)

ALEKSEI. But as if that wasn't enough, at the same time as that swindler was on his way, another swindler took off in the same direction—His Excellency the Commander of the Army, Prince Belorukov. So that, my friends, there's not only nobody to defend but there's nobody to take command, for the Prince's staff scooted away with him.

(*A din.*)

CADETS. Impossible!

This is impossible!

It's a lie!

ALEKSEI. Who said lie? Who said lie? I was at headquarters just now. I checked all the information. I swear each word I said is true! . . . And so, gentlemen! Here we are, two hundred men. And there's Petlura. Hold it, what am I saying—not there, but here! My friends, his cavalry's on the edge of town! He's got an army of two hundred thousand, and we have right here ourselves, two or three infantry detachments and three batteries. Y'understand? One of you just now pulled out a revolver and pointed it at me. He scared me dreadfully. Little boy!

THIRD OFFICER. Colonel . . .

ALEKSEI. Shut up! So that's how it is. If all of you now, under these conditions, carried out your instructions to defend . . . what? whom? . . . in short, went into battle—I wouldn't lead you, because I don't have anything to do with puppet shows, especially when you have to pay for the puppet show with your blood and all of you are absolutely crazy!

NIKOLKA. The bastards on the staff!

(*Din and shouting.*)

CADETS. What'll we do now?

Climb into the grave!

Disgraceful! . . .

You go to hell! . . . What do you think this is, a meeting? Stand at attention!

Drove us into a trap!

THIRD CADET (*runs in crying*). They kept shouting, forward! forward! and now it's, back! I'll find that Hetman and kill him!

FIRST OFFICER. Get that old woman the hell out of here! Cadets, listen: if what the Colonel says is true, fall in behind me! We'll reach the troop trains—and go down to the Don, to Denikin!

CADETS. To the Don! To Denikin! . . .

It's easy enough . . . what you're doing!

To the Don is impossible! . . .

STUDZINSKY. Aleksei Vasilyevich, truly, we ought to drop everything and take the division down to the Don.

ALEKSEI. Captain Studzinsky! Don't be so forward! I'm in command of this division! I'll give the orders—and you'll carry them out! To the Don? Listen, all of you! Down there, on the Don, you'll find the very same thing, *if* you can even get that far. There you'll find the same generals and the same headquarters bunch.

NIKOLKA. The same headquarters bastards!

ALEKSEI. Absolutely right. They'll make you fight against

your own people. And when your heads are split open, they'll run off abroad ... I know that in Rostov it's the same as in Kiev. There the divisions have no shells, the cadets have no boots, and the officers sit around in the cafés. Listen to me, my friends! They assigned me, a front-line officer, to take you into the fray. If only there was some reason! But there's no point. I make the public announcement that I won't lead you and won't let you go! I repeat: the movement of the Whites in the Ukraine is finished. It's finished in Rostov-on-the-Don, everywhere! The people aren't with us. They're against us. That means it's done! Coffin! Shut the lid! And so I, Aleksei Turbin, an officer in the regular army, having fought through the whole war with the Germans, as Captain Studzinsky and Lieutenant Myshlayevsky can testify, I take everything on my own conscience and responsibility, take everything, give you warning and, in my heart fond of you, send you home. I'm through.

(*A roar of voices. A sudden explosion.*)

Pull off your shoulder loops, throw down your rifles, and go home right away!

(*The* CADETS *rip off their shoulder loops, throw down their rifles.*)

MYSHLAYEVSKY (*shouts*). Quiet! Colonel, may I have permission to set fire to the school?

ALEKSEI. No.

(*A cannon goes off. The windows rattle.*)

MYSHLAYEVSKY. A machine gun!

STUDZINSKY. Cadets, go home!

MYSHLAYEVSKY. Cadets, beat retreat, go home!

(*A bugle sounds backstage. The* CADETS *and officers break up in a run.* NIKOLKA *hits the switch box with his rifle and runs out. The lights go out.* ALEKSEI, *by the stove, tears up papers and burns them. A long pause.* MAKSIM *comes in.*)

ALEKSEI. Who're you?

MAKSIM. I'm the watchman here.

ALEKSEI. Get out of here, you'll get killed here.

MAKSIM. Your Excellency, where'll I go? I've got no business leaving government property. They broke up the desks in two classrooms, caused such ruin as I can't even tell you.

And the light . . . There've been lots of soldiers here, but such as these—I'm sorry . . .

ALEKSEI. Old man, get away from me.

MAKSIM. Cut me down with a sword now, even, I won't go. I was told by the director . . .

ALEKSEI. Well, what were you told by the director?

MAKSIM. Maksim, you're the only one who's staying . . . Maksim, watch out . . . But now you . . .

ALEKSEI. You understand Russian, old man? You'll get killed. Go off into the cellar some place, hide there, so there's not a trace of you.

MAKSIM. Who'll be responsible? Maksim, you be responsible for everything. There've been all kinds—some for the tsar and some against, soldiers with no shame, but as to breaking up desks . . .

ALEKSEI. Where did the rolls go? (*Smashes the cupboard with his foot.*)

MAKSIM. Your Excellency, you know, there's a key for it. A school cupboard, but you—just with your foot. (*Steps back, makes the sign of the cross.*)

(*A cannon goes off.*)

Mother of Heaven . . . Mary Almighty . . . Lord Jesus save us . . .

ALEKSEI. Give it to him! That's it! That's it! Concert! Music! Ah, I'll get you in my hands some time, Mr. Hetman! You rotten . . .

(MYSHLAYEVSKY *appears up above. A light red glow shines through the windows.*)

MAKSIM. Your Excellency, maybe you can tell him. What is this? Broke the cupboard with his foot!

MYSHLAYEVSKY. Old man, don't get underfoot. Clear out.

MAKSIM. Tartars, absolute Tartars. (*Disappears.*)

MYSHLAYEVSKY (*from a distance*). Alyosha! I set fire to the storeroom! It's not coats Petlura'll find waiting but a long nose!

ALEKSEI. For God's sake, don't you stay here too long. Run on home.

MYSHLAYEVSKY. Got just a little business first. I'll toss two more grenades now into the hay—and then I'm off. What are you sitting here for?

ALEKSEI. I can't go until the pickets have come in.
MYSHLAYEVSKY. Alyosha, you have to? eh?
ALEKSEI. What do you think, Lieutenant!
MYSHLAYEVSKY. Then I'm staying with you.
ALEKSEI. What do I need you for, Viktor? I'm ordering you: off to Elena at once! Protect her! I'll be right after you. Come, what're you doing, you gone mad, is that it? Are you going to obey or not?
MYSHLAYEVSKY. All right, Alyosha. I'll run over to Lenka!
ALEKSEI. Take a look see if Nikolka's gone. Kick him out, for God's sake.
MYSHLAYEVSKY. All right! Alyosha, be careful, don't take chances!
ALEKSEI. Go teach the teacher!
  (MYSHLAYEVSKY *disappears*.)
  Very serious. "Extremely serious . . ." And when we're taken up to heaven . . . up along the whitened stairs . . . Hope the pickets haven't run into trouble . . .
NIKOLKA (*appears, up above, crawling*). Alyosha!
ALEKSEI. What're you doing, trying to play tricks on me, is that it?! Get home this instant, take off your shoulder loops! Out of here!
NIKOLKA. I'm not going without you, Colonel.
ALEKSEI. What! (*Pulls out his revolver.*)
NIKOLKA. Shoot, go ahead shoot your own brother!
ALEKSEI. You idiot!
NIKOLKA. Call your own brother names, go ahead. I know what you're sitting here for! I know, you, the Commander, are waiting for death from the disgrace, that's what! Well, I'm going to guard you. Lenka'll kill me.
ALEKSEI. Hey, somebody! Take Cadet Turbin away! Lieutenant Myshlayevsky!
NIKOLKA. Everybody's already gone.
ALEKSEI. Just you wait, you bastard, I'll deal with you at home!
  (*Noise and hoofbeats. The* CADETS *run in—those who were on picket duty.*)
CADETS (*running through*). Petlura's cavalry's right behind! . . .
ALEKSEI. Cadets! Listen to my order! Take the underground

passage to Podol! I'll cover you. Rip off your shoulder loops on the way!

(*Backstage a bold whistle comes closer and closer, an accordion dully sounds: "With a noise and a clamor . . ."*)

Run, run! I'll cover you! (*Rushes to the upstairs window. To* NIKOLKA.) Run, I beg you. Have pity on Lenka!

(*A shell explodes close by. The windows are smashed.* ALEKSEI *falls.*)

NIKOLKA. Colonel! Alyoshka, Alyoshka, what have you done?!

ALEKSEI. Cadet Turbin, now send heroism to hell! (*Falls silent.*)

NIKOLKA. Colonel, it just can't be! Alyosha, get up!

(*Hoofbeats and much noise. Cossack soldiers run in.*)

URAGAN. Here! This way! Here! Shoot him, boys! Shoot him!

(KIRPATY *shoots at* NIKOLKA.)

GALANBA (*running in*). Alive! Take him alive, boys!

(NIKOLKA *crawls off up the stairs, grinning.*)

KIRPATY. Look at him, the little wolf! Ah, son of a bitch!

URAGAN. You won't get away! You won't!

(*Cossack soldiers appear.*)

NIKOLKA. You gallows birds, I'll not surrender! Never will, you bandits! (*Flings himself from the railing and vanishes.*)

KIRPATY. Ah, the clown! (*Shoots.*) That's the last of them.

GALANBA. What did you let him go for, boys? Eh, no-goods! . . .

(*The accordion: "With a noise and a clamor . . ." Backstage, a shout: "Glory! Praise!" Bugles backstage.* BOLBOTUN *comes in followed by soldiers with standards. The standards and flags flow up the stairs. A deafening march.*)

SCENE 2

The Turbin's apartment. Dawn. There is no electricity. A candle burns on a card table.

LARIOSIK. Elena Vasilyevna, dear lady! Do what you want to with me! You want me to, I'll put my things on and go look for them.

ELENA. Oh, no, no! What're you talking about, Lariosik! You'll be killed on the street. We'll wait. My Lord, it's dawn already. What a horrible light! What's happening there? I only want to know where they are.

LARIOSIK. Good Lord, the civil war's terrible!

ELENA. You know what: I'm a woman, they won't touch me. I'll go have a look what's happening outside.

LARIOSIK. Elena Vasilyevna, I won't let you! Indeed I . . . I just won't let you! . . . What would Aleksei Vasilyevich say to me! He told me not to let you out on the street no matter what, and I gave him my word of honor.

ELENA. I'd stay close . . .

LARIOSIK. Elena Vasilyevna!

ELENA. Just to find out what's happening . . .

LARIOSIK. I'll go myself . . .

ELENA. Don't any more . . . We'll wait . . .

LARIOSIK. Your husband was very clever to have left. That's a very smart move. Now he'll wait out this terrible mess in Berlin and then come back.

ELENA. My husband? My husband? . . . Don't mention my husband's name in this house again. You hear?

LARIOSIK. Very well, Elena Vasilyevna . . . I always find something to say at just the wrong time . . . Maybe you'd like some tea? I could put up the samovar . . .

ELENA. No, don't bother . . .

(*A knock.*)

LARIOSIK. Wait, wait, don't open; have to find out who's there. Who's there?

SHERVINSKY. It's me! Me . . . Shervinsky . . .

ELENA. Thank God! (*Opens.*) What's this mean? Something terrible?

SHERVINSKY. Petlura's taken the city.

LARIOSIK. Taken it? God, how terrible!

ELENA. Where are they? Fighting?

SHERVINSKY. Don't be upset, Elena Vasilyevna! I warned Aleksei Vasilyevich several hours ago. Everything's perfectly all right now.

ELENA. What do you mean, everything's all right? And the Hetman? The army?

SHERVINSKY. The Hetman fled during the night.

ELENA. Fled? Abandoned the army?

SHERVINSKY. Precisely. And Prince Belokurov did, too. (*Takes off his coat.*)

ELENA. The rats!

SHERVINSKY. Unspeakable scoundrels!

LARIOSIK. But why isn't there any electricity?

SHERVINSKY. They shelled the power station.

LARIOSIK. Oh-oh-oh . . .

SHERVINSKY. Elena Vasilyevna, may I hide here at your place? They'll be looking for officers now.

ELENA. Why, of course!

SHERVINSKY. Elena Vasilyevna, if only you knew how happy I am that you're alive and well.

(*A knock on the door.*)

Larion, find out who's there . . .

LARIOSIK. Who's there?

MYSHLAYEVSKY'S VOICE. Your own, your own . . .

(LARIOSIK *opens the door.* MYSHLAYEVSKY *and* STUDZINSKY *come in.*)

ELENA. Thank the good Lord! But where are Alyosha and Nikolai?

MYSHLAYEVSKY. Steady, steady, Lena, they'll be here in a minute. Don't be afraid at all, the streets are still open. The pickets will bring them both. Ah, and he's here? Means, then, you know everything. . . .

ELENA. Thanks, everything. Oh, the Germans! The Germans!

STUDZINSKY. No matter . . . no matter, some day we'll remind 'em of it all . . . No matter!

MYSHLAYEVSKY. Hello, Larion!

LARIOSIK. What terrible things are happening, Vitenka!

MYSHLAYEVSKY. Sure, really first class.

ELENA. Just look at you both! Go get warm; I'll put up the samovar right away.

SHERVINSKY (*from the fireplace*). May I help you, Lena?

ELENA. Don't bother. I can do it myself. (*Runs out.*)

MYSHLAYEVSKY. Hope everything's happy, Mr. Personal Aide. How come you've no aiguillettes? "Go, gentlemen of the officer corps, to the Ukraine and assemble your detachments . . ." And burst into tears. I'd take your Mama by the hind legs!

SHERVINSKY. What signifies this coarse, side-show tone?

MYSHLAYEVSKY. It ended up a puppet show, and that's why the tone goes to match. You're the one promised a sovereign emperor and drank to the health of his eminence. By the way, where is that eminence now, right this minute?

SHERVINSKY. What's it to you?

MYSHLAYEVSKY. Here's what: if I just got hold this minute of that very same eminence, I'd take it by its legs and pound its head on the pavement until I felt myself I'd had all I wanted. And your whole headquarters gang ought to be stuck down the toilet!

SHERVINSKY. Mr. Myshlayevsky, I ask you not to forget yourself!

MYSHLAYEVSKY. Bastards!

SHERVINSKY. Wha-at?

LARIOSIK. Why quarrel?

STUDZINSKY. As senior, I ask you to stop this conversation this instant! It's absolutely absurd and pointless! Why are you, in fact, bothering the man? (*To* SHERVINSKY.) Lieutenant, relax.

SHERVINSKY. Lieutenant Myshlayevsky's behavior recently has been unbearable . . . And the main thing is—boorishness! Is it my fault, now, everything collapsed? On the contrary, I warned you all. If it hadn't been for me, it's still a question whether or not he'd be sitting here right now alive!

STUDZINSKY. Absolutely right, Lieutenant. And we're very grateful to you.

ELENA (*enters*). What's happening? What's the matter?

STUDZINSKY. Elena Vasilyevna, don't worry, everything's just as it ought to be. I promise you. Go to your room.

(ELENA *goes out.*)

Viktor, apologize, you have absolutely no right.

MYSHLAYEVSKY. All right, let's drop it, Leonid! I lost my temper. It's such an insult, you know!

SHERVINSKY. Sort of strange . . .

STUDZINSKY. Drop it, that's enough of that. (*Sits down by the fire. A pause.*)

MYSHLAYEVSKY. Where are Alyosha and Nikolka, as a matter of fact?

STUDZINSKY. I'm worried myself . . . I'll wait five minutes, and after that I'll go meet them . . . (*A pause.*)

MYSHLAYEVSKY. That mean he took off right in front of you?

SHERVINSKY. In front of me: I was there to the last minute.

MYSHLAYEVSKY. What a great sight! I'd have given a lot to have been there to see it! Why didn't you whack him like a dog?

SHERVINSKY. You should have gone and done it yourself!

MYSHLAYEVSKY. I would have, don't worry. And did he say anything to you as he was leaving?

SHERVINSKY. Sure he did! Put his arm around me, thanked me for faithful service . . .

MYSHLAYEVSKY. And shed tears?

SHERVINSKY. Yes, he did . . .

LARIOSIK. Shed tears? What do you know about that!

MYSHLAYEVSKY. Maybe he gave you something to remember him by? Like, for example, a gold cigarette case with his monogram?

SHERVINSKY. Yes, he did.

MYSHLAYEVSKY. Oh, come on, now, damn it! . . . I'm sorry, Leonid, I'm afraid you'll get angry again. Basically, you're not a bad fellow at all, but you have some strange . . .

SHERVINSKY. What do you mean by that?

MYSHLAYEVSKY. Well, how'll I put it . . . You ought to be a writer . . . You got a rich imagination . . . Shed tears . . . Well, just supposing I said now: show me the cigarette case!

(*Without speaking,* SHERVINSKY *shows him the cigarette case.*)

You got me! And actually with a monogram!

SHERVINSKY. What do you have to say, Lieutenant Myshlayevsky?

MYSHLAYEVSKY. Right away. In front of you all, gentlemen, I beg his pardon.

LARIOSIK. I never saw anything so beautiful in my life! Probably weighs a whole pound?

SHERVINSKY. Seven-eighths.

(*A knock on the window.*)

Gentlemen! . . .

(*They rise.*)

THE DAYS OF THE TURBINS 317

MYSHLAYEVSKY. I don't like tricks . . . Why not in through the door? . . .

SHERVINSKY. Gentlemen . . . your revolvers . . . are better discarded. (*Hides the cigarette case behind the fireplace.*)

(STUDZINSKY *and* MYSHLAYEVSKY *go to the window and, having cautiously raised the shade, look out.*)

STUDZINSKY. Ah, I'll never forgive myself!

MYSHLAYEVSKY. What kind of dirty work is this!

LARIOSIK. Oh, my God! (*Rushes off to tell* ELENA.) Elena . . .

MYSHLAYEVSKY. Where the hell are you going! . . . You mad! . . . What made you think you could! . . . (*Puts his hand over his mouth.*)

(*All run out. A pause. They carry* NIKOLKA *in.*)

Lenka, Lenka has to be taken away someplace . . . Good Lord! And where's Alyosha? . . . Shooting me wouldn't do! . . . Put him down, put him down . . . right on the floor . . .

STUDZINSKY. The sofa'd be better. Find where he's hit, find the wound!

SHERVINSKY. His head's all bashed!

STUDZINSKY. There's blood in his boot . . . Take off his boots . . .

SHERVINSKY. Let's move him . . . over there . . . The floor's no good, actually . . .

STUDZINSKY. Lariosik! Hurry get a pillow and a blanket. (*To the others.*) Put him on the sofa.

(*They carry* NIKOLKA *over to the sofa.*)

Cut his boot off! Cut it off! Aleksei Vasilyevich has some bandage in his study.

(SHERVINSKY *runs out.*)

Get some spirits! Good God in heaven, how did he ever get back? What's happened? . . . Where's Aleksei Vasilyevich? . . .

(SHERVINSKY *runs in with iodine and bandage.* STUDZINSKY *bandages* NIKOLKA'S *head.*)

LARIOSIK. Is he dying?

NIKOLKA (*coming to*). Oh! . . .

MYSHLAYEVSKY. It'd drive you mad! . . . Just tell us one thing: where's Alyoshka?

STUDZINSKY. Where's Aleksei Vasilyevich?

NIKOLKA. Gentlemen . . .

MYSHLAYEVSKY. What?

(ELENA *comes rushing in.*)

Lenochka, don't get upset. He fell and hit his head. Nothing serious.

ELENA. Why, he's wounded! What do you mean?

NIKOLKA. No, Lenochka, no . . .

ELENA. And where's Aleksei? Where's Aleksei? (*Insistently.*) You were with him. Just tell me one thing: where's Aleksei?

MYSHLAYEVSKY. What can we do now? . . .

STUDZINSKY (*to* MYSHLAYEVSKY). That's impossible! Impossible! . . .

ELENA. Why won't you talk?

NIKOLKA. Lenochka . . . Just a minute . . .

ELENA. Don't lie! Only don't lie!

(MYSHLAYEVSKY *makes a sign to* NIKOLKA—"*Keep quiet.*")

STUDZINSKY. Elena Vasilyevna . . .

SHERVINSKY. Lena, what're you . . .

ELENA. It's all clear! Aleksei's been killed!

MYSHLAYEVSKY. What do you mean, what do you mean, Lena! What makes you think so?

ELENA. Just look at his face. Look. Besides, I don't even need to look. I knew it, I felt it, even as he was going out, I knew it would end like this!

STUDZINSKY (*to* NIKOLKA). Tell us what's happened to him!

ELENA. Larion! Alyosha's been killed . . .

SHERVINSKY. Get some water . . .

ELENA. Larion! Alyosha's been killed! Yesterday you were sitting at the table with him—remember? But now he's killed.

LARIOSIK. Elena Vasilyevna, dearest . . .

SHERVINSKY. Lena, Lena . . .

ELENA. And you? You senior officers! Senior officers! You all came home, but the Commander got killed? . . .

MYSHLAYEVSKY. Lena, spare us, what're you saying! We all carried out his orders. All of us!

STUDZINSKY. No, she's absolutely right! I'm completely to blame! He shouldn't have been left! I'm the senior officer, and I'll correct my mistake! (*Takes his revolver.*)

MYSHLAYEVSKY. Where you going? No, stop! No, stop!

STUDZINSKY. Take your hands off!

MYSHLAYEVSKY. What, am I going to be the only one left? You're not to blame in absolutely anything! Nothing at all! I was the last to see him, warned him, and did all I was supposed to. Lena!

STUDZINSKY. Lieutenant Myshlayevsky, let go of me this instant!

MYSHLAYEVSKY. Hand over your revolver! Shervinsky!

SHERVINSKY. You haven't the right to! What, you want to make things still worse? You haven't the right to! (*Holds* STUDZINSKY *back.*)

MYSHLAYEVSKY. Lena, order him to! It's all because of what you said. Take his revolver away from him!

ELENA. I talked like that out of grief. I felt sort of dizzy. Give me your revolver!

STUDZINSKY (*hysterically*). Nobody has the right to reproach me! Nobody! Nobody! I carried out all of Colonel Turbin's orders!

ELENA. Nobody! . . . Nobody! . . . I lost my senses for a moment.

MYSHLAYEVSKY. Nikolka, tell us . . . Lena, be brave. We'll find him . . . Find him . . . Say it out . . .

NIKOLKA. The Commander was killed . . .

(ELENA *faints*)

(*Curtain*)

ACT IV

Two months have passed. It is Twelfth-night (The Eve of the Epiphany), 1919. The apartment is brightly lit. ELENA *and* LARIOSIK *are decorating the Christmas tree.*

LARIOSIK (*on a ladder*). I think that this star . . . (*Mysteriously listens to something.*)

ELENA. What do you hear?

LARIOSIK. Nothing, I just thought I did . . . Elena Vasilyevna, I assure you this is the end. They'll take the city.

ELENA. Don't be so quick, Lariosik, nothing's known for sure yet.

LARIOSIK. A sure sign is that there's no shooting. I must tell you frankly, Elena Vasilyevna, that during these past two months I've gotten terribly fed up with the shooting. I don't like . . .

ELENA. I share your taste.

LARIOSIK. I think that this star here will be just in the right place.

ELENA. Come on down, Lariosik, or I'm afraid you'll fall and break your head.

LARIOSIK. Now what do you mean, Elena Vasilyevna! The tree's done to a T, as Vitenka says. I'd just like to meet the man who'd say the tree doesn't look lovely! Ah, Elena Vasilyevna, if you only knew! . . . The tree reminds me of the bygone days of my childhood in Zhitomir . . . The lights . . . the green Christman tree . . . (*A pause.*) However, I like it here better—a lot better—than where I grew up. I'd never go away from here any place . . . Just sit for centuries under the tree at your feet and not go any place . . .

ELENA. You'd get bored. You're terribly much a poet, Larion.

LARIOSIK. No, what kind of a poet am I! What the he . . . Ah, excuse me, Elena Vasilyevna!

ELENA. Recite, recite something new of yours. Come, recite something. I like your poems very much. You have a lot of ability.

LARIOSIK. You mean that seriously?

ELENA. Absolutely seriously.

LARIOSIK. Well, all right . . . I'll recite . . . I'll recite . . . It's dedicated . . . Well, in short, it's dedicated to . . . No, I won't recite you any of my poems.

ELENA. Why not?

LARIOSIK. No, what for?

ELENA. And who is it dedicated to?

LARIOSIK. Some woman.

ELENA. A secret?

LARIOSIK. A secret. You.

ELENA. Thank you, dear boy.

LARIOSIK. Why thank me! . . . You can't make a coat out of thank-yous . . . Oh, excuse me, Elena Vasilyevna, I've caught all that from Myshlayevsky. You know, expressions like that just come right out . . .

ELENA. So I see. I think you're in love with Myshlayevsky.

LARIOSIK. No. I'm in love with you.

ELENA. Don't be, Larion, don't.

LARIOSIK. You know what? Marry me.

ELENA. You're a very touching person. Only that's impossible.

LARIOSIK. He won't come back! . . . And how can you live alone? Alone, without help, without sympathy. Oh, sure, as far as help goes I'm rather stink . . . weak, though on the other hand I'll love you very much. All my life. You're my ideal. He won't come. Now especially when the Bolsheviks are moving in . . . He won't come back!

ELENA. He won't. But that's not the point. Even if he did, my life with him would still be all through.

LARIOSIK. He's been cut off . . . I couldn't stand looking at you when he left. My heart was bleeding. It was just terrible to look at you, you know, honest to God . . .

ELENA. Was I really so bad?

LARIOSIK. Dreadful! It was a nightmare! Thin as a rail . . . Your face—all sunken and yellow . . .

ELENA. What you won't think up, Larion!

LARIOSIK. Oh . . . really, damn it . . . But now you're better, much better . . . Now you're all pink and rosy . . .

ELENA. Lariosik, you're inimitable. Come over here. I'll kiss your forehead.

LARIOSIK. Forehead? Well, that's better than nothing!
  (ELENA *kisses him on the forehead.*)
  Sure, how could anyone fall in love with me!
ELENA. Very easily. Only I already am in love.
LARIOSIK. What? In love? With whom? You are? You're in love? Impossible!
ELENA. Won't I do?
LARIOSIK. You're—divine! You . . . Who is he? Do I know him?
ELENA. Very well.
LARIOSIK. I know him very well? Wait . . . Who, now? Wait, wait, wait! . . . "Young man . . . you didn't see a thing! . . ." "Play the king, but don't touch the queens . . ." And I thought that it was a dream. Damn the lucky man!
ELENA. Lariosik! That's indiscreet!
LARIOSIK. I'm going . . . I'm going . . .
ELENA. Where, where?
LARIOSIK. Over to the Armenian's for vodka and I'll drink myself senseless . . .
ELENA. And so I let you . . . Larion, I'll be your friend.
LARIOSIK. I've read, I've read novels . . . This "I'll be your friend" means it's finished, the lid's shut! All over! (*Puts on his coat.*)
ELENA. Lariosik! Hurry back! The guests will be here soon!
  (LARIOSIK, *having opened the door, bumps into* SHERVINSKY *in the hallway as he is coming in.* SHERVINSKY *wears an abominable hat, a tattered coat and dark glasses.*)
SHERVINSKY. Hello, Elena Vasilyevna! Hello, Larion!
LARIOSIK. A-a . . . hello . . . hello . . . (*Disappears.*)
ELENA. My hero! Just what do you look like!
SHERVINSKY. Well, thank you, Elena Vasilyevna. That's what I was trying for! I was riding along in a cab today and some proletarians going along the sidewalks kept looking at me and peering. And one says in such a sticky little voice: "Hey, look at the Ukrainian gent! Just wait," he says, "till tomorrow. Tomorrow we'll haul you down out of that cab!" I have a keen eye. I just looked at him and right away understood that I had to go home and disguise myself. Congratulations, the lid's come down on Petlura!

ELENA. Really?!

SHERVINSKY. The Reds will be here tonight. That means Soviet authority and all the rest!

ELENA. Why are you so glad? One might think you were a Bolshevik yourself!

SHERVINSKY. I'm a sympathizer! And this overcoat I hired from the yardman. It's a non-party coat.

ELENA. Please take that repulsive thing off this instant!

SHERVINSKY. Yes, ma'am! (*Takes off the coat, the hat, his galoshes, and his glasses and remains in splendid evening dress.*) Now, congratulate me, I've just come from my tryout. I sang and was taken.

ELENA. Congratulations.

SHERVINSKY. Lena, nobody home? How's Nikolka?

ELENA. Asleep . . .

SHERVINSKY. Lena, Lena . . .

ELENA. Don't . . . Wait, why have you shaved off your side whiskers?

SHERVINSKY. Easier to put on make-up.

ELENA. Easier to make yourself up like a Bolshevik. Ah, you sly, fainthearted creature! Don't worry, nobody'll touch you.

SHERVINSKY. Just let them try to touch a man who has a range of two full octaves and two notes on top of that! . . . Lenochka! May I talk to you?

ELENA. Do.

SHERVINSKY. Lena! Everything's over now . . . Nikolka's getting well . . . Petlura's being chased out . . . I've made my debut . . . A new life's beginning now. We can't go on pining away any more. He won't come. He's been cut off, Lena! I'm not so bad, honest to God! . . . Not so bad . . . Take a look at yourself. You're all alone. You're withering away . . .

ELENA. Will you get cured?

SHERVINSKY. What should I get cured of, Lenochka?

ELENA. Leonid, I'll become your wife if you'll turn over a new leaf. And first of all stop lying!

SHERVINSKY. Am I really such a liar, Lenochka?

ELENA. You're not a liar, but God knows what you are, all sort of hollow, like a nut . . . What is all this! Saw the emperor behind the portiere, and he shed tears . . . There was never anything like that! And this skinny girl is a mezzo-soprano, but it turns out she's just a waitress in Semadeni's café . . .

SHERVINSKY. Lenochka, she didn't work there long at all, just while she didn't have an engagement.

ELENA. Seems she certainly did have one!

SHERVINSKY. Lena! I swear by my mother's dead body, and my father's, too, there was never anything between us. After all, I'm an orphan.

ELENA. I don't care. I'm not interested in your dirty secrets. What's important is something else: that you stop boasting and lying. The only time you've ever told the truth was when you told about the cigarette case, and then nobody believed you and you had to prove it. Fie! . . . Shame . . . Shame . . .

SHERVINSKY. It was precisely about the cigarette case that I made everything up. The Hetman didn't give it to me, didn't put his arm around me or shed tears. He simply forgot it on the table, and I pocketed it.

ELENA. Swiped it off the table?

SHERVINSKY. *Pocketed* it. It's a historical thing of value.

ELENA. Good Lord, this was all we needed! Let me have it! (*Takes the cigarette case and puts it away.*)

SHERVINSKY. Lenochka, the cigarettes in it are mine.

ELENA. Thank your lucky stars that you realized you had to tell me about this. For if I'd found out myself . . .

SHERVINSKY. But how would you have?

ELENA. You savage!

SHERVINSKY. Not a bit. Lenochka, I've changed terrifically. I don't recognize myself, word of honor! Whether it's the whole catastrophe has had an affect on me, or Alyosha's death . . . I'm different now. And don't worry about material things, Lenusha, because you know I—oho-ho . . . I sang at my debut today, and the director says to me: "Leonid Yuryevich," he says, "you give wonderful promise. You ought to go to Moscow," he says, "to the Bolshoi . . ." He came up to me, put his arm around me, and . . .

ELENA. And what?

SHERVINSKY. And nothing . . . Went off down the corridor . . .

ELENA. Incorrigible!

SHERVINSKY. Lena!

ELENA. What are we going to do about Talberg?

SHERVINSKY. Divorce. Get a divorce. You know his address? Send him a telegram and a letter that it's all over! All over!

ELENA. All right! It's tiresome for me, and lonely. Depressing. All right! I agree!

SHERVINSKY. You've won, Galilean! Lena! (*Sings.*) *And you'll be the queen of the wo-or-rld* . . . Pure "G"! (*Points to* TALBERG'S *portrait.*) I insist that it be thrown out! I can't stand seeing it!

ELENA. Oho, what a tone!

SHERVINSKY (*affectionately*). I can't stand seeing it, Lenochka. (*Breaks the portrait out of its frame and throws it into the fireplace.*) The rat! And my conscience is clean and at rest!

ELENA. A jabot will look very good on you . . . You are handsome, I must say! . . .

SHERVINSKY. We won't perish . . .

ELENA. Oh, I'm not worried about you! . . . You'll never!

SHERVINSKY. Lena, let's go into your room . . . I'll sing a little, and you'll accompany on the piano . . . Why, we haven't seen each other really for two months. Always in public, and more public.

ELENA. But they'll be here in a minute.

SHERVINSKY. Well, then we'll come back. (*They go out, shut the door. The piano is heard. In a splendid voice,* SHERVINSKY *sings the epithalamion from* Nero.)

NIKOLKA (*comes in, in a black cap, on crutches. He is pale and feeble. Wears a student jacket*). Ah! . . . They're rehearsing! (*Sees the portrait frame.*) Ah! . . . Knocked it out. I get it . . . Guessed it long ago. (*Lies down on the sofa.*)

LARIOSIK (*appears in the hallway*). Nikolasha! You up? Alone? Wait, I'll bring you a pillow right away. (*Brings* NIKOLKA *a pillow.*)

NIKOLKA. Don't bother, Larion, don't. Thanks. It's clear, Larion, I'm a cripple and going to stay one.

LARIOSIK. Now, what're you talking about, what're you talking about, Nikolasha, you ought to be ashamed of yourself!

NIKOLKA. Listen, Larion, how come they're not here yet?

LARIOSIK. They're not here yet, but they soon will be. You know, I was coming along the street just now—there were lines and lines of carts, and these people on 'em, and long lines of stragglers. It's clear the Bolsheviks really gave 'em a good beating.

NIKOLKA. That's what they had coming!

LARIOSIK. But all the same I got some vodka! The only time in my life I had real luck! I thought there wasn't a chance of my getting it. I'm that sort of person! The weather was splendid when I went out. A clear sky, the stars were shining, the cannons weren't shooting . . . Everything in nature was just fine. But just let me show my face on the street and it absolutely has to snow. And sure enough it did—and the wet snow was sticking right on your face. But I got a bottle! . . . Let Myshlayevsky know I can do things. Fell down twice, clonked my head, but I kept holding the bottle in my hands.

SHERVINSKY'S VOICE. "*You give your blessing to our love . . .*"

NIKOLKA. Look, see? Astounding news! Elena's getting divorced from her husband. She's going to marry Shervinsky.

LARIOSIK (*drops the bottle*). Already?

NIKOLKA. Eh, Lariosik, eh-eh! . . . Come, now, Larion, come . . . Ah-ah . . . I get it! You're smitten, too?

LARIOSIK. Nikol, when talking about Elena Vasilyevna, words like "smitten" are out of place. You understand? She's precious-special!

NIKOLKA. She's a redhead, Larion, a redhead. A real misfortune! So everybody likes her, because she's a redhead. Just somebody lay eyes on her, he starts hauling in the bouquets right away. So we've always had bouquets around in the apartment all the time, like little brooms. And Talberg would get angry. Come on, you better pick up the pieces or Myshlayevsky'll show up in a minute and kill you.

LARIOSIK. Don't you tell him. (*Picks up the pieces.*)

(*The doorbell rings.* LARIOSIK *lets in* MYSHLAYEVSKY *and* STUDZINSKY. *Both are in civilian clothes.*)

MYSHLAYEVSKY. The Reds have crushed Petlura! Petlura's troops are leaving the city!

STUDZINSKY. Yes, indeed! The Reds are already in Slobodka. In a half hour they'll be here.

MYSHLAYEVSKY. So tomorrow there'll be a Soviet Republic here . . . So help me, it smells of vodka! Who was drinking vodka ahead of time? 'Fess up. What's going on here in this god-protected house! . . . You washing the floors with vodka?! . . . I know whose work this is! What are you breaking everything for? What are you breaking everything for! This is the work of real skillful fingers, in the full sense of the word! Whatever's touched—crash, bang, pieces! Well, if you got such an itch, go smash the tea set! (*All the while the piano is playing backstage.*)

LARIOSIK. What right have you to scold me! I don't like it!

MYSHALYEVSKY. Why am I being shouted at all the time? Soon they'll start smashing me! However, I'm in a good mood today, for some reason. Peace, Larion, I'm not angry at you.

NIKOLKA. But why is there no shooting?

MYSHLAYEVSKY. They're going along quietly, nicely. And without any fighting!

LARIOSIK. But the main thing is, most surprising of all, is that everybody's glad, even the leftover bourgeois. That's how much they all were fed up with Petlura!

NIKOLKA. Interesting to know what the Bolsheviks look like.

MYSHLAYEVSKY. You'll see, you'll see.

LARIOSIK. What do you think, Captain?

STUDZINSKY. I don't know, I don't understand anything now. The best thing to do would be to pull ourselves together and go off behind Petlura. How are we, White Guardsmen, going to get on with the Bolsheviks, I just can't imagine!

MYSHLAYEVSKY. Go where behind Petlura?

STUDZINSKY. Latch on to some cart transport and go off to Galicia.

MYSHLAYEVSKY. And then where?

STUDZINSKY. And then to the Don, to Denikin, and fight the Bolsheviks.

MYSHLAYEVSKY. Under the command of the generals again, that means? That's a mighty smart plan. It's a shame

Alyosha's lying in the ground, or else he could say a lot of interesting things about the generals. But it's a shame, the Commander's resting easy.

STUDZINSKY. Don't rend my heart, don't remind me.

MYSHLAYEVSKY. No, if you don't mind, he's gone, if you don't mind, I'll say something . . . Go back in the army, go fight again? . . . And he shed tears? . . . Thanks, thanks a lot, I've already done my laughing. Especially when I saw Alyoshka in the anatomical theater.

(NIKOLKA *cries*.)

LARIOSIK. Nikolasha, Nikolasha, come now, stop!

MYSHLAYEVSKY. Enough! I've been fighting since '14. For what? For my country? How can I call this my country when it's left me to disgrace! . . . And I ought to go back to join these eminences? No, sir. You see this? (*Makes a fig.*) A fig for them!

STUDZINSKY. Express yourself verbally, please.

MYSHLAYEVSKY. I'll express myself, all right, right now, you can be sure. What am I, an idiot, actually? No. I, Viktor Myshlayevsky, inform one and all that I have nothing more to do with all those general bastards. I'm through!

LARIOSIK. Viktor Myshlayevsky's become a Bolshevik.

MYSHLAYEVSKY. Yes, if you want to put it that way, I'm for the Bolsheviks!

STUDZINSKY. Viktor, what're you saying!

MYSHLAYEVSKY. I'm for the Bolsheviks, but against the Communists.

STUDZINSKY. That's ridiculous. You have to understand what you're talking about.

LARIOSIK. Let me point out to you that they're one and the same, Bolshevism and Communism.

MYSHLAYEVSKY (*mimicking*). "Bolshevism and Communism." Well, then I'm for the Communists . . .

STUDZINSKY. Listen, Lieutenant, you mentioned the word "country." What kind of country have we, when there are the Bolsheviks? Russia is finished. Remember how our Commander spoke, and the Commander was right: there they are, the Bolsheviks! . . .

MYSHLAYEVSKY. Bolsheviks? . . . Great! Very glad!

STUDZINSKY. But they'll draft you.

MYSHLAYEVSKY. And I'll go, and I'll serve. Sure!

STUDZINSKY. Why!

MYSHLAYEVSKY. Here's why! Because! Because Petlura has—how many did you say?—two hundred thousand! And here these two hundred thousand have greased their heels and faded away just on the mention of the word "Bolsheviks." You saw it? Neat! Because there are peasants in swarms behind the Bolsheviks . . . And what can I put up against 'em all? A pair of riding breeches with piping on 'em? They can't stand the sight of that piping . . . They'll go for the machineguns right away. Won't this do? . . . Red Army men in front, like a wall; speculators and all kinds of riffraff with the Hetman behind; and me in the middle? Your humble servant! No, I'm fed up with being used like manure or stopping up holes. Let 'em call me up! At least I'll know I'll be serving in a Russian army. The people aren't with us. The people are against us. Alyoshka was right!

STUDZINSKY. But what the hell kind of a Russian army is it that's finished Russia off! And besides, we'll be shot all the same!

MYSHLAYEVSKY. And good work! They'll haul us into the Chekà,[8] set the fine and write us off. And they'll feel easier, and so will we . . .

STUDZINSKY. I'm going to fight them!

MYSHLAYEVSKY. Go ahead, put on your overcoat! Take off! Hurry! . . . Fire away at the Bolsheviks, shout at 'em: won't let you! Nikolka's already been tossed down stairs once! Seen his head? And they'll pull yours off all the way. And rightly so—keep out of it! It's not our cause is underway now!

LARIOSIK. I'm against the horrors of the civil war. Actually, why spill blood?

MYSHLAYEVSKY. You ever in the war?

LARIOSIK. I have a white card, Vitenka. Weak lungs. And, besides, I'm Mama's only son.

MYSHLAYEVSKY. Right you are, Comrade Whitecard.

---

[8] Chekà—usually abbreviated by the two letters Ch K, standing for the second and third words of the All-Russian Extraordinary Commission for the Fight Against Counterrevolution, Sabotage, and Speculation, operative 1917–21.

STUDZINSKY. Our Russia once—was a great power! . . .
MYSHLAYEVSKY. And will be! . . . It will be!
STUDZINSKY. Sure, will be, will be—you wait!
MYSHLAYEVSKY. Won't be like before; it'll be something new. New! Here, you tell me something. When you all get smashed apart on the Don—and I predict now that you will be—and when your Denikin skips off abroad—and I predict that, too—then where'll you go?
STUDZINSKY. Also abroad.
MYSHLAYEVSKY. They need you there like a cannon needs a third wheel! No matter where you show up, they'll spit in your mug from Singapore to Paris. I'm not going, I'm going to stay here in Russia. And let come what may! . . . Well, that's that, it's finished, I close the meeting.
STUDZINSKY. I see I'm alone.
SHERVINSKY (*runs in*). Wait, wait, don't close the meeting. I have an announcement to make out of order. Elena Vasilyevna Talberg is going to get divorced from her husband, former Colonel Talberg of the General Staff, and marry . . . (*Bows, pointing to himself.*)
(ELENA *comes in.*)
LARIOSIK. Ah! . . .
MYSHLAYEVSKY. Forget it, Larion. What business have we got sticking our big, fat faces in what they do? Lena serene, let me hug you and kiss you.
STUDZINSKY. Congratulations, Elena Vasilyevna.
MYSHLAYEVSKY (*goes after* LARIOSIK, *who has run out into the hallway*). Larion, congratulate them—you can't do this! Then you'll come back here again.
LARIOSIK (*to* ELENA). I congratulate you and wish you happiness. (*To* SHERVINSKY.) I congratulate you . . . congratulate you.
MYSHLAYEVSKY. Good boy, that's a good boy! Oh, what a woman! Speaks English, plays the piano, and at the same time can put up the samovar. I'd be glad to marry you myself, Lena.
ELENA. But, Vitenka, I wouldn't marry you.
MYSHLAYEVSKY. And there's no need to. I love you anyway. Myself, by my own choice, I'm a bachelor and army man. Like things comfortable at home, without women and

children, the way they are in the barracks . . . Larion, fill the glasses! Got to drink their health!

SHERVINSKY. Wait, gentlemen! Don't drink that! I'll bring you in some right away. You know what this wine is like? Oho-ho! . . . (*Glances at* ELENA, *wilts.*) Oh, so, just a regular little wine. An ordinary Abrau-Dyurso.[9]

MYSHLAYEVSKY. Lena, that's your doing! Shervinsky, get married . . . you're completely cured! So, congratulations to you both and I wish you . . .

(*The hallway door opens,* TALBERG *walks in, in a civilian overcoat, with a suitcase.*)

STUDZINSKY. Gentlemen! Vladimir Robertovich . . . Vladimir Robertovich . . .

TALBERG. My compliments.

(*Dead silence.*)

MYSHLAYEVSKY. It's a trick!

TALBERG. Hello, Lena! You all seem surprised? (*A pause.*) That's a little strange! I would have thought that I should be the more surprised, coming upon such a gay gathering in my place in such a difficult time. Hello, Lena. What does this mean?

SHERVINSKY. Why this, that . . .

ELENA. Wait . . . Gentlemen, all of you step out a moment, leave Vladimir Robertovich and me alone.

SHERVINSKY. Lena, I don't like to!

MYSHLAYEVSKY. Stop, stop . . . We'll fix everything. Keep calm . . . We ought to clear out, Lenochka?

ELENA. Yes.

MYSHLAYEVSKY. I know you've got a good head on you. In case anything happens, give me a call. Personally. Well, so, gentlemen, let's have a smoke, let's go to Larion's room. Larion, grab a pillow and let's go.

(*All go out,* LARION, *for some reason, on tiptoe.*)

ELENA. Please.[10]

---

[9] A cheap sparkling wine from the Don region.
[10] When Talberg left for Germany, Lena addressed him, her husband, not by his first name but by his first name and patronymic. Now, on his return, though he speaks to her in the singular, "intimate" form, she uses the polite plural; this by itself indicates irreconcilable differences.

TALBERG. What does this all mean? Please explain to me. (*A pause.*) What's the joke? Where's Aleksei?

ELENA. Aleksei was killed.

TALBERG. Impossible! . . . When?

ELENA. Two months ago. Two days after you left.

TALBERG. Ah, good Lord, that's dreadful! But, you know, I warned him. You remember?

ELENA. Yes, I do. And Nikolka's a cripple.

TALBERG. Of course, it's all dreadful . . . But, surely, I'm not to blame for all this business . . . And agree that it's in no sense an excuse for arranging such a—I would say—stupid demonstration. (*A pause.*)

ELENA. Tell me how you came back. Because the Bolsheviks will be here today . . .

TALBERG. I'm absolutely up on things. The business with the Hetman turned out to be a silly operetta. The Germans tricked us. But in Berlin I managed to wrangle an assignment to the Don, to General Krasnov. We have to get out of Kiev at once . . . there's no time to lose . . . I've come to get you.

ELENA. Well, you see, I'm getting divorced from you and going to marry Shervinsky.

TALBERG (*after a long pause*). Very well! Very, very well! To take advantage of my absence for setting up some foul affair . . .

ELENA. Viktor! . . .

(MYSHLAYEVSKY *comes in.*)

MYSHLAYEVSKY. Lena, you authorize me to do the explaining?

ELENA. Yes! (*Goes out.*)

MYSHLAYEVSKY. Right. (*Goes over to* TALBERG.) Well? Get out! . . . (*Hits him.*)

(TALBERG *is confused. He goes into the hallway, goes out.*)
Lena! Just you!

(ELENA *enters.*)

He's gone. Agrees to the divorce. We had a very nice talk.

ELENA. Thank you, Viktor! (*Kisses him and runs out.*)

MYSHLAYEVSKY. Larion!

LARIOSIK (*comes in*). Already gone?

MYSHLAYEVSKY. Gone!

LARIOSIK. You're a genius, Vitenka!

MYSHLAYEVSKY. "I'm a genius—Igor Severyanin." Put the lights out, light up the tree, and play some march or other.

(LARIOSIK *puts out the lights in the room, turns on the electric lights on the tree, runs out into the next room. A march.*)

Gentlemen, please!

(SHERVINSKY, STUDZINSKY, NIKOLKA, *and* ELENA *come in.*)

STUDZINSKY. Very lovely! And how cozy it has become right away!

MYSHLAYEVSKY. Larion's doing. Well, now let's really congratulate you. Larion, that'll do!

(LARIOSIK *comes in with the guitar, hands it to* NIKOLKA.)

Congratulations to you, Lena dearest, once and for all. Forget everything. And in general—the health of you both! (*Drinks.*)

NIKOLKA (*plucks the guitar strings, sings*).
Tell me now, wizard, you pet of the gods,
What is to happen to me in life?
To the enemy's joy will I soon be dead,
And buried deep in a grave in the earth?
Now louder, you music, play us the victory,
We are the victors; the enemy flees, flees, flees!

MYSHLAYEVSKY (*sings*).
Now to the Council of People's Commissars . . .

ALL (*except* STUDZINSKY *join in*).
We shout out a loud Hurrah! Hurrah! Hurrah!

STUDZINSKY. Why, what the hell is this! . . . You ought to be ashamed of yourselves!

NIKOLKA (*sets the tune*).
Coming to meet him from the dark woods
The wizard goes on, his heart inspired . . .

LARIOSIK. Wonderful! . . . The lights . . . the little tree . . .

MYSHLAYEVSKY. Larion! Give us a speech!

NIKOLKA. Right, a speech! . . .

LARIOSIK. Really, gentlemen, I don't know how. And besides, I'm very bashful.

MYSHLAYEVSKY. Larion's making a speech!

LARIOSIK. Well, if everybody wants it, I will. Only please excuse the fact that I'm not prepared, you know. Gentlemen! We have come together in a most difficult and terrible time, and we have all lived through a great, great deal . . . and that includes me. I have lived through a real-life drama . . . And my fragile bark was long tossed about on the stormy waves of the civil war . . .

MYSHLAYEVSKY. That's very good about the bark . . .

LARIOSIK. Yes, the bark . . . Until thrown into this harbor with the cream-colored shades, among people whom I like so much . . . However, with them, too, I found drama . . . But there is no need to talk about sad things. The times have changed. Petlura has vanished . . . Everyone's alive . . . yes . . . and we're all together again . . . And even in addition: there's Elena Vasilyevna; she's also lived through a great, great deal and deserves happiness, because she's a wonderful woman. And I'd like to say to her, in the words of the writer, "We'll rest, we'll rest . . . "[11]

(*Cannons go off, far away.*)

MYSHLAYEVSKY. So, now! . . . We've rested! . . . Five . . . six . . . nine! . . .

ELENA. Not fighting again?

SHERVINSKY. No. That's a salute!

MYSHLAYEVSKY. Absolutely right: that's the six-inch battery saluting.

(*Backstage, far away in the distance, coming closer and closer, a band plays the "International."*)

Gentlemen, you hear that? That's the Reds coming!

(*All go to the window.*)

NIKOLKA. Gentlemen, this evening is a great prologue to a new historical drama.

STUDZINSKY. For some, the prologue; for others, the epilogue.

(*Curtain*)

[11] The phrase comes from Sonya's final speech in Chekhov's play *Uncle Vanya*, in which it is the last line.

The Bedbug

A FANTASY IN
NINE SCENES

**Vladimir Vladimirovich
Mayakovsky**

A NOTE ON THE PLAY

On October 29, 1927, Mayakovsky signed a contract with the Leningrad studios of *Sovkino* to write the scenario for a film celebrating technological advances, part of the title of which was taken from an old song—"Forget about the Fireplace—Remember the Steam Heat." The studio directors gave Mayakovsky a free hand but, nevertheless, felt unprepared to film the scenario he delivered to them. As late as July, 1928, the film was still listed as part of the plan proposed by the studios, but it was never made: " 'Forget about the Fireplace.' Scenario by Mayakovsky. Director—Schmidthof. The bourgeoisie in the workers' world and the struggle against it. A semi-utopian portrayal of the way of life of the future."

In the fall of 1928 Mayakovsky took the theme, plot, main characters, setting—the city Tambov—and topics, and turned them into *The Bedbug*. "The material I have treated and put into my comedy," Mayakovsky wrote in an article about his play, "is an agglomerate of everyday facts that I thought of or came across all over, all the time I was doing my newspaper and advertising work, especially while I was working on *The Komsomol Pravda*." This material, he adds, is concentrated in the characters Prisypkin—"who for the sake of elegance changes his name to Pierre Skripkin"—and Oleg Bayan. He says that the central problem of the play is the exposure of the contemporary bourgeoisie. Russian critics have pointed out the use—or rather re-use—in the play of early, romantic materials and motifs, now ridiculed. Roman Jakobson has several times emphasized the inversion here of Mayakovsky's young, flamboyant world—of Mayakovsky's seemingly deliberate parody or mockery of himself. "Of course," said Mayakovsky on December 30, 1928, "I don't portray socialist society." One may read that literally, and, equally, one may read it as applying to the world of 1979.

On December 26, 1928, Mayakovsky read the play to his friend, V. E. Meyerhold, to whom it is dedicated. On December thirtieth, he read it to a meeting of the full staff of the V. Meyerhold State Theater, of which Meyerhold was the director. It was approved for presentation, and Mayakovsky was appointed official assistant to Meyerhold in charge of textual revisions. As usually happens, a number of minor changes were made during rehearsals. Because Mayakovsky entered them in whatever copy he happened to have in hand, there is some discrepancy among the many typed manuscripts now available. The final version, printed during Mayakovsky's lifetime, however, serves as the basis for the text printed in Volume XI of *Polnoe sobranie sochinenii*, Moscow, 1958, from which the present translation was made and many of the notes were taken.

The Bedbug received its première at the V. Meyerhold State Theater on February 13, 1929, with Ilyinsky in the role of Prisypkin and Temerin as Bayan. Shostakovich composed incidental music for it, and Kukryniksy and Rodchenko did the sets. The play was a wild success. Performed almost daily for the remainder of the season, it soon entered the repertoire of other theaters as well. It was first performed in New York in 1931.

Its best advertisement, other than its own excellence, seems still to be a poster Mayakovsky wrote for it back in 1929:

PEOPLE GUFFAW
          AND WRINKLE THEIR FOREHEADS
IN MEYERHOLD'S THEATER
               AT THE COMEDY *Bedbug*.

CITIZEN!
     HURRY
          AND CATCH *The Bedbug*.
THERE'S A LINE FOR TICKETS
            AND A MOB IN THE HOUSE.
ONLY DON'T
       YOU GET SORE
             AT THE INSECT'S BITES.
THEY'RE NOT MEANT FOR YOU
            BUT FOR THE NEXT GUY.

DRAMATIS PERSONAE

Prisypkin [Pierre Skripkin], a former workingman, a former party member, now a fiancé
Zoya Beryozkina, a working girl
Elzevira Davidovna, a fiancée, a manicurist, cashier in a beauty parlor ⎫
Rozaliya Pavlovna, her mother, a hair dresser ⎬ Renaissance family
David Osipovich, her father, a hair dresser ⎭
Oleg Bayan, a man of natural talents, from a family of landlords
Policeman
Professor
Director of the Zoo
Fire Chief
Firemen
Wedding attendant (Man of Honor)
Reporter
Workmen in the auditorium
Chairman of the City Council
Orator
University students
Master of ceremonies
City Council presidium, Hunters, Children, Old men

SCENE I

Center stage, the huge revolving door of a department store, the sides glassed in, the store windows filled with goods. People go in empty-handed, come out with packages. Independent vendors wander all through the theater.

BUTTON VENDOR. No point getting married on account of a
   button, on account of a button no point getting divorced!
   Just a squeeze of the thumb and the index finger, and the
   citizens' pants won't ever fall down.
   Dutch,
   mechanical,
   self-sewing buttons,
   six for 20 kopeks . . .
   Help yerself, *Moosieu!*
DOLL VENDOR. A dancing crowd
   from the ballet studios.
   Best toy of all
   in the house and outdoors,
   dances along
   on the Education Commissar's order!
APPLE VENDOR. Got no
                         pineapples!
   Got no
          bananas!
   Got Antonov apples at four for 15.
   Let's have your order, lady!
WHETSTONE VENDOR. An unbreakable
                                   German
                                           whetstone,
30
   kopeks
          for any
                  one.

Sharpens
> in any
>> direction
>>> the way you like

razors,
> knives
>> and tongues for talk!

Help yerselves, citizens!

LAMPSHADE VENDOR. Shades
> of every
>> hue and complexion.

Light blue for comfort,
> red for real passion.

Come pick what you want, Comrades!

BALLOON SELLER. Balloons like sausages.

Fly without cautiousness.

This is
> the kind
>> General Nobile needed[1]—

he could have stayed on the Pole
> a lot longer indeed.

Pick yours, Citizens . . .

SALTED-HERRING VENDOR. Now here are
> the best
>> republican salted herrings,

that you can't do without
> with pancakes and vodka-drinking!

HABERDASHERY VENDOR. Fur-lined bras,
> fur-lined bras!

GLUE SELLER. Here
> and abroad
>> and all over

people
> throw out
>> their broken dishes.

---

[1] Umberto Nobile, leader of the 1928 Italian expedition to the North Pole in the dirigible "Italia." Their airship wrecked, the men were rescued by the Russian icebreaker "Krasin." Mayakovsky wrote two poems about it.

The great
> Excelsior,
>> the powder glue,
glues
> both the Venus de Milo
>> and your chamber pot.

You want some, madam?

PERFUME VENDOR. Coty perfume
> in real ounce bottles!

Coty perfume
> in real ounce bottles![2]

BOOKSELLER. What the little woman does when her man is not home, one hundred five amusing stories by former Count Lev Nikolayevich Tolstoy reduced from a ruble 20 to 15 kopeks.

HABERDASHERY VENDOR. Fur-lined bras,
> fur-lined bras!

(PRISYPKIN, ROZALIYA PAVLOVNA *and* BAYAN *come in.*)

Fur-lined . . .

PRISYPKIN (*ecstatically*). What aristocratic little caps!

ROZALIYA PAVLOVNA. What do you mean "caps," they're . . .

PRISYPKIN. You think I haven't got eyes, hunh? And what if we have twins? This is for Dorothy, and this is for Lilian—I've decided to give them aristocratic names like in the movies—and so they'll be going out together. Right! My home has got to be a place of plenty. Get some, Rozaliya Pavlovna!

BAYAN (*giggling*). Grab them, grab them, Rozaliya Pavlovna! How could he really have a dirty idea in his head? He's a youngster still, takes everything his own way. He comes to you of ancient, unsullied proletarian stock and brings a union card into your house, and you grudge a ruble! His home has got to be a place of plenty.

(*Sighing*, ROZALIYA PAVLOVNA *buys them.*)

I'll take them . . . they're light . . . don't worry . . . for the same price . . .

---

[2] In the original, "by the zolotnik"—a pre-metric Russian measure equal to about 4.25 grams, used for small but valuable things.

TOY VENDOR. A dancing crowd from the ballet studios . . .

PRISYPKIN. My future heirs and descendants must be brought up in elegance. Right! Get some, Rozaliya Pavlovna!

ROZALIYA PAVLOVNA. Comrade Prisypkin . . .

PRISYPKIN. Don't "Comrade" me, Citizen, you haven't yet got into the proletariat.

ROZALIYA PAVLOVNA. Future Comrade, Citizen Prisypkin, for this much money fifteen men can get shaved—not counting the change—mustache and all. It'd be better to have an extra dozen beers at the wedding. Eh?

PRISYPKIN (*sternly*). Rozaliya Pavlovna! My home . . .

BAYAN. His home has got to be a place of plenty. With dancing and beer squirting like a fountain, like out of a cornucopia.

(ROZALIYA PAVLOVNA *buys them.*)

(*Taking the bundles.*) Don't worry, for the same price.

BUTTON VENDOR. No point getting married on account of a button!

On account of a button no point getting divorced!

PRISYPKIN. Our Red family must have no bourgeois ways in it or trouble with pants. Right! Get some, Rozaliya Pavlovna!

BAYAN. As long as you haven't got a union card, don't cross him, Rozaliya Pavlovna. He's the class that won, and he sweeps everything before him, like lava, and Comrade Skripkin's pants have got to be a place of plenty.

(*With a sigh,* ROZALIYA PAVLOVNA *buys them.*)

Let me, I'll carry them for the same . . .

HERRING VENDOR. The best republican herring!

You can't do without them

with any vodka-drinking!

ROZALIYA PAVLOVNA (*pushing everyone aside, loudly and gaily*). Herring—now that—yes! This is something you'll be having for your wedding. Sure I'll buy this! You go on, you *moosieu* men! What does this sardine cost?

VENDOR. This salmon costs 2.60 a kilo.

ROZALIYA PAVLOVNA. 2.60 for this overgrown sprat?

VENDOR. What are you talking about, madame, only 2.60 for this future sturgeon!

ROZALIYA PAVLOVNA. 2.60 for these pickled corset bones? You hear that, Comrade Skripkin? You were right when you killed the tsar and kicked out Mr. Ryabushinsky![2] Oh, these robbers! I'll get my citizen's rights and my *own* herring in the Government Soviet Social Co-op!

BAYAN. Let's wait here, Comrade Skripkin. Why should you mingle with this petty-bourgeois world and buy herring in such a loud-mouthed way? For 15 rubles and a bottle of vodka I'll set up a little wedding for you to a T.

PRISYPKIN. Comrade Bayan, I'm against this bourgeois way of living—canaries and all the rest. I'm a man with great demands . . . I'm—interested in a wardrobe with a mirror . . .

(ZOYA BERYOZKINA *practically runs into them as they talk, steps back in surprise, listening.*)

BAYAN. When your wedding *cortège* . . .

PRISYPKIN. What are you mumbling? What kind of cardplay?

BAYAN. I said "*cortège*." That, Comrade Skripkin, is what, in beautiful foreign languages, any and especially such a triumphant wedding procession is called.

PRISYPKIN. Ah! Well, well! So . . .

BAYAN. So then, when the *cortège* drives up, I'll sing you Hymen's "Epithalamion." [4]

PRISYPKIN. What are you muttering? What are these Himalayas now?

BAYAN. Not Himalayas but the epithalamion for the god Hymen. The Greeks had a god of love like that—not these yellow ones, the wild followers of Venizelos,[5] but the ancient ones, the republicans.

PRISYPKIN. Comrade Bayan, for my money I require that the wedding be Red and without any gods! Got me?

BAYAN. Come on now, Comrade Skripkin, I not only got you, but on the strength of the expression, following Plekhanov, permitted to Marxists, I see, as if through a prism, your noble, elegant, intoxicating, class triumph! The bride climbs

---

[3] P. P. Ryabushinsky was one of the richest capitalists and patrons of the arts in tsarist Russia.

[4] One of the favorite concert numbers was the "Epithalamion" from Rubinstein's opera *Nero*.

[5] Elefterios Venizelos (1864–1936) was long the Greek Prime Minister.

out of the carriage—the Red bride—all red, means she got steamed up; she's led out by her red wedding-father, bookkeeper Erylakov—he happens to be a puffy, red, apoplectic man—you're escorted by red men of honor, the whole table is covered with red ham and bottles with red tops.

PRISYPKIN (*sympathetically*). Right! Right!

BAYAN. Red guests shout "Kiss, kiss," and now the Red—already married—girl puts her red, red little lips out toward you . . .

ZOYA (*distraught, takes them both by the sleeve; they both take her hands off, and flick off the dust*). Vanya! What's he talking about! What's this bandy-legged roly-poly in a necktie muttering about? What wedding? Whose?

BAYAN. The Red Marriage Bonds of Labor of Elzevira Davidovna Renaissance and . . .

PRISYPKIN. Zoya Vanna, I love another.
She's slimmer and lots fancier,
And a really snappy vest
Tightly holds her lovely breast.

ZOYA. Vanya! But what about me? This mean you got a girl in every port?

PRISYPKIN (*stretching out his hand in rejection*). We drifted apart, like two
ships at sea . . .

ROZALIYA PAVLOVNA (*bursts out of the store carrying a herring above her head*). Whales! Porpoises! (*To the* HERRING VENDOR) Well, show me, come on, compare your snail! (*She compares them; the street vendor's herring is bigger; she clasps her hands.*) A tail-length bigger? What did we fight for, hey, Citizen Skripkin? What did we kill the emperor for and kick out Mr. Ryabushinsky, hey? Your Soviet state is driving me to my grave. A tail-length, a whole tail bigger!

BAYAN. My good Rozaliya Pavlovna, compare it from the other end. It's only a head bigger, and what do you want the head for? You can't eat it, you have to cut it off and throw it out.

ROZALIYA PAVLOVNA. You hear what he said? Cut off the head. It's your head that ought to be cut off, Citizen Bayan, it's worth nothing and there'll be no loss. But cutting off its head costs ten kopeks more a kilo. So there! Home! I really need a union card in the house, but a daughter with a regular income—that's nothing to spit at, neither.

ZOYA. We wanted to live, to work . . . This means, everything . . .

PRISYPKIN. Citizen! Our love is liquidated. Don't interfere with free civil sentiment, or I'll call the police.

(ZOYA, *in tears, fastens onto his sleeve.* PRISYPKIN *breaks away.* ROZALIYA PAVLOVNA *stands between him and* ZOYA, *dropping her bundles.*)

ROZALIYA PAVLOVNA. What does this slob want? What are you clinging to my son-in-law for?

ZOYA. He's mine!

ROZALIYA PAVLOVNA. Ah! She's expecting! I'll pay her support, but I'll bash her mug in!

POLICEMAN. Citizens, cut out this hideous scene!

SCENE II

A Molodnyatskoe dormitory.[6] *An* INVENTOR *wheezes and keeps drawing designs. A* FELLOW *lounges around; on the edge of the bed, a* GIRL. SPECTACLES *has his head buried in a book. When the doors open, you can see a corridor with doors and light bulbs.*

BAREFOOT FELLOW (*yells*). Where are my boots? Someone's swiped my boots again. What have I got to do, take them every night to the Hand and Foot Baggage Room in the Kursky Station—is that it?

CLEANING MAN. It was Prisypkin tramped off in them to see his old she-camel. Put them on—cursed like hell. "This is

[6] "Molodnyatskoe" refers both to a district and to a young animal ("molodnyak"), as well as to young people collectively.

the last time," he says. "In the evening," he says, "I'll show up in new things, better suited to my new social position."

BAREFOOT. The bastard!

YOUNG WORKINGMAN (*cleaning up*). Even the dirt after him has become somehow noble, delicate like. What did there used to be? Old beer bottles and a catfish tail, but now there are little Tezhe[7] bottles and perfumed ribbons.

GIRL. Stop talking stupid; the guy bought a tie, so now you swear at him for being MacDonald.[8]

FELLOW. He *is* MacDonald! It's not the tie, but the fact that what is tied, is not the tie to him, but him to the tie. Doesn't even think—afraid to muss up his brains.

CLEANING MAN. Covers up holes with varnish; was in a hurry, saw a hole in his sock, so as he was going he blacked up his leg with an indelible pencil.

FELLOW. His is black anyway without the pencil.

INVENTOR. Maybe not in that place. He should have changed his socks.

CLEANING MAN. Got it right away—that's an inventor for you. Take out a patent! Look out somebody doesn't steal your idea. (*Swishes a rag over the table, knocks a little box down— visiting cards fall out in a fan-shape. He bends down to pick them up, takes them over to the light, dissolves in laughter, barely able to beckon his comrades over.*)

ALL (*reading again and again, repeating*). Pierre Skripkin. Pierre Skripkin!

INVENTOR. That's the name he invented for himself. Prisypkin. Why, what's Prisypkin? What for? What's the good of it? Who wants it? But Pierre Skripkin—that's not just a name, but a romance!

GIRL (*dreamily*). Why that's true: Pierre Skripkin—that's very elegant and wonderful. You laugh now, but maybe he'll work a cultural revolution in the house.

FELLOW. He's outdone even Pushkin's ugly mug. His sideburns hang down like a dog's tail, doesn't wash even— afraid of messing them up.

---

[7] The name of a perfume shop.
[8] The British Laborite Prime Minister.

GIRL. Harry Piehl has the same cultural value all over his cheeks, too.[9]

INVENTOR. That's what his teacher in the field of hair is developing.

FELLOW. But just what does this teacher's hair hang onto: no head at all but all the curliness you want. You get hair like that from dampness, is that it?

FELLOW WITH THE BOOK. No-o-o. He's a writer. I've got no idea what he's written, I just know he's famous! *Evening Moscow* wrote him up three times: they say he passed off Apukhtin's poems as his own, and when Apukhtin got sore, he wrote a denial. "You idiots," he says, "it's all wrong—I copied from Nadson.[10] Who's right I don't know. They don't print him any more, but he's very famous now— teaches young people. Some poetry, some singing, some dancing, some . . . how to borrow money.

FELLOW WITH THE BROOM. That's no workingman's way— cover up a corn with varnish.

(A LOCKSMITH, *all grimy, enters in the middle of the sentence, washes his hands, turns around.*)

LOCKSMITH. He's got nothing to do with workingmen, got himself paid off today, marries a girl, a hairdresser's daughter—she's the cashier and the manicurist, too. He'll get his claws trimmed now by *Mademoiselle* Elzevira Renaissance.

INVENTOR. Elzevir—there's a type font called that.

LOCKSMITH. I don't know about fonts, but she's got other parts—that's for sure. Showed her photo to the bookkeeper for speedy reckoning.

Hey, my sweetie, hey, my own—
Her breasts weigh eighty pounds alone.

BAREFOOT. He made it!

GIRL. Aha! Jealousy got you?

BAREFOOT. So what. Me, too, when I become a technician and get everyday boots, I'll fix myself up with a fine little place, too.

[9] Harry Piehl—a widely popular, swashbuckling German movie star.

[10] A. N. Apukhtin (1841–93) and S. Y. Nadson (1862–87) were popular, sentimental, "Parnassian" Russian poets.

LOCKSMITH. Here's what I advise you: you rig yourself up some little curtains. Open the curtain, you have a look at the street: shut the curtain, you pocket a bribe. It's just working alone is no good, but eating your chicken all by yourself is good enough. Right? That's the kind would run away from the trenches to fix it up, too, only we slapped them back. So, now—take off!

BAREFOOT. I'm going, I'm going. But why are you trying to make like Karl Liebknecht?[11] Wave at you from a window with some little flowers and I bet you'd go up, too. Big hero!

LOCKSMITH. I'm not going anywhere. You think I like all these rags and the stink? No. There's a lot of us, see. You can't set up enough little NEP girls for us all. We'll build ourselves houses and move right away—all of us right away. But we aren't crawling out of this stinking trench with white flags.

BAREFOOT. You and your damned trenches! This isn't '19. People want to live for themselves now.

LOCKSMITH. What do you mean—aren't these trenches?

BAREFOOT. Bull!

LOCKSMITH. It's lousy as hell!

BAREFOOT. Bull!

LOCKSMITH. But they're shooting with noiseless powder.

BAREFOOT. Bull!

LOCKSMITH. And Prisypkin's already been peppered by a double-eyed shotgun.

(PRISYPKIN *enters in patent-leather shoes; in his outstretched hand he holds the worn-out boots by their laces, throws them to* BAREFOOT. BAYAN *comes in with the packages. He pushes in between* SKRIPKIN *and the* LOCKSMITH, *who has begun a fast dance.*)

BAYAN. Now, Comrade Skripkin, pay no attention to these vulgar dances; they'll only spoil your growing sophistication. (*The dormitory fellows turn away.*)

LOCKSMITH. Cut the bowing! You'll crack your bean.

BAYAN. I understand you, Comrade Skripkin: it's hard for you, it's impossible for you, with your tender heart, in their

[11] Karl Liebknecht (1871–1919)—one of the German Social Democratic leaders, murdered in 1919.

vulgar company. Don't let your patience bust for just one more lesson. The step in life most fraught with responsibility is the first fox trot after the marriage ceremony. You've got to make an impression to last a lifetime. So, move forward now with a make-believe lady. What're you stomping for, like in the May Day parade?

PRISYPKIN. Comrade Bayan, I'm going to take off my shoes. In the first place, they pinch; and secondly, the heels are getting worn down.

BAYAN. There you go, that's it! That's it, slowly, like you're coming home from the tavern on a moonlit night lost in dreams and melancholy. That's it, that's it! But don't wiggle your lower parts, you're not pushing a cart but a *mademoiselle*. That's it, that's it! Where's your hand? Your hand's too low!

PRISYPKIN (*sliding over an imaginary shoulder*). It won't stay up in the air for me.

BAYAN. Now, Comrade Prisypkin, find the brassiere with a little light reconnoitering and, as if to take a breath, push in with your thumb; the lady likes your feeling for her, and it makes things easier for you—you can think about your other hand. What're you shaking your shoulders for? That's no fox trot, you've started doing a shimmy.

PRISYPKIN. No. I was just . . . scratching myself on the way.

BAYAN. How can you, Comrade Prisypkin! If during your inspirational dancing such an occurrence befalls you, roll your eyes, as if you're jealous of the lady, step back like the Spanish to the wall, quickly rub yourself on a piece of statuary—in the fashionable society in which you'll be traveling, different vases and statues of this sort are all over hell. Rub yourself, adjust your suit, flash your eyes, and say: "I got you, devilish woman, you're teasing me . . . but . . ." and set off dancing again, as if slowly cooling off and calming down.

PRISYPKIN. Like this?

BAYAN. Bravo! Fine! You've got talent, Comrade Prisypkin! With the bourgeois encirclement and the building of socialism in one country, you've got no place to go. Is our little Middle Goat Alley a worthy field for you? You need a World Revolution, you need an out into Europe, you just

have to knock off the Chamberlains and Poincarés and
you'll be thrilling the *Moulin Rouges* and *Panthéons* with
the beauty of your bodily movements. Remember that,
stand still like that! Splendid! Well, I'm off. Got to keep
an eye on those Men of Honor; they get a glass as advance
before the wedding and not a drop more, but once they've
done their job, then they can drink right from the bottle.
Au revoir. (*Goes out, shouting from the door.*) Don't put on
two ties at once, especially different-colored, and stick this
in your bonnet: you can't wear a starched shirt with the
tails out!

(PRISYPKIN *tries on the new things.*)

FELLOW. Vanka, cut out all this fuss! Why make yourself such
a stuffed dummy?

PRISYPKIN. It's none of your goddamned business, most
worthy Comrade! What did I fight for? I fought for the
good life. And here it is in my hands: a wife, a house, and
the proper style. I can always do my duty if I have to. He
who fought has won the right to rest by the gentle stream.
So there! Maybe I'll raise my whole class by my own good
arrangement. There!

LOCKSMITH. Fighter! Suvorov![12] Right you are!
Took the high road,
                      took the low,
built the bridge to socialism,
didn't finish,
        tired out,
and sat down beside the bridge.
Grass grew up beside the bridge.
Little lambkins go across it.
Very simply
            we'd now like to
take a rest beside this stream . . .
That's it, isn't it?

PRISYPKIN. Go to hell! Leave me alone with your foul prop-
aganda. So there! (*Sits down on the bed, sings to the guitar.*)
On Lunacharsky Street
there's a house that I remember—

---

[12] A. Suvorov (1729–1800)—a great Russian general, famous
for his campaigns in the Alps.

*with a wonderful wide stair
and the loveliest window.*

(*A shot. They rush to the door.*)

FELLOW (*from the doorway*). Zoya Beryozkina has shot herself!
(*They all rush to the door.*)
Oh, they'll give it to her now in the party cell!

VOICES. Hurry . . .
Hurry . . .
Ambulance . . .
Ambulance . . .

VOICE. Ambulance! Hurry! What? Shot herself! The breast. Right through. Middle Goat, 16.

(PRISYPKIN *alone hurriedly collects his things.*)

LOCKSMITH. On account of you, you hairy ape, a woman like that killed herself! Get out! (*Takes* PRISYPKIN *by his jacket, tosses him out the door, and throws the things after him.*)

CLEANING MAN (*running in with the doctor; halts and picks* PRISYPKIN *up, handing him his hat which flew off*). You sure are busting out of your class with a bang, pal!

PRISYPKIN (*turning away, shouts*). Cabbie, Lunacharsky Street, 17! And the things!

SCENE III

A big room in a beauty parlor. Mirrors on the sides. Big paper flowers in front of the mirrors. Bottles stand on little barber's tables. Downstage left is a piano with its jaw open; on the right, a stove, its pipes twisted around all over the room. In the middle of the room, a round wedding table is set. At the table: PIERRE SKRIPKIN, ELZEVIRA RENAISSANCE, *two* MEN OF HONOR *and* MAIDS OF HONOR, MOMMY *and* DADDY RENAISSANCE, *the* WEDDING-FATHER—BOOKKEEPER *and, likewise, the* MOTHER. OLEG BAYAN *takes charge of things in the center, his back to the audience.*

ELZEVIRA. Shall we begin, Skripochka?

SKRIPKIN. Wait a little. (*Pause.*)

ELZEVIRA. Skripochka, shall we begin?

SKRIPKIN. Wait a little. I want to get married in regular order and in the presence of honored guests and especially in the personal presence of the Secretary of the Factory Committee, honored Comrade Lassalchenko. So there!

GUEST (*running in*). Honored newlyweds, generously forgive my being late, but I'm entrusted with giving you good wishes on your marriage from our honored leader, Comrade Lassalchenko. Tomorrow, he says, he'd go even to church, but today, he says, he can't come. Today, he says, is the Party's day, and whether he wants to or not, he's got to go, he says, to the Party cell. Now let's get on, so to speak, with the regular business.

PRISYPKIN. I declare the wedding open.

ROZALIYA PAVLOVNA. Comrades and *Moosieu*, start eating, please. Where'll you find such pigs now? I bought this side of ham three years ago in case of war either with Greece or Poland. But . . . there's no war yet, and the ham's going bad. Eat up, *Moosieu*.

ALL (*raise their glasses and wineglasses*). Kiss! Kiss!

(ELZEVIRA *and* PIERRE *kiss.*)

Kiss! K-i-i-s-s-s!

(ELZEVIRA *drapes herself on* PIERRE. PIERRE *kisses her importantly and with a sense of class dignity.*)

BOOKKEEPER. Beethoven! Shake-his-pair! Please play something! We don't celebrate your jubilees every day just for nothing!

(*They pull out the piano.*)

VOICES. By the end, take her by the end! Ah, what ivories, what ivories! Like to pound them in!

PRISYPKIN. Don't kick my piano's legs.

BAYAN (*gets up, sways, and spills from his wineglass*). I'm happy, I'm happy to see the elegant fruition in this present instant of time of Comrade Skripkin's battle-fraught path in life. True, on this path he lost one personal Party card, but he acquired, however, many government loan coupons. We managed to reconcile and untangle his class and other contradictions, in which whoever is armed with a Marxist eye can't help seeing, as in a drop of water, so to speak, mankind's future happiness, among simple folks called Socialism.

ALL. Kiss! Kiss!

(ELZEVIRA *and* SKRIPKIN *kiss*.)

BAYAN. With what capital steps we march ahead down the path of building our family! When we were dying at Perekop,[13] and a lot of guys were already dead, could we actually suppose that these roses would bloom and smell sweet for us in this present instant of time? When we groaned under the yoke of autocracy, could even our great teachers, Marx and Engels, have really supposedly dreamed or even supposed as in a dream that we would tie with Hymen's bonds unknown, though great, labor with overthrown, though enchanting, capital?

ALL. Kiss! Kiss!

BAYAN. Honored Citizens! Beauty is the motor of progress! What would I be as a simple workingman? A cooper—that's all! What could I do as a cooper? Moo! And that's all! But as a Bayan—I can do what I please![14] For example:
Oleg Bayan, boy,
Is clobbered from joy.

And here I am now, Oleg Bayan, and I enjoy, as a member of society with equal rights, all the delights of culture, and I can let go—I mean, no, I can't let go, but I can keep conversing away, just like the ancient Greeks: "Elzevira Skripkina, pass the fishies now." And the whole country can answer me, like any old troubadours:

To wet your little whistle,
for pleasure and delight,
we pass the herring-tail and bottle
to Oleg on our right.

ALL. Bravo! Hurrah! Kiss!

BAYAN. Beauty is the screw . . .

MAN OF HONOR (*sullenly and jumping up*). Screw! Who said "screw?" No swearing, please, in front of newlyweds.

(*They push the* MAN OF HONOR *back*.)

---

[13] Perekop—a small town in the Crimea where the Red Army decisively defeated the Whites in 1920.

[14] Bayàn—an ancient Russian minstrel-poet and, now, a large, first-class accordion.

ALL. Beethoven! Kamarinsky!

(BAYAN *is hauled to the piano.*)

BAYAN. *The trolleys gathered at the marriage bureau—*
There was a Red wedding there . . .[15]

ALL (*joining in*). *The groom was in his working clothes,*
his union card was sticking out!

BOOKKEEPER. Got it! Got everything! That means:
God bless you, Oleg Bayan-chik,
you curly little ram-chik . . .

HAIRDRESSER (*heads with his fork toward the* WEDDING-MOTHER). No, madame, after the Revolution, now, there are no more real curly-haired people. A chignon *gaufré* is done like this: you take the curling-irons (*spins the fork*) warm them in a weak flame *à la étoile* (*sticks the fork into the stove's fire*) and whip up on the crown a hairy *soufflé* like this.

WEDDING-MOTHER. You're offending my dignity as a mother and lady! Stop it! You son of a bitch!

MAN OF HONOR. Who said "son of a bitch?" No swearing, please, in front of newlyweds!

(*The* BOOKKEEPER *separates them, singing away, trying to crank the handle of the cash register, which he is turning like a hand organ.*)

ELZEVIRA (*to* BAYAN). Oh! Play something. Oh! The "Makarov's Longing for Vera Kholodnaya"[16] waltz. Oh, it's so *charmant*, oh, it's simply a *petite histoire*.

MAN OF HONOR (*armed with a guitar*). Who said "*pissoir?*" In front of newlyweds, please . . .

MAN OF HONOR (*glaring, threateningly*). What're you playing on just the black keys for? On just half for the proletariat, is that it, but for the bourgeoisie, on all of 'em?

BAYAN. What do you mean, what do you mean, citizen? I'm trying especially on the whites.

MAN OF HONOR. So again it turns out the Whites are better, is that it? Play on all of 'em!

BAYAN. But I am!

---

[15] A parody of the song "The carriages stood by the church, An elegant wedding was there."

[16] Vera Kholodnaya—a star of the early Russian cinema.

MAN OF HONOR. You're with the Whites, you opportunist—is that it?

BAYAN. Comrade . . . now this is . . . a D-flat.

MAN OF HONOR. Who said "idiot?" In front of newlyweds! Take that! (*Clonks him on the back of the head with the guitar.*)

(*The* HAIRDRESSER *winds the* WEDDING-MOTHER'S *hair on his fork.* PRISYPKIN *comes between the* BOOKKEEPER *and his wife.*)

PRISYPKIN. What're you doing sticking a herring into my wife's bosom? That's not a flower bed for you, but a bosom, and that's no chrysanthemum but a herring!

BOOKKEEPER. And did you treat us to salmon? Did you? Hunh? And now you're screaming yourelf—hunh?

(*In the struggle they knock the gauze-veiled bride onto the stove, the stove is turned over—flames, smoke.*)

SHOUTS. We're burning! Who said "burning?" Fire! Salmon . . . The trolleys gathered from the marriage bureau . . .

SCENE IV

A FIREMAN'S *helmet shines in the light of nearby flames in the pitch dark. The* CHIEF *is alone.* FIREMEN *reporting come and go.*

1ST FIREMAN. Can't get it under control, Comrade Chief! Didn't call us for two hours. The drunken bastards! It's burning like a powder keg. (*Goes out.*)

CHIEF. Why shouldn't it burn? Cobwebs and liquor.

2ND FIREMAN. It's dying down; the water's freezing in the air. We flooded up the cellar smoother than a skating rink. (*Goes out.*)

CHIEF. Found any bodies?

3RD FIREMAN. Carted off one, the whole skull bashed in. Must have been cracked by a beam. Straight to the morgue. (*Goes out.*)

4TH FIREMAN. Carted off . . . one burned body of unidentifiable sex with a fork in its head.

1ST FIREMAN. Under the stove we turned up what was once a woman with a wire crown on her skull.

3RD FIREMAN. Found some man of pre-war build with a cash register in his hands—obviously in life was a robber.

2ND FIREMAN. Not one left alive. Among the bodies there's one short, so since we didn't find it I figure it burned to pieces.

1ST FIREMAN. Some fireworks! Real theater, only all the actors have burned up!

3RD FIREMAN. Their carriage drove off from the wedding, The Red Cross carriage carrying them.

(*The Trumpet Player signals to the* FIREMEN. *They line up. They parade through the theater, calling out.*)

FIREMEN. Comrades and Citizens,

                        vodka'll kill you.

Drunkards
     will burn
          the republic up just like that!

Living with fireplaces,
          living with primuses,

you'll fire your house
          and burn yourself up!

You happen to fall
     asleep—
          that's the cause of fires—

To fall asleep
     don't read
          Allsleep and Fiery![17]

---

[17] In the Russian, "Nadson" and "Zharov," Russian poets. *Son* means sleep; *pozhar* means fire. The lines read: "*sluchainy son—prichina pozharov,—na son ne chitaite Nadsòna i Zharova!*"

SCENE V

A huge high-ceilinged meeting hall, with seats slanting up in an amphitheater. Instead of people's voices—loudspeakers; beside them, several hanging arms like those stuck out automobile windows. On top of every loudspeaker, colored electric bulbs; right under the ceiling, a screen. In the center, a rostrum with a microphone. On both sides of the rostrum, selector panels and controls for the voices and colors. Two MECHANICS—*one old, one young—are working away in the dark auditorium.*

OLD ONE (*with a tattered feather duster, brushing the dust off the loudspeakers*). Today is the important vote. Oil it up and check the voting receiver of the agricultural sections. Last time there was a hitch. They voted with a squeak.

YOUNG ONE. The agricultural? OK! I'll oil the central. I'll rub the Smolensk receivers' throats with a chamois. Last week they were hoarse again. Got to tighten up the screws on the arms of the capital officials, because otherwise they're a bit off: the right keeps getting caught in the left.

OLD ONE. The Ural factories are set. We'll plug in the Kursk metallurgical works; there they set up a new receiver of 62,000 votes of the second group of the Zaporozhe power station. No trouble with them, the work is easy.

YOUNG ONE. You still remember what it was like before? Ridiculous, I bet?

OLD ONE. Mama carried me in her arms to a meeting once. Hardly anybody there—maybe a thousand all together, sitting around, like spongers, and listening. The question was somehow important and with lots of talking, got passed by one vote. Mother was against but couldn't vote, because she was carrying me in her arms.

YOUNG ONE. Well, sure! Real amateurish!

OLD ONE. Before, a rig like this wouldn't have worked. Used to be, the *first* man had to raise his hand so as to be recognized, so he'd stick it under the chairman's nose, stick them both right up under his nostrils, and just feel sorry he wasn't the old goddess Izida so he could vote with twelve. But a lot of people steered clear of it all. They say one guy sat out a whole important discussion in the toilet—was scared to vote. Sat there and thought, saving his skin for his job, see.

YOUNG ONE. Did he?

OLD ONE. Did he! Only got assigned another job. People saw his love for toilets, so they made him headman in charge of soap and towels. Is it ready?

YOUNG ONE. Ready!

(*They run down to the selector panels and wires. The Man with Glasses and Beard, having flung the door open, marches onstage, his back to the audience, his hands raised high.*)

ORATOR. Switch on simultaneously all the Federation districts!

OLD ONE and YOUNG ONE. Aye-aye, sir!

(*Simultaneously all the red, green, and blue lights of the auditorium light up.*)

ORATOR. Hello! Hello! This is the president of the Institute of Human Resurrection speaking! The question has been made public in telegrams, been discussed, is clear and simple. At the intersection of 62nd Street and 17th Prospect, in the former Tambov, the squad digging the foundations at a depth of seven meters turned up an earth-strewn, ice-covered cellar. Through the ice of this phenomenon one could discern the frozen figure of a man. The Institute considers possible the resurrection of this individuum, frozen stiff fifty years ago. Let's adjust the difference of opinions. The Institute believes that every life of a worker must be used to the last second. Radioscopy showed that on the creature's hands there were calluses, formerly, half a century ago, the sign of a workingman. Let me remind you that after the wars occurring all over the world, the civil wars creating the federation of the earth, by the decree of November 7, 1965, man's life is inviolable. I bring to your attention the objections of the epidemic section, fearing the threat of the spread of bacteria which filled the former creatures of what formerly was Russia. Fully conscious of my responsibility, I now ask for a decision. Comrades, remember, remember, and once more remember:

We're
    voting
        human life!
(*The lights go out; there is a piercing ring; the resolution, repeated by the* ORATOR, *flashes on the screen.*)
"In the name of research on the laboring skills of working humanity, in the name of a visual comparative study of everyday life, we demand resurrection."

> (*Voices of half the loudspeakers:* "*Right, adopted!*" *Some of the voices:* "*Down with it!*" *The voices fall silent instantly. The screen darkens. A second ring; a new resolution lights up. The* ORATOR *repeats it.*)

"The resolution of the sanitation control-station of the Donbas metallurgical and chemical works. In order to avoid the danger of spreading the bacteria of toadyism and playing big, characteristic of '29, we demand the exhibit be left in its frozen state."

> (*Voices of the loudspeakers:* "*Down with it!*" *Isolated outcries:* "*Right!*")

Are there other resolutions and amendments?

(*A third screen lights up, the* ORATOR *repeats what is on it.*)
"The Siberian agricultural regions request resurrection in the fall, when the work in the fields is done, to help assure the possibility of the presence of broad masses of people who want to take part."

> (*The overwhelming majority of voices-and-speakers:* "*Down with it!*" "*Rejected!*" *The lights come on.*)

I put it to a vote: who's for the first resolution? Please raise your hands!

> (*An overwhelming majority of the iron hands goes up.*)

Put them down! Who's for Siberia's amendment?

> (*Two lone hands go up.*)

The assembly of the federation has adopted "Resurrection!"

> (*A roar from all the loudspeakers:* "*Hurrah!*" *The voices fall silent.*)

The meeting is closed!

> (REPORTERS *burst in through two flung-open doors. The* ORATOR *breaks off, tossing in all directions delightedly:*)

Resurrection! Resurrection!! Resurrection!!!

(*The* REPORTERS *pull microphones out of their pockets, shouting as they go along:*)

1ST REPORTER. Hello! Wavelength 472½ meters . . . *The Chukchi News* . . . Resurrection!

2ND REPORTER. Hello! Hello! Wavelength 376 meters . . . *The Vitebsk Evening Pravda* . . . Resurrection!

3RD REPORTER. Hello! Hello! Hello! Wavelength 211 meters . . . *The Warsaw Komsomolskaya Pravda* . . . Resurrection!

4TH REPORTER. *The Armavir Monday Literary.* Hello! Hello!

5TH REPORTER. Hello! Hello! Hello! Wavelength 44 meters. *The Chicago Council News* . . . Resurrection!

6TH REPORTER. Hello! Hello! Hello! Wavelength 115 meters . . . *The Rome Red Gazette* . . . Resurrection!

7TH REPORTER. Hello! Hello! Hello! Wavelength 78 meters . . . *The Shanghai Pauper* . . . Resurrection!

8TH REPORTER. Hello! Hello! Hello! Wavelength 220 meters . . . *The Madrid Farm Girl* . . . Resurrection!

9TH REPORTER. Hello! Hello! Hello! Wavelength 11 meters . . . *The Kabul Pioneer* . . . Resurrection!

(NEWSBOYS *burst in with ready "extras."*)

1ST NEWSBOY. To thaw him out
                    or not to thaw?
Editorials
      in verse and prose!

2ND NEWSBOY. Worldwide questionnaire
                         on the crucial topic—
the possibility of a pile-up
                of toadyism epidemics!

3RD NEWSBOY. Articles on ancient
                    guitars and romances
and other devices
           for dumbfounding the masses!

4TH NEWSBOY. The latest news! Interview! Interview!

5TH NEWSBOY. Science News—
                  please don't be scared!
Here's a full list
      of how you so-called swear!

6TH NEWSBOY. The latest radio report!

7TH NEWSBOY. The theoretical side
>>>>>>>>>>>>>>>>>>>>of the historical question:
can
>>>a cigarette
>>>>>>>knock off
>>>>>>>>>>>a pachyderm!
8TH NEWSBOY. Makes you shed tears,
>>>>>>>>>>>>>>>>>>>makes you laugh till you're sick:
the complete explanation
>>>>>>>>>>>>>>>>of the word "alcoholic!"

SCENE VI

A frosted-glass double door; the metal parts of medical instruments shine through the wall. In front of the wall, an old PROFESSOR *and an aged Assistant, still preserving features that characterize* ZOYA BERYOZKINA. *Both in hospital whites.*

ZOYA BERYOZKINA. Comrade! Comrade Professor, please, don't do this experiment. Comrade Professor, there'll be a blowup again . . .

PROFESSOR. Comrade Beryozkina, you've started living in your memories and speaking an incomprehensible language. An absolute dictionary of dead words. What's "blowup?" (*Looks in a dictionary.*) Blowup . . . Blowup . . . Blowup . . . Bureaucracy, Beseeching,[18] Bagels, Bohemia, Bulgakov . . . Blowup—this is a kind of activity of people who interfere with every kind of activity . . .

ZOYA BERYOZKINA. This "activity" of his fifty years ago nearly cost me my life. I even went so far as . . . to try suicide.

PROFESSOR. Suicide? What's "suicide?" (*Looks in the dic-*

[18] *Bogoiskatelstvo*—literally, "god-seeking," a religious movement with socio-philosophic aims particularly strong after the 1905 revolution.

tionary.) Self-surrender,[19] self-advertisement, sovereignty, space-sharing . . .[20] Found it. "Suicide." (*Amazed*.) You shot yourself? Were sentenced? A court? A revolutionary tribunal?

ZOYA BERYOZKINA. No . . . Did it myself.

PROFESSOR. Yourself? Out of carelessness?

ZOYA BERYOZKINA. No . . . Out of love.

PROFESSOR. Nonsense . . . Out of love one must build bridges and bear children . . . But you . . . Indeed! Indeed! Indeed!

ZOYA BERYOZKINA. Let me go, really, I can't.

PROFESSOR. That's it all right! How did you put it? Blowup. Indeed! Indeed! Indeed! Indeed! Blowup! Society proposes you express all the feelings you have for the maximum ease of the thawed-out subject's overcoming fifty anabiological years. Yes! Yes! Yes! Yes! Your presence is very, very important. I'm delighted you were here and came. He—that's him! And you—that's her! Tell me, now, were his eyelashes soft? In case of breakage under fast thawing.

ZOYA BERYOZKINA. Comrade Professor, how can I remember eyelashes some fifty years ago?

PROFESSOR. What? Fifty years ago? It was yesterday! How do I remember the color of the hair on the tail of a mastodon five hundred thousand years ago! Indeed! Indeed! Indeed! But you don't remember if he opened his nostrils wide when inhaling in exciting company?

ZOYA BERYOZKINA. Comrade Professor, how could I? For thirty years now nobody has opened his nostrils wide in such cases.

PROFESSOR. Right! Right! Right! And you have no information with regard to the capacity of the stomach and liver, in case of elimination of a possible content of alcohol and vodka, capable of catching fire under the necessary high voltage?

ZOYA BERYOZKINA. How could I possibly recall that, Comrade Professor! I remember there *was* a belly of sorts . . .

---

[19] *Samooblozhenie*—voluntary delivery of goods and produce to satisfy common needs as collectively determined.

[20] *Samouplotnenie*—voluntary sharing of living quarters according to one's own choice.

THE BEDBUG   363

PROFESSOR. Ah, you don't remember a thing, Comrade Beryozkina! At least, was he impetuous or not?

ZOYA BERYOZKINA. I don't know. Possibly, but . . . only not with me.

PROFESSOR. Right! Right! Right! I'm afraid that while we're getting him unfrozen, in the meantime you got frostbitten yourself. Yes! Yes! Yes! Well, now to work.

(He pushes a button, the glass wall quietly opens. In the middle, on an operating table, there is a shiny galvanized box the size of a man. On the box there are faucets; under the faucets, buckets. Electric wires lead to the box. Cylinders of oxygen. Around the box are six DOCTORS, *dressed in white and relaxed. Downstage on the apron in front of the box are six doctor's washstands. On an invisible wire, hang—as if in thin air—six towels.)*

PROFESSOR *(going from doctor to doctor and speaking. To the First.)* Switch the current on when I signal.

(To the Second.) Bring the heat up to 36.4°—fifteen seconds for every tenth.

(To the Third.) The oxygen pillows are ready?

(To the Fourth.) Let the water out gradually, replacing the ice with air pressure.

(To the Fifth.) Open the lid right away.

(To the Sixth.) Observe, in the mirror, the stages of animation.

    (The DOCTORS *bow their heads to indicate that they have understood and go to their stations.)*

Let's begin!

(The current is switched on; they watch the temperature. Water drips. The SIXTH DOCTOR *is glued to the mirror in the little right-hand wall.)*

SIXTH DOCTOR. Natural color is beginning to show! *(Pause.)* He's clear of the ice! *(Pause.)* The chest's vibrating! *(Pause. Frightened.)* Professor, come look at the unnatural violence . . .

PROFESSOR *(comes over, peers in, reassuringly).* The movements are normal, he's scratching—evidently certain parasites pertaining to such individuums are coming alive.

SIXTH DOCTOR. Professor, something incomprehensible: by a

movement of the left hand something is being separated from the body.

PROFESSOR (*peering in*). He and music fused together: they used to call that having a "sensitive soul." In ancient times there lived Stradivarius and Utkin.[21] Stradivarius made violins, and Utkin made this, and it's called a guitar. (*The* PROFESSOR *glances at the thermometer and at the instrument recording the blood pressure.*)

FIRST DOCTOR. 36.1.

SECOND DOCTOR. Pulse 68.

SIXTH DOCTOR. Breathing even.

PROFESSOR. To your stations!

(*The* DOCTORS *move away from the box. The lid is instantly thrown off, and out of the box comes a dishevelled and bewildered* PRISYPKIN, *looks around, hugging his guitar.*)

PRISYPKIN. Well, what a good nap! Excuse me, Comrades, of course I was tight! This is which division of the police?

PROFESSOR. No, this is a different division altogether! This is the division from ice of the skin teguments which you froze . . .

PRISYPKIN. What? It's you yourself got frozen. We'll see which of us was drunk. As big doctor specialists, you're always hanging around liquor yourselves. And I, as an individual, can always identify myself. Got my papers on me. (*Jumps out, turns his pockets inside out.*) Got 17 rubles, 60 kopeks on me. Owe IOARF?[22] Paid 'em. SADACC?[23] Paid up. "Down with Illiteracy?"[24] Maybe. What's this? A registration from the Marriage Bureau! (*Whistles.*) That's right, I got married yesterday! Where are you now; who's kissing your fingers?[25] I'll get hell when I get home! Here are the signatures of the Men of Honor. Here's my union card. (*His eye falls on the calendar; he rubs his eyes, stares in terror.*) May 12, 1979! I owe union dues for all that time! Fifty

[21] I. P. Utkin—a Russian poet (1903–44) whose poem "The Guitar" was once widely popular with young people.

[22] Translated abbreviation for MOPR—International Organization for Assistance to Revolutionary Fighters.

[23] Translated abbreviation for OSOAVIAKHIM—Society for Assisting Defense and Aviational-Chemical Construction.

[24] Such groups existed on a wide scale "among the masses."

[25] The first line of a popular song.

years! They'll want receipts, the receipts! The Provsec! The CC![26] Good god! My wife!! Let me go! (*Shakes hands all around, rushes for the door.*)

(BERYOZKINA, *nervous, follows him. The* DOCTORS *surround the* PROFESSOR.)

ALL TOGETHER. What was that he did with his hands? Stuck them out and shook them, stuck them out and shook them . . .

PROFESSOR. In antiquity such an unsanitary custom existed. (*The six* DOCTORS *and the* PROFESSOR *pensively wash their hands.*)

PRISYPKIN (*running into* ZOYA). What are you all really, citizens? Who am I? Where am I? You wouldn't by any chance be Zoya Beryozkina's mother, would you?

(*The wail of a siren makes* PRISYPKIN *turn his head.*)

What have I gotten into? What's happened to me? What *is* this? Moscow? Paris? New York? Cabbie!

(*The loud honking of automobile horns.*)

No people, no horses! AAA, AAA, AAA![27] (*Presses against the door, scratches his back, looks for something with his hand open wide, turns around; on the white wall sees a bedbug crawling out from his collar.*) Bedbug, bedbuggy, beddybug! (*Plucks his guitar, sings.*) "Don't go away, stay with me a while . . ." (*Tries to catch the bedbug with his open palm; the bedbug crawls away.*) We've drifted apart, like two ships at sea. Crawled away! Alone! But no one answers me, I'm alone again. Alone! Cabbie! AAA! Lunacharsky Street, 17! Never mind the things! (*Grabs his head, faints into the arms of* BERYOZKINA, *who has run in from the doorway.*)

[26] *Provsec*—a division of the provincial government; *CC*—the Central Committee of the Party.

[27] *AAA*—Association for Assistance in Developing Automotive Transport.

SCENE VII

The center of the stage is a triangular town green. On the green are three artificial trees. The first tree has huge plates on square, green leaves; on the plates, tangerines. The second tree has paper plates; on the plates, apples. The third is green and has open perfume bottles, like pine cones. The sides are the glass-and-veneer walls of houses. Along the edges of the green are long benches. A REPORTER *comes in; behind him, a foursome:* MEN *and* WOMEN.

REPORTER. Comrades, over here, come over here! In the shade! I'll tell you about all these devious and marvellous events one by one. First: give me a tangerine. The City Council did right in putting tangerines on the trees today, because yesterday there were just pears—neither juicy, nor tasty, nor nourishing . . .
(*A* GIRL *takes a plate of tangerines off the tree; the rest, sitting down, peel them, eat them, leaning toward the* REPORTER *intently.*)

1ST MAN. Come on, Comrade, tell us everything in detail and in order.

REPORTER. So, now . . . What juicy little slices! Do you want some? All right, all right, I'll tell you. Just think, what impatience! Of course, I myself, as chief of the news section, know it all . . . Just look there; see, see . . .
   (*A Man with a Doctor's Bag with Thermometers walks quickly by.*)
That's a veterinary. The epidemic's spreading. Left alone, this resurrected mammal got into contact with all the domestic animals of the skyscraper, and now all the dogs are mad. It taught them how to stand on their hind legs. The dogs don't bark and don't play, but just sit up and beg. The beasts pester everybody who's eating, nuzzle up to them and beg for attention. The doctors say that people bitten by such beasts acquire all the basic traits of this toadyism epidemic.

PEOPLE SEATED. O—o—o!!

REPORTER. Look, look! (*A Staggering Man goes by, loaded down with baskets full of bottles of beer.*)

PASSER-BY (*sings*). *In the nineteenth century
People lived real wondrously—
downed their vodka, downed their beer,
their purple noses big as pears.*

REPORTER. Look at him, a sick, finished man! He's one of the hundred seventy-five workers in the second medical lab. In an attempt to ease its transitional existence, the doctors prescribed, for the resurrected mammal, drinking a mixture, poisonous in large doses and repulsive in little, otherwise known as beer. These workers went dizzy from the poisonous fumes and by mistake swallowed some of this cooling mixture. And since then they've already begun replacing the third batch. Five hundred twenty workers are in the hospital, but the terrible epidemic bubbles up as ever like the "local beer plague,"[28] boils away, and mows 'em down.

PEOPLE SEATED. A—a—a—a!!

MAN (*dreamily and wearily*). I'd sacrifice myself for science—let 'em inject me, too, with this bewildering disease!

REPORTER. Ready! That one's ready, too! Take it easy! Don't frighten this lunatic . . .

(*A GIRL goes by, her feet weave in and out in a fox trot and Charleston; she mumbles verses from a book held up by two fingers of her outstretched hand. In two fingers of her other hand she holds an imaginary rose; raises it to her nose and sniffs it.*)

Poor thing, she lives right beside it, beside this mad mammal, and at night now, when the city sleeps, she's begun hearing guitar plunkings through the wall, followed by long, soul-wearying sighs and wailings like singing—what do they call this? "Love songs," don't they? There's more and more as time goes on, and the poor girl's started going out of her mind. Her parents, nearly dead from grief, call in the doctors. The professors say it's the onset of a severe case of "falling in love"—that's what the old disease used to be

---

[28] *Tryokhgornaya chuma*—a slang expression for being drunk on beer; literally, the "Tryokhgornaya plague," from the former Moscow brewery "Tryokhgornaya."

called when human sexual energy, rationally distributed over one's whole life, suddenly wells up and condenses in one week in a single inflammatory process, leading to irrational and incredible actions.

GIRL (*covers her eyes with her hands*). I better not look; I can feel how these dreadful love microbes are going around through the air.

REPORTER. Ready, she's ready, too . . . The epidemic's surging on . . .

(*Thirty dancing chorus girls go by.*)

Look at that thirty-headed sixty-legged thing! Just think —they even used to label this leg-raising (*to the audience*) art!

(*A* COUPLE, *foxtrotting.*)

The epidemic's reached its . . . reached its . . . What's it reached? (*Looks in the dictionary.*) Its a-po-gee, well . . . it's already become a bisexual quadruped.

(*The* DIRECTOR OF THE ZOO *runs in with a little glass case in his hands. Behind the* DIRECTOR *comes a crowd armed with telescopes, cameras, and firemen's ladders.*)

DIRECTOR (*to everyone*). Did you see it? Did you see it? Where is it? Ah, you didn't see a thing! A band of hunters reported seeing it here a quarter of an hour ago; it was scrambling up to the fourth floor. Considering that its average speed is a meter and a half an hour, it can't have gone far. Comrades, search along the walls at once!

(*The Watchers open up their telescopes, jump down from the benches, look searchingly, shading their eyes. The* DIRECTOR *forms them into groups, directs the search.*)

VOICES. How'll you find it?

Got to stick somebody naked on a mattress in every window --it'll go for a man.

Don't shout, you'll scare it!

If I find it, I won't hand it over to anyone . . .

You wouldn't dare: it's community property . . .

VOICE (*excited*). Found it! It's here! Crawling!

(*The binoculars and telescopes are all focussed on one spot. Silence, broken by the clicking of still and movie cameras.*)

PROFESSOR (*in a restrained whisper*). Yes! That's it! Position the guards and ready the ambush. Firemen, over here!

(*People with nets surround the place. The firemen extend a ladder, people scramble up single-file.*)

DIRECTOR (*lowering his telescope, in a plaintive voice*). It's gone . . . Went across to the other wall . . . S O S! If it falls off, it'll kill itself! Daredevils, volunteers, heroes!! Over here!

(*A ladder goes up against the second wall, people clamber up. The spectators are frozen still.*)

VOICE (*from above; excited*). I got it! Hurrah!!

DIRECTOR. Hurry up!! Be careful!! Don't let it get away, don't crush the thing's paws . . .

(*The creature is handed down the ladder from one person to the next, finally ending up in the* DIRECTOR's *hands. The* DIRECTOR *stuffs the creature away in the case and raises the case over his head.*)

Thank you, inconspicuous servants of science! Our zoological park is delighted and *chef-d'oeuvred*. We've captured a very rare specimen of an extinct insect very popular in the beginning of this century. Our city can well be proud—scholars and tourists will flock here! Here, in my hands, lies the only living *bedbugus normalis*. Citizens, step back: the animal has fallen asleep, it has crossed its paws, it wants to rest! I invite you all to the gala opening in the zoo. A most significant, most nervewracking capture has been accomplished!

SCENE VIII

The flush, opal, semi-transparent walls of a room. From the cornice above falls an even band of light-blue light. On the left, a big window. In front of the window, a drafting board. A radio. A screen. Three or four books. On the right, a bed pulled out of the wall; on the bed, under the cleanest possible blanket, the dirtiest possible PRISYPKIN. *Electric fans. The corner of the room near*

PRISYPKIN *is all littered up. There are cigarette butts on the table and overturned bottles. There is a torn-off piece of pink paper on the lamp.* PRISYPKIN *is groaning. A* DOCTOR *nervously paces the room.*

PROFESSOR (*entering*). How are things with the patient?
DOCTOR. I don't know about the patient, but with me they're rotten! If you don't arrange for relief every half hour, he'll infect us all. He just breathes and my legs start giving way under me. I've put in seven fans already: to dispel his breath.
PRISYPKIN. O—o—o!
   (*The* PROFESSOR *rushes to* PRISYPKIN.)
   Professor, oh Professor!
   (*The* PROFESSOR *gets a whiff and reels back dizzy, pawing the air with his hands.*)
   One for the morning after . . .
   (*The* PROFESSOR *pours some beer into the bottom of a glass and gives it to him.*)
   (PRISYPKIN *raising himself onto his elbows; reproachful.*)
   Resurrected me . . . and now they make fun of me! What's that—no more than lemonade to an elephant!
PROFESSOR. Society hopes to raise you up to human status.
PRISYPKIN. The hell with you and your society! I didn't ask you to resurrect me. Freeze me up again! So there!
PROFESSOR. I don't understand what you're talking about! Our life belongs to the collective, and neither I nor anyone else can make this life . . .
PRISYPKIN. But what kind of a life is it when you can't even pin your girl's photo on the wall? All the thumbtacks break on this damned glass. Comrade Professor, give me one for the morning after.
PROFESSOR (*pours a glass*). Only don't breathe in my direction.
   (ZOYA BERYOZKINA *comes in with two piles of books. The doctors confer with her in a whisper, then go out.*)
ZOYA BERYOZKINA (*sits down beside* PRISYPKIN, *unties the books*). I don't know if this will do. There isn't any of what you were talking about and nobody knows about it. There's something about roses only in the gardening texts, about daydreams only in the medical books in the section about

dreams. Here are two really interesting books from about that time. A translation from English: Hoover's "How I Was President."[29]

PRISYPKIN (*takes the book, throws it away*). No, this doesn't touch the heart; got to have one that stops it still . . .

ZOYA BERYOZKINA. Here's the other—by some Mussolini or other: "Letters from Exile."

PRISYPKIN (*takes it, throws it down*). No, this doesn't touch the soul. Leave off all your vulgar propagandizing. Got to have one that really pricks . . .

ZOYA BERYOZKINA. I don't know what all that means. Stops it still, really pricks . . . really pricks, stops it still . . .

PRISYPKIN. What *is* this? What did we struggle for, spill our blood for, now, if I, the power behind it all, in my own society, doing a newly-learned dance, can't even dance my fill?

ZOYA BERYOZKINA. I showed your gymnastics even to the Director of the Central Kinetic Institute. He says he saw the same kind of thing in old collections of French postcards, but now, he says, there's nobody around who you could ask about it. There's a pair of old ladies—they remember, but they can't show how on account of their rheumatism.

PRISYPKIN. So why did I get myself a real elegant education that I could pass on? I was working enough even before the Revolution.

ZOYA BERYOZKINA. Tomorrow I'll take you to see a dance by ten thousand male and female workers; they'll be moving around in the city square. It'll be a gay rehearsal of a new system of field work.

PRISYPKIN. Comrades, I protest! I didn't get thawed so you could then dry me out. (*Rips off the blanket, jumps up, grabs the pile of books and shakes them out of their wrappers. Begins to tear up the paper and suddenly stares at the letters, as he runs from one lamp to another.*) Where? Where did you get this? . . .

ZOYA BERYOZKINA. They were handed out to everybody on the street. I suppose they put it in the books in the library.

---

[29] Translated from the Russian; the original English is *An Ex-President Speaks*.

PRISYPKIN. Saved! Hurrah! (*Rushes for the door, waving the paper in his hand like a flag.*)

ZOYA BERYOZKINA (*alone*). I've lived fifty years ahead, but fifty years back I could have died on account of this slob.

SCENE IX

The Zoo. In the center, on a pedestal, a cage covered with cloths and flags. Behind the cage are two trees. Behind the trees are cages with elephants and giraffes. On the left of the cage, a rostrum; on the right, raised stands for guests of honor. Musicians are all around. Spectators come up in groups. Ushers with armbands assign them places—according to occupation and height.

MASTER OF CEREMONIES. Comrade foreign correspondents, over here! Closer to the stands! Step aside and give the Brazilians room! Their airship is now landing at Central Airport. (*Steps back, admires the scene.*) Comrade Negroes, mix in with the Englishmen in pretty colored bunches; the Anglo-Saxon whiteness will set off your olive hue even better . . . University students—to the left; three old women and three old men from the Century Union are going to join you. They'll fill out all your professors' explanations with eyewitness accounts.

(*The old men and old women ride in in wheel chairs.*)

FIRST OLD WOMAN. I remember as if it were now . . .

FIRST OLD MAN. No—*I* remember as if it were now . . .

SECOND OLD WOMAN. You remember it as if it were now, but I remember how it was.

SECOND OLD MAN. And I remember how it was as if it were now.

THIRD OLD WOMAN. And I remember how it was even before that, way, way before.

THIRD OLD MAN. And I remember both as if it were now and how it was before.

THE BEDBUG

MASTER OF CEREMONIES. Quiet, eyewitnesses, stop whispering! Make way, Comrades, for the children! Over here, Comrades! Hurry up! Hurry up!

CHILDREN (*marching in a column, singing*). We study
>   real hard

to what was called "T"!
But we also
> do better than

all the rest
> at a spree.

X's and Y's
were long
> ago done.

We're going
> where
>> tigers

and elephants
> run!

Here,
> where there's lots of beasts,

to the zoological
> park

we, too,
> with the rest

Come march!
> March!!
>> March!!!

MASTER OF CEREMONIES. Citizens wishing to afford the exhibits pleasure, or likewise to employ them in scientific studies, will please obtain scientific apparatus and exotic products in the proper dosage only from the official park attendants. Dilettantism and hyperbole in large amounts are fatal. You are requested to use only those products and apparatuses put out by the Central Medical Institute and by the City Precision Equipment Laboratories.

(ZOO ATTENDANTS *walk through the park and the theater.*)

FIRST ATTENDANT. It's stupid to peer
>   through your fist
>> at microbes!

Comrades,
> get hold of
>> magnifying glasses and 'scopes!

SECOND ATTENDANT. Doctor Tobolkin[30]
>> suggests you have
>>> as precaution,
in case you get spat on,
> carbolic acid solution.

THIRD ATTENDANT. Feeding the exhibits—
>> it's an unforgettable scene!
Bring 'em
> doses
>> of alcohol and nicotine!

FOURTH ATTENDANT. Give 'em some liquor
>> and the creatures are sure of
podagra,
> idiocy,
>> and cirrhosis of the liver.

FIFTH ATTENDANT. A flaming carnation
>> and a smoky rose
guarantee
> a one hundred
>> percent
>>> sclerosis.

SIXTH ATTENDANT. Be sure
> your ears
>> have the best equipment on.
Earphones
> muffle
>> dirty expressions.

MASTER OF CEREMONIES (*clears the way for the City Council to the rostrum*). Comrade Chairman and his closest co-workers have left their crucial work behind and, to an ancient state march, have come to our celebration. Greetings to our Comrades!

(*All applaud; a group with briefcases goes by, importantly bowing and singing.*)

---

[30] Y. A. Tobolkin—a Moscow veterinary who took care of Mayakovsky's dog.

ALL. The weight
    of work
 hasn't
   got us down.
There's time
    for work,
but now's
   for fun!
Greetings to you
     from the city,
brave, audacious trappers!
We're proud
   of you,
we, the
  city fathers!!!

CHAIRMAN (*steps up onto the rostrum, waves a flag, everything quiets down*). Comrades, I declare the ceremony open. Our age is fraught with profound disturbances and experiences of an internal nature. External events are rare. Mankind, exhausted by the preceding events, is even glad of this relative tranquillity. We, however, never refuse a sight which, though it be fantastic externally, conceals under all its rainbow-colored plumage profound scientific import. Lamentable accidents in our city, the results of incautiously allowing two parasites to sojourn in it—these accidents have been overcome by my efforts and by the efforts of world medicine. These accidents, however, containing as they did the vaguest suggestion of the past, emphasize the horror of that rejected period and the power and laboriousness of the cultural struggle of working-class mankind. Let the hearts and souls of our young be tempered by the sight of these ominous examples! I cannot help but express gratitude to, and yield the rostrum to, our glorious Director, who figured out the significance of these strange phenomena and made, out of dire phenomena, a scientific and amusing pastime.

Hurrah!!

(*All cry "Hurrah," the band strikes up a fanfare, the* ZOO DIRECTOR *climbs up onto the rostrum, bowing in all directions.*)

DIRECTOR. Comrades! I'm delighted and embarrassed by your attention. Even considering my own part, I still can't help but express gratitude to the loyal Hunters' Union workers who were the on-the-spot heroes of our search; also, to our honored Professor of the Institute of Resurrection, who conquered death-by-freezing. All the same, I can't help but point out that our honored professor's first mistake was the indirect cause of calamities well known to you. According to external, camouflaging signs—calluses, clothing and so on—our honored professor erroneously assigned the defrozen mammal to the species *homo sapiens* and to its highest form—the working class. I don't ascribe my success only to my long dealings with animals and my penetration of their psychology. Chance helped me out. A vague, subconscious hope kept insisting: "Write and publish an advertisement." So I did: "Following the tenets of the Zoological Garden, I seek a live human body which may be continually bitten and which may be used to support and to develop a newly obtained insect under conditions habitual and normal for it."

VOICE (*from the crowd*). Ah, what horror!

DIRECTOR. I know it's horrible; I didn't even believe my own absurdity; when suddenly . . . a creature appeared! His appearance was almost human . . . Well, like you and me . . .

COUNCIL CHAIRMAN (*rings a bell*). Comrade Director, come to order!

DIRECTOR. Excuse me, excuse me! Of course, I immediately ascertained, by means of inquiry and comparative bestiology, that we were dealing with a terrible, human-like fraud and that this was the most incredible parasite. I won't go into details, especially since you'll see them for yourselves right away in this, in the full sense of the word, incredible cage. There are two of them—of different sizes but essentially identical: they are the famous *bedbugus normalis* and . . . and the *inhabitantus vulgaris*. Both are to be found in the rotten mattresses of time. *Bedbugus normalis*, fattened and drunk on the body of one man, falls *under* the bed. *Inhabitantus vulgaris*, fattened and drunk on the body of all mankind, falls *on* the bed. That's the the whole difference!

When the Revolutionary Working Class was scratching itself and squirming to scrape the mud off itself, they built themselves nests and little houses right in that mud, beat their wives and swore by Bebel[31] and rested and took their ease in the tents of their own Galliffets.[32] But *inhabitantus vulgaris* is worse. With his monstrous camouflage he lures on things he can bite, sometimes seeming to be a cricket-like rhymester and sometimes a love-song-singing bird. In those days even their clothes were camouflage—all bird style— little wings and a tail coat and a white-white little breast. Birds like that built themselves nests in theater loges, piled together on the oak trees of opera, rubbed one leg against the other at the ballet of the "International,"[33] hung down from the branches of verses, shaved Tolstoy á la Marx, shrieked and wailed in appalling numbers and—excuse the expression, but this is a scientific report—defecated in quantities which cannot be considered mere bird droppings. Comrades! However . . . see for yourselves!

(*He gives a signal; the Attendants uncover the cage. The bedbug case is on a pedestal; behind it, a raised platform with a double bed. On the bed is* PRISYPKIN *with his guitar. A lamp with a yellow shade hangs above the cage. Over* PRISYPKIN'S *head is a shiny little wreath—a fan of photo-postcards. Bottles are standing on the floor and lying around. The cage is surrounded by spittoons. On the cage walls are inscriptions; on the sides, filters and ozonizers. The inscriptions: 1. "Caution—it spits!" 2. "No unannounced entering." 3. "Hold your ears—it lets go!" A fanfare; Bengal lighting; the crowd, having stepped back at first, draws closer, dumb from excitement.*)

PRISYPKIN. I think of that old house
on Lunacharsky Street—

---

[31] August Bebel (1840–1913)—a German socialist, one of the founders of the Second International.

[32] Riding breeches, named after a French cavalry general, famous for his cruelty to the Paris Commune.

[33] Isadora Duncan, when she visited Russia after the Revolution, danced a ballet to the music of the "International."

with the staircase dark and neat
and the window curtains closed! . . .

DIRECTOR. Comrades, go on up to it; don't be afraid; it's completely tame. Go on, go on! Don't worry: four filters on the sides keep all expressions inside the cage and only a few get outside, the completely clean ones. The filters are cleaned daily by special attendants in gas masks. Look, it's going to do what's called "smoke."

VOICE (*from the crowd*). Ah, how dreadful!

DIRECTOR. Don't be afraid! Now it's going to do what's called "have a swig." Skripkin—bottoms up!

(SKRIPKIN *tries to reach a vodka bottle.*)

VOICE (*from the crowd*). Ah, don't, don't! Don't torment the poor creature!

DIRECTOR. Comrades, there's nothing frightening at all: it's tame. See, I'll bring it out to the rostrum right now. (*Goes to the cage, puts on gloves, examines his pistols, opens the door, leads* SKRIPKIN *out, places him on the rostrum, turns him around to face the guests of honor.*) So, now, say a little something in imitation of human expression, voice, and language.

(*Stands submissively, coughs, raises his guitar and suddenly turns and looks hard at the audience.* SKRIPKIN'S *face changes, he becomes excited.* SKRIPKIN *pushes the* DIRECTOR *back, hurls his guitar away, and bellows into the theater.*)

SKRIPKIN. Citizens! Pals! My guys! My own! Where did you come from? How many of you! When did you all get thawed out? How come I'm in the cage alone? Boys, my pals, come on in! Why am I suffering! Citizens! . . .

VOICES. The children, take the children away . . .

A muzzle . . . Put a muzzle on him . . .

Ah, how dreadful!

Professor, stop this!

Ah, only don't shoot!

(*The* DIRECTOR, *accompanied by two* ATTENDANTS, *runs onto the stage with a fan. The* ATTENDANTS *pull* SKRIPKIN *back. The* DIRECTOR *ventilates the rostrum. The Musicians play a fanfare. The Attendants cover the cage.*)

DIRECTOR. Sorry, Comrades . . . Excuse me . . . The insect's dead tired. The noise and all the lights made him have

hallucinations. Don't worry. There's nothing to it. Tomorrow he'll calm down . . . Go home quietly, now, citizens. Until tomorrow.
Music! March!

(The End)

The Shadow

A FAIRY TALE IN
THREE ACTS

**Evgeny Lvovich
Shvarts**

A NOTE ON THE PLAY

Long unknown except amoung a relatively small circle of brilliant writers and editors, Evgeny Shvarts achieved sudden and extraordinary, but posthumous, success with the presentation of two of his plays in 1960–61. For much of his life, he was one of Samuil Marshak's right-hand men in the editorial offices of the Children's Publishing House in Leningrad. He was one of those who, in 1929, signed a strong protest against the attack on the fresh and vigorous writings for young people by Marshak and Kornei Chukovsky. He was at one point an editor of the magazine *Yozh* (*The Hedgehog*). Marshak had surrounded himself with many of the cleverest and most talented literary men of his day. Among them, Shvarts was famous for his biting wit and deep, genuine humor. Lidiya Chukovskaya, long one of Marshak's editors, tells of a time Shvarts and Oleynikov together came into the office:

"Evgeny Lvovich has created a terribly impressive work of art," Oleynikov says sententiously. "It's the only thing of its kind in three genres: it's a satire, an ode, and, perhaps, even partly a fable.

'A Zoilus I know

Went out to milk the cow,'

Shvarts begins, and the room immediately echoes with laughter; Zabolotsky smiles graciously, and Yura Vladimirov is simply rolling with laughter. But the fabulist's thin lips and yellow eyes remain serious.

'A Zoilus I know

Went out to milk the cow

And gloomily sat reasoning by the pail:

Books for younger readers is something I don't like,

Books for younger readers is something I mean to spike.

Without commotion or complaint.

But pow!—the cow had kicked him in the head;

The poor old man collapsed like a piece of lead.

Our Zoilus had set all nature against his creed
By cursing books that youngsters read . . .' "

Oleynikov and Shvarts, still completely serious, bow deeply to their audience. At that moment Marshak comes in. The fable is recited to him afresh (it's also a satire and an ode), and he laughs so hard he has to take off his glasses and wipe the tears of laughter from them.

Shvarts wrote a number of children's stories, in addition to his editorial work, and retold a number of others. His "Little Red Riding-Hood," "The Snow Queen," and "The Two Maples," perhaps some of his better known works, are included in a 1959 collection of his stories for younger readers. He published children's stories throughout his life.

With one exception, however, his plays were not published until 1960, a little over a year after he died. In 1934 he completed the play *The Naked King*, based on "The Emperor's New Clothes." All of the "original" that is retained in the play is the skeleton of the plot; the rest is a bright fabric of witty dialogue, robust farce and keen social satire that pokes fun at, and also, at times, scathingly ridicules, all such inhuman and pompous pretension as the King's. The play was first performed in Moscow in two theaters during the 1960–61 season and was a wild success. At present, it is still in the repertoire of the Sovremennik (Contemporary) Theater.

Of Shvarts' half-dozen other plays, including plays for children's theater, perhaps the three most important are *The Shadow* (1940), *The Dragon* (1943)—a powerful anti-fascist, anti-tyranny drama of high seriousness—and *The Story of the Young Marrieds* (1955)—his last play, a sensitive study of two young people's adjustment to each other and to the postwar world. *The Dragon* opened in Leningrad in the fall of 1962.

The Shadow, probably the most vivid, the most flamboyant, the most imaginative, and the most profoundly shocking comedy or modern satire on social manners, was written in 1939–40, and first published in March, 1940, in the magazine *Literaturny sovremennik (The Literary Contemporary)*. In May of that year it was published in a separate volume, *The Shadow*, by the Leningrad State Comic Theater in an acting version, which was introduced into the theater's repertoire that fall, but almost immediately taken off the stage. Twenty years went by; much in the world changed; but nothing could detract from the brilliance and humanistic independence of the play. N. P. Akimov, the celebrated managing director of the Comic Theater in Leningrad, who first presented the play in 1940, presented it again—the same text, the same costumes, the same set and staging—in the 1960–61 season. Its success was great, and it is still part of the theater's repertoire, both in Leningrad and on tour in Moscow and other cities.

The present translation was made from the text appearing in the posthumous collection of Shvarts' work, *Plays*, Leningrad, 1960.

DRAMATIS PERSONAE

A scholar
His shadow
Pietro, a hotel keeper
Annunziata, his daughter
Julia Juli, a singer
A Princess
The Prime Minister
The Minister of Finance
Caesar Borgia, a newspaperman
A Privy Councillor
A doctor
An executioner
A Major-domo
A Corporal
Ladies of the court
Courtiers
Health resorters
A Sister of Pleasure
A Sister of Mercy
Royal heralds
The valets[1] of the Minister of Finances
The watch
Townspeople

[1] The 1940 text as well as the program for the 1960–61 performances refers to them as "Bodyguards."

. . . And the scholar became angry not so much because his shadow had left him as because he remembered the well-known story about the man without a shadow, a story which each and every person in his native land knew. Just let him go home now and tell his story, why everybody would say that he had started copying others . . .

                        H. C. Andersen, "The Shadow."

. . . A strange plot seemed somehow to have gotten into my flesh and blood; I re-created it and only then published it to the world.

                        H. C. Andersen, *The Story of My Life*, ch. VIII.

ACT I

A small room in a hotel in a southern country. There are two doors—one into the corridor, the other onto a balcony. It is twilight. The SCHOLAR *is half reclining on a sofa, a young man of twenty-six. He is fumbling around on the table with his hand—looking for his glasses.*

SCHOLAR. When you lose your glasses, it's, of course, unpleasant. But at the same time it's wonderful, too—in the twilight, my whole room seems different from usual. This plaid blanket, thrown over the armchair, now seems to me a very sweet and kind princess. I'm in love with her, and she's come to visit me. She's not alone, of course. A princess isn't supposed to go around without a retinue. This tall, skinny clock in its wooden case isn't a clock at all. It's the princess' eternal companion, the privy councillor. His heart pounds regularly like a pendulum, his counsels change in accordance with the requirements of the time, and he gives them in a whisper. It's not for nothing, of course, that he's privy. And if the counsels of the privy councillor turn out to be ruinous, he later repudiates them completely. He insists that people simply didn't catch what he said, and that's very practical of him. But who's this? Who's this stranger, thin and slender, all in black with a white face? Why do I suddenly have the idea that that's the princess' fiancé? Now, you know, it's me who's in love with the princess! I'm so much in love with her that it will be simply monstrous if she marries somebody else. (*Laughs.*) The charm of all these fancies is that I'll have no sooner put my glasses on when everything will be back in place. The blanket will be a blanket, the clock a clock, and this sinister stranger will vanish. (*Rummages around on the table with his hands.*) Now, here are my glasses. (*Puts on his glasses and shrieks.*) What's this?
(*A very beautiful, splendidly dressed* GIRL *is sitting in the armchair. Behind her is a bald* OLD MAN *in a frock coat with a star on it. And pressed flat against the wall is a stringy,*

emaciated, pale man in a black tail coat and dazzling linen. A diamond ring is on his hand.)

SCHOLAR (*mumbles, lighting a candle*). What wonder of wonders! I'm a humble scholar—how do I have such important guests? Good evening, ladies and gentlemen! I'm very glad you're here, but . . . won't you explain to me to what I owe such an honor? You don't talk? Ah, it's all clear. I dozed off. I'm having a dream.

GIRL IN THE MASK. No, it's not a dream.

SCHOLAR. Really! But then what is it?

GIRL. It's a fairy tale. Good-bye, Mr. Scholar! We'll meet again, you and I.

MAN IN THE TAIL COAT. Good-bye, scholar! We'll meet again!

OLD MAN WITH THE STAR (*in a whisper*). Good-bye, my dear Scholar! We'll meet again, and perhaps everything will end entirely happily, if you're sensible.

(*A knock on the door; all three disappear.*)

SCHOLAR. Isn't that something!

(*The knock is repeated.*)

Come in!

(ANNUNZIATA *comes into the room, a black-haired girl with big, black eyes. Her face is in the highest degree mobile and expressive, but her voice and manner are soft and hesitant. She is very beautiful. She is about seventeen.*)

ANNUNZIATA. Excuse me, sir, you have guests . . . Ah!

SCHOLAR. What's the matter, Annunziata?

ANNUNZIATA. But I clearly heard voices in your room!

SCHOLAR. I fell asleep and was talking in my sleep.

ANNUNZIATA. But . . . excuse me . . . I heard a woman's voice.

SCHOLAR. I dreamed I saw a princess.

ANNUNZIATA. And there was an old man mumbling something in a low voice.

SCHOLAR. I dreamed I saw a privy councillor.

ANNUNZIATA. And some man, so it seemed to me, was shouting at you.

SCHOLAR. That was the princess' fiancé. Well? Now do you see that it was a dream? Would such unpleasant guests come see me when I'm awake?

ANNUNZIATA. You're joking?

SCHOLAR. Yes.

ANNUNZIATA. I'm glad of that, thank you. You're always so nice to me. Probably I heard voices in the room next door and got it all confused. But . . . you won't get angry at me? Can I tell you something?

SCHOLAR. Of course, Annunziata.

ANNUNZIATA. I've wanted to warn you about something for a long time . . . Don't be angry . . . You're a scholar, and I'm just a simple girl. But it's just . . . I can tell you something I know which you don't. (*Curtsies.*) Excuse me being so forward.

SCHOLAR. Not at all! Speak up! Teach me! I may be a scholar, but scholars study all their lives.

ANNUNZIATA. You're joking?

SCHOLAR. No, I'm absolutely serious.

ANNUNZIATA. I'm glad of that, thank you. (*Looks around at the door.*) In the books about our country there's a lot written about the healthful climate, fresh air, wonderful views, hot sun, well . . . in short, you yourself know what's written in the books about our country . . .

SCHOLAR. Of course, I do. That's exactly why I came here.

ANNUNZIATA. Sure. You know what's written about us in the books, but what's not written about us there, you don't know.

SCHOLAR. That sometimes happens to scholars.

ANNUNZIATA. You don't know that you're living in a wholly special country. Everything that's told as happening in fairy tales, everything that in other nations seems made-up —actually occurs here every day. Why, for example, Sleeping Beauty used to live just a five hours' walk from the tobacco store—from the one that's on the right of the fountain. Only now Sleeping Beauty is dead. The Ogre is still alive and working as an appraiser in the municipal pawnshop. Tom Thumb married a very tall woman nicknamed Grenadier, and their children are people of normal height, just like you and me. And you know what's surprising? That woman nicknamed Grenadier is completely under his thumb. She even takes him to the market with her. Tom Thumb sits in the pocket of her apron and haggles away for all he's worth. However, they get on very well together. The wife is so considerate toward her husband. Whenever they dance a minuet on the holidays, she puts on extra glasses so as not to step on her man accidentally.

SCHOLAR. Now, that's very interesting, you know; why isn't that written up in the books about your country?

ANNUNZIATA (*glancing at the door*). Not everybody likes fairy tales.

SCHOLAR. Really?

ANNUNZIATA. Indeed, can you imagine! (*Glances round at the door.*) We're terribly afraid that if everybody finds this out, they'll stop coming to us. That would be such a disadvantage! Don't give us away, please.

SCHOLAR. No, I won't tell a soul.

ANNUNZIATA. I'm glad of that, thank you. My poor father just loves money, and I'll be desperate if he earns less than he expects. When he's upset, he swears terribly.

SCHOLAR. But, nevertheless, it seems to me the number of visitors will only increase once they find out that in your country fairy tales are true.

ANNUNZIATA. No. If it were children who came here, that would be one thing. But grown-ups are a cautious lot. They very well know that many fairy tales end sadly. That's just what I wanted to talk to you about. Be careful.

SCHOLAR. How do you mean? Not to catch cold you have to dress warmly. Not to fall down you have to watch where you're going. But how do you avoid fairy tales with sad endings?

ANNUNZIATA. Well . . . I don't know . . . You oughtn't to talk with people you don't know well enough.

SCHOLAR. Then I'll have to keep quiet the whole time. Because I'm a visitor.

ANNUNZIATA. No, really, please, do be careful. You're a very good man, and it's just people like that who most often have something bad happen to them.

SCHOLAR. How do you know that I'm a good man?

ANNUNZIATA. You know, I'm often doing something in the kitchen. And our cook has a dozen friends. And they all know everything that is, was, and will be. Nothing stays hidden from them. They know what's going on in every family, as if the houses had glass walls. Down in the kitchen we laugh and cry and are horrified. On days of specially interesting events everything on the stove gets ruined. They all say in a chorus that you're a wonderful man.

SCHOLAR. It was they who told you that in your country a fairy tale is true?

ANNUNZIATA. Yes.

SCHOLAR. You know, in the evening, and especially when my glasses are off, I'm ready to believe it. But in the morning, once I'm out of the house, I see something completely different. Your country—alas!—is like all the other countries in the world. Wealth and poverty, nobility and slavery, death and misery, love and happiness, intelligence and stupidity, holiness, crime, conscience, shamelessness—it's all so closely mixed up together that a man is simply horrified. It will be very hard to untangle it all, sort it out and put it in order in such a way as not to harm any living thing. In fairy tales it's all much simpler.

ANNUNZIATA (*curtsying*). Thank you.

SCHOLAR. For what?

ANNUNZIATA. For talking so finely to me, a simple girl.

SCHOLAR. That's quite all right; that happens to scholars. But now tell me: my friend Hans Christian Andersen, who lived here in this room before me—did he know about the fairy tales?

ANNUNZIATA. Yes, he somehow found out about it.

SCHOLAR. And what did he say to that?

ANNUNZIATA. He said: "All my life I've had a suspicion that I've been writing the simple truth." He liked our house very much. He liked the fact that it's so quiet here.

(*A deafening shot.*)

SCHOLAR. What's that?

ANNUNZIATA. Oh, pay no attention. That's just my father having an argument with somebody. He's very quick-tempered and, at the least little thing, shoots his pistol. But so far he hasn't killed anybody. He's nervous and therefore always misses.

SCHOLAR. I see. That's a phenomenon familiar to me. If he hit the mark, he wouldn't fire so often.

(*Backstage a roar: "Annunziata!"*)

ANNUNZIATA (*meekly*). Coming, Papa dear! Good-bye! Oh, I completely forgot what I came for. What would you wish served to you—coffee or milk?

(*The door is flung open with a crash. A young-looking man, well-built and broad-shouldered, runs into the room. His face resembles* ANNUNZIATA'S. *Sullen, he does not look people in the eye. This is the proprietor of the furnished rooms,* ANNUNZIATA'S *father,* PIETRO.)

PIETRO. Why don't you come when you're called! Go right away and reload my pistol. 'Cause you heard, didn't you, your father's shooting. Got to explain everything, got to stick his nose into everything. I'll kill him!

(ANNUNZIATA *calmly and boldly goes up to her father and kisses him on the forehead.*)

ANNUNZIATA. I'm going, Papa. Good-bye, sir! (*Goes out.*)

SCHOLAR. As one can see, your daughter isn't afraid of you, Signor Pietro.

PIETRO. No, damn my hide. She treats me as if I was the lovingest father in town.

SCHOLAR. Maybe you really are?

PIETRO. None of her business to know that. I can't stand people guessing about my feelings and thoughts. A little slut like that! There's nothing but unpleasantness all around. The lodger in number fifteen just now refused again to pay. Out of fury I took a shot at the lodger in number fourteen.

SCHOLAR. He doesn't pay either?

PIETRO. He pays. But he, fourteen, now, is a worthless fellow. Our Prime Minister can't stand him. And the other, that damned cheapskate, fifteen, works on our triply foul newspaper. Oh, let the whole world go to hell! I spin around like a corkscrew, pulling money out of the lodgers of my miserable hotel and can't make ends meet. I've got to have an office job besides, so as not to die of cold.

SCHOLAR. But do you work in an office?

PIETRO. Yes.

SCHOLAR. Where?

PIETRO. I'm appraiser in the municipal pawnshop.

(*Music suddenly begins playing—sometimes barely audibly, sometimes as if it were being played right in the room.*)

SCHOLAR. Tell me . . . tell me . . . Tell me, please, where is that being played?

PIETRO. 'Cross the way.

SCHOLAR. And who lives there?

PIETRO. Don't know. They say some kind of a damned princess.

SCHOLAR. A princess?

PIETRO. That's what they say. I came in here on business. This damned number fifteen asks you to receive him. This newspaper fellow. This thief who's trying to fix it up so he lives free in a lovely room. Can he?

SCHOLAR. Please. I'll be happy to see him.

PIETRO. Don't be so happy ahead of time. Good-bye! (*Goes out.*)

SCHOLAR. The proprietor of the hotel is an appraiser in the municipal pawnshop. The Ogre? Think of that!

(*Opens the door leading out onto the balcony. The wall of the opposite house can be seen. A narrow street. The balcony of the opposite house almost touches the balcony of the* SCHOLAR'S *room. He has barely opened the door when the noise from the street bursts into the room. Separate voices stand out from the general uproar.*)

VOICES. Watermelons, watermelons! In slices!

Water, water, ice-water!

Here y'have murderers' knives! Who wants some murderers' knives?

Flowers, flowers! Roses! Lilies! Tulips!

Let the ass through, let the ass through! Step aside, everybody—here comes an ass!

Help a poor deaf man!

Poisons, poisons, fresh poisons!

SCHOLAR. Our street is bubbling, like a real kettle. How much I like it here! If it weren't for my everlasting restlessness, if it didn't strike me that the whole world is unhappy because I have not yet thought up the way to save it, it would be perfect. And when the girl who lives across there comes out on her balcony, I think I have to make just one, just one little effort and everything will become clear.

(*A very beautiful young* WOMAN *comes into the room,*

splendidly dressed. She squints, looks around. The SCHOLAR *does not notice her.*)

If there is harmony in the sea, in the mountains, in the forest and in yourself, then it means the world is more wisely arranged than out there on the street.

WOMAN. No one's going to buy that.

SCHOLAR (*turns around*). Excuse me!

WOMAN. No, they won't. In what you were just mumbling there isn't even a shadow of wit. Is that your new article? Where are you? What's the matter with you today? You don't recognize me, is that it?

SCHOLAR. I'm sorry, I don't.

WOMAN. That's enough making fun of my nearsightedness. It's not gracious. Where are you, there?

SCHOLAR. I'm here.

WOMAN. Come over a little closer.

SCHOLAR. Here I am. (*Goes up to the stranger.*)

WOMAN (*she is genuinely surprised*). Who are you?

SCHOLAR. I'm a visiting scholar, living here in the hotel. That's who I am.

WOMAN. Excuse me—my eyes have played a bad trick on me again—this isn't number fifteen?

SCHOLAR. No, unfortunately.

WOMAN. What a nice, kind face you have! Why haven't you yet joined our circle, the circle of real people?

SCHOLAR. And what sort of circle is that?

WOMAN. Oh, it's actors, writers, courtiers. There's even one minister who keeps coming. We're elegant, devoid of prejudices, and understand everything. Are you famous?

SCHOLAR. No.

WOMAN. What a pity! It isn't done here. But . . . but I guess I'm ready to forgive you that—I've suddenly taken such a liking to you. Are you angry at me?

SCHOLAR. No, what do you mean!

WOMAN. I'll just sit here for a while. May I?

SCHOLAR. Of course.

WOMAN. It suddenly struck me that you're just exactly the man I've been looking for all my life. It used to seem—by his voice and what he said—that there he was, just such a man, but he'd come up closer and you'd see it wasn't the right thing at all. But it was already too late to retreat, he had come too close. It's a terrible thing to be beautiful and nearsighted. Am I boring you?

SCHOLAR. No, what do you mean!

WOMAN. How simply and serenely you answer me! But he irritates me.

SCHOLAR. Who?

WOMAN. The one I came to see. He's a terribly restless man. He wants to please everybody in the world. He's a slave to fashion. Just for example, when it was the fashion to get sun tanned, he got so tanned he was as black as a Negro. But then suddenly sun tans went out of fashion. And he decided to have an operation. The doctors grafted skin from under his bathing suit—that was the only white place on his body—onto his face.

SCHOLAR. I hope it didn't hurt him?

WOMAN. No. He just became extraordinarily shameless and now he calls a slap in the face simply a smack on the bottom.

SCHOLAR. Why do you keep visiting him?

WOMAN. Well, still, he's a man of our circle, the circle of real people. And besides he works on the newspaper. You know who I am?

SCHOLAR. No.

WOMAN. I'm a singer. My name is Julia Juli.

SCHOLAR. You're very famous in this country!

JULIA. Yes. Everybody knows my songs: "Mama, What's Love?" "Girls, Hurry Find Your Happiness," "But I Remain Unmoved By the Languor of His Love," and "Ah, How Come I'm Not a Meadow." Are you a doctor?

SCHOLAR. No, I'm an historian.

JULIA. You vacationing here?

SCHOLAR. I'm studying the history of your country.

JULIA. Our country's little.

SCHOLAR. Yes, but its history is like that of all the rest. And that delights me.

JULIA. Why?

SCHOLAR. That means that in the world there are general laws for everyone. When you live in one place for a long time, in one and the same room, and see only the same people, whom you yourself chose as friends, then the world seems very simple to you. But once you're just out of the house, there's already too much variety. And this . . .

(*Somebody screams frightenedly behind the door. There is the sound of broken glass.*)

Who's there?

(*Shaking himself, an elegant* YOUNG MAN *comes in. Behind him—an embarrassed* ANNUNZIATA.)

YOUNG MAN. How do you do. I was standing here by your door, and Annunziata scared me. Am I really so frightening?

ANNUNZIATA (*to the* SCHOLAR). I'm sorry, I broke the glass of milk which I was bringing you.

YOUNG MAN. And aren't you going to tell me you're sorry?

ANNUNZIATA. But it's your own fault, sir! Why were you hiding by somebody else's door and just standing still?

YOUNG MAN. I was eavesdropping. (*To the* SCHOLAR.) You like my frankness? All scholars are straightforward people. You must like it. Right? Well then, tell me, do you like my frankness? Do you like me?

JULIA. Don't answer. If you say "yes," he'll despise you; if you say "no," he'll be filled with hatred for you.

YOUNG MAN. Julia, Julia, wicked Julia! (*To the* SCHOLAR.) Allow me to introduce myself: Caesar Borgia. You've heard of me?

SCHOLAR. Yes.

CAESAR BORGIA. So? Really? And just exactly what have you heard?

SCHOLAR. A lot.

CAESAR BORGIA. Was I praised? Or criticized? By whom specifically?

SCHOLAR. I myself read your critical and political articles in the local paper.

CAESAR BORGIA. They're successful. But somebody's always displeased. You criticize a man roundly and he's displeased. I'd like to find the secret of complete success. I'm ready to do anything for this secret. You like my frankness?

JULIA. Let's go. We've come calling on the scholar, but scholars are eternally busy.

CAESAR BORGIA. I warned our scholarly gentleman. Our hotelkeeper told him I was coming. But you, glorious Julia, made a mistake about the room?

JULIA. No, I think I've come just exactly where I should have.

CAESAR BORGIA. But you know you were coming to me! I'm just finishing up an article about you. You'll like it, but—alas!—your friends won't. (*To the* SCHOLAR.) Will you allow me to call on you once more today?

SCHOLAR. Please do.

CAESAR BORGIA. I want to write an article about you.

SCHOLAR. Thank you. That will stand me in good stead in working in your archives. I'll be more respected there.

CAESAR BORGIA. You old fox! Don't think I don't know why you've come here. It has nothing to do with the archives.

SCHOLAR. Well, what does it with, then?

CAESAR BORGIA. You old fox! You're always looking over at that neighboring balcony.

SCHOLAR. Do I look over there?

CAESAR BORGIA. Yes. You think there's where she lives.

SCHOLAR. Who?

CAESAR BORGIA. No need being so secretive. You're an historian, aren't you, studying our country; so, it follows that you know the testament of our last King, Louis the Ninth, the Dreamy.

SCHOLAR. I'm sorry, I've reached only the end of the sixteenth century.

CAESAR BORGIA. Really? And you haven't heard anything about the testament?

SCHOLAR. No, I assure you.

CAESAR BORGIA. That's strange. Then why did you ask the hotelkeeper to give you precisely this room?

SCHOLAR. Because my friend Hans Christian Andersen lived here.

CAESAR BORGIA. That's the only reason?

SCHOLAR. My word of honor, that's it. What does my room have to do with the testament of the late king?

CAESAR BORGIA. Oh, very much. Good-bye! Let me show you the way, glorious Julia.

SCHOLAR. Let me ask you: exactly what was written in that mysterious testament?

CAESAR BORGIA. Oh no, I won't tell. I've got an interest in it myself. I want power, esteem, and I haven't got nearly enough money. You know that I, Caesar Borgia, whose name is known throughout the land, must still work as a simple appraiser in the municipal pawnshop. You like my frankness?

JULIA. Let's go! Let's go, now! Everybody here likes you. He never leaves right away. (*To the* SCHOLAR.) We'll meet again.

SCHOLAR. I'll be happy to see you.

CAESAR BORGIA. Don't be so happy ahead of time. (CAESAR BORGIA *and* JULIA JULI *go out*.)

SCHOLAR. Annunziata, how many appraisers are there in your municipal pawnshop?

ANNUNZIATA. Lots.

SCHOLAR. And they're all ex-cannibals?

ANNUNZIATA. Almost all.

SCHOLAR. What's the matter with you? Why are you so sad?

ANNUNZIATA. Oh! You know I asked you to be careful. They say that that singer Julia Juli is the same little girl who walked on bread so as not to spoil her new shoes.

SCHOLAR. But, as far as I remember, that little girl was punished for it.

ANNUNZIATA. Yes, the earth swallowed her up, but then she crawled back out again and ever since she's kept right on walking on good people, on her best friends, and even on herself—all just so as not to spoil her new little shoes, stockings, and dresses. I'll bring you another glass of milk right away.

SCHOLAR. Wait! I don't want anything to drink, I want to talk to you.

ANNUNZIATA. I'm glad of that, thank you.

SCHOLAR. Tell me, please, what sort of testament did your late king, Louis the Ninth, the Dreamy, leave?

ANNUNZIATA. Oh, that's a secret, a terrible secret! The testament was sealed in seven envelopes with seven wax seals and countersigned with the signatures of seven Privy Councillors. The Princess opened and read the testament in complete isolation. Guards stood at the windows and the doors, their ears stopped up just in case, though the

Princess was reading the testament just to herself. Nobody knows what's said in this secret document except the Princess and the whole town.

SCHOLAR. The whole town?

ANNUNZIATA. Yes.

SCHOLAR. How come?

ANNUNZIATA. Nobody can explain it. All the precautions were observed, it seems. It's simply a miracle. Everybody knows the testament. Even the little street urchins.

SCHOLAR. Well, then, what does it say?

ANNUNZIATA. Oh, don't ask me.

SCHOLAR. Why?

ANNUNZIATA. I'm very afraid that that testament is the beginning of a new fairy tale that will end sadly.

SCHOLAR. Annunziata, you know I'm a visitor. Your King's testament has nothing to do with me, in any way. Tell me about it. Otherwise things go badly: I'm a scholar, an historian—and suddenly I don't know what every little urchin knows! Tell me, please.

ANNUNZIATA (*sighing*). All right, I will. When a good man asks me a favor, I can't refuse him. Our cook says that that's going to get me into a lot of trouble. But let it all fall on my head, and not on yours. And so . . . You're not listening to me?

SCHOLAR. Of course. What do you mean!

ANNUNZIATA. But why are you looking at the balcony of the house opposite us?

SCHOLAR. No, no . . . Here, you see, I've settled down, lit my pipe, and I'm not taking my eyes off your face.

ANNUNZIATA. Thanks. And so, our King, Louis the Ninth, the Dreamy, died five years ago. The street urchins used to call him not The Dreamy but The Idiot, but that's not true. It is true he often stuck his tongue out at them, poking his head through the window vent,[2] but the boys themselves were to blame. Why did they tease him? The late King was a clever man, but being a king is such a position that it spoils a man's character. In the very beginning of his reign,

---

[2] In Russian, *fortochka*—a diminutive, from the German *Pförtchen*, and meaning a small, hinged pane in a window, used for ventilation.

the Prime Minister, who the King trusted more than his own father, poisoned the King's favorite sister. The King executed the Prime Minister. The second Prime Minister wasn't a poisoner, but he lied to the King so much that the King stopped trusting everybody, including himself. The third Prime Minister wasn't a liar, but he was terrifically sly. He wove and wove and wove the finest webs around the very simplest things. During his final report, the King started to say "I authorize" and suddenly began buzzing thinly like a fly that's fallen into a spiderweb. And the Minister fell at the insistence of the King's doctor. The fourth Prime Minister wasn't sly. He was straightforward and simple. He stole the King's gold snuffbox and ran away. And the King gave up on this business of running things. Since then the Prime Ministers themselves have done the replacing of each other. And the King took up the theater. But they say that that's even worse than running a government. After a year of working in the theater the King began turning stiff.

SCHOLAR. What do you mean "turning stiff?"

ANNUNZIATA. Simply that. He'd be going along—and he'd suddenly become all stiff—with one foot raised. And at the same time his face would show despair. The doctor explained it by the fact that the King had been incurably mixed up, trying to understand the relations of theater people to each other. You know there are so many!

SCHOLAR. The doctor was right.

ANNUNZIATA. He recommended a simple cure, which would surely have worked for the poor King. He recommended executing half the company, but the King didn't agree.

SCHOLAR. Why?

ANNUNZIATA. He couldn't possibly make up his mind which half of the company needed killing. And finally the King gave up on the whole thing and started going after loose women, and they were the only ones who didn't deceive him.

SCHOLAR. Really?

ANNUNZIATA. Yes, oh yes! They turned out to be indeed loose women. That is to say, precisely the kind they were described as being. And that comforted the King a lot, but in the end it ruined his health. And his legs became paralyzed. And after that they started pulling him around the palace in a chair, and he was silent the whole time, thinking, thinking, thinking. He didn't tell anybody what he was thinking about. Sometimes the King ordered them to take him over to the window and, opening the window vent, he'd stick his tongue out at the street urchins who were jumping up and down and shouting, "Idiot! Idiot! Idiot!" And then the King drew up his testament. And then he died.

SCHOLAR. At last we've come to the real crux of the matter.

ANNUNZIATA. When the King died, his only daughter, the Princess, was thirteen. "My dear," he wrote her in his testament, "I've lived my life badly, haven't done a thing. You're not going to do anything either—you've been poisoned by the palace air. I don't want you to marry a prince. I can count off to you all the princes in the world. They're all much too big fools for such a little country as ours. When you become eighteen, find yourself a little place in town and go looking, looking, looking. Find yourself a good, honest, educated, and intelligent husband. Let him be a commoner. Maybe he'll suddenly be able to do what not one of the noblest has ever managed? Perhaps he'll suddenly be able to rule, and rule well? Eh? Wouldn't that be good! Try to do that, please. Papa."

SCHOLAR. Is that what he wrote?

ANNUNZIATA. To the letter. The testament has been repeated in the kitchen so many times that I've memorized it word for word.

SCHOLAR. And the Princess now lives in town?

ANNUNZIATA. Yes. But it's not that easy to find her.

SCHOLAR. Why?

ANNUNZIATA. A whole lot of loose women have rented whole floors in houses and pretend to be princesses.

SCHOLAR. But don't you know your Princess when you see her?

ANNUNZIATA. No. After she'd read the testament, the Princess began wearing a mask so she wouldn't be recognized when she went out looking for a husband.

SCHOLAR. Tell me, she . . . (*Falls silent.*)

(*A* GIRL *with blonde hair, in a dark and modest outfit, comes out onto the balcony of the house opposite.*)

But tell me, she . . . What was I going to ask you? However . . . No, nothing.

ANNUNZIATA. Again you're not looking at me!

SCHOLAR. What do you mean I'm not looking? Where am I looking then?

ANNUNZIATA. Over there . . . Ah! Let me close the door onto the balcony.

SCHOLAR. Why, now? Don't! You know it's only just become really cool.

ANNUNZIATA. After the sun has gone down the windows and doors ought to be shut. Otherwise you can get malaria. No, it's not a question of malaria at this point! Don't look over there. Please . . . Are you angry at me? Don't be . . . Don't look at that girl. Let me shut the door onto the balcony. You know you're no better than a little child. Here, you don't like soup, and what kind of a dinner is it without soup! You send your clothes to the laundry without a list. And with the same good-natured, cheerful face you'll go straight to your death. I'm talking so freely, that I'm beginning not to understand what I'm saying myself: it's impudence, but I can't help warning you. They say about that girl that she's a bad woman. Wait, wait . . . I don't think that's so terrible . . . I'm afraid there's something worse to it.

SCHOLAR. You think so?

ANNUNZIATA. Yes. Maybe, suddenly, this girl is the Princess? What then? What are you going to do then?

SCHOLAR. Of course, of course.

ANNUNZIATA. You didn't hear what I said?

SCHOLAR. Really!

ANNUNZIATA. You know if she's really the Princess, everybody's going to want to marry her and you'll be trampled in the crush.

SCHOLAR. Yes, yes, of course.

ANNUNZIATA. No, I see there's nothing I can do at this point. What an unhappy girl I am, sir.

SCHOLAR. Isn't it so?

(ANNUNZIATA *goes to the exit, the* SCHOLAR, *to the door leading to the balcony.* ANNUNZIATA *turns and looks around. She stops.*)

ANNUNZIATA. Good-bye, sir. (*Softly, with unexpected intensity.*) I won't let anybody hurt you. Not under any conditions. Ever. (*Goes out.*)

(*The* SCHOLAR *looks at the* GIRL *standing on the balcony opposite; she looks down on the street. The* SCHOLAR *begins talking quietly, then louder and louder. By the end of his monologue, the* GIRL *is looking at him uninterruptedly.*)

SCHOLAR. Of course, the world is more wisely arranged than it seems. Just a bit more—another two or three days of work—and I'll understand how to make all people happy. Everybody'll be happy, but not the way I am. Only here, in the evening, when you stand on the balcony, have I begun to understand that I can be anybody like nobody else. I know you—one can't help knowing you. I understand you, as I understand good weather, the moon, a path in the mountains. It's so simple, you know. I can't say just exactly what you're thinking about, but nevertheless I absolutely know that your thoughts would delight me, like your face, your braids and your eyelashes. Thank you for everything: for having chosen that house for yourself, for having been born and for living at the same time I am. What would I do if I hadn't suddenly met you! It's awful to think!

GIRL. Are you saying all that by heart?

SCHOLAR. I . . . I . . .

GIRL. Go on.

SCHOLAR. You talked to me!

GIRL. Did you make all that up yourself or did you have somebody do it for you?

SCHOLAR. I'm sorry, but your voice has startled me so, that I don't understand a thing.

GIRL. You rather cleverly evade a direct answer. Probably you yourself made up what you told me. But perhaps not. Well, all right, we'll drop this. I'm bored today. How do you have the patience to sit in the one room all day? Is this your study?

SCHOLAR. Excuse me?

GIRL. Is this your study, or the cloakroom, or the drawing room, or one of the reception rooms?

SCHOLAR. It's just my room. My only room.

GIRL. You're a beggar?

SCHOLAR. No, I'm a scholar.

GIRL. Oh, very well. You have a very odd face.

SCHOLAR. In what way?

GIRL. When you talk it seems as if you weren't lying.

SCHOLAR. And in fact I'm not.

GIRL. All people are liars.

SCHOLAR. That's not true.

GIRL. No, it is. Maybe they don't lie to you, you have only one room, but they're forever lying to me. I feel sorry for myself.

SCHOLAR. Why, what are you saying? Do they insult you? Who?

GIRL. You're so clever at pretending to be attentive and kind, that I feel like complaining to you.

SCHOLAR. Are you so unhappy?

GIRL. I don't know. Yes.

SCHOLAR. Why?

GIRL. I just am. Everybody's a scoundrel.

SCHOLAR. Don't talk like that. That's the way those talk who've chosen for themselves the most horrible path in life. They strangle, crush, rob, slander mercilessly: who's there to be sorry for—why, everybody's a scoundrel!

GIRL. So, you mean, not everybody is?

SCHOLAR. No.

GIRL. It would be all right if that were so. I'm terribly afraid of turning into a frog.

SCHOLAR. Why into a frog?

GIRL. You've heard the fairy tale about the frog-princess? They tell it wrong. In fact, it was all different. I know that for sure. The frog-princess is my aunt.

SCHOLAR. Your aunt?

GIRL. Yes. By blood. They say the frog-princess was kissed by a man who had fallen in love with her despite her hideous appearance. And from that the frog turned into a beautiful woman. Right?

SCHOLAR. Yes, as far as I remember.

GIRL. But in fact my aunt was a beautiful girl and she married a scoundrel who was only pretending that he loved her. And his kisses were cold and so repulsive that in a short while the beautiful girl turned into a cold and repulsive frog. For us, her relatives, that was very unpleasant. They say that such things happen much more often than you might suppose. Only my aunt didn't manage to hide her transformation. She was extremely impetuous. That's horrible. Isn't that so?

SCHOLAR. Yes, that's very sad.

GIRL. You see! And suddenly maybe that's in store for me, too? You know I have to get married. You know for sure that not everybody's a scoundrel?

SCHOLAR. I know absolutely for sure. After all, I'm an historian.

GIRL. Now wouldn't that be good! However, I don't trust you.

SCHOLAR. Why not?

GIRL. In general I don't trust anybody or anything.

SCHOLAR. No, that's impossible. You have such a healthy color to your face, such quick eyes. Not to trust anything—why, you know, that's death!

GIRL. Ah, I understand everything.

SCHOLAR. To understand everything—that's death, too.

GIRL. Everything in the world's the same. The one side's right, and the other's right and, after all, it all makes no difference to me.

SCHOLAR. It all makes no difference—but you know that's even worse than death! You just can't think like that. No! How you've distressed me!

GIRL. It's all the same to me. No, it isn't all the same, I guess. Now you're not going to be looking at me every night any more?

SCHOLAR. I will. Everything's not so simple as it seems. It seemed to me your thoughts were harmonious, like yourself. But there they are before me . . . They're not at all like those I was expecting . . . And still . . . still I love you . . .

GIRL. You do?

SCHOLAR. I love you . . .

GIRL. Well, there you are . . . I understood everything, didn't believe anything, nothing made any difference to me, but now everything's all mixed up . . .

SCHOLAR. I love you.

GIRL. Go away . . . Or no . . . No, go away and close the door . . . No, I'll go . . . But . . . if you dare tomorrow evening . . . dare not come out here on the balcony, I . . . I'll . . . order . . . No . . . I'll just be hurt. (*Goes to the door, turns around.*) I don't even know your name.

SCHOLAR. I'm called Christian-Theodore.

GIRL. Good-bye, Christian-Theodore, darling. Don't smile! Don't think you've slyly tricked me. No, cheer up! I'm just talking like that . . . When you said it just like that, suddenly, straight out, that you love me, I felt all warm, though I came out on the balcony in a muslin dress. Don't dare talk to me! Enough! If I hear just one more word, I'll burst into tears . . . Good-bye! What an unhappy girl I am, sir. (*Goes out.*)

SCHOLAR. Well, now . . . I thought that just another moment and I'd understand everything, but now I think that another moment and I'll be completely confused. I fear that girl is really the Princess. "Everybody's a scoundrel, everything in the world's the same, nothing makes any difference to me, I don't believe in anything"—what clear signs of that malignant anaemia common to delicate people brought up in a hothouse atmosphere! Her . . . She . . . But still, you know, she suddenly felt warm when I confessed that I love her! Means she's still got enough blood in her veins, doesn't it? (*Laughs.*) I'm sure, I'm sure that everything will end wonderfully. Shadow, my good, obedient shadow! You lie so humbly at my feet. Your head looks out the door through which the unknown girl passed. Shadow, you ought to get up and go over there to her. What trouble is it for you? Just go and tell her: "This is all nonsense. My master loves you, loves you so, that everything will be wonderful. If you're the frog-princess, he'll bring you to life and turn you into a beautiful woman." In short, you know what you have to say; after all, we grew up together. (*Laughs.*) Go on!

(*The SCHOLAR moves away from the door. The SCHOLAR'S SHADOW suddenly separates itself from him. It stretches out to full height on the balcony opposite. It plunges through the door which the girl, going out, left half open.*)

What's this? I have a sort of strange feeling in my legs . . .

in my whole body . . . I . . . am I sick? I . . . (*Staggers, falls into the armchair, rings.*)

(ANNUNZIATA *runs in.*)

Annunziata! It seems you were right.

ANNUNZIATA. It was the Princess?

SCHOLAR. No! I've gotten sick. (*Shuts his eyes.*)

ANNUNZIATA (*runs to the door*). Father!

(PIETRO *comes in.*)

PIETRO. Don't shout. Don't you know, really, that your father's listening here by the door?

ANNUNZIATA. I didn't notice.

PIETRO. Doesn't notice her own father . . . What we've come to! Well? What're you batting your eyes for? Got an idea to start wailing?

ANNUNZIATA. He's gotten sick.

PIETRO. Let me help you get into bed, sir.

SCHOLAR (*gets up*). No. I'll do it myself. Don't touch me, please . . .

PIETRO. What're you afraid of? I'm not going to eat you up!

SCHOLAR. I don't know. I've suddenly become so weak. (*Goes toward the screen behind which is his bed.*)

ANNUNZIATA (*softly, in horror*). Look!

PIETRO. What now?

ANNUNZIATA. He has no shadow!

PIETRO. Well, so? Really doesn't . . . Damned climate! How in hell did he do that? There'll be talk. People'll think it's an epidemic . . .

(*The* SCHOLAR *disappears behind the screen.*)

Not a word to anybody! You hear?

ANNUNZIATA (*by the screen*). He's fainted.

PIETRO. So much the better. Run and get the doctor. The doctor'll put the idiot in bed for a week or two, and in the meantime he'll grow a new shadow. And nobody'll be the wiser.

ANNUNZIATA. A man without a shadow—why, that's one of the very saddest fairy tales in the world.

PIETRO. I tell you he'll grow a new one! He'll get out of it . . . Hurry up!

(ANNUNZIATA *runs out.*)

Damn it . . . It's a good thing that newspaper boy's busy with his lady and hasn't smelled a thing.

(CAESAR BORGIA *enters.*)

CAESAR BORGIA. Good evening!

PIETRO. Ah, so you're here after all . . . Devil . . . Where's your old woman?

CAESAR BORGIA. Went to a concert.

PIETRO. The hell with all concerts!

CAESAR BORGIA. The Scholar's fainted?

PIETRO. Yes, God damn him.

CAESAR BORGIA. Did you hear?

PIETRO. What exactly?

CAESAR BORGIA. His conversation with the Princess?

PIETRO. Yes.

CAESAR BORGIA. That's a short answer. How come you aren't damning everything and everyone, shooting off your pistol, shouting?

PIETRO. In serious things I'm calm.

CAESAR BORGIA. Looks like it was the real Princess.

PIETRO. Yes. It was.

CAESAR BORGIA. I see you'd like him to marry the Princess.

PIETRO. Me? I'll eat him up at the first opportunity.

CAESAR BORGIA. He'll have to be eaten. Yes, have to be, have to be. As I see it, now's just the right moment. A man's easiest of all to eat up when he's sick or gone off on a vacation. Why, then he himself doesn't know who has eaten him and you can stay on the most splendid terms with him.

PIETRO. The shadow.

CAESAR BORGIA. What about the shadow?

PIETRO. We'll have to find his shadow.

CAESAR BORGIA. What for?

PIETRO. It'll help us. It'll never in its life forgive him that once upon a time it was his shadow.

CAESAR BORGIA. Yes, it will help us eat him up.

PIETRO. The shadow's the exact antithesis to the Scholar.

CAESAR BORGIA. But . . . But, you know, then it might turn out to be stronger than you'd expect . . .

PIETRO. So what. The shadow won't forget that we'll have helped it come up in the world. And we'll eat him.

CAESAR BORGIA. Yes, he'll have to be eaten, have to be, have to be.

PIETRO. Hush!

(ANNUNZIATA *runs in.*)

ANNUNZIATA. Get out of here! What do you want here?

PIETRO. Daughter! (*Gets his pistol.*) But let's go into my room, though. We can talk there. The doctor's coming?

ANNUNZIATA. Yes, he's hurrying as fast as he can. He says it's a serious thing.

PIETRO. All right. (*Goes out together with* CAESAR BORGIA.)

ANNUNZIATA (*peeking behind the screen*). I knew it! His face is peaceful, kind, as if he was dreaming that he's taking a walk under the trees in the forest. No, they're not going to forgive him for being such a good man! Something's going to happen, something's going to happen!

(*Curtain*)

ACT II

A park. A little square strewn with sand, surrounded by clipped trees. Far back, a pavilion. The MAJOR-DOMO *and his* ASSISTANT *are busy downstage.*

MAJOR-DOMO. Put the table here. And the armchairs here. Put the chess set on the table. There. Now everything's ready for the conference.

ASSISTANT. But tell me, Mr. Major-domo, why do the Ministers confer here, in the park, and not in the palace?

MAJOR-DOMO. Because the palace has walls. Get it?

ASSISTANT. Not at all.

MAJOR-DOMO. And the walls have ears. Get it?

ASSISTANT. Yes, now I do.

MAJOR-DOMO. What did I tell you? Put the pillows on this armchair.

ASSISTANT. These are for the Prime Minister?

MAJOR-DOMO. No, for the Minister of Finance. He's seriously ill.

ASSISTANT. What's wrong with him?

MAJOR-DOMO. He's the very richest businessman in the country. His rivals hate him terrificly. And last year one of them, now, went so far as to commit a crime. He resolved to poison the Minister of Finance.

ASSISTANT. How horrible!

MAJOR-DOMO. Don't be so pained ahead of time. The Minister of Finance found out about it in good time and bought up all the poisons in the country.

ASSISTANT. How wonderful!

MAJOR-DOMO. Don't be so happy ahead of time. Then the criminal came to the Minister of Finance and offered an unusually large sum for the poisons. And the Minister behaved completely naturally. For you know the Minister is a realistic politician. He figured out the profit and sold the scoundrel his whole store of poisons. And the scoundrel poisoned the Minister. His Excellency's entire family allowed itself to give up the ghost in terrible torments.

And he himself has been hardly alive ever since then, but he made a clear two hundred per cent on it. Business is business. Get it?

ASSISTANT. Yes, now I do.

MAJOR-DOMO. Well, what did I tell you! And so, everything's ready? The armchairs. The chess set. It will be a specially important consultation here today.

ASSISTANT. Why do you think so?

MAJOR-DOMO. First of all, only the two chief Ministers will meet—the Prime Minister and the Minister of Finance, and secondly they'll make believe they're playing chess and not conferring. Everybody knows what that means. The bushes, probably, are swarming with people who are curious.

ASSISTANT. But suddenly they may overhear what the Ministers are saying?

MAJOR-DOMO. The curious won't find out anything.

ASSISTANT. Why not?

MAJOR-DOMO. Because the Ministers understand each other at just a hint. A lot you'll catch on to from just hints! (*Suddenly bends down in a low bow.*) They're coming. I've served in the Court so long that my waist bends all by itself at the approach of the great. I don't see them yet, or hear them, but I'm already bowing. That's why I'm head man. Get it? Now bow . . . Deeper.

(*The* MAJOR-DOMO *bends down to the ground. His* ASSISTANT *does likewise. From both sides of the stage, two ministers come out simultaneously—the* PRIME MINISTER *and the* MINISTER OF FINANCE. *The* PRIME MINISTER *is a short man with a paunch, a bald patch, rosy-faced, over fifty. The* MINISTER OF FINANCE *is withered, stringy, looks around in horror, is lame in both legs. He is carried along under his arms by two husky* VALETS. *The ministers reach the table simultaneously, simultaneously sit down and immediately start playing chess. The* VALETS, *having brought the* MINISTER OF FINANCE *in and having seated him, noiselessly withdraw. The* MAJOR-DOMO *and his* ASSISTANT *remain on stage. They stand at attention.*)

PRIME MINISTER. Health?

MINISTER OF FINANCE. Awf.

PRIME MINISTER. Business?

MINISTER OF FINANCE. Very ba.

PRIME MINISTER. Why?

MINISTER OF FINANCE. Competi.

(*They silently play chess.*)

MAJOR-DOMO (*in a whisper*). See, I told you, they understand each other at just a hint.

PRIME MINISTER. Heard about Princess?

MINISTER OF FINANCE. Yes, was to[ld].

PRIME MINISTER. This visiting scholar has stolen her heart.

MINISTER OF FINANCE. Stolen? Just a moment . . . Valet! No, not you . . . My valet!

(ONE OF THE VALETS *who brought the* MINISTER *in comes on.*)

Valet! Did you shut all the doors when we left?

VALET. All of them, Your Excellency.

MINISTER OF FINANCE. And the iron one?

VALET. Yes, indeed.

MINISTER OF FINANCE. And the bronze one?

VALET. Yes, indeed.

MINISTER OF FINANCE. And the cast-iron one?

VALET. Yes, indeed.

MINISTER OF FINANCE. And set out the traps? Don't forget, you answer with your life for the very littlest loss.

VALET. I won't forget, Your Excellency.

MINISTER OF FINANCE. Go away . . .

(*The* VALET *goes out.*)

I'm listening.

PRIME MINISTER. According to the reports of the Privy Counsellors on duty, the day before yesterday the Princess looked into the mirror for a long time, then burst into tears and said: (*Takes out a notebook, reads.*) "Ah, why am I perishing in vain?"—and for the fifth time sent to find out about the Scholar's health. Having learned that no particular changes had occurred, the Princess stamped her foot and whispered: (*Reads.*) "God damn it!" And today she set a rendezvous with him in the park. There you have it. How do you li[ke it]?

MINISTER OF FINANCE. Not a bi. Who's this scholar?

PRIME MINISTER. Ah, I've made a study of him right down to the minutest details.

MINISTER OF FINANCE. A blackmailer?
PRIME MINISTER. Worse . . .
MINISTER OF FINANCE. A thief?
PRIME MINISTER. Even worse . . .
MINISTER OF FINANCE. An adventurer, an old fox, an artful dodger?
PRIME MINISTER. Oh, if only . . .
MINISTER OF FINANCE. Well, what is he then, after all?
PRIME MINISTER. A simple, naïve man.
MINISTER OF FINANCE. Check to your king.
PRIME MINISTER. I'm castling . . .
MINISTER OF FINANCE. Check to the queen.
PRIME MINISTER. The poor Princess! We would expose a blackmailer, we would catch a thief, we would outsmart an old fox or an artful dodger, but this . . . The things that simple and honest people do are sometimes so puzzling!
MINISTER OF FINANCE. He must be either bo[ught] or ki[lled].
PRIME MINISTER. Indeed, there's no other way out.
MINISTER OF FINANCE. The town has gotten wi[nd of this]?
PRIME MINISTER. I'll say!
MINISTER OF FINANCE. I knew it. That's why sensible people are transferring their gold abroad in such quantity. The day before yesterday one banker even had his gold teeth sent abroad. And now he's continually going abroad and coming back. In his own country he has nothing to chew things over with.
PRIME MINISTER. It seems to me your banker showed needless nervousness.
MINISTER OF FINANCE. That's sensitivity! There's no more sensitive organism in the world than business circles! The King's testament alone provoked seven bankruptcies, seven suicides, and all securities fell seven points. But now . . . Oh, what will happen now! There'll be no change, Mr. Prime Minister! Life must go on regularly, like a clock.
PRIME MINISTER. Speaking of clocks, what time is it?
MINISTER OF FINANCE. My gold watch has been sent abroad. And if I wear a silver one, people will start saying that I've gone broke, and that'll cause a panic in business circles.
PRIME MINISTER. Is there absolutely no gold left in our country?

MINISTER OF FINANCE. There's more than we need.

PRIME MINISTER. Where from?

MINISTER OF FINANCE. From abroad. Foreign business circles are uneasy for their own foreign reasons and transfer gold here to us. And so we make out. Let me sum up now. Consequently, we'll buy the Scholar off.

PRIME MINISTER. Or kill him.

MINISTER OF FINANCE. How will we do that?

PRIME MINISTER. The most tactful and ticklish way! You know the business has such a feeling as love mixed into it! I'm planning to make short work of the scholar with the help of friendship.

MINISTER OF FINANCE. Friendship?

PRIME MINISTER. Yes. For this it's essential to find a man whom our scholar is friendly with. A friend knows what he loves, what he can be bought with. A friend knows what he hates, what's sheer death for him. I've given orders in the office to dig up a friend.

MINISTER OF FINANCE. That's dreadful.

PRIME MINISTER. Why?

MINISTER OF FINANCE. You know the Scholar is a visitor; that means he'll have to send for a friend from abroad. And in what column will I enter that expense? Every violation of the estimate provokes bitter tears from my head bookkeeper. He'll sob like a baby and then fall into a delirious condition. For a while he'll stop giving out money altogether. To everybody. Even to me. Even you.

PRIME MINISTER. Yes, but? . . . That's unpleasant. You know the fate of the whole kingdom is at stake. What will we do?

MINISTER OF FINANCE. I don't know.

PRIME MINISTER. Then who does?

ASSISTANT (*coming forward*). I do.

MINISTER OF FINANCE (*jumping up*). What's that? Has it begun?

PRIME MINISTER. Relax, please. If it ever does begin some time, it won't be from palace footmen.

MINISTER OF FINANCE. So it's not a revolt?

PRIME MINISTER. No. It's simply impudence. Who are you?

ASSISTANT. I'm the man you're looking for. I'm a friend of the

Scholar, his closest friend. We were never apart from our days in the cradle until just recently.

PRIME MINISTER. Listen, good friend, you know who you're talking to?

ASSISTANT. Yes.

PRIME MINISTER. Why don't you call me "Your Excellency"?

ASSISTANT (*with a deep bow*). I'm sorry, Your Excellency.

PRIME MINISTER. You a visitor?

ASSISTANT. I came into the world in this town, Your Excellency.

PRIME MINISTER. And nevertheless you're a friend of the visiting scholar?

ASSISTANT. I'm just exactly the man you need, Your Excellency. I know him as nobody else does, and he doesn't know me at all, Your Excellency.

PRIME MINISTER. Strange.

ASSISTANT. If you wish, I'll tell you who I am, Your Excellency.

PRIME MINISTER. Do. What are you looking around for?

ASSISTANT. Let me write in the sand who I am, Your Excellency.

PRIME MINISTER. Go ahead.

(*The* ASSISTANT *traces something in the sand. The* MINISTERS *read it and look at each other.*)

What do you thi?

MINISTER OF FINANCE. Will d[o]. But be caref! Or he'll ask an exorbitant pri.

PRIME MINISTER. Right. Who arranged a palace job for you?

ASSISTANT. Mr. Caesar Borgia and Mr. Pietro, Your Excellency.

PRIME MINISTER (*to the* MINISTER OF FINANCE). Are these names familiar to you?

MINISTER OF FINANCE. Yes, completely reliable ogres.

PRIME MINISTER. All right, my good man, we'll think it over.

ASSISTANT. I make bold to remind you that we're in the South, Your Excellency.

PRIME MINISTER. Well, what of it?

ASSISTANT. In the South everything grows so fast, Your Excellency. The Scholar and the Princess first talked to each other only two weeks ago and haven't seen each other once since then, but just look how their love has grown, Your Excellency. We musn't be too late, Your Excellency!

PRIME MINISTER. But I've told you we'll think it over. Step to one side. (*The* MINISTERS *fall to thinking.*) Come over here, my good man.

(*The* ASSISTANT *does as he is bid.*)

We've thought it over and decided to take you on in the Prime Minister's office.

ASSISTANT. Thanks, Your Excellency. As I see it, what has to be done about the Scholar is . . .

PRIME MINISTER. What's the matter with you, my good man? Are you starting to do things before you've even been formally put on the staff? Why, you've gone mad! You don't know what an office is, is that it?

ASSISTANT. I'm sorry, Your Excellency.

(*There is a burst of laughter behind the wings.*)

PRIME MINISTER. Here come the health resorters. They'll be in our way. Let's go into the office, and there I'll draw up your appointment. And after that—very well, we'll listen to what you have to say.

ASSISTANT. Thanks, Your Excellency.

MINISTER OF FINANCE. Valets!

(*The* VALETS *appear.*)

Take me away.

(*They go out. The doors of the pavilion are flung open and out comes the* DOCTOR, *a young man, in the highest degree sullen and preoccupied. He is surrounded by* HEALTH RESORTERS, *lightly but sumptuously dressed.*)

FIRST LADY RESORTER. Doctor, why in back of my knee do I sometimes have a feeling something like thoughtfulness?

DOCTOR. In back of which knee?

FIRST LADY RESORTER. The right.

DOCTOR. It'll go away.

SECOND LADY RESORTER. But why at mealtimes, between the eighth and ninth dishes, do I have melancholic thoughts?

DOCTOR. What kind, for example?

SECOND LADY RESORTER. Well, I suddenly feel like going far away into a desert and there giving myself up to fasting and prayers.

DOCTOR. It'll go away.

FIRST GENTLEMAN RESORTER. Doctor, why after the fortieth bath did I suddenly stop liking brunettes?

DOCTOR. And whom do you like now?

FIRST GENTLEMAN RESORTER. Just one blonde.

DOCTOR. It'll go away. Ladies and gentlemen, let me remind you that the medicinal hour is over. Sister of Mercy, you're excused. Sister of Pleasure, commence your duties.

SISTER OF PLEASURE. Who wants the ball? Who, the skip rope? The hoops, the hoops, ladies and gentlemen! Who wants to play tag? hy-spy? cat-and-mouse? Time's flying, ladies and gentlemen, exult and triumph now, ladies and gentlemen, play!

(*The* HEALTH RESORTERS *disperse, playing games. The* SCHOLAR *and* ANNUNZIATA *come in.*)

ANNUNZIATA. Doctor, he just bought a whole trayful of fruit drops.

SCHOLAR. But you know I gave them away to the little boys on the street.

ANNUNZIATA. Makes no difference! After all, can a sick person buy sweets?

DOCTOR (*to the* SCHOLAR). Stand facing the sun. That's it. Your shadow has grown to normal proportions. That's what was to be expected—in the South everything grows so fast. How do you feel?

SCHOLAR. I feel I'm perfectly well.

DOCTOR. Still, I want to listen to you. No, no need to take your coat off: I have very sensitive ears. (*Takes a stethoscope from a table in the pavilion.*) Now. Breathe in. Breathe in deeply. Heave a deep sigh. Once more. Give a deep sigh of relief. Once more. Look at everything through your fingers. Give a wave of your hand in disgust at everything. Once more. Shrug your shoulders. That's it. (*Sits down and becomes thoughtful.*)

(*The* SCHOLAR *takes a bundle of letters out of a side pocket of his coat. He searches through them.*)

ANNUNZIATA. Well, what do you think, Doctor? How are things going with him?

DOCTOR. Badly.

ANNUNZIATA. Well, there you are, and he says he's perfectly well.

DOCTOR. Indeed he is. But things are going badly with him. And they'll get still worse, as long as he doesn't learn how to look at the world through his fingers, wave his hand in disgust at everything, and possess the art of shrugging his shoulders.

ANNUNZIATA. What's to be done, Doctor? How can he be taught all this?

(*Without speaking, the* DOCTOR *shrugs his shoulders.*)

Answer me, Doctor. Oh, please. You know all the same I won't leave you alone, you know how stubborn I am. What does he have to do?

DOCTOR. Take care!

ANNUNZIATA. But he smiles.

DOCTOR. Yes, that happens.

ANNUNZIATA. He's a scholar, he's intelligent, he's older than me, but sometimes I just simply feel like spanking him. Now you talk to him!

(*The* DOCTOR *waves his hand in disgust.*)

Doctor!

DOCTOR. You see he doesn't listen to me. He's buried his nose in some notes.

ANNUNZIATA. Those are letters from the Princess. Sir! The Doctor wants to talk to you but you're not listening.

SCHOLAR. What do you mean not listening! I've heard everything.

ANNUNZIATA. And what do you have to say to it?

SCHOLAR. I'd say, I'd say . . .

ANNUNZIATA. Sir!

SCHOLAR. Right away! I can't find here . . . (*Mumbles.*) How did she put it—"ever yours" or "forever yours"?

ANNUNZIATA (*plaintively*). I'll shoot you!

SCHOLAR. Yes, yes, please.

DOCTOR. Christian-Theodore! Now you're a scholar . . . Listen to me. After all, I'm still your friend.

SCHOLAR (*putting the letters away*). Yes, yes. I'm sorry.

DOCTOR. In folk legends about the man who lost his shadow, in the monographs of Chamisso and your friend Hans Christian Andersen it says that . . .

SCHOLAR. We won't bring up what it says there. Everything with me ends differently.

DOCTOR. Answer me as your doctor—are you planning to marry the Princess?

SCHOLAR. Of course.

DOCTOR. But I heard that you were dreaming of making as many people as possible happy.

SCHOLAR. That's correct, too.

DOCTOR. They both can't be.

SCHOLAR. Why not?

DOCTOR. Having married the Princess, you'll become King.

SCHOLAR. That's just the great thing about it—I won't be King! The Princess loves me, and she'll go away with me. And we'll renounce the crown—you see how good that is! And I'll explain to anybody who asks, and I'll make even the least interested understand, that royal power is meaningless and worthless. And therefore I even abdicated the throne.

DOCTOR. And people will understand you?

SCHOLAR. Of course! Why, I'll prove it to them by a living example!

(*The* DOCTOR *silently waves his hand in disgust.*)

A man can have anything explained to him. Why, he knows the alphabet, and this is even simpler than the alphabet, and, most importantly, comes so close to home for him himself!

(*The* HEALTH RESORTERS, *playing their games, run across the stage.*)

DOCTOR (*pointing to them*). And these will understand you, too?

SCHOLAR. Of course! Every man has a quick. Just have to sting him to the quick—and it's all right there.

DOCTOR. Child! I know them better. After all, they're my patients.

SCHOLAR. What are they sick with?

DOCTOR. Satiety, in an acute form.

SCHOLAR. Is that dangerous?

DOCTOR. Yes, for those around them.

SCHOLAR. In what way?

DOCTOR. Satiety in its acute form suddenly takes hold of even virtuous people. A man has earned a lot of money honestly. And then suddenly the ominous symptom appears: the particular, restive, hungry look of the well-to-do man.

That's the end of him. From that day forth he's sterile, blind and cruel.

SCHOLAR. But haven't you tried to explain everything to them?

DOCTOR. Now that was one of the things I wanted to warn you against. Woe to the man who tries to make them think about anything except money. That drives them really wild.

(*The* HEALTH RESORTERS *run through.*)

SCHOLAR. Just look how gay they are!

DOCTOR. They're relaxing!

(JULIA JULI *comes in quickly.*)

JULIA (*to the* DOCTOR). At last, here you are. Are you all well?

DOCTOR. Yes, Julia.

JULIA. Ah, that's the Doctor.

DOCTOR. Yes, it's me, Julia.

JULIA. Why're you batting your eyes at me like some rabbit in love? Clear out!

(*The* DOCTOR *begins to answer, but goes out into the pavilion, having silently given a wave of his hand in disgust.*)

Where are you, Christian-Theodore?

SCHOLAR. Here I am.

JULIA (*goes up to him*). Yes, it's you. (*Smiles.*) How glad I am to see you! Well, what did that worthless doctor tell you?

SCHOLAR. He told me I'm well. Why do you call him worthless?

JULIA. Ah, once upon a time I loved him, and then afterward I hate people like that terrificly.

SCHOLAR. It was an ill-fated love?

JULIA. Worse. This very same doctor has a hideous and wicked wife whom he's scared to death of. He could be kissed only on the back of his head.

SCHOLAR. Why?

JULIA. He kept turning around all the time to see if his wife was coming. But that's enough about him. I came here to . . . to warn you, Christian-Theodore. Trouble's threatening you.

SCHOLAR. Impossible. Why, I'm so happy!

JULIA. Nevertheless, trouble's threatening you.

ANNUNZIATA. Don't smile, madam, I beg you. Otherwise, we won't understand whether you're talking seriously or joking and will even perish on account of that.

JULIA. Pay no attention to my smiling. In our circle, the circle of real people, they always smile at everything. Because then, you know, no matter what you say, it can be taken either this way or that. I'm speaking seriously, Christian-Theodore. Trouble's threatening you.

SCHOLAR. What kind?

JULIA. I've told you that there's a certain Minister in our circle?

SCHOLAR. Yes.

JULIA. He's the Minister of Finance. He comes to our circle because of me. He's courting me and every moment prepared to propose to me.

ANNUNZIATA. Him? Why, he can't even walk!

JULIA. He's escorted by splendidly dressed valets. And you know he's so rich. I just met him. He asked where I was going. Hearing your name, he frowned, Christian-Theodore.

ANNUNZIATA. How terrible!

JULIA. In our circle we all possess a certain art—we know how to read dignitaries' expressions amazingly. Even me, with my nearsightedness, I just read on the Minister's face that there's something being cooked up against you, Christian-Theodore.

SCHOLAR. Well, let it be.

JULIA. Ah, you've ruined me in these last two weeks. Why was I the only one to visit you? I've turned into a sentimental middle-class woman! It's such a nuisance. Annunziata, take him away.

SCHOLAR. Why?

JULIA. The Minister of Finance will be here any minute, and I'll turn on all my charm and find out what they're cooking up. I'll even try to save you, Christian-Theodore.

ANNUNZIATA. How can I show you my gratitude, madam?

JULIA. Not a word to a soul, if you're really grateful. Go on.

ANNUNZIATA. Let's go, sir.

SCHOLAR. But, Annunziata, you know very well that I'm supposed to meet the Princess here.

JULIA. You still have an hour. Go away, if you love the Princess and have any feeling for me.

SCHOLAR. Good-bye, poor Julia. You're both so worried! And I'm the only one who knows that everything will be wonderful!

ANNUNZIATA. He's coming. Madam, I beg you . . .

JULIA. Shh! I've already told you I'll try.

(*The* SCHOLAR *and* ANNUNZIATA *go out. The* MINISTER OF FINANCE *appears, transported by his* VALETS.)

MINISTER OF FINANCE. Valets! Set me down beside this bewitching woman! Give me a pose conducive to light, witty conversation.

(*The* VALETS *obey.*)

Good, now go away.

(*The* VALETS *go out.*)

Julia, I want to make you happy.

JULIA. That's easy for you to do.

MINISTER OF FINANCE. Enchantress! Circe! Aphrodite! We were just talking about you in the Prime Minister's office.

JULIA. Naughty boys!

MINISTER OF FINANCE. I swear we were! And we all agreed on one thing: you're a clever, practical nymph!

JULIA. Oh you courtiers!

MINISTER OF FINANCE. And we decided that you're just the person who would help us in a certain thing.

JULIA. Tell me what. If it's not too hard, I'm ready to do everything for you.

MINISTER OF FINANCE. It's nothing! You'll have to help us get rid of the visiting scholar called Theodore-Christian. After all, you know him, don't you? You'll help us?

(JULIA *does not reply.*)

Valets!

(*The* VALETS *appear.*)

The pose of extreme amazement!

(*The* VALETS *obey.*)

Julia, I'm extremely amazed. Why do you keep looking at me as if you didn't know what to answer me?

JULIA. I actually don't know what to tell you. These two weeks are simply ruining me.

MINISTER OF FINANCE. I don't understand.

JULIA. Myself, I don't understand myself.
MINISTER OF FINANCE. Is this a refusal?
JULIA. I don't know.
MINISTER OF FINANCE. Valets!

(*The* VALETS *run in.*)

The pose of extreme indignation!

(*The* VALETS *obey.*)

I'm extremely indignant, Madame Julia Juli! What does this mean? You haven't fallen in love with this little beggar boy, have you? Shut up! Get up! Attention! In front of you, you have not a man but the Minister of Finance. Your refusal shows that you lack respect for our whole State System. Silence! Shut up! Under arrest!

JULIA. Wait a minute!
MINISTER OF FINANCE. I won't! "Ah, How Come I'm Not a Meadow!" Only now do I understand what you mean by that. You're hinting that the farmers have too little land. Ah? Well? Indeed I . . . Yes I did . . . Tomorrow the papers will tear to shreds your figure, your way of singing, your private life. Valets! Stamp!

(*The* VALETS *stamp their feet.*)

No, not your own, you idiots, mine!

(*The* VALETS *obey.*)

Good-bye, former celebrity.

JULIA. But wait!
MINISTER OF FINANCE. I won't!
JULIA. Look at me!
MINISTER OF FINANCE. Kindly call me "Your Excellency"!
JULIA. Look at me, Your Excellency.
MINISTER OF FINANCE. Well?
JULIA. Really, don't you understand that for me you're more a man than a Minister of Finance?
MINISTER OF FINANCE (*flattered*). Come now, stop it!
JULIA. I swear. And can you say "yes" to a man right away?
MINISTER OF FINANCE. Aphrodite! Let's be precise: you agree?
JULIA. Now I'll answer you—yes.
MINISTER OF FINANCE. Valets! Embrace her!

(*The* VALETS *embrace* JULIA.)

You idiots! *I* want to embrace her! There. Dear Julia, many thanks. Tomorrow in an office memorandum I'll announce myself your chief patron. Valets! Set me down beside this Aphrodite. Give me the pose of extreme lightheartedness. And you, Julia, assume a lighthearted pose but listen to me with both ears. So, in a little while you'll find the Scholar here, animatedly talking to the Official in Charge of Specially Important Business. And under any pretext you want, you'll take the Scholar away from here for twenty minutes. That's all there is to it.

JULIA. That's all?

MINISTER OF FINANCE. You see how easy! And just these twenty minutes will finish him off for keeps. Let's go to the jeweler's; I'll buy you a ring of inestimable value. Let's go. Valets! Carry us away.

(*They go off. The* ASSISTANT *comes in with* PIETRO *and* CAESAR BORGIA.)

ASSISTANT. Good morning, gentlemen!

PIETRO. But we already saw each other this morning.

ASSISTANT. I advise you to forget that we met this morning. I won't forget that at one point you found me, got me a job in the palace, helped me along in the world. But you, gentlemen, forget once and for all who I was and remember who I've become.

CAESAR BORGIA. Who are you now?

ASSISTANT. I'm now the Official in Charge of Specially Important Business in the Office of His Excellency the Prime Minister.

CAESAR BORGIA. How did you get that? That's real success! God knows what the hell it is! Here we go again!

ASSISTANT. I achieved this success by my own efforts. Therefore I remind you once again: forget who I was.

PIETRO. That can be done. If we ever fall out, what's the use of remembering!

CAESAR BORGIA. It's hard to forget about this. But a man can keep his face shut until the right time. You get what I'm hinting at?

ASSISTANT. I get you, gentlemen. We won't have a falling out as long as you keep quiet about who I was. Now listen carefully. I've been assigned Business Number 8989. (*Shows a file.*) Here it is.

PIETRO (*reads*). The Business of the Princess' Married Life.

ASSISTANT. Right. Here, in this file, there's everything: the Princess, and him, and you, and the present, and the future.

CAESAR BORGIA. Who's been selected as the fiancé of this lofty person is something that doesn't worry me much, like everything else in this, as they say, earthly life, but still . . .

ASSISTANT. You two have been selected as the Princess' fiancé.

PIETRO. I'll be! How can it be the two of us!

CAESAR BORGIA. Me and him?

ASSISTANT. Yes. Nevertheless, the Princess has to have a choice . . .

CAESAR BORGIA. But you yourself must be able to see!

PIETRO. What's she need some devil for when it's me!

ASSISTANT. Quiet! The definitive decision. I propose that the Princess choose. Pietro, take your daughter home. I have to talk to the Scholar, and she protects him like a whole regiment of Guards.

CAESAR BORGIA. She's in love with him. And Pietro's blind, as a father ought to be!

PIETRO. I'll be! I'll kill them both!

CAESAR BORGIA. Should have long ago.

PIETRO. Damnation! You're tempting me on purpose! I'll be arrested for murder and you'll be the only fiancé left? Is that what you're after?

CAESAR BORGIA. Yes, it is. And it's a perfectly natural desire. Good-bye.

PIETRO. No you don't, you're not leaving. I know where you're headed.

CAESAR BORGIA. Where?

PIETRO. You want to eat me up one way or another. It won't work. I won't let you out of my sight.

ASSISTANT. Shh! He's coming this way. Here's what we'll agree on: the one of you who'll be King will buy the other off with a good reward. He'll fix as the victim, say, the King's First Secretary or the Commander of the Watch. Careful: he's coming. He feels cheerful.

CAESAR BORGIA. And how are you going to talk to him?

ASSISTANT. I talk to every man in his own language.

(*The* SCHOLAR *and* ANNUNZIATA *come in.*)

SCHOLAR. What a wonderful day, gentlemen!

PIETRO. Sure, there's nothing wrong with the day, God damn it. Annunziata, home!

ANNUNZIATA. Papa . . .

PIETRO. Home! Or else you'll be in trouble and so will somebody else. You didn't even tell the cook what to make for supper tonight.

ANNUNZIATA. It's all the same to me.

PIETRO. What do you say, you monster? Mr. Caesar Borgia, let's you and I go home, my friend, or, I swear on my word of honor, I'll polish you off on the sly with a dagger.

(*They go out. The* ASSISTANT, *having kept on the side during the preceding conversation, goes up to the* SCHOLAR.)

ASSISTANT. You don't recognize me?

SCHOLAR. I'm sorry, I don't.

ASSISTANT. Look more closely.

SCHOLAR. What is this? I feel as if I knew you, and knew you well, but . . .

ASSISTANT. And we spent so many years together.

SCHOLAR. You don't say!

ASSISTANT. I assure you. I used to follow you relentlessly, but you would only casually glance at me from time to time. And you know I was often higher than you, going way up to the roofs of the highest houses. Usually that happened on moonlit nights.

SCHOLAR. So, that means, you . . .

ASSISTANT. Shh! Yes, I'm your shadow . . . Why do you look at me distrustfully? You know how tied I was to you your whole life, right from the day you were born.

SCHOLAR. Oh yes, I was just . . .

SHADOW. You're angry at me for leaving you. But you yourself asked me to go over to the Princess, and I immediately did what you asked. After all, we grew up together among the very same people. When you would say "Mama," I would soundlessly repeat the same word. I loved the people you did, and your enemies were mine. When you were sick, I, too, couldn't raise my head from the pillow. You got well, and I got well, too. Really, after a whole life lived in such close friendship, could I suddenly become your enemy?

SCHOLAR. Why no! What do you mean? Sit down, old friend.

Without you I was sick, but now I'm well again . . . I feel fine. It's such a wonderful day today. I'm happy; today my heart is wide open—that's what I'll tell you, though, you know, I don't like phrases like that. But you've really moved me . . . But what about you, what have you been doing all this time? Or no, wait, let's first switch to the familiar form.[3]

SHADOW (*holding his hand out to the* SCHOLAR). Thanks. I stayed your shadow—that's what I was doing all this time.

SCHOLAR. I don't understand you.

SHADOW. You sent me to the Princess. I first got myself set up as Assistant to the Chief Valet in the Palace, then worked my way up higher and higher, and from today on I'm the Official in Charge of Specially Important Business under the Prime Minister.

SCHOLAR. You poor soul! I can imagine how hard it is among those people! But why did you do it?

SHADOW. For your sake.

SCHOLAR. For my sake?

SHADOW. You yourself don't know what a terrible hatred has surrounded you ever since you fell in love with the Princess, and the Princess with you. They're all ready to eat you up, and they would have today, if it hadn't been for me.

SCHOLAR. What are you talking about!

SHADOW. I'm with them in order to save you. They trust me. They've assigned me Business Number 8989.

SCHOLAR. What kind of business is that?

SHADOW. It's the Business of the Princess' Married Life.

SCHOLAR. Impossible.

SHADOW. And our luck is that this business is in good hands. The Prime Minister himself sent me to you. I'm commissioned to buy you off.

SCHOLAR. To buy me? (*Laughs.*) For how much?

SHADOW. It doesn't matter. You're promised fame, honor, and wealth if you'll turn the Princess down.

SCHOLAR. And if I won't sell myself?

---

[3] Because English does not admit "thou" any longer, this line must seem out of place in translation.

SHADOW. You'll be killed today.

SCHOLAR. I'll never in my life believe that I might die, especially today.

SHADOW. Christian, my friend, old man, you'll be killed, believe me. Do they know the paths we ran along in our childhood, the mill where we talked to the water sprite, the forest where we met the teacher's daughter and fell in love—you with her, and I with her shadow? They can't even imagine that you're a living man. For them you're an obstacle, like a stump or an old log. Believe me, the sun won't have set, before you're dead.

SCHOLAR. So what do you advise me to do?

SHADOW (*takes a document out of the file*). Sign this.

SCHOLAR (*reads*). "I, the undersigned, positively, irrevocably and definitively refuse to enter into marriage with the Princess, heiress to the throne, if in return I am guaranteed fame, honor, and wealth." Are you seriously suggesting I sign this?

SHADOW. Sign it, if you're not a foolish boy, if you're a real man.

SCHOLAR. Why, what's the matter with you?

SHADOW. Understand, we have no other way out. On the one side there's just the three of us; on the other, the Ministers, the Privy Councillors, all the officials of the kingdom, the police and the army. In an open fight we couldn't win. Believe me, I was always closer to the ground than you. Listen: this little piece of paper will calm them down. This evening you'll hire a carriage, nobody will follow you. And we'll get into your carriage in the forest—the Princess and I. And in a few hours we'll be free. You understand—free. Here's the portable inkwell, here's the pen. Sign.

SCHOLAR. Well, all right. The Princess will be here in just a minute, I'll talk it over with her, and if there's no other way out, I'll sign.

SHADOW. It can't be put off! The Prime Minister gave me only twenty minutes. He doesn't believe you can be bought off; He thinks this conversation of ours is just a formality. He's already got the assassins on duty sitting outside and waiting for the order. Sign.

SCHOLAR. I really don't feel like it.

SHADOW. You're also a murderer! By refusing to sign this miserable little scrap of paper you're killing me, your best friend, and the poor, helpless Princess. Could we survive your death?

SCHOLAR. Well, all right, all right. Give it to me, I'll sign. Only . . . I'm never going to get so close to palaces again in my life . . . (*Signs the paper.*)

SHADOW. And there's the royal seal. (*Affixes the seal.*)

(JULIA *runs in. The* SHADOW *modestly moves to one side.*)

JULIA. Christian! I'm lost.

SCHOLAR. What happened?

JULIA. Help me!

SCHOLAR. I'm ready . . . But how? You're not joking?

JULIA. No! Am I smiling? That's just habit. Come with me right away! Come!

SCHOLAR. Word of honor, I can't leave here. The Princess will be here any minute.

JULIA. It's a question of life and death!

SCHOLAR. Aha, I can guess what it's about . . . You found out from the Minister of Finance what trouble is threatening me and you want to warn me. Thank you, Julia, but . . .

JULIA. Ah, you don't understand . . . All right, then, stay. No! I don't want to be a virtuous, sentimental, middle-class girl. I have no thought at all of warning you. It's about me! Christian, please . . . Come with me, or else I'm done for. You want me to get down on my knees to you? Let's go!

SCHOLAR. All right. I just have to say two words to my friend. (*Goes over to the* SHADOW.) Listen, the Princess will be here any minute.

SHADOW. Right.

SCHOLAR. Tell her that I'll be right back in just a few minutes. I can't say no to this woman. There's been some misfortune.

SHADOW. Go ahead and don't worry. I'll explain everything to the Princess.

SCHOLAR. Thanks. (*They go out.*)

SHADOW. Damned habit! My arms and legs and neck ache. All the time I kept wanting to repeat his every movement.

It's just dangerous . . . (*Opens the file.*) So . . . Item four—done . . . (*Becomes absorbed in reading.*)

(*The* PRINCESS *and the* PRIVY COUNCILLOR *come in. The* SHADOW *comes to attention and stares intently at the* PRINCESS.)

PRINCESS. Privy Councillor, where is he? Why isn't he here?

PRIVY COUNCILLOR (*in a whisper*). He'll be here in a minute, Princess, and everything will be fine.

PRINCESS. No, this is a terrible misfortune! Be quiet, you don't understand a thing. You're not in love; it's easy for you to say that everything's going fine. And besides, I'm a Princess, I don't know how to wait. What's that music?

PRIVY COUNCILLOR. It's in the restaurant, Princess.

PRINCESS. Why do we always have music in the restaurant?

PRIVY COUNCILLOR. So you can't hear people chewing, Princess.

PRINCESS. Leave me alone . . . Now what's this? (*To the* SHADOW.) Hey, you, why are you looking at me with such big eyes?

SHADOW. I must talk to you and I don't dare, Princess.

PRINCESS. Who are you?

SHADOW. I'm his best friend.

PRINCESS. Whose?

SHADOW. I'm the best friend of the man you're waiting for, Princess.

PRINCESS. Really? Why don't you talk?

SHADOW. My answer will seem impudent to you, Princess.

PRINCESS. That's all right, go ahead.

SHADOW. I didn't say anything because your beauty overwhelmed me.

PRINCESS. Oh, that's not impudent at all. Did he send you to me?

SHADOW. Yes. He asked me to tell you that he'll be here right away, Princess. Some very important business detained him. Everything's all right, Princess.

PRINCESS. But he'll be here soon?

SHADOW. Yes.

PRINCESS. Well, now I feel cheerful again. You'll entertain me until he comes. Well?

(*The* SHADOW *is silent.*)

Well now! I feel awkward having to remind you of it, but after all I am the Princess. I'm used to being entertained . . .

SHADOW. Very well, I'll do your bidding. I'll tell you dreams, Princess.

PRINCESS. Are your dreams interesting?

SHADOW. I'll tell you your dreams, Princess.

PRINCESS. Mine?

SHADOW. Yes. The night before last you dreamed that the palace walls had suddenly turned into waves on the sea. You cried out, "Christian!"—and he appeared in a boat and stretched his hand out toward you . . .

PRINCESS. But, you know, I didn't tell anybody this dream!

SHADOW. And you found yourself in a forest . . . And a wolf suddenly rose up from the bushes. But Christian said: "Don't be afraid, it's a good wolf"—and patted it. And then there's one more dream. You were galloping across a field on a fine horse. As you rode along, the grass was higher and higher and finally was a wall all around you. This seemed to you beautiful, amazingly beautiful, so beautiful that you began crying and woke up in tears.

PRINCESS. But how do you know all this?

SHADOW. Love works wonders, Princess.

PRINCESS. Love?

SHADOW. Yes. For I'm a very wretched man, Princess. I love you.

PRINCESS. Really . . . Councillor!

PRIVY COUNCILLOR. Yes, Princess.

PRINCESS. Call . . . No, step back five paces.

(*The* COUNCILLOR *counts off the paces.*)

I . . .

SHADOW. You wanted him to call the Watch, Princess, and, yourself not understanding how it happened, ordered him to move five paces away.

PRINCESS. You . . .

SHADOW. I love you, Princess. And you sense that yourself. I'm so filled with you that your soul is as clear to me as my own. I've told you only two of your dreams, but of course I remember them all. I know your terrifying dreams, and your silly ones, and the ones that can only be whispered into your ear.

PRINCESS. There aren't . . .

SHADOW. I'll tell you that dream which amazed you—want me too? You remember? In that dream it wasn't he was with you, not Christian, but a completely different man with an unfamiliar face, and it was just that that you liked, Princess. And with him you . . .

PRINCESS. Councillor, call the Watch.

PRIVY COUNCILLOR. Very good, Princess.

PRINCESS. But for the time being let the Watch stand there behind the bushes. Tell some more. I'm listening because . . . because I'm just bored waiting for him.

SHADOW. People don't know the shady side of things, but it's precisely in the shadows, in the semi-darkness, in the depths that there lurks that which gives poignancy to our feelings. In the depths of your soul there is me.

PRINCESS. That will do. I've suddenly come to. Right now the Watch will seize you and tonight you'll be beheaded.

SHADOW. Read this! (*Takes from his file the document which the* SCHOLAR *signed. The* PRINCESS *reads it.*) He's a nice man, a fine man, but he's petty. He was trying to persuade you to run away with him because he's afraid of becoming King—you know, that's dangerous. And he sold you. The coward!

PRINCESS. I don't trust this document.

SHADOW. But here's the royal seal. I bought off your no-good fiancé, I took you by force. Order my head cut off.

PRINCESS. You're not letting me collect myself. How should I know—perhaps you, too, don't love me. What an unhappy girl I am!

SHADOW. But the dreams? You've forgotten the dreams, Princess. How did I find out your dreams? You know only love can work such wonders.

PRINCESS. Ah, indeed, that's true . . .

SHADOW. Farewell, Princess.

PRINCESS. You . . . you're going? How dare you! Come over here to me, give me your hand! It's . . . it's all . . . so . . . so interesting . . . (*A kiss.*) I . . . I don't even know what your name is.

SHADOW. Theodore-Christian.

PRINCESS. How fine! It's almost . . . almost exactly the same. (*They kiss.*)

(*The* SCHOLAR *runs in and stops dead.*)

PRIVY COUNCILLOR. I advise you to go away; here the Princess is giving an audience to one of her subjects.

SCHOLAR. Louise!

PRINCESS. Go away, you're a petty man.

SCHOLAR. What do you mean, Louise?

PRINCESS. Did you sign a document in which you turned me down?

SCHOLAR. Yes . . . but . . .

PRINCESS. That'll do. You're a nice man, but you're a nobody. Let's go, Theodore-Christian, dearest.

SCHOLAR. Scoundrel! (*Rushes at the* SHADOW.)

PRINCESS. Watch! Guard!

(*The* WATCH *runs out of the bushes.*)

Take us to the palace.

(*They go out. The* SCHOLAR *sinks down onto the bench. The* DOCTOR *quickly comes out of the pavilion.*)

DOCTOR. Wave your hand in disgust at all this. Wave it right this minute, or else you'll go mad.

SCHOLAR. So you know what happened?

DOCTOR. Yes, I have very sensitive ears. I heard it all.

SCHOLAR. How did he get to the point where she kissed him?

DOCTOR. He dumfounded her. He told her all her dreams.

SCHOLAR. How did he find out her dreams?

DOCTOR. Why, you know, dreams and shadows are closely related. I think they're cousins.

SCHOLAR. You heard it all and didn't interfere?

DOCTOR. What do you mean! You know he's the Official in Charge of Specially Important Business. Don't you know what a terrific power that is? I used to know a man of unusual courage. He would go bear hunting with just a knife; once he even went after a lion with his bare hands—true, somehow he didn't come back from that last expedition. And once this man fainted, having accidentally bumped the Privy Councillor. It's a special fear. Is it surprising that I, too, am afraid of him? No, I didn't get involved in this business, and you wave your hand in disgust at it all.

SCHOLAR. Don't want to.

DOCTOR. But what can you do?

SCHOLAR. I'll rub him out.

DOCTOR. No. Listen to me: you obviously don't know, and nobody in the world knows, that I made a great discovery. I found a spring of running carbonaceous water. Not far away. Right beside the palace itself. This water cures all diseases, any kind there is on earth, and even resurrects the dead, if they're good people. And what came of it? The Minister of Finance ordered me to cover the spring up. If we cure all the sick, who'll come visit us? I fought with the Minister like a madman—and that's when the officials started moving in on me. Nothing makes any difference to them. Either life or death or great discoveries. And that's exactly why they won out. And I waved my hand in disgust at it all. And right away it was a lot easier for me to live in the world. And now you wave your hand in disgust at it all and live as I do.

SCHOLAR. What do you live by? What for?

DOCTOR. Oh, there's lots . . . Here a patient's got well. Here the wife's gone away for two days. Here it's written in the paper that nevertheless I give them something to hope for.

SCHOLAR. That's all?

DOCTOR. But you want to live in order to make as many people as possible happy? The officials will certainly take care of you! And the people themselves can't stand it. Wave your hand in disgust at them. Look through your fingers at this mad, unhappy world.

SCHOLAR. I can't.

(*Backstage, a drum and horns.*)

DOCTOR. He's coming back. (*Hurriedly goes out into the pavilion.*)

(*A large detachment of the* WATCH *appears, with* TRUMPETERS *and* DRUMMERS. *At the head of the detachment is the* SHADOW, *in a black tail coat with dazzling linen. The procession halts in the middle of the stage.*)

SHADOW. Christian! I'll hand out two or three orders and then get down to business with you!

(*The* PRIME MINISTER *runs in, out of breath.* VALETS *practically fly in, carrying the* MINISTER OF FINANCE. PIETRO *and* CAESAR BORGIA *appear arm-in-arm.*)

PRIME MINISTER. What's this all mean? You know we've already decided.

SHADOW. But I've revised the decision in my way.

PRIME MINISTER. Now listen . . .

SHADOW. No, you listen, my good man. You know who you're talking to?

PRIME MINISTER. Yes.

SHADOW. Then why don't you call me "Your Excellency"? You haven't been in the office yet?

PRIME MINISTER. No, I was dining, Your Excellency.

SHADOW. Go down there. Business Number 8989 is finished. Filed in the back of it are the Princess' gracious instructions and my order Number 0001. There it's ordered that I be called "Your Excellency" until we adopt a new and proper title for ourselves.

PRIME MINISTER. That means, then, that everything is drawn up and regularized?

SHADOW. Yes.

PRIME MINISTER. Then there's no help for it. I congratulate you, Your Excellency.

SHADOW. Why are you frowning, Minister of Finance?

MINISTER OF FINANCE. I don't know how this will be received in business circles. You're nevertheless from the world of scholars. All kinds of changes will start, and we just can't stand that.

SHADOW. No changes at all. Let things be as they were. No plans. No dreaming. There you have the latest conclusions of my scholarship.

MINISTER OF FINANCE. In that case, I congratulate you, Your Excellency.

SHADOW. Pietro! The Princess has chosen a fiancé, only it's not you.

PIETRO. The hell with it, Your Excellency, you just pay me something.

SHADOW. Caesar Borgia! Nor are you to be King.

CAESAR BORGIA. I've only one thing left—to write my memoirs, Your Excellency.

SHADOW. Cheer up. I value old friends who knew me when I was still the simple Official in Charge of Specially Important Business. You're appointed Royal Secretary. You—Commander of the Royal Watch.

(PIETRO *and* CAESAR BORGIA *bow*.)

Gentlemen, you're excused! (*All go out bowing. The* SHADOW *goes over to the* SCHOLAR.) Did you see?

SCHOLAR. Yes.

SHADOW. What do you think?

SCHOLAR. I think: immediately refuse the Princess and the throne, or I'll make you.

SHADOW. Listen, you nobody. Tomorrow I'll hand out a whole series of orders—and you'll find yourself alone against the entire world. Friends will turn away from you in disgust. Your enemies will laugh at you. And you'll come crawling to me and beg for mercy.

SCHOLAR. No.

SHADOW. We'll see. At twelve o'clock midnight between Tuesday and Wednesday you'll come to the palace and send me a note: "I give up, Christian-Theodore." And I, mark my words, will give you a job around my person. Watch, follow me! (*Drums and horns. The* SHADOW *goes out with his retinue*.)

SCHOLAR. Annunziata! Annunziata!

(ANNUNZIATA *runs in*.)

ANNUNZIATA. I'm here, sir! Maybe . . . maybe you'll do what the Doctor says? Maybe you'll wave your hand in disgust at all this? I'm sorry . . . Don't be angry at me. I'll help you. I'm a very reliable girl, sir.

SCHOLAR. Annunziata, what a sad fairy tale!

(*Curtain*)

ACT III

SCENE 1

Night. Torches are burning. Lampions are burning on the cornices, columns, the balconies of the palace. A CROWD, *animated and noisy.*

VERY TALL MAN. Who wants to hear about what I see? All about it for a penny. Now who wants to hear? Oh, it's interesting!
SHORT MAN. Don't listen to him. Listen to me; I hop through everywhere, I know everything. Now who wants the news, all the news for a penny? How they first met, got acquainted, how the first fiancé was retired.
FIRST WOMAN. But over at our place they say the first fiancé was a very good man.
SECOND WOMAN. Now really! Very good! He turned her down for a million.
FIRST WOMAN. Really? What're you talking about?
SECOND WOMAN. Everybody knows that! She says to him: "You queer fellow, you wouldn't be working for no less, if you was King, you wouldn't." And he says: "And work on top of it!"
FIRST WOMAN. People like that ought to be drowned!
SECOND WOMAN. I'll say! It'd be hard for him to be King. But he could give it a try around the house!
TALL MAN. And who wants to hear about what I see in the window? The Royal Head Valet is going down the corridor and . . . well, who wants to know what comes next? All about it for a penny.
SHORT MAN. And who wants a portrait of the new King? Life size! With the crown on his head! With a kind smile on his lips! With good will in his eyes!
FIRST MAN. We have a King; now life'll be a lot better.
SECOND MAN. Why's that?
FIRST MAN. I'll explain right away. See that?
SECOND MAN. What?

FIRST MAN. See who's standing there?

SECOND MAN. Seems it's the Commander of the Watch.

FIRST MAN. Why, sure, it's him, in disguise.

SECOND MAN. Aha, I see. (*At the top of his voice.*) We have a King, now we will live. (*Quietly.*) Disguised himself, but he's got boots with spurs on his feet. (*Loudly.*) Oh, how good it feels inside!

FIRST MAN (*at the top of his voice*). Sure, what kind of a life was that without a King! We just missed him terribly!

CROWD. Long live our new King, Theodore the First! Hurrah! (*Little by little they disperse, apprehensively looking at* PIETRO. *He remains alone. The figure of a man in a cloak stands clear of the wall.*)

PIETRO. Well, what's up, Corporal?

CORPORAL. Nothing, everything's quiet. Arrested two of 'em.

PIETRO. What for?

CORPORAL. Instead of "Long live the King" one of 'em was shouting "Long live the cow."

PIETRO. And the other?

CORPORAL. The other's my neighbor.

PIETRO. But what did he do?

CORPORAL. Well, nothing, actually. He's got a foul nature. Nicknamed my wife "The Melon." I've been after him for a long time. And how're things with you, Mr. Commander?

PIETRO. Everything's quiet. The people are celebrating.

CORPORAL. Allow me to point something out to you, Mr. Commander. The boots.

PIETRO. What about the boots?

CORPORAL. Again you forgot to change your boots. The spurs jangle so!

PIETRO. Well, so? That's something nobody expected!

CORPORAL. The people guess who you are. You see how it's become empty all around?

PIETRO. Yes . . . But, however . . . You're one of us, I can make a confession to you: I came out in boots with spurs on purpose.

CORPORAL. Impossible!

PIETRO. Really. It's better if they find out who I am, or else you'll hear such things as'll keep you from sleeping three nights in a row.

CORPORAL. Indeed, that happens.

PIETRO. It's much more peaceful in boots. You walk along, jangle your spurs—and all around hear only what you ought to.

CORPORAL. Indeed, that's so.

PIETRO. It's easy for them there, in the office. They deal only with papers. But how is it for me dealing with the people?

CORPORAL. Indeed, the people . . .

PIETRO (*in a whisper*). You know what, let me tell you: the people go their own way.

CORPORAL. What do you mean?

PIETRO. You can take my word for it. Here the sovereign is celebrating his coronation, the gala marriage of noble persons is coming up, but what're the people doing with themselves? Lots of boys and girls are kissing each other just two steps from the palace, having picked out the darker corners. In house number eight, the tailor's wife got the idea of having a baby right now. Such a big event going on in the kingdom, but she just goes right on roaring as if there was nothing happening! The old blacksmith in house number three, up and died. A holiday feast in the palace, but he's lying in his coffin and not giving a damn. It's disorder!

CORPORAL. What number is she having the baby in? I'll fine her.

PIETRO. That's not the point, Corporal. What scares me is how they dare behave like that. What kind of stubbornness is this, eh, Corporal? And suddenly they'll just as peacefully, stubbornly, all at once . . . What're you doing there?

CORPORAL. Me? Nothing . . .

PIETRO. Look out, boy . . . How're you standing?

(*The* CORPORAL *pulls himself to attention.*)

I'll sho-ow y-y-you! You old devil . . . You've got out of hand! Thinking about things! Now really, Jean-Jacques Rousseau! What time is it?

CORPORAL. Quarter of twelve, Mr. Commander.

PIETRO. You remember what you have to shout out exactly at midnight?

CORPORAL. Yes, indeed, Mr. Commander.

PIETRO. I'm going to go into the office now, rest a bit, calm down, read some different documents, and you announce here what you're supposed to, don't forget! (*Goes out.*) (*The* SCHOLAR *appears.*)

SCHOLAR. I very much like the way these little lanterns are burning. I think my head has never been working so clearly in my life. I see all the lanterns together at once and each lantern separately. And I like all the lanterns together at once and each lantern separately. I know that toward morning you'll go out, my friends, but you don't mind this. You've been burning all the same, and burning merrily—nobody can take this from you.

A MAN, CLOAKED FROM HEAD TO FOOT. Christian!

SCHOLAR. Who's that? Why, now, it's the Doctor.

DOCTOR. You recognized me so easily . . . (*Looks around.*) Let's go over here to one side. Turn away from me! No, that's just ringing in my ears, but I thought it was spurs. Don't be angry. I have such a big family, you know.

SCHOLAR. I'm not angry. (*They go down onto the apron.*)

DOCTOR. Tell me as a doctor, have you decided to give up?

SCHOLAR. No. I'm a man with scruples; I have to go and tell them what I know.

DOCTOR. But you know that's suicide.

SCHOLAR. Possibly.

DOCTOR. I beg you, give up.

SCHOLAR. I can't.

DOCTOR. They'll cut off your head.

SCHOLAR. I don't believe it. On the one hand—a real life; on the other—a shadow. All my knowledge says that the shadow can win only for a while. After all, the world is kept going by us, by people who work! Good-bye!

DOCTOR. Listen, people are horrible when you fight with them. But if you live with them peacefully, why, they can seem all right.

SCHOLAR. Is that what you wanted to tell me?

DOCTOR. No! Maybe I've gone mad, but I can't stand seeing you go there unarmed. Shhh! Remember these words: "Shadow, know your place."

SCHOLAR. I don't understand you!

DOCTOR. All these days I've been digging in old studies of people who lost their shadow. In one analysis, the author, a reputable professor, recommends this: the owner of the shadow must shout at it: "Shadow, know your place!" and then again, for a while, it turns back into a shadow.

SCHOLAR. Is that really so! Why, that's wonderful! Everybody will see that he's a shadow. Right! Didn't I tell you that he would end up badly! Life's against him. We . . .

DOCTOR. Not a word about me . . . Good-bye. (*Quickly goes out.*)

SCHOLAR. Very well. I was thinking about perishing with honor, but to win—that's much better. They'll see that he's a shadow, and they'll understand . . . Why, in short, they'll understand everything . . . I . . .

(*A crowd of* PEOPLE *run in.*)

What's happened?

FIRST MAN. Here comes the Corporal with a trumpet.

SCHOLAR. What for?

FIRST MAN. He's going to announce something . . . Here he is. Hush!

CORPORAL. Christian-Theodore! Christian-Theodore!

SCHOLAR. What's the matter? I seem to be scared!

CORPORAL. Christian-Theodore! Christian-Theodore!

SCHOLAR (*loudly*). Here I am.

CORPORAL. Do you have a letter for the King?

SCHOLAR. Here it is.

CORPORAL. Follow me!

(*Curtain*)

SCENE 2

The presence chamber of the royal palace. COURTIERS *sit around in groups. There is quiet talk. The* MAJOR-DOMO *and* ASSISTANTS *carry refreshments around on trays.*

FIRST COURTIER (*gray-haired, with a handsome, sad face*). They used to serve the ice cream in the shape of enchanting little lambs, or rabbits, or kittens. The blood would freeze in your veins whenever you'd happen to bite off the head of a meek, innocent, little creature.

FIRST LADY. Oh yes, yes! My blood would freeze in my veins, too; the ice cream is so cold, you know!

FIRST COURTIER. Now the ice cream is served in the shape of beautiful fruit—it's much more humane.

FIRST LADY. You're right! What a kind heart you have. How are your sweet little canaries?

FIRST COURTIER. Oh, one of them, little Gold Drop, caught cold and coughed so, that I practically fell ill myself from compassion. Now it's better. It's even trying to sing, but I won't let it.

(PIETRO *comes in.*)

PIETRO. How are you doing! What're you eating there, ladies and gentlemen?

SECOND COURTIER. Ice cream, Mr. Commander of the Royal Watch.

PIETRO. Hey! Give me a serving. Hurry up, damn it! Put more on, you devil!

SECOND COURTIER. You're so very fond of ice cream, Mr. Commander?

PIETRO. Hate it. But since they're serving it, got to take it, the damned stuff.

MAJOR-DOMO. Sweet buns with pink cream filling! Who would like some, ladies and gentlemen of the court? (*Quietly to the* LACKEYS.) Serve the dukes first, then the counts, then the barons. Six buns for the dukes, four for the counts, two for the barons—and for the rest, whatever's left over. Don't mix things up.

LACKEY. How many buns for the new Royal Secretaries?

MAJOR-DOMO. Six and a half.

(CAESAR BORGIA *comes in.*)

CAESAR BORGIA. Hello, ladies and gentlemen. Look at me. Well? So? How do you like my tie, ladies and gentlemen? This tie is more than fashionable. It will only become fashionable in two weeks.

THIRD COURTIER. But how did you manage to obtain this work of art?

CAESAR BORGIA. Oh, very simply. My outfitter of ties is the Admiral of the Royal Navy. He imports the ties for me from abroad and brings them on shore hidden in his cocked hat.

THIRD COURTIER. That's brilliantly simple!

CAESAR BORGIA. As the Royal Secretary, I'll arrange for you to get a dozen ties. Ladies and gentlemen, I want to make you rejoice. All right? Then come with me, I'll show you my apartments. Mahogany, Chinese porcelain. You want to take a look?

COURTIERS. Of course! We're dying of impatience! How kind of you, Mr. Royal Secretary!

(CAESAR BORGIA *goes out, the* COURTIERS *after him.* ANNUNZIATA *comes in, followed by* JULIA JULI.)

JULIA. Annunziata! Are you angry at me? Don't deny it! Now that you're the daughter of a high official, I can see perfectly plainly all over your face that you're angry at me. Isn't that so?

ANNUNZIATA. Oh, really, I've no time for that, ma'am.

JULIA. You're still thinking about him all the time? About the Scholar?

ANNUNZIATA. Yes.

JULIA. Do you really think he might win?

ANNUNZIATA. I don't care.

JULIA. You're wrong there. You're still a girl. You don't know that a real man is the one who wins. The only thing that's terrible is that you can never know for sure who's going to win in the end. Christian-Theodore is so strange! Do you know anything about him?

ANNUNZIATA. Oh, what a catastrophe! We moved into the palace and father ordered the servants not to let me out. I can't even send letters to the Scholar. And he thinks, probably, that I, too, have left him. Every day Caesar Borgia reduces him to nothing in the papers; Papa reads it and licks his lips, but I read it and practically cry. Just now I bumped into this Caesar Borgia in the corridor and didn't even say I was sorry.

JULIA. He didn't notice, believe me.

ANNUNZIATA. Maybe. Do you know something about the Scholar, ma'am?

JULIA. Yes, I do. My friends the Ministers tell me everything. Christian-Theodore has wound up in complete isolation. And yet in spite of all that, he keeps walking around smiling.

ANNUNZIATA. It's dreadful!

JULIA. Of course. Who ever behaves like that under such oppressive circumstances? It makes no sense. I had my life arranged so easily, so elegantly, and now suddenly—I'm practically suffering. Suffering—why, you know, that's unpleasant! (*Laughs loudly and coquettishly.*)

ANNUNZIATA. What's the matter, madam?

JULIA. The Courtiers are coming back. Mr. Minister, here you are at last! I was really bored to death without you. How do you do?

(*The* VALETS *carry in the* MINISTER OF FINANCE.)

MINISTER OF FINANCE. One, two, three, four . . . right. All the diamonds are in place. One, two, three . . . and the pearls. And the rubies. Hello, Julia! Where are you going?

JULIA. Oh, your nearness makes me too nervous . . . The world might notice . . .

MINISTER OF FINANCE. But after all, our relations have been drawn up and regularized in the order . . .

JULIA. All the same . . . I'm going to leave you. That will be much more elegant. (*Leaves.*)

MINISTER OF FINANCE. She's a real goddess. Valets! Seat me over by the wall. Give me the pose of complete satisfaction with what's going on. Hurry up!

(*The* VALETS *do as they are bid.*)

Be off!

(*The* VALETS *go out. The* PRIME MINISTER, *seemingly out for a stroll, draws close to the* MINISTER OF FINANCE.)

(*Smiling, quietly.*) How are things, Prime Minister?

PRIME MINISTER. Everything seems in order. (*Smiles.*)

MINISTER OF FINANCE. Why—seems?

PRIME MINISTER. In my long years of service I have discovered one not particularly pleasant law. Just when we are winning completely, life suddenly raises its head.

MINISTER OF FINANCE. Raises its head? You've summoned the Royal Executioner?

PRIME MINISTER. Yes, he's here. Smile, we're being watched.

MINISTER OF FINANCE (*smiles*). But the axe and the block?

PRIME MINISTER. Already brought. The block has been put up in the pink drawing room, beside a statue of Cupid, and disguised with forget-me-nots.

MINISTER OF FINANCE. What can the Scholar do?

PRIME MINISTER. Nothing. He's alone and helpless. But these honest, naïve people sometimes do such unexpected things!

MINISTER OF FINANCE. Why wasn't he executed at once?

PRIME MINISTER. The King's against it. Smile! (*Moves away, smiling.*)

(*The* PRIVY COUNCILLOR *comes in.*)

PRIVY COUNCILLOR. Ladies and gentlemen of the court, I congratulate you! His Majesty with his most august Crown Princess are directing their feet toward this presence chamber. There's good news for you!

(*All rise. The door is flung open wide. The* SHADOW *and the* PRINCESS *enter arm-in-arm.*)

SHADOW (*with an elegant and majestic wave of his hand*). Be seated!

COURTIERS (*all together*). We won't.

SHADOW. Be seated!

COURTIERS. We daren't.

SHADOW. Be seated!

COURTIERS. Oh, very well. (*They sit down.*)

SHADOW. Prime Minister!

PRIME MINISTER. Here I am, Your Majesty!

SHADOW. What time is it?

PRIME MINISTER. A quarter to twelve, Your Majesty!

SHADOW. You may go.

PRINCESS. Where are we, in which room?

SHADOW. In the small throne room, Princess. Do you see?

PRINCESS. I see nothing except you. I don't recognize the rooms in which I grew up, the people with whom I spent so many years. I'd like to throw them all out and just be with you.

SHADOW. Me, too.

PRINCESS. Are you worried by something?

SHADOW. Yes. I promised to forgive Christian if he came here himself tonight at midnight. He's an unlucky failure, but I was a close friend of his for many years . . .

PRINCESS. How can you think about anybody else except me? You know our wedding is in an hour.

SHADOW. But we met each other thanks to Christian!

PRINCESS. Oh, yes. What a kind man you are, Theodore. Yes, we'll forgive him. He's an unlucky failure, but you were a close friend of his for many years.

SHADOW. Privy Councillor!

PRIVY COUNCILLOR. Here I am, Your Majesty!

SHADOW. In just a moment a man will come here whom I want to talk to alone.

PRIVY COUNCILLOR. Yes, Your Majesty! Ladies and gentlemen of the court! His Majesty has been pleased to grant an audience in this chamber to one of his subjects. There's a lucky man for you!

(*The* COURTIERS *rise and go out bowing.*)

PRINCESS. You think he'll come?

SHADOW. And what else can he do? (*Kisses the* PRINCESS' *hand.*) I'll call you just as soon as I've comforted him and quieted him down.

PRINCESS. I'll leave you, my darling. What an unusual man you are! (*Goes out after the* COURTIERS.)

(*The* SHADOW *opens a window. He listens. In the room next door, a clock strikes.*)

SHADOW. Midnight. He'll be here any minute.

(*Far, far away down below, the* CORPORAL *shouts.*)

CORPORAL. Christian-Theodore! Christian-Theodore!

SHADOW. What's the matter? I seem to be scared!

CORPORAL. Christian-Theodore! Christian-Theodore!

SCHOLAR'S VOICE. Here I am.

CORPORAL. Do you have a letter for the King?

SCHOLAR. Here it is.

CORPORAL. Follow me!

SHADOW (*slams the window shut, goes to the throne and sits down*). I can stretch out across the floor, go up the wall and fall through the window at one and the same time—is he capable of such suppleness? I can lie on the pavement, and pedestrians, wheels, horses' hoofs don't hurt me in the slightest—but could he so adjust himself to a place? In two weeks I've learned about life a thousand times better than he. Inaudibly, like a shadow, I slipped through everywhere, and looked, and listened, and read other people's letters. I know the whole shady side of things. And here I am now sitting on the throne, and he's lying at my feet.

(*The door is flung open, the* COMMANDER OF THE WATCH *enters.*)

PIETRO. A letter, Your Majesty.

SHADOW. Give it here. (*Reads.*) "I have come. Christian-Theodore." Where is he?

PIETRO. Outside the door, Your Majesty.

SHADOW. Show him in.

(*The* COMMANDER OF THE WATCH *goes out. The* SCHOLAR *appears. He stops in front of the throne.*)

Well, how are things going with you, Christian-Theodore?

SCHOLAR. Badly, Theodore-Christian.

SHADOW. What's wrong?

SCHOLAR. I've suddenly found myself in complete isolation.

SHADOW. But what about your friends?

SCHOLAR. I've been slandered to them.

SHADOW. But where's that girl you loved?

SCHOLAR. She's now your bride-to-be.

SHADOW. Whose fault is all this, Christian-Theodore?

SCHOLAR. Yours, Theodore-Christian.

SHADOW. Now there's a real conversation between a man and his shadow. Privy Councillor!

(*The* PRIVY COUNCILLOR *runs in.*)

Call everyone here! Hurry up!

(*The* PRINCESS *comes in, sits down beside the* SHADOW. *The* COURTIERS *come in and pause in a semi-circle. The* DOCTOR *is among them.*)

Be seated!

COURTIERS. We won't!

SHADOW. Be seated!

COURTIERS. We daren't!

SHADOW. Be seated!

COURTIERS. Oh, very well. (*They sit down.*)

SHADOW. Ladies and gentlemen, before you is a man whom I wish to make happy. All his life he has been an unlucky failure. Finally, to his good fortune, I ascended the throne.

I appoint him my shadow. Congratulate him, ladies and gentlemen of the court!

(*The* COURTIERS *rise and bow.*)

I assign him the same rank and honors as the Royal Secretaries!

MAJOR-DOMO (*in a loud whisper*). Get six and a half buns ready for him!

SHADOW. Don't be embarrassed, Christian-Theodore! If it's rather hard for you in the beginning, I'll give you some good lessons like those you've had recently. And soon you'll turn into a real shadow, Christian-Theodore. Take your place at our feet.

PRIME MINISTER. Your Majesty, his appointment has not yet been drawn up and regularized. With your permission I'll order the Commander of the Watch to take him away until tomorrow.

SHADOW. No! Christian-Theodore! Take your place at our feet!

SCHOLAR. Under no conditions! Ladies and gentlemen! Listen seriously to what I have to say! There's the real shadow. My shadow! A shadow has seized the throne. You hear?

PRIME MINISTER. I knew it. Your Majesty!

SHADOW (*calmly*). Prime Minister, hush! Speak, you unlucky failure! I'll have a good look at the last failure in your life.

SCHOLAR. Princess, I never refused you. He deceived and confused both you and me.

PRINCESS. I won't talk!

SCHOLAR. But you know you wrote me that you were ready to leave the palace and go away with me wherever I wanted.

PRINCESS. I won't, I won't, I won't talk!

SCHOLAR. But I've come for you, Princess. Give me your hand—and we'll run away. To be the wife of a shadow—that means turning into a hideous, wicked frog.

PRINCESS. What you're saying is unpleasant. Why should I listen to you?

SCHOLAR. Louise!

PRINCESS. I'm not saying a word!

SCHOLAR. Ladies and gentlemen!

PRIVY COUNCILLOR. I advise you not to listen to him. Real,

cultured people simply pay no attention to the behavior of the uneducated.

SCHOLAR. Ladies and gentlemen! This cruel creature will ruin you all. He's at the peak of power, but he's hollow. He's already weary now and doesn't know what he should do. And so he'll start tormenting you all out of boredom and having nothing to do.

FIRST COURTIER. My little meadowlark eats out of my hand. And my little starling calls me Papa.

SCHOLAR. Julia! You know you and I became such friends; after all, you know who I am. Tell them.

MINISTER OF FINANCE. Julia, I worship you, but if you go too far, I'll grind you into powder.

SCHOLAR. Julia, tell them.

JULIA (*points at the* SCHOLAR). The shadow—that's you!

SCHOLAR. But am I really talking in a wilderness?

ANNUNZIATA. No, no! Father was threatening all the time to kill you and therefore I kept quiet. Ladies and gentlemen, listen to me! (*Points to the* SHADOW.) There's the Shadow! Word of honor!

(*A slight movement among the* COURTIERS.)

I saw with my own eyes how he left the Scholar. I'm not lying. The whole town knows I'm an honest girl.

PIETRO. She can't be a witness!

SCHOLAR. Why not?

PIETRO. She's in love with you.

SCHOLAR. Is that true, Annunziata?

ANNUNZIATA. Yes, please forgive me for it. And all the same listen to what I have to say, ladies and gentlemen.

SCHOLAR. That's enough, Annunziata. Thank you. Hey, you! You didn't want to believe me, well now believe your eyes! Shadow! Know your place!

(*The* SHADOW *rises with difficulty, struggling with himself, and goes over to the* SCHOLAR.)

PRIME MINISTER. Look! He's copying all his movements. Guard!

SCHOLAR. A shadow! It's simply a shadow. You're a shadow, Theodore-Christian?

SHADOW. Yes, I am, Christian-Theodore! Don't you all believe it! It's a lie! (*To the* SCHOLAR.) I'll have you executed!

SCHOLAR. You wouldn't dare, Theodore-Christian!

SHADOW (*falls*). I wouldn't, Christian-Theodore!

PRIME MINISTER. That'll do! Everything is clear to me! This Scholar's mad! And his disease is contagious. His Majesty has fallen ill, but he'll get well. Footmen, take His Majesty out.

(*The* FOOTMEN *carry out the order. The* PRINCESS *runs after them.*)

Men of the Watch!

(*The* CORPORAL *comes in with a detachment of* SOLDIERS.)

Grab him!

(*The* SCHOLAR *is surrounded.*)

Doctor!

(*The* DOCTOR *comes out of the crowd of* COURTIERS. *The* MINISTER *points to the* SCHOLAR.)

Is this man insane?

DOCTOR (*waves his hand in disgust*). I told him long ago that this was madness.

PRIME MINISTER. Is his madness contagious?

DOCTOR. Yes. I practically caught this madness myself.

PRIME MINISTER. Is it curable?

DOCTOR. No.

PRIME MINISTER. That means we must cut off his head.

PRIVY COUNCILLOR. If you please, Mr. Prime Minister, after all I, as Master of Ceremonies, am responsible for the festivities.

PRIME MINISTER. Well, well!

PRIVY COUNCILLOR. It would be vulgar, it would be inhumane to cut off a poor madman's head. I protest execution, but instead it's essential to make a small medical operation on the poor man's head right away. A medical operation won't spoil the festivities.

PRIME MINISTER. Splendidly put.

PRIVY COUNCILLOR. Our honored doctor, as is well known, is a therapeutist and not a surgeon. Therefore, in this case, in order to amputate the diseased part, I advise using the services of the Royal Executioner.

PRIME MINISTER. Royal Executioner!

FIRST COURTIER. Just a moment. (*Gets up. Speaks to the lady beside him, putting on his white gloves.*) Please excuse me. I'll be back soon and I'll tell you how I saved the lives of my white rabbits. (*To the* PRIME MINISTER.) I'm ready.

ANNUNZIATA. Let me say good-bye to him! Good-bye, Christian-Theodore!

SCHOLAR. Good-bye, Annunziata!

ANNUNZIATA. Are you terrified, Christian-Theodore?

SCHOLAR. Yes. But I ask no mercy. I . . .

PRIME MINISTER. The drums!

PIETRO. The drums!

(*The* DRUMMERS *beat the drums.*)

PRIME MINISTER. Forward, march!

PIETRO. Forward, march!

CORPORAL. Forward, march!

(*The* GUARD *goes out and escorts the* SCHOLAR. *The* EXECUTIONER *follows behind.*)

PRIME MINISTER. Ladies and gentlemen, I invite you to the balcony—to watch the fireworks. And in the meantime some cool and soothing beverages will be prepared here. (*All rise, move toward the exit.* ANNUNZIATA *and* JULIA *remain on stage.*)

JULIA. Annunziata, I couldn't do anything else. I'm sorry.

ANNUNZIATA. He's completely well—and suddenly he has to die!

JULIA. It's terribly, terribly unpleasant for me, too, believe me. But what a scoundrel that doctor is! To betray your good friend like that!

ANNUNZIATA. And you?

JULIA. How can you make a comparison! That no-good doctor had nothing to lose. But I'm so fond of the stage. Are you crying?

ANNUNZIATA. No. I'll cry by myself in my room.

JULIA. You have to learn to get out of your head everything that makes you suffer. A light shake of the head—and that's it. Like this. Try it.

ANNUNZIATA. I don't want to.

JULIA. You're making a mistake. Don't turn away from me. I swear I'm ready to kill myself, I feel so sorry for him. But that's between you and me.

ANNUNZIATA. Is he still alive?

JULIA. Of course, of course! When it's all over they'll beat the drums.

ANNUNZIATA. I don't believe that there's nothing to be done. I beg you, Julia, let's put a stop to all this. We have to go there . . . as fast as we can!

JULIA. Shhh!

(*The* DOCTOR *comes in quickly.*)

DOCTOR. Some wine!

MAJOR-DOMO. Some wine for the Doctor!

JULIA. Annunziata, if you give me your word of honor that you won't say a thing, I'll try to help you . . .

ANNUNZIATA. I won't tell a soul! Word of honor! Only hurry up!

JULIA. There's no need to hurry at all. My way can help only when everything's over. Quiet. Listen carefully. (*Goes over to the* DOCTOR.) Doctor!

DOCTOR. Yes, Julia.

JULIA. I bet I know what you're thinking about.

DOCTOR. About wine.

JULIA. No, about water . . .

DOCTOR. I'm not in the mood for joking now, Julia.

JULIA. You know I'm not joking.

DOCTOR. Give me just a minute at least to relax.

JULIA. Unfortunately, that's impossible. Right now one of our mutual friends . . . Well, in short, you understand me.

DOCTOR. What can I do?

JULIA. But the water?

DOCTOR. Which?

JULIA. Remember the time when we were so close . . . Once the moon was bright, the stars were shining, and you were telling me you had discovered some running water which cured all diseases and even resurrected the dead, if they were good people.

ANNUNZIATA. Doctor, is that true? Is there such water?

DOCTOR. Julia's joking, as always.

ANNUNZIATA. You're lying, I can see it. I'll kill you this minute!

DOCTOR. I'll be very glad if you do.

ANNUNZIATA. Doctor, you'll wake up tomorrow, but he never will. He used to call you his friend, his comrade!

DOCTOR. Silly, unhappy girl! What can I do? They have all the water behind seven doors with seven locks, and the Minister of Finance has the keys.

JULIA. I—I bet you set a bottle aside for yourself for a rainy day.

DOCTOR. No, Julia! I'm at least that honest. I didn't set a drop aside for myself, once I couldn't cure everybody.

JULIA. You no-good man.

DOCTOR. But you know the Minister loves you; ask him for the keys, Julia!

JULIA. Me? The egotist! He wants to dump everything in my lap.

ANNUNZIATA. Madam!

JULIA. Not a word more! I've done everything I could.

ANNUNZIATA. Doctor!

DOCTOR. What can I do?

MAJOR-DOMO. His Majesty!

(*The chamber fills with* COURTIERS. *Slowly the* SHADOW *enters with the* PRINCESS. *They sit down on the throne. The* PRIME MINISTER *makes a sign to the* MAJOR-DOMO.)

Now His Majesty's soloist, under the patronage of His Eminence, the Minister of Finance, Madame Julia Juli will perform the refreshing and soothing little song "It's Not Worth-While To Lose Your Head."

SHADOW. It's not worth-while to lose your head—splendid!

JULIA (*makes a low curtsy to the* KING. *Bows to the* COURTIERS. *Sings*).

Once there lived a dragonfly,
She was a fickle woman.
Her absolutely charming eyes
Brought many flies to ruin.
She loved to say and often said:
"It's not worth-while to lose your head . . ."

(*The thunder of drums interrupts the song.*)

SHADOW (*jumps up, staggering*). Water!

(*The* MAJOR-DOMO *rushes toward the* SHADOW *and stops, stunned. The* SHADOW'S *head suddenly flies off his shoulders. A headless* SHADOW *sits motionlessly on the throne.*)

ANNUNZIATA. Look!

MINISTER OF FINANCE. What's this?

PRIME MINISTER. My god! We didn't calculate this. Why, it's his own personal shadow. Ladies and gentlemen, you are at a formal assembly in the Royal Palace. You must be enjoying yourselves, enjoying yourselves no matter what!

PRINCESS (*runs up to the* MINISTER). This minute! This minute! This minute!

PRIME MINISTER. What, Your Excellency?

PRINCESS. Fix him this minute! I don't want it like this! Don't want it! Don't want it!

PRIME MINISTER. Princess, I beg you, stop it.

PRINCESS. But what would you say if the man you were going to marry lost his head?

PRIVY COUNCILLOR. It happened out of love, Princess.

PRINCESS. If you don't fix him, I'll have your head cut off this minute. All the princesses in the world have husbands all in one piece, but look at what I have! What a stinking, dirty trick!

PRIME MINISTER. The spring water, quickly, quickly, quickly!

MINISTER OF FINANCE. For whom? For him? But it resurrects only good people.

PRIME MINISTER. Then we'll have to resurrect the good one. Oh, I really don't want to.

MINISTER OF FINANCE. There's no other way out. Doctor! Follow me. Valets! Take me. (*Goes out.*)

PRIME MINISTER. Relax, Princess, everything will be taken care of.

(*The* FIRST COURTIER *comes in, taking off his gloves on his way. Having noticed the headless* KING, *he stops in his tracks.*)

FIRST COURTIER. If you please . . . Now who did this? You just go out of the room for thirty minutes—and they start taking your job away from you—the plotters!

(*The door is flung open, and a whole procession moves across stage. In front* VALETS *conduct the* MINISTER OF FINANCE. *Behind him four* SOLDIERS *are carrying a huge barrel. The barrel shines all by itself. Tongues of flame come out from between the cracks. Shining drops fall onto the parquet floor. The* DOCTOR *walks along behind the barrel. The procession passes across the stage and disappears.*)

JULIA. Annunziata, you were right.

ANNUNZIATA. About what?

JULIA. He'll win! Right now he'll win. They've taken the spring water. It will resurrect him.

ANNUNZIATA. Why should they resurrect a good man?

JULIA. So that the bad one can live. You're a lucky girl, Annunziata.

ANNUNZIATA. I don't believe it; something's going to happen still. After all, we're in the palace.

JULIA. Oh, I'm afraid nothing more is going to happen. Is it really going to become fashionable to be a good man? You know that's so much bother!

CAESAR BORGIA. Mr. Commander of the Royal Watch!

PIETRO. Now what?

CAESAR BORGIA. The Courtiers are sort of giving us dirty looks. Maybe we ought to clear out?

PIETRO. Damned if I know. We'd still be caught . . .

CAESAR BORGIA. We hooked up with an unlucky failure.

PIETRO. I'll never forgive myself, damn it all!

CAESAR BORGIA. To lose your head at such an important moment!

PIETRO. The lunkhead! And in front of everybody, too! Ought to have gone into his study and there lost anything he wanted to, the pig!

CAESAR BORGIA. The tactless creature!

PIETRO. The ass!

CAESAR BORGIA. Really, he'll have to be eaten. Have to be, have to be.

PIETRO. Yes, that has to be done.

(*The thunder of drums. Suddenly the* SHADOW's *head appears on his shoulders.*)

CAESAR BORGIA. I congratulate you, Your Majesty!

PIETRO. Hurrah, Your Majesty!

MAJOR-DOMO. Some water, Your Majesty!

SHADOW. Why is it so empty in the chamber? Where is everybody? Louise?

(*The* PRINCESS *runs in. Behind her, the* COURTIERS.)

PRINCESS. A head is so becoming to you, darling!

SHADOW. Louise, where is he?

PRINCESS. I don't know. How do you feel, darling?

SHADOW. It hurts to swallow.

PRINCESS. I'll make you a compress for the night.

SHADOW. Thank you. But where is he? Call him in.

(*The* PRIME MINISTER *and the* MINISTER OF FINANCE *run in.*)

PRIME MINISTER. Excellent. Everything's in place.

MINISTER OF FINANCE. No changes at all!

PRIME MINISTER. Your Majesty, do me a favor, nod your head.

SHADOW. Where is he?

PRIME MINISTER. Splendid! The head works! Hurrah! Everything's in good shape.

SHADOW. I'm asking you: where is he?

PRIME MINISTER. And I'm giving you the answer: everything's in good shape, Your Majesty. He'll be shut up in the dungeon right away.

SHADOW. Why, you're out of your mind! How can you even dare think of doing that! Guard of Honor!

PIETRO. Guard of Honor!

SHADOW. Go, ask, beg him to come here.

PIETRO. Ask him and beg him—forward, march! (*Goes out with the* GUARD.)

PRINCESS. Why are you calling him, Theodore-Christian?

SHADOW. I want to live.

PRINCESS. But you used to say that he was an unlucky failure.

SHADOW. That's all true, but I can't live without him!

(*The* DOCTOR *runs in.*)

DOCTOR. He's all well. Listen to me, all of you: he behaved like a madman, walked straight ahead, without turning one way or the other, was executed—and here he is now alive, alive, like any one of you.

MAJOR-DOMO. His Illustrious Excellency, Mr. Scholar.

(*The* SCHOLAR *enters. The* SHADOW *jumps up and reaches out his arms. The* SCHOLAR *pays him no attention.*)

SCHOLAR. Annunziata!

ANNUNZIATA. Here I am.

SCHOLAR. Annunziata, they didn't let me finish talking. Yes, Annunziata. I was terrified of dying. After all I'm so young!

SHADOW. Christian!

SCHOLAR. Keep quiet. But I went to my death, Annunziata. You know, in order to win, you even have to go to your death. And so—I won. Let's get out of here, Annunziata.

SHADOW. No! Stay with me, Christian! Live in the palace.

Not a hair on your head will be touched. I'll make you Prime Minister; you want me to?

PRIME MINISTER. Now why specifically Prime Minister? The Minister of Finance, here, is ailing.

MINISTER OF FINANCE. Me, ailing? Look here. (*Jumps lightly around the chamber.*)

PRIME MINISTER. He got well!

MINISTER OF FINANCE. In a moment of real danger, we men of business have wings that grow on our feet.

SHADOW. You want me to, I'll chase them all out, Christian? I'll let you rule—within, of course, reasonable limits. I'll help you make a certain number of people happy. You're not going to answer me? Louise! Order him to!

PRINCESS. Be quiet, you coward! What have you all done, ladies and gentlemen? For once in my life I met a good man, but you all rushed at him like dogs. Clear out, get out of here, Shadow!

(*The* SHADOW *descends from the throne, clings to the wall, wrapped in his cloak.*)

You can take any pitiful pose you want. You won't make me feel sorry for you. Ladies and gentlemen! He's not my bridegroom any more. I'll find myself a new one.

PRIVY COUNCILLOR. There's good news for you!

PRINCESS. Now I understand everything, Christian, darling. Hey! Commander of the Watch, grab him! (*Points to the* SHADOW.)

PIETRO. Please. Grab him. (*Goes toward the* SHADOW.)

PRIME MINISTER. I'll help you.

MINISTER OF FINANCE. Me, too; me, too.

CAESAR BORGIA. Down with the Shadow!

(*They seize the* SHADOW, *but there is no* SHADOW; *an empty cloak is hanging in their hands.*)

PRINCESS. He escaped!

SCHOLAR. He disappeared so that time and again he might be with me on the road. But I'll recognize him, I'll recognize him anywhere. Annunziata, give me your hand, let's get out of here.

ANNUNZIATA. How do you feel, Christian-Theodore, darling?

SCHOLAR. It's hard to swallow. Good-bye, ladies and gentlemen!

PRINCESS. Christian-Theodore, forgive me; after all, it's the only time I've made a mistake. And I'm already punished—that's enough. Stay, or take me with you. I'll behave very well. You'll see.

SCHOLAR. No, Princess.

PRINCESS. Don't go! What an unhappy girl I am! Ladies and gentlemen, you ask him.

COURTIERS. Now where are you going?

Stay . . .

Sit here just a moment, please . . .

What's your hurry? You don't have to go to bed yet!

SCHOLAR. I'm sorry, ladies and gentlemen, but I'm so busy. (*Going with* ANNUNZIATA, *holding hands.*)

PRINCESS. Christian-Theodore! It's raining outdoors! It's dark. But in the palace it's warm and comfortable. I'll have all the stoves lit. Stay.

SCHOLAR. No. We'll dress more warmly and go. Don't hold us up, ladies and gentlemen.

CAESAR BORGIA. Let them through, let them through! Here are your galoshes, Mr. Professor!

PIETRO. Here's your cloak. (*To* ANNUNZIATA.) Put in a good word for your father, you monster!

CORPORAL. The carriage is at the gate.

SCHOLAR. Annunziata, let's go!

(*Curtain*)